Social Connections in China

Guanxi, loosely translated as "social connections" or "social networks," is among the most important, talked about, and studied phenomena in China today. *Guanxi* lies at the heart of China's social order, its economic structure, and its changing institutional landscape. It is considered important in almost every realm of life, from politics to business, and from officialdom to street life. *Social Connections in China* offers the latest scholarly thinking on the subject by leading China sociologists whose work on *guanxi* has been influential, and by new scholars offering the most current insights on the topic.

The authors present a history and taxonomy of *guanxi* as it has evolved in scholarly and business communities and offer new theoretical and methodological assessments of this important phenomenon. Their findings address fundamental questions surrounding the current debate about the role and origins of *guanxi*: What forms does *guanxi* take today? How is it shaping and changing China's economy and economic reforms, business deals, and legal system? Is *guanxi* a fundamentally Chinese phenomenon in form and function? Or is it simply another word for the personal networks, social capital, and gift economies that can be found in other societies?

Drawing from a number of groundbreaking studies of contemporary China (from the perspectives of sociology, political science, and economics), the chapters examine the role of *guanxi* in business decisions among managers and entrepreneurs, the decisions and practices of workers, the construction of new legal institutions, and the new social order. Scholars and students of China will find this not only a rich source of detailed information on the workings of Chinese social relationships, but also a valuable, new interpretation of the meaning and place of *guanxi* today.

Thomas Gold is a member of the Sociology Department of the University of California, Berkeley; Executive Director of the Inter-University Program for Chinese Language Studies; and former Chair of Berkeley's Center for Chinese Studies (1990–4 and 1998). He is the author of *State and Society in the Taiwan Miracle* (1986) and the forthcoming Cambridge book *Remaking Taiwan: Society and the State since the End of Martial Law.*

Doug Guthrie is Associate Professor of Sociology at New York University. He is the author of *Dragon in a Three-Piece Suit: The Emergence of Capitalism in China* (1999), as well as several articles on the economic reforms in China.

David Wank is Associate Professor of Sociology at Sophia University, Tokyo, and the author of *Commodifying Communism: Business, Trust and Politics in a Chinese City* (Cambridge, 1999).

Structural Analysis in the Social Sciences
Mark Granovetter, editor

The *Structural Analysis in the Social Sciences* series presents approaches that explain social behavior and institutions by reference to *relationships* between such concrete entities as persons and organizations. This contrasts with at least four other popular strategies: (1) reductionist attempts at explanation by focusing on individuals alone; (2) explanations stressing the causal primacy of ideas, values, and cognitions; (3) technological and material determinism; (4) explanations using "variables" as the main analytical concept, as in "structural equation" models, where the structure connects variables rather than actual social entities.

An important example of structural analysis is the "social network" approach. However, the series also features social science theory and research that is not framed explicitly in network terms, but stresses the importance of relationships rather than the atomization of reductionism or the determinism of ideas, technology, or material conditions. Such efforts typically deal with the complex balance between structure and agency, increasingly a key issue in the human sciences. Examples of the structural approach are scattered across many disciplines, and it is the goal of the *Structural Analysis* series to expose this very fruitful style of analysis to a wider public by bringing all the approaches together under a single rubric.

Other books in the series:

1. Mark S. Mizruchi and Michael Schwartz, eds., *Intercorporate Relations: The Structural Analysis of Business*
2. Barry Wellman and S. D. Berkowitz, eds., *Social Structures: A Network Approach*
3. Ronald L. Breiger, ed., *Social Mobility and Social Structure*
4. David Knoke, *Political Networks: The Structural Perspective*
5. John L. Campbell, J. Rogers Hollingsworth and Leon N. Lindberg, eds., *Governance of the American Economy*
6. Kyriakos Kontopoulos, *The Logics of Social Structure*
7. Philippa Pattison, *Alegebraic Models for Social Networks*
8. Stanley Wasserman and Katherine Faust, *Social Network Analysis: Methods and Applications*
9. Gary Herrigel, *Industrial Constructions: The Sources of German Industrial Power*
10. Philipe Bourgois, *In Search of Respect: Selling Crack in El Barrio*
11. Per Hage and Frank Harary, *Island Networks: Communication, Kinship, and Classification Structures in Oceania*
12. Thomas Schweizer and Douglas R. White, eds., *Kinship, Networks and Exchange*
13. Noah E. Friedkin, *A Structural Theory of Social Influence*

Continued on page following the Index

Social Connections in China

Institutions, Culture, and the Changing
Nature of *Guanxi*

Edited by

Thomas Gold
University of California, Berkeley

Doug Guthrie
New York University

David Wank
Sophia University

CAMBRIDGE
UNIVERSITY PRESS

PUBLISHED BY THE PRESS SYNDICATE OF THE UNIVERSITY OF CAMBRIDGE
The Pitt Building, Trumpington Street, Cambridge, United Kingdom

CAMBRIDGE UNIVERSITY PRESS
The Edinburgh Building, Cambridge CB2 2RU, UK
40 West 20th Street, New York, NY 10011-4211, USA
477 Williamstown Road, Port Melbourne, VIC 3207, Australia
Ruiz de Alarcón 13, 28014 Madrid, Spain
Dock House, The Waterfront, Cape Town 8001, South Africa

http://www.cambridge.org

First published 2002

Printed in the United Kingdom at the University Press, Cambridge

Typeface Times Roman 10/12 pt.   *System* LATEX 2_ε [TB]

A catalog record for this book is available from the British Library.

Library of Congress Cataloging in Publication Data
Social connections in China : institutions, culture, and the changing nature of
Guanxi / edited by Thomas Gold, Doug Guthrie, David Wank.
    p.   cm. – (Structural analysis in the social sciences; 21)
Includes bibliographical references and index.
ISBN 0-521-81233-X
I. Title: Institutions, culture, and the changing nature of Guanxi.
II. Gold, Thomas, 1948–   III. Guthrie, Doug, 1969–
IV. Wank, David L., 1957–   V. Series.
HN740.G825 S63   2002
306′.0951′28–dc21   2001037922

ISBN 0 521 81233 X hardback
ISBN 0 521 53031 8 paperback

CONTENTS

Contributors   *page* ix
List of Figures and Tables   xiii
Prologue   xv

Introduction
    An Introduction to the Study of *Guanxi*   *Thomas Gold,*
    Doug Guthrie, and David Wank   3
1 Practices of *Guanxi* Production and Practices of
    Ganqing Avoidance   *Andrew Kipnis*   21

Methodological and Conceptual Considerations
2 Information Asymmetries and the Problem of Perception:
    The Significance of Structural Position in Assessing
    the Importance of *Guanxi* in China   *Doug Guthrie*   37
3 Beyond Dyadic Social Exchange: *Guanxi* and Third-Party
    Effects   *Yi-min Lin*   57

New Substantive Studies of *Guanxi*
4 *Guanxi* in Business Groups: Social Ties and the Formation
    of Economic Relations   *Lisa A. Keister*   77
5 Business-State Clientelism in China:
    Decline or Evolution?   *David Wank*   97
6 Institutional Holes and Job Mobility Processes: *Guanxi*
    Mechanisms in China's Emergent Labor Markets   *Yanjie Bian*   117
7 Youth Job Searches in Urban China: The Use of Social
    Connections in a Changing Labor Market   *Amy Hanser*   137
8 Face, Norms, and Instrumentality   *Scott Wilson*   163
9 *Guanxi* and the PRC Legal System: From Contradiction to
    Complementarity   *Pitman B. Potter*   179

10 "Idle Talk": Neighborhood Gossip as a Medium of Social
Communication in Reform Era Shanghai   *James Farrer*   197

Conclusions
11 Networking *Guanxi*   *Barry Wellman, Wenhong Chen,*
   and Dong Weizhen   221

References   243
Index   273

CONTRIBUTORS

Yanjie Bian: Associate Professor of Sociology at the University of Minnesota and Associate Professor of Social Science and Director of the Survey Research Center at Hong Kong University of Science and Technology. He is the author of *Work and Inequality in Urban China* (SUNY Press, 1994) and co-editor of *Market Transition and Social Stratification* (Beijing: Joint Publishing Co, 2000, with Hanlong Lu and Liping Sun) and *Survey Research in Chinese Societies* (Oxford University Press [HK], 2001, with Edward Tu and Alvin So). He is the author of numerous articles on the subject of *guanxi* and is currently extending his research on social capital, *guanxi* networks, and employment processes in Chinese cities.

Wenhong Chen: Graduate student in the Department of Sociology at the University of Toronto. She received her BA in economics from the University of International Business and International Economics, Beijing, and has also studied sociology at the University of Munich. Her research interests include social stratification and social change. She is currently studying the global digital divide and the evolution of the new economy in China and Europe.

James Farrer: Lecturer in Sociology in the Faculty of Comparative Culture of Sophia University in Tokyo. He is author of *Opening Up: Sex, Love and Money in Shanghai*, forthcoming from the University of Chicago Press.

Thomas Gold: Member of the Sociology Department of the University of California, Berkeley; Executive Director of the Inter-University Program for Chinese Language Studies; and former Chair of Berkeley's Center for Chinese Studies (1990–4 and 1998). He is the author of *State and Society in the Taiwan Miracle* (1986) and the forthcoming Cambridge book *Remaking Taiwan: Society and the State since the End of Martial Law.* He also wrote "After Comradeship: Personal Relations in China after the Cultural Revolution" (*China Quarterly*, 1985), among many other articles on Taiwan's political economy and ongoing democratization, as well as on private business in mainland China.

Doug Guthrie: Associate Professor of Sociology at New York University. He is the author of *Dragon in a Three-Piece Suit: The Emergence of Capitalism in China* (Princeton, 1999), as well as several articles on the economic reforms in China, including "The Declining Significance of *Guanxi* in China's Economic Transition" (*The China Quarterly*, 1998). His current research focuses on the relationship between economic and political change in China.

Amy Hanser: Doctoral candidate in the Department of Sociology at the University of California, Berkeley. She is currently writing a dissertation on service sector employment in China's northeast.

Lisa A. Keister: Assistant Professor of Sociology at the Ohio State University. She received her PhD from Cornell University in 1997 and conducts research in economic sociology, inequality, and organizational behavior. She is the recipient of the National Science Foundation's Faculty Early Development Career Award and author of the books *Chinese Business Groups* (Oxford, 2000) and *Wealth in America* (Cambridge, 2000).

Andrew Kipnis: Research Fellow in the Contemporary China Center of the Australian National University. He is author of *Producing Guanxi: Sentiment, Self, and Subculture in a North China Village*. He is currently doing research on education reform as a sociocultural process in East Asia and writing a book about sociocultural theory in the post-socialist era.

Yi-min Lin: Teaches at the Social Science Division, Hong Kong University of Science and Technology. He is the author of *Between Politics and Markets: Firms, Competition, and Institutional Change in Post-Mao China* (Cambridge, 2001).

Pitman B. Potter: Director of the Institute of Asian Research at the University of British Columbia. He is also Professor of Law and Director of Chinese Legal Studies at UBC's Faculty of Law. Dr. Potter's teaching and research activities focus on law and legal culture in the PRC and Taiwan.

David Wank: Associate Professor of Sociology at Sophia University, Tokyo. He is the author of *Commodifying Communism: Business Trust and Politics in a Chinese City* (Cambridge, 1999) and is currently researching the institutional politics of China's Buddhist resurgence.

Dong Weizhen: PhD candidate at the Department of Sociology, University of Toronto. She received her MA in Development Studies from the Institute of Social Studies, The Hague. She has been a researcher at the Asian Institute of Technology, Bangkok, and the Shanghai Academy of Social Sciences. Her publications have been in the areas of employment, industrialization, women's psychology, and gender socialization. She is also interested in migration, the private economy, and social network analysis.

Barry Wellman: Student of networks since his teenage gang days in New York City. He has continued networking as Professor of Sociology at the University of Toronto. Wellman founded the International Network for Social Network Analysis in 1977 and led it for a dozen years. He has co-edited *Social Structures: A Network Approach* (2nd ed, JAI Press, 1998) and edited *Networks in the Global Village* (Westview Press, 1999).

Scott Wilson: Assistant Professor of Political Science at The University of the South. His dissertation and subsequent publications have focused on changing social relations in peri-urban Shanghai villages caused by the Deng era economic reforms. Currently he is researching the impact of foreign investments from Japan, the United States, and Hong Kong on their Shanghai host business environment.

LIST OF FIGURES AND TABLES

FIGURES

2.1 Proportion of firms by administrative rank that rely on *guanxi* (in markets) and *guanxi xue* (in official procedures) in four sectors in industrial Shanghai, 1995. *page* 54

11.1 Graphical and matrix representation of a network. 227

11.2 A network of networks: From an interpersonal to an interorganizational network. Copyright © Barry Wellman 1988. 231

11.3 Typical North American network. Copyright © Barry Wellman 1988. 233

TABLES

2.1 Logistic coefficients for the determinants of the use of connections [*guanxi*] in hiring decisions in four industrial sectors, Shanghai, 1995. 50

4.1 *Guanxi* in lending and trade relations: Logistic regression results. 90

6.1 Basic characteristics of a sample of 100 interviewees. 120

6.2 Job changes experienced by a sample of 100 interviewees. 121

11.1 Block model of seeking advice. 230

PROLOGUE

In the fall of 1998, the Center for Chinese Studies at the University of California, Berkeley, under the direction of Thomas Gold, brought several scholars from around the world to talk about *guanxi*, a phenomenon we had all written about in one way or another. We wanted not only to explore several substantive issues – the importance of *guanxi* in Chinese societies, the conditions under which it is alive and thriving in China today, the extent to which it is linked to Chinese culture, its fate in China's economic reforms – but also to examine the ways this important Chinese phenomenon had been treated in academic scholarship and popular discourse over the years. As these discussions got under way, we were struck by something else: While actual research that discussed the phenomenon of *guanxi* in China was relatively young – scholars have really only been discussing the topic directly since the mid-1970s – there has been an absolute explosion of scholarship on the topic in recent years.

Though not the first to write about the phenomenon, Thomas Gold published one of the early essays in 1985 that addressed the issue directly from the perspective of its changing role in China's economic reforms. And while the early works of Andrew Walder (1986) and Jean Oi (1989) do not spend much time discussing *guanxi* per se, the issue of social relations in China is clearly central in their examinations of Chinese political economy. In the 1990s, three seminal books were published that focused wholly and exclusively on understanding and explaining the phenomena of *guanxi* and *guanxixue* (social relations and the "art" of social relations, respectively) in Chinese society. In 1994, Mayfair Yang published *Gifts, Favors, and Banquets: The Art of Social Relationships in China*, which would prove to be the reference point for many future studies of *guanxi*. In 1996, Yunxiang Yan published *The Flow of Gifts: Reciprocity and Social Networks in a Chinese Village*, and in 1997, Andrew Kipnis published *Producing Guanxi: Sentiment, Self, and Subculture in a North China Village*. Each of these projects was based on intensive fieldwork in China, and each considered different aspects of *guanxi* in Chinese society. Another scholar, Yanjie Bian, has through a series of articles also established an important body of work on the role of *guanxi* in past and current Chinese labor markets. Finally, in 1998, a two-volume set simply titled *Guanxixue Quanshu* (Dong 1998), was published in Beijing, promoting its contents on the jacket by promising to "teach you how to grasp China's most complex yet most practical body of knowledge (*xuewen*) . . . These two characters, '*guan xi*' are endlessly subtle; if you learn how to manage all forms of human and social *guanxi*, it will be like planting a large tree from which you can obtain mounds of fruit you never imagined."

From the academic and even abstruse treatments of *guanxi* to the practical (and clearly business-oriented) examinations of the issue, *guanxi* has clearly entered into the mainstream of both of these worlds. Yet there are many questions that remain unanswered. There is still quite a lively and unresolved debate about the extent to which *guanxi* is a uniquely Chinese phenomenon, inextricably tied to and deeply rooted in Chinese culture. Is *guanxi* fundamentally Chinese? Or is it produced by certain institutional arrangements and historical circumstances that happen to be common to China's experience? The rapid economic and institutional changes that have occurred over the course of the last two decades in China actually provide interesting fodder for this discussion: How is *guanxi* changing in China's economic reforms? What does *guanxi* look like today? If the nature of *guanxi* is changing in reform-era China, what do these changes tell us about the relationship between *guanxi* and Chinese culture? And, perhaps most importantly, what kinds of research strategies and methods provide us with the best tools for answering these questions?

It would be presumptuous to suggest that we have actually provided definitive answers to these questions. However, we do believe that this volume brings together some of the scholars whose work has been influential on the views of *guanxi* thus far and new scholars whose work provides the most current insights on the topic. While many of the chapters in this volume are grounded in the literature that has defined past research on *guanxi*, it is our hope that the volume will push research on social networks in China beyond the current divides in the literature. As such, this book has two goals. First, we have sought to push some of the boundaries of current work on *guanxi* both theoretically and methodologically. We have asked some authors to reconsider conceptual work they have done in the past, and we have invited some scholars to think methodologically about the ways in which we approach the study of *guanxi*. Second, we have attempted to push the work on *guanxi* in new directions substantively. With the dramatic changes occurring throughout China, there are many different settings and prisms through which to view the changing role of social networks there. In this study, we have brought together work that considers the situation of social connections within classical settings and settings that have not been closely examined in past studies of *guanxi*. At the very least, we hope that this volume provides a good mix of assessments of the past research, current insights from the field, and a research agenda for future generations of China scholars.

In the course of producing this book, we have expanded our own *guanxiwang*, and in the process we have incurred multitudinous obligations from colleagues too numerous to name individually. We sincerely thank all of them for their contributions. We do want to single out Professor Hishida Masaharu of the University of Shizuoka and Professor Shigeto Sonoda of Chuo University, who joined the editors in a roundtable at the Asian Studies Conference in Tokyo in June 1999 where we discussed some of the central issues in this book.

Thanks to the Center for Chinese Studies at Berkeley for its financial support of the initial workshop and to Shiping Tang for research assistance on the Introduction.

We would also like to thank series editor Mark Granovetter and our editor at Cambridge, Mary Child, for support and encouragement as we developed this project.

INTRODUCTION

AN INTRODUCTION TO THE STUDY
OF *GUANXI*

Thomas Gold, Doug Guthrie, and David Wank

Guanxi[1] (pronounced "gwan-shee"), loosely translated as "connections," is the latest Chinese word to gain entry into English parlance. While the term was virtually unknown to non-Chinese speakers a decade ago, today it is used by Chinese and non-Chinese speakers alike, and it has made its way into many popular venues. Indeed, Internet search engines such as Yahoo and Altavista yield some 2,000 references under the heading "*guanxi.*" Conventional wisdom among Chinese and foreigners holds that in the People's Republic of China (PRC), *guanxi* is absolutely essential to successfully complete any task in virtually all spheres of social life. *Guanxi* purportedly performs a critical lubricating function in Mainland China, and also in the peripheral Chinese societies of Hong Kong and Taiwan, among minority Chinese communities in Southeast Asia and elsewhere, and as a means of linking together the global Chinese diaspora.

Guanxi has both positive and negative connotations, with the latter dominating most of the discussions. Critics see it as fueling the country's rampant corruption, and as an obstacle to China's becoming a modern society based on the rule of law. Those who see it in a more favorable light contend that *guanxi* adds an element of humanity to otherwise cold transactions, and comes to the rescue in the absence of consistent regulations or guidelines for social conduct. There is also disagreement over the extent to which *guanxi* is something unique to China: To some observers and practitioners, *guanxi* is an essential and defining element of Chinese culture, handed down relatively unchanged through time and space. To others, *guanxi* is little more than a Chinese word for the personal networks, social capital, and gift economies found in all societies. Finally, but not least of all, there is considerable disagreement over the fate of *guanxi* in the period of economic reforms: Some scholars argue that as the state has loosened its grip on the economy, the role of

---

[1] This book utilizes the *pinyin* system of romanization developed on the Mainland. Many of the works cited utilize the older Wade-Giles system. When a Chinese term first appears, we will indicate the alternative romanization when appropriate, in parentheses.

guanxi has expanded in Chinese society. They argue that its role will continue to expand, leading to an economic system that is substantially different from the rational-legal systems that define Western market economies. Others believe that the role of *guanxi* is declining in the era of economic reforms, and that eventually formal rational law will supplant the norms of the personal economy.

The contributors to this volume stake out a variety of positions within these debates. Our goal has been to bring together several of the individuals who have contributed to the scholarship and debate over what *guanxi* means in Chinese society and how it is changing in the period of economic reforms. While we all generally agree that *guanxi* is a specifically Chinese idiom of social networks, integrally linked to other building blocks of Chinese sociality such as *ganqing* (sentiment), *renqing* (human feelings), *mianzi* (face), and *bao* (reciprocity), our views vary on the extent to which *guanxi* is shaped by institutional contexts and on its future in the reform era. In this volume, we have pushed ourselves to focus on demonstrating and explaining the dynamic interrelations between cultural traits and institutional contexts surrounding *guanxi* in Chinese society.

The PRC presents an extreme case for understanding this complicated interaction of culture and institutions. Given the Chinese Communists' relentless and sustained attacks on what they saw as such "feudal" and backward traits as the reliance on particularistic *guanxi*-type rather than universalistic "modern" orientations to the social world, and their efforts to build a set of institutions based on radically different principles, the stubborn persistence of *guanxi* in practice and in the popular mind requires explanation. Though coming from different academic disciplines, all of the authors assembled here have conducted extended fieldwork in Mainland China, and many have also done research in Hong Kong or Taiwan. Some set out explicitly to study the operation of *guanxi*; more commonly, in the course of fieldwork on other topics, they were struck by the centrality of the term "*guanxi*" in everyday discourse, popular culture, and political debate, and then began to examine it more concretely and systematically. Rather than seeing *guanxi* as an unchanging and fixed cultural trait, their research demonstrates both the persistence of *guanxi* and how it is changing in the midst of the rapid institutional transformations that have swept across China since the late 1970s.

A detailed look at *guanxi* will shed light on one of the most dominant aspects of contemporary Chinese life, but it has larger implications for the social sciences as well. First among these is the issue of institutional change in a rapidly transforming economy and the extent to which what appear to be indigenous features of Chinese social, political, and economic landscapes will endure in the face of dramatic upheaval and change. The seeming persistence of *guanxi* in Chinese society, in spite of conscious and conscientious efforts to eradicate it by Communists and capitalists alike, offers interesting insights into the complex interaction of culture, institutions, and social practice in a modernizing society (Dickson 1992; Nathan and Tsai 1995). Study of *guanxi* can shed light on issues of political culture, such as the operations of informal politics and the potential for social networks to evolve into something resembling civil society (Lo and Otis 1999). Understanding the role of *guanxi* in economic life can also contribute to the debates about the embeddedness of economic practices in institutions (Granovetter 1985; Uzzi 1996; Polanyi 1957).

In this introductory chapter, we will begin by laying out the basic lexicon of *guanxi* and its evolution within Chinese society as well as its evolution in academic scholarship. Following that discussion, we examine some of the literature that has been put forward on this topic, focusing on the debate over whether *guanxi* is a distinctly Chinese phenomenon, inextricably linked to Chinese culture and society, or whether it is a general phenomenon, produced by institutional arrangements that happen to exist in China. Finally, we will suggest ways that the examination of this concept might be pushed forward and how the chapters of this volume attempt to achieve this goal.

DISENTANGLING *GUANXI*

Chinese and foreign scholars have long noted the centrality of personal networks in Chinese life, historically and in modern times. Since the late 1970s, along with the Chinese Communists' introduction of market practices into their socialist economy and their opening of the country to the outside world, foreign scholars and professionals have enjoyed unprecedented access to Chinese daily life on the Mainland after a break of more than three decades. It is no exaggeration to state that especially in the early years of this opening, most foreigners have been struck by the prevalence of *guanxi* as a topic and an analytical category in conversation, scholarship, and the state-controlled media. Its significance as a distinctive social phenomenon constraining individual behavior while also becoming internalized – that is to say, becoming a "social fact" in Durkheim's terms – has earned *guanxi* a status where now foreign scholars and laypersons utilize the untranslated Chinese word unself-consciously when discussing and explaining China.[2] Interestingly, although foreign scholars prior to the access afforded by the Chinese reform era wrote a great deal about the importance of personal relations and networks, and did employ a handful of Chinese terms, it was only with the opportunity to engage in extended fieldwork and to experience the pervasiveness of *guanxi* in everyday practice and discourse that the Chinese word entered the popular and scholarly English lexicon.[3]

2   We disagree with Ong's (1997, p. 181) statement that "key terms such as *guanxi* (interpersonal relations) . . . have been constructed by Western academics to define Chinese culture." The other terms in her list (networks, neo-Confucianism, tribes and multiculturalism) aside, in the case of *guanxi* it is clear that Western academics (and business people) picked the term up because Chinese people use it themselves. We do agree with the "*self-orientalization*" (her term), which grants Asians "the agency to maneuver and manipulate meanings within different power domains" (p. 195).
3   Scholars who conducted interviews in Hong Kong prior to the Cultural Revolution recall Chinese emigres using the term *guanxi*, but without the significance detected after the reforms began (personal communication with Gold). One scholar (personal communication with Gold) said that as a form of political correctness, foreign scholars avoided the term because they were aware that the Chinese were embarrassed about the practice, seeing it as a weakness. Important studies of

"Guanxi" (*kuan-hsi*) literally means "relation" or "relationship," as a noun, and "relate to" as a verb, though as commonly used in contemporary Chinese societies, it refers more narrowly to "particularistic ties" (Jacobs 1979, 1980).[4] These ties are based on ascribed or primordial traits such as kinship, native place, and ethnicity, and also on achieved characteristics such as attending the same school (even if not at the same time), serving together in the same military unit, having shared experiences, such as the Long March, and doing business together.[5] Particularly in this last instance, potential business partners may consciously establish or seek to manufacture *guanxi* when no prior basis exists, either by relying on intermediaries or establishing a relationship directly. While the bases for *guanxi* may be naturally occurring or created, the important point is that *guanxi* must be consciously produced, cultivated, and maintained over time (Kipnis 1997; Yan 1996a; Yang 1994).

A set of specialized terms has arisen in China related to *guanxi* (Yang 1994, esp. ch. 1). The art or science of manipulating and utilizing *guanxi* is *guanxixue*.[6] If we see *guanxi* as an established relationship, then *guanxixue* is the art of putting that relationship to use, of actualizing it (Chen 2000). This term usually has a negative connotation, implying "going through the back door" to get something done, though it undeniably performs a positive function as well, especially if there is no formal "front door" available. The person who has the power to achieve a desired goal for another, is a *guanxihu*, sometimes translated as an "under the table relationship."[7] Utilizing such relationships is referred to as "to pull" (*la*) or to "do" (*gao*) *guanxi*. *"Gao"* is commonly used as an all-purpose verb on the Mainland, but in Taiwan it is disparaged as vulgar slang indicating poor upbringing. The sum total or extent of one's *guanxi* is a *guanxiwang*, which might be loosely translated as a network. A person proficient in *guanxixue* can *la guanxi* with closer intermediaries in order to reach *guanxihu* either in one's own or someone else's *guanxiwang*.

---

informal politics, factions, and career paths (Nathan 1973, 1976a; Oksenberg 1970, 1976; Tsou 1976) discuss personal relations and networks but do not use the Chinese word *guanxi*, although they do use other Chinese words. Nathan (1976b) has *kuan-hsi* in parentheses in his Index after "Connections," but does not use it in the actual text.

4 Because none of the translations completely captures the cultural essence of the term, we will, following Jacobs, leave it untranslated.

5 "Native place" can range from a village up to a province, depending on the context in which people try to establish some common trait. Outside of China, the mere fact of being "Chinese" can serve the same function. For another listing of the bases of *guanxi*, see Qiao (1982). He emphasizes that people who perceive they have a relationship use the words *tong* (same) or *lao* (a term of familiarity, literally "old") to identify partners. These terms recall Talcott Parsons's contrasting of traditional and modern orientations to the world characteristic of whole societies. "Particularism," according to Parsons, includes an affective component, and this is opposed to "universalism," which is based on objective standards devoid of affect.

6 Yang (1994) translates *"xue"* as "ology." It literally means "study." See also Xin (1983). Other Chinese scholars who have been active in proposing taxonomies of *guanxi* include Sun (1996) and Yang (1995).

7 See, for example: Central Discipline Inspection Commission of the CCP's August 6, 1981, Circular on Enforcing Party Discipline and Eliminating the Unhealthy Practice of Under-the-Table Relationships (*guanxihu*); *Foreign Broadcast Information Report*, August 7, 1981, pp. K2–3.

In a very general sense, *guanxi* resembles Pierre Bourdieu's concept of "social capital," which, according to Bourdieu (1986, pp. 248–249), "is the aggregate of the actual or potential resources which are linked to possession of a durable network of more or less institutionalized relationships of mutual acquaintance and recognition – or in other words, to membership in a group – which provides each of its members with the backing of the collectivity-owned capital, a 'credential' which entitles them to credit, in the various senses of the word."[8] As with other forms of capital, Bourdieu is interested in the ability to convert one form of capital into another. Clearly, in China, *guanxi* as social capital is accumulated with the intention of converting it into economic, political, or symbolic capital.[9]

However, there are important aspects of *guanxi* that set it apart from a generalized notion of social capital, imparting a special significance to interpersonal relations that turns *guanxi* into the "indigenous Chinese category" (Yan 1996a, p. 14). First is that it is "based implicitly (rather than explicitly) on mutual interest and benefit. Once *guanxi* is recognized between two people, each can ask a favor of the other with the expectation that the debt incurred will be repaid sometime in the future" (Yang 1994, pp. 1–2). The notion of reciprocal obligation and indebtedness is central to the system of *guanxi* in China. Thus, this is more than simply an issue of social embeddedness and social connections; it is a system of gifts and favors in which obligation and indebtedness are manufactured, and there is no time limit on repayment (Yang 1994; see also Yang 1957).[10] In other words, *guanxi* is the basis for a gift economy that exists in China, and this economy has specific rites, rituals, and rules attached to it. The other distinctive aspect is the importance of affect or sentiment – *ganqing (kan-ch'ing)* – in *guanxi*. Although many foreign commentators (business people prominent among them) believe that *guanxi* functions almost exclusively for instrumental purposes, Chinese frequently stress that true *guanxi* must possess an affective component. The most extended discussion of *ganqing* in

8   Bourdieu's concept of social capital actually falls in line with those in this volume who see *guanxi* not as a cultural or social given but as a system that is closely tied to institutions and structures of power. Indeed, Bourdieu (1986, p. 249) goes on to note that "the existence of a network of connections is not a natural given, or even a social given . . . It is the product of an endless effort at institution." For more elaboration, see Smart (1993). Bourdieu also mentions "institution rites" (1986, p. 249), which is a critically important aspect of correctly establishing *guanxi* in China without causing undue embarrassment or humiliation. See Kipnis (1997), Yan (1996a), and Yang (1994) for more discussion of rituals.

9   While not using Bourdieu's terms, Hwang (1987) discusses the "conversion" of *guanxi* into face (symbolic capital) and *renqing* (human feelings). See also the discussion in Yan (1996a), esp. ch. 6. With symbolic capital, prestige is gained both by demonstrating that one's *guanxi* enables one to solicit favors and that one can deliver when solicited by others.

10   In his classic essay, Lien-sheng Yang (1957) elaborates the concept of *bao (pao)*, meaning "reciprocity of actions." He writes: "Favors done for others are often considered what may be termed 'social investments,' for which handsome returns are expected" (p. 291). He emphasizes that "the response or return in social relations need not always be immediate" (p. 292), but notations are kept on a "social balance sheet" (p. 292), which is held by a family, not just an individual. Several anthropologists have elaborated on this idea, specifically relating it to *guanxi*, utilizing Mauss's concept of "the gift" (Liu 1998; Smart 1993, 1998; Yan 1996a; and Yang 1989, 1994).

interpersonal relations is Fried's (1953) classic ethnography of a village in Anhui province. He defines it as "the quality of the relationship" between two parties that varies "in warmth and intensity" (p. 103).[11] Some Chinese engage in the practice of *guanxi* for the intrinsic enjoyment of the ongoing personal relationship itself, although the aspect of implied obligations is never entirely absent. Instrumentalism and sentiment come together in *guanxi*, as cultivating *guanxi* successfully over time creates a basis of trust in a relationship (Smart 1993, p. 402).[12]

Not surprisingly, this combination of instrumentalism and sentiment strikes many observers (and practitioners) as contradictory at best, cynical at worst.[13] One can see it as part of a larger moral economy, often difficult for outsiders to comprehend, much less appreciate (Geertz 1973). To explain this, Kipnis (1997, p. 23) states that "in *guanxi*, feelings and instrumentality are a totality," while Smart (1993, p. 404) concludes that "the stability of interpersonal relationships even those implicated in capitalist relations of production, is supported by the utilization of an idiom capable of encompassing divergent motivations and forms of exchange. This idiom is the vocabulary of *guanxi*, of *ganqing*, of accomplishing tasks, and of long-term social relationships." It is significant, though not surprising, that anthropologists who have done intensive field work in a discrete rural field site appear likelier to stress the sentimental component than people who have conducted research (or business) in urban areas. The latter often believe that *guanxi* serves purely instrumental functions and is little more than a euphemistic gloss for corruption and back door dealing.

It is also possible that timing has something to do with this negative view of *guanxi*. Because the concept initially made it into foreign perspectives of China during the early period of opening up, when China had few laws or regulations governing the headlong, often ill-prepared onslaught of foreign trade and investment, the centrality of *guanxi* was quite pronounced, and any protestations of an equal element of sentiment were scoffed at. The early reform years coincided with Deng Xiaoping's efforts to purge the followers of the radical Gang of Four, itself, by definition, a *guanxiwang*. In a major 1980 address, "On the Reform of the System of Party and State Leadership," Deng lambasted many unhealthy practices of cadres such as "bureaucracy, over-concentration of power, patriarchal methods,

---

11 Fried draws a careful distinction between *ganqing* and friendship. The latter is "a relationship between two or more persons based on mutual affection and sympathy and devoid of the object of exploitation," while the former "differs from friendship in that it presumes a much more specific common interest, much less warmth and more formality of contact, and includes a recognized degree of exploitation" (p. 226). In this book, he uses numerous Chinese terms but does not mention the term "*guanxi*."

12 For an extended discussion of trust in Chinese societies (or the lack thereof), in comparison with other societies, see Fukuyama (1995).

13 Research by psychologists comparing East Asians and Americans suggests that Asians have a higher tolerance for such contradictions: In one study, "'Asians tended to be more 'holistic,' showing greater attention to context, a tolerance for contradiction, and less dependence on logic'" ("Tomayto, Tomahto, Potayto . . ." *New York Times Week in Review*, August 13, 2000, p. 2); see also Ji et al. (2000).

life tenure in leading posts, and privileges of various kinds" (Deng 1984, p. 309). Personal networks pervade these practices and had been strengthened by the law-lessness of the Cultural Revolution decade (1966–1976). Now these networks were being used to protect their members from the purge. Of course, Deng was also mobilizing his own networks to oust those of his enemies. The Chinese media at the time were replete with attacks on *guanxi*-related unhealthy practices, fueling perceptions of *guanxi*'s ubiquity among Chinese and foreigners alike.[14]

Guanxi relationships are by definition unequal, although the locus of power shifts and may never be in complete balance (Hwang 1987; Wang 1979; Zhai 1996). Because of the intrinsic element of reciprocity and obligation, one party seeks some favor, which then obligates both parties to continue the relationship. (Of course, it is possible to break off a relationship, although there is a risk to the reputation of both parties.) Effective use of *guanxi* can provide face (*mianzi*) – that is, prestige and status. Pye (1992b, pp. 207–208) argues that "the advantaged position is that of the person who can 'pull *guanxi*' – that is, extract favors from the more fortunate partner" – and Yan (1996a, p. 21, and ch. 7) concludes that gift-receiving rather than gift-giving generates power and prestige: "In some contexts, gifts flow only up the social status hierarchy with the recipient always superior in status to the giver." Inequality is also apparent in the exclusionary nature of *guanxi*, as it indicates who is in a network and who is not. Although networks are far-flung, they do constitute a boundary for a circle of exchange.

SCHOLARSHIP ON *GUANXI*[15]

The Chinese can hardly claim to have the only society where networks play an important role in social life. Yet, many observers and scholars of China recognize *guanxi* as something special or crucial within Chinese society and Chinese circles more broadly. How do we explain its significance? And what does it actually tell us about Chinese society? In answer to these enduring questions, a growing body of literature has emerged over the last two decades that can be broken down into two perspectives. On one side of the debate sit those who see *guanxi* as an essential element of Chinese culture, a phenomenon deeply rooted in the Chinese psyche. On the other side of the debate are scholars who see *guanxi* as a response to specific institutional and historical conditions that happen to exist in China. According to this latter group of scholars, the conditions that have produced *guanxi* have been extreme enough and enduring enough that the phenomenon has over time become inextricably linked to Chinese society, but it is the institutional conditions that have driven the emergence of the phenomenon. Thus, from this view, any perception of the particular Chineseness of *guanxi* is an artifact of historical and institutional conditions.

14 Examples include: Liu Binyan's (1983) "People or Monsters?"; fiction by Jiang Zilong (1980, 1983); poetry by Ye Wenfu (1983); drama by Sha Yexin et. al. (1983) and Xing Yixun (1980); comedians' cross-talk by Wang Minglu (1986); and news items with critical commentary such as *Renmin Ribao* August 7, 1981.

15 For an extensive literature review, see Nathan (1993).

Is Guanxi a Chinese phenomenon?

Scholars who view this phenomenon as fundamentally Chinese trace *guanxi* to its enduring significance in traditional Chinese philosophy, in particular its stress on the centrality of social interaction in the formation of the individual's identity and sense of fulfillment as a "person." In contrast to someone in the Judeo-Christian tradition who derives identity and fulfillment from a direct spiritual relation to God, for a Chinese "there can be no fulfillment for the individual in isolation from his fellow men" (King 1985, p. 57; see also deBary 1985, p. 33). The self is realized in the social sphere. "*The* key concept in Confucianism is *jen* [*ren*], or human heartedness" (Mei 1967, p. 328), which involves self-cultivation and education, in particular, learning how to treat other people.[16]

It follows that understanding and successfully managing interpersonal relationships are essential elements of being authentically "Chinese," regardless of time or place. The noted Chinese scholar Liang Shuming argued that "Chinese society is neither *ko-jen pen-wei* [*geren benwei*] (individual-based) nor *she-hui pen-wei* [*shehui benwei*] (society-based), but *kuan-hsi pen-wei* [*guanxi benwei*] (relation-based). In a relation-based social system, the emphasis is placed on the relation between particular individuals: "The focus is not fixed on any particular individual, but on the particular nature of the relations between individuals who interact with each other. The focus is placed upon the relationship" (King 1985, p. 63). Wei-ming Tu (1981, p. 114) argues that "the human mind may resemble a tabula rasa, but a person is always born to a complex social network." The main point within this view is that "the self so conceived is not a static structure but a dynamic process. It is a *center* of relationships, not an enclosed world of private thoughts and feelings. It needs to reach out, to be in touch with other selves and to communicate through an ever-expanding network of human-relatedness" (ibid, p. 113).

To characterize the essential Chinese approach to social relationships, China's eminent sociologist Fei Xiaotong (1992, p. 65) utilized the image of "ripples formed from a stone thrown into a lake, each circle spreading out from the center becomes more distant and at the same time more insignificant." Fei refers to this as *chaxu geju*, his neologism awkwardly translated as "differential mode of association." Within this mode of association, the society is composed not of discrete organizations, as in the modern West, but of overlapping networks of people linked together through differentially categorized social relationships" (ibid, p. 20). Each individual is at the center of an egocentric network with no explicit boundaries, always involved in social interactions (*guanxi*) of varying strength. People are

---

16 This *jen* (*ren*) is the same Chinese character as the *ren* in *renqing* (*jen-ch'ing*) translated above as human feelings. *Ren* is made up of a radical for "person" with the number 2, indicating that to be a fully realized "person" involves interacting properly with other people. Contrast this with the "Lockean individualism" at the root of the American concept of "self" (Bellah et al., 1991, esp. pp. 85–90). In his fabulously politically incorrect 1894 book, Arthur Smith wrote on the concept of *ren*, which he translated as "benevolence": "It is unnecessary to remark that the theory which the form of the character seems to favour, is not at all substantiated by the facts of life among the Chinese" (p. 186).

continuously evaluating and managing – through reciprocity – their relations with others.

From this perspective, the centrality of *guanxi* in Chinese society at any time or place is an essential part of "China's national character" (Hwang 1987, p. 959). "That the Chinese are preoccupied with *kuan-hsi* building has indeed a built-in cultural imperative behind it" (King 1985, p. 68). One need not anchor an explanation of the persistence of *guanxi* in any particular institutional arrangement; Chinese just are that way. It is "part of the essential 'stock knowledge' . . . of Chinese adults in their management of everyday life" (ibid, p. 63). While these elements singly and as a complex are not unique to China, contemporary or historically, scholars in this tradition believe that the pervasiveness of *guanxi* as a social fact in China gives credence to claims that it occupies a special place in Chinese life, well beyond its status elsewhere.

These often-unquestioned assumptions about the centrality of *guanxi* to the Chinese worldview have informed the work of scholars and business consultants. Prominent among scholars have been political scientists examining topics such as factionalism, patron-client relations, and informal politics.[17] The work of Lucian Pye (1968) and Richard Solomon (1969, 1971) on political culture stands out, in particular their emphasis on Chinese psychological dependency on strong personalized authority figures. Pye starts from the Chinese "compulsive need to avoid disorder and confusion, to seek predictability and the comforts of dependency, and to accept the importance of authority," which makes "them anxious to seek out any acceptable basis for orderly human relationships" (1968, p. 174). According to Pye, the very basis of a Chinese person's understanding of the world is the "web" of relationships in which he is embedded, a fact that naturalizes the manipulation of relationships to accomplish tasks. As Pye puts it, "The Chinese tend to see the manipulation of human relationships as the natural and normal approach for accomplishing most things in life" because they perceive "society as a web of human relationships and associations" (ibid, pp. 173–74). From this view, Chinese culture creates a deep psychological proclivity for individuals to actively cultivate and manipulate social relations for instrumental ends.[17a]

The unanticipated rise of industrial East Asia generated a great deal of interest in explaining how collectivity-oriented peoples could exhibit such dynamic entrepreneurial energy, something presumed to reside only in heroic individuals. The work of S. Gordon Redding, in delineating the contours of "the spirit of Chinese capitalism" (1990), focuses on "the psycho-social legacy of China" to explain how networks can be made to serve business. As with Pye and Solomon,

17   While the early scholars working in this area studied issues related to *guanxi*, many did not use the term or address the issue specifically. However, it appears that the first scholarly work to explore *guanxi* explicitly was in the area of politics: J. Bruce Jacobs (1979, 1980) took up the issue in his study of factions in Taiwanese politics. While his approach was essentialist, Bosco (1994a) later, also studied *guanxi* in Taiwanese factional politics from an institutionalist perspective.

17a Pye (1992a) and Solomon (1999) have discussed the Chinese use of *guanxi* as central to their negotiating style in diplomacy and business.

Redding stresses the insecurity at the root of the Chinese psyche and the need to be part of a collectivity and deal to the greatest extent possible only with familiar people one can trust. Gary Hamilton (1989) coined the term "*guanxi* capitalism" as a distinct form of business practice derived primarily from the Chinese kinship system.[17b] The role of *guanxi* also figures prominently in studies of the rise of Taiwan's business class (Kao 1991; Fields 1995; Luo 1997; Numazaki 1992).[18] Studies of the predominance of Overseas Chinese in the economies of Southeast Asia emphasize *guanxi* as the fundamental principle undergirding business activity (Kao 1993; Simons and Zielenziger 1994; Tanzer 1994; Weidenbaum 1996).

China's opening to the outside world also spawned a cohort of consultants to explain the mysteries of doing business in China. No "how to" book or seminar on doing business in China fails to cover the necessity and tactics for establishing, cultivating, and making use of *guanxi*.[18a] Not surprisingly many of the consultants promote themselves as repositories of invaluable *guanxi* at the highest level, able to clinch any deal.[19] Some scholarly studies of inter-firm activity first assumed the importance of *guanxi* in doing business in China, and then, tautologically, set out to prove how important it was, urging foreign investors to master the skill (Gomez Arias 1998; Luo and Chen 1997; Tung and Worm 1997). In this way, *guanxi* often becomes a self-fulfilling prophecy.

Other prominent scholars of *guanxi* maintain the view that *guanxi* is a cultural phenomenon in China, though for many the assumptions about the Chineseness of *guanxi* are more implicit than explicit. One important example can be found in the work of Mayfair Yang, whose book, *Gifts, Favors, and Banquets: The Art of Social Relationships in China* (1994), is in many ways *the* seminal book in contemporary research on *guanxi*. While Yang links China's contemporary gift economy to the institutional upheaval of the Cultural Revolution, she nevertheless stakes out an unambiguous position on the Chineseness of *guanxi*. Yang explicitly links the current incarnations of *guanxixue* (i.e., China's gift economy) to "the ancestral forms of *guanxixue* gifts and etiquette." Yang is thorough in this endeavor,

---

17b   Hsu and Saxenian (2000) apply this term critically in their study of linkages between Taiwanese and Silicon Valley firms.

18   Enterprise groups in Taiwan are referred to as *guanxi qiye* – literally, related enterprises.

18a   Consider the promotion for *Doing Business in China*, Ambler and Witzel (2000): "This work . . . emphasizes the importance of '*guanxi*' (relationships) as the underpinning of virtually all business in China."

19   In a form of self-orientalization, a two-volume set attributed to Dong Fangzhi (an obvious pseudonym meaning Eastern Wisdom) entitled *Guanxixue* published in Beijing promises readers that "if you learn how to manage all forms of human and social *guanxi*, it will be like planting a large tree from which you can obtain mounds of fruit you never imagined" (1998, cover). Alan Turley, America's Senior Commercial Officer in Beijing, in his "Turley's Top Ten Tips on Doing Business in China," advised business people to "pay attention to *guanxi*," while quickly adding that most of what is said about *guanxi* is "garbage." As the reforms deepened and rule of law gained ground, assumptions that manipulating *guanxi* was the only way to conduct business could prove destructive (Gilley 1999a, 1999b; Saywell 1999). The commercial office of the American Institute in Taiwan published a journal entitled "Kwanhsi" to introduce Americans to business practices in Taiwan.

devoting a full chapter of her book to tracing the contemporary gift economy's origins "to an ancient past ... when a conflict between two discourses, *Rujia* (later called Confucian) and *Fajia* (or Legalist), first took place" (Yang 1994, pp. 208–9). Through a detailed discussion of the *Rujia* discourse, Yang argues that the antecedent of China's current gift economy is the early Confucian discourse on a ritualized state and society that placed social relations (as opposed to a rationalized objective legal system) at its center. As Yang (1994, p. 229) puts it, "Therefore the implications of the *Rujia* discourse on government based on ritual is a society of social relations. . . ." From this perspective, it is China's distant past that has reemerged to shape the practices of the gift economy in contemporary Chinese society.

Others, such as Yanjie Bian, are subtler in their cultural orientation toward understanding this phenomenon, yet the assumptions about the basic Chineseness of *guanxi* are still evident. Bian, who has done significant work on the institutional underpinnings of the role of *guanxi* in job allocation, stops short of the essentialist view, but nevertheless seems to be informed by a view that there is something fundamentally Chinese about *guanxi*. While clearly interested in the structural factors that shape certain social practices (such as hiring practices), Bian begins with the assumption that the reliance on social relations is fundamental in China, stating his baseline assumptions in the following way: "The assumption ... is that all Chinese live in a web of social relationships. People's family, kinship networks, work colleagues, neighbours, classmates, friendship circles and even casual acquaintances are the social communities into which they grow and on which they depend ... Rationally, individuals cultivate and utilize their social connections in order to satisfy their personal interests. As an exchange, they have an obligation to assist others who are connected to them" (Bian 1994b, p. 972). Thus, while Bian mentions nothing of Confucianism, *Rujia*, or the philosophical roots of *guanxi*, the *assumption* of Chinese social embeddedness and the notion that Chinese people have a natural tendency to manufacture reciprocal obligation within this "web of social relationships" is the starting point for all further analyses. What unites this body of research is the beginning assumptions about Chinese society and Chinese social interaction.

The institutional turn in analyses of Guanxi

A growing body of scholarship has taken the position that *guanxi* has emerged from a particular set of social institutions that happen to exist in China (but also exist in other societies) and that there is nothing fundamentally Chinese about this phenomenon.[20] Where many of the scholars discussed earlier see *guanxi* as essentially Chinese, tracing its origins to philosophical antecedents millennia old, others hold the view that there is nothing Chinese about *guanxi*, but rather that this system is the result of the institutional structure of Chinese society. That is,

20   In other words, *guanxi* is a Chinese idiom for a general phenomenon.

the structure of Chinese society facilitates or encourages the reliance on networks to accomplish tasks; it is the institutional configuration of society that leads to the patterns of behavior that prevail in Chinese society. From this perspective, *guanxi* is no different from its Russian analog, *blat*, and the gift economy that is built around this concept in Russia (Ledeneva 1998) is very similar to the one that exists in China. What these societies share, the institutionalists would argue, is that they are both shortage economies with weak legal infrastructures, so networking and trust become fundamental parts of economic transactions. Institutionalists would further predict that as the institutions of these developing economies and societies change, so too should the reliance on social networks. The fascinating thing about China today is that it presents us with a remarkable laboratory in which to examine our ideas about the role of culture and different institutional configurations in shaping the reliance on *guanxi* in Chinese societies. For example, one way scholars have gained analytical leverage over the issue lies in the study of cross-societal uses of *guanxi*, asking questions about the appearance of and reliance on *guanxi* in Chinese societies that vary institutionally, such as China, Taiwan, and Singapore.[21] Another analytical strategy, especially among institutionalists, has been to study the role of *guanxi* in Mainland China, paying close attention to the stability of *guanxi* in the face of China's rapidly changing institutions.

The most clearly institutionalist position on the existence of *guanxi* has been staked out by the influential works of Andrew Walder (1986) and Jean Oi (1989). For Walder, the use of *guanxi* in the form of patron-client relations within the work unit (*danwei*) is a response to the situation where powerful officials controlled access to scarce, rationed necessities such as housing, non-wage benefits, and even promotions. But this can also be seen in other socialist economies of shortage such as the Soviet Union. Walder terms this set of relationships "neo-traditional," by which he means to imply "traditional" as opposed to "modern" or personal and particularistic as opposed to rational-legal.[22] In Oi's analysis of rural politics, she concludes that although "parallels exist" between the type of clientelistic politics that she has described and "similar accounts of official malfeasance and the importance of personal ties in imperial China . . . this behavior is neither inherently Chinese nor traditional" (1989, p. 228) as it can be found in a wide variety of other societies. Guthrie (1998a) follows Walder and Oi in looking at the structural causes underlying the utilization of *guanxi*, tracing the prevalence of *guanxi* to the problems inherent

---

21   This book's focus is on the PRC, but it would be valuable to conduct rigorous systematic comparative research on *guanxi* in different "Chinese" societies, including the diaspora, to see how, if one holds culture constant, *guanxi* adapts to different economic, social, and political environments (see, e.g., Bian and Ang 1997). Another interesting issue is why *guanxi* is such a pejorative term in the PRC but has a much less negative connotation in other societies, such as Taiwan, where the affective element is stressed. Alston (1989) and Sonoda (1995) do some of this across Confucian societies.

22   "It is not intended to convey a proposition that is a virtual truism – that authority relations in contemporary industry reflect the influence of prerevolutionary cultural traditions" (1986, p. 9). The term "neo-traditional" comes from Ken Jowitt (1983). On the role of *guanxi* in the workplace, see also Ruan (1993).

in shortage economies. Guthrie extends this position to argue that the emergence of rational law and a market economy in China are diminishing the importance of *guanxi* in Chinese society, a position, he asserts, that underlines the institutional roots of this phenomenon. The central notion for all of these scholars is that there are specific structural and institutional conditions that have given rise to the reliance on *guanxi* to accomplish tasks in China's transforming economy, and this phenomenon has little if anything to do with Chinese culture or Chinese society per se.

Other scholars, examining different sectors of Chinese society, have walked a line that acknowledges Chinese cultural and historical particularities, while refraining from making them central explanatory variables. Many of these studies have demonstrated how Chinese people have used *guanxi* to cope with the lack of the rule of law and the arbitrary and discretionary nature of the use of power. For example, although not using the Chinese term *guanxi*, analysts of factions, interest groups, and elites prior to and during the Cultural Revolution consistently held up the use of personal networks based on such things as common native place, military service, schooling, time in the Soviet Union, and so on, as a means utilized by political figures as a key mechanism of self-protection, career advancement, and survival particularly during the rough and tumble Cultural Revolution era when whatever regularized procedures had been established in effect collapsed. In a pair of book-end articles on "the ladder of success" (1970) and "the exit pattern" (1976), Michel Oksenberg enumerates a number of important political skills under the larger rubric "managing personal relations" (1970, p. 330 ff). These involve finding correct people to associate with as well as knowing whom to avoid. And Lucian Pye's later work, while still stressing Chinese cultural proclivities, has been more firmly situated in specific structural causes, such as the lack of formal regulations and the "danger-filled political environment" (1995, p. 35). A special issue of *The China Journal* (No. 34, July 1995) featured a lively debate about informal politics in China and the role of *guanxi* therein.[23]

The use of *guanxi* to navigate institutionally uncertain environments also relates to the issue of foreigners attempting to trade with or invest in China. Although the Chinese have been attempting to promulgate and implement a set of regulations and laws, Chinese business practices still approach such bedrock Western concepts as "contracts" from a perspective where the contract is seen as a cage that appropriate *guanxi* can unlock (Lubman 1998, pp. 3–43; see also Lubman 1996). For those viewing *guanxi* as a mechanism for coping with the absence of a formal and reliable system of laws and regulations in the economy, the socialist legacy of a shortage economy combined with the subsequent problems derived from the co-existence of two systems (redistributive and market) to create both the need and opportunity for using *guanxi* (Wang 1989; Zheng 1986). David Wank's (1995, 1999a) research on Xiamen uncovered the existence of what he labeled "symbiotic clientelism" between private businessmen and officials. The businessmen, whose

23 In particular, the contributions of Dittmer, Pye, and Nathan, and Tsai. See also the special issue of *Asian Survey* (36[3], March 1996) on "Informal Politics in East Asia." In the articles by Fewsmith on the elite and Dittmer and Lu on the *danwei, guanxi* is a key analytical concept.

social and legal standing were still very tenuous, needed official assistance to get access to licenses, resources, venues, protection, and other favors, while the officials needed the businessmen to stimulate the economy to demonstrate the official's competence in the new reform environment.[24] Wank argues that the more marketized regions of China have not eliminated clientelism, as some had predicted, but on the contrary, had just marked a "transformation *within* a clientelist political order" (1995, p. 176).

Hsing (1998), and Smart and Smart (1998) have shown how *guanxi* operates in the foreign-investment sector of the reform economy, using case studies of Taiwanese and Hong Kong investors on the Mainland. When Beijing urged local officials to solicit foreign investment, many of them turned first to Overseas Chinese whose ancestors originated from their jurisdiction, such as Taiwanese from Fujian or Hong Kongese from Guangdong. This also resulted in a form of symbiotic relationship between the investors and local officials. Bosco (1994b) has shown how Taiwanese investors also use *guanxi* with other Taiwanese investors in China "as a defense against what are viewed as unpredictable Mainland Chinese" (p. 16). In all of these studies, while the study of *guanxi* networks becomes important to the research these scholars present, each is interested in presenting the institutional configurations that lead to the importance of *guanxi* in the various economic settings they are studying.

Studies of rural society have unearthed the tangled effects of traditional kin relations and transitional institutions. Kipnis (1997) and Yan (1996a, b) conducted detailed ethnographies examining the structure of *guanxi* as well as its meaning to the villagers they lived among. These scholars do not deny the particularities of Chinese culture or history, but they ground their work in a more recent past than that found in the work of Yang.[25] In this body of work, the focus is on the ways that traditional categories are mobilized and employed in the practices of today. In his study of local corporatism in the notorious village of Daqiuzhuang, Lin (1995) discovered how the "inequality of opportunity and rewards structures" (p. 312) gave salience to the importance of kin networks. He and others highlight *guanxi* as a resource, often called "*guanxi* capital," which can be profitably invested in the reform era economy. And while marriage has traditionally been seen as a means of linking family networks together, Riley (1994, p. 793) argues that "certain elements of modern Chinese society have actually increased the necessity for maintaining kin ties," and passing *guanxi* down through the generations. These elements include the need for *guanxi* to find jobs and housing. Her conclusions, like Gold's (1985), stress the instrumental side of *guanxi*, where the social, economic,

---

24   Bruun (1993; 1995), Chen (2000), Hertz (1998), Li (1997), Whiting (1998), Xin and Pearce (1996), and Young (1995) make similar arguments. It is beyond the scope of this book, but work by Hamilton and Kao (1990), on Taiwanese business, as well as Hamilton and Biggart (1988) attempts to offer an institutional alternative to both overly cultural and overly economic explanations for the structure of business groups and management styles in Taiwan and elsewhere in East Asia.

25   As Kipnis puts it, *guanxi* "must be understood in the context of more than 40 years of Chinese Communist Party policy ... rather than [as] a manifestation of ancient textual tradition" (Kipnis 1997, p. 7).

and political systems require that one accumulate *guanxi* to get almost anything done. Chinese scholars generally concurred, at least in the early 1980s, that the upheavals of the Cultural Revolution left institutions and values in such disarray that people everywhere concentrated their energies on accumulating *guanxi* and mastering the art of *guanxixue* as a basic strategy for survival and mobility (Chen 1997; Peng 1996; Zhai 1996).

Contributions to current scholarship

With a critical mass of scholarship on this topic, the study of *guanxi* has begun to unearth many of the most interesting and challenging questions for understanding Chinese society. In our assessment, however, there are at least four critical directions in which research on social networks in China must evolve, and it is our hope that this book begins to address each of these directions. First, on a conceptual level, the important insights in research on *guanxi* are going to come from work that extends beyond the recent debate over whether *guanxi* is a uniquely Chinese phenomenon or whether it is a general phenomenon that extends across different cultural settings. The debate has been set up in an either-or framework, but the reality is that both culture and institutions matter for the functioning of *guanxi* in China. While this debate has produced some lively exchanges, a continued consideration of the "Chineseness" of *guanxi* is not going to advance research on or understanding of the social structure of Chinese society. What will advance research is a focus on the specific ways this phenomenon functions across different social settings in China today. In other words, conceptual work on *current practice* and the intermingling of institutions and culture in the current era will be the key to advancing insights on the study of social networks in China. It is along these lines that the work of Andrew Kipnis has been among the most interesting in its analytical approach to the study of *guanxi*. Kipnis's work has focused more explicitly than most on the *practices* of *guanxi*, rather than on trying to find a definition of *guanxi* itself. For Kipnis, the phenomenon and the practices through which it is manifested are so intricately intertwined that it is impossible to try to define *guanxi* independent of its practices. Kipnis's work has been built on an in-depth consideration of the relationship between the practices associated with *guanxi* and those associated with *ganqing*, and in his chapter in this volume he pushes that analysis further. Where previously Kipnis argued that *ganqing* was central to the production of *guanxi*, he now sees the relationship between the two concepts as a much more complex one, a relationship subject to the complex and multifaceted intentions of the individuals involved in the exchange. His new insights into the data he analyzed in his earlier work illustrate the ways that a sustained and careful focus on specific practices and the cultural concepts they embody can advance our understanding of this complex social phenomenon.

A second direction for development in this area of research will come through careful methodological consideration about how exactly we should approach the study of *guanxi*. In their respective chapters, Guthrie and Lin take up some of these issues directly. Guthrie points to what he sees as a fundamental problem in the study of *guanxi*, centering his analysis on the problem of information asymmetries in perceptions of *guanxi* exchange. Focusing primarily on the research that examines the role of *guanxi* in labor markets, he argues that it makes little sense to ask individuals who seek to use *guanxi* to gain an advantage in the marketplace whether *guanxi* is important in these processes. Studies on the role of *guanxi* in labor market processes, without exception, use data gathered from employees or job *seekers*. While these individuals certainly know if they *attempted* to use *guanxi* to gain an advantage on the labor market, they have no information on how much the *guanxi* tie actually figured into the decision or outcome. In other words, while an individual who attempts to *la guanxi* ("pull" *guanxi* strings) to get a job might perceive that *guanxi* was instrumental in his job attainment (and thereby present such a picture of Chinese society), it is equally possible that he got the job for his qualifications and that the *guanxi* tie had little or nothing to do with the final outcome. However, the employee or job seeker has no way of distinguishing between these circumstances, because he is not privy to the decision-making process. Thus, as long as this information asymmetry exists, this research tack must remain suspect. Lin also deals with an under-theorized and under-studied part of *guanxi* exchanges – "third-party effects" – which he argues are absolutely crucial to these exchanges. Lin begins with the simple question: "Given similarly strong ties and networking skills, why are some actors more capable of making effective use of *guanxi* than others?" The answer, he argues, lies in individuals who are positioned outside of the dyad involved in the *guanxi* exchange. A third party can be a mutual friend, an intermediary, or even a competitor in the marketplace, and all of these, according to Lin, have crucial implications for how *guanxi* functions as an exchange system in the era of economic reforms.

A third step forward in the research on *guanxi* will come from an examination of new types of data and heretofore-unexamined contexts in which *guanxi* can be found. The interesting challenge before us now lies in figuring out the specific ways and under what set of circumstances *guanxi* matters in China's transforming economy, and it is only through an in-depth examination of new research sites and new cases that we can begin to uncover the ways that *guanxi* matters in China today. This is perhaps where the new insights generated by this volume will be most fruitful. For example, Lisa Keister brings to bear an entirely original data set on the study of *guanxi* to examine the ways that *guanxi* ties influence the economic decisions of state managers in reform-era China. Her analysis of trading relations among the 535 member firms of China's 40 largest business groups, coupled with the qualitative data she gathered through in-depth interviews with the managers from a sub-sample of these firms, provide excellent concrete evidence of the ways that social relations shape economic relations and economic decisions. Keister finds that while social relations seem to hold little sway in the structuring of obligation and indebtedness or in attempting to avoid complying with formal laws and regulations, "managers [in the 535 member firms] relied on the social ties they already had to reduce the uncertainty that characterized China's economy in the early stages of reform." She also finds, however, that prior social ties reduced the likelihood that managers would try to cultivate dependent relations with weaker firms in the economy, a fact that has interesting implications for the specific ways that social relations might influence the type of market economy emerging in China. In other words, social ties appear to reduce the likelihood of predatory market strategies, regardless of the advantages such strategies might provide. Wank also embeds his work in the study of social relations among economic actors, but his focus is on the private economy, rather than the transforming state sector as in Keister. Wank's objective is to place power squarely in the center of the analysis of *guanxi*, arguing that the necessity of cultivating relationships with powerful state actors is central to the experience of entrepreneurs in China's emerging private economy. More than this, however, Wank makes the case that this is about more than simply the experiences of small-scale entrepreneurs in China; it is fundamentally about the type of market economy that is emerging in China in the first place. According to Wank, China's market economy will be one that is centrally organized around the types of network relations that economic actors see as essential to their desire to get ahead in China's transitional economy.

Research on the role of *guanxi* in labor market processes has formed a well-beaten path, but Yanjie Bian and Amy Hanser both bring new data to the table. In his chapter, Bian argues that *guanxi* remains a persistent and important factor in the allocation of jobs in urban China. Based on an in-depth study of 100 job seekers, who acquired 392 jobs between 1992 and 1997, Bian finds that more than half of these job shifts used *guanxi* (i.e., "strong" as opposed to "weak" ties) to gain employment. Bian argues that there are still many "institutional holes" in the Chinese labor market, and with the lack of formal institutions by which labor markets operate, individuals still rely on their social networks to gain advantages in the employment process. Hanser uses an in-depth interviewing method and a rich repository of qualitative data to explore the salience of *guanxi* among urban youth in China in the 1990s. Contra Bian, Hanser employs her data to argue that individuals do not rely heavily on *guanxi* to secure jobs in urban China today. In line with Guthrie's position on the issue, Hanser argues that when individuals do talk about *guanxi*, they are generally talking about social ties that generate no sense of reciprocal obligation (such as simple advice or information exchanges), rather than the instrumental use of their social ties in the gift economy.

Scott Wilson, James Farrer, and Pitman Potter each break new substantive ground and bring to bear new conceptual issues, as they explore the linkages between *guanxi* and different types of social norms – from the formal to the informal – and the way current changes in China are transforming the normative environment in which *guanxi* operates. Beginning with the formal, Potter argues that as formal law emerges in China, there is a growing complementarity between the formal rules of the legal system and the informal rules and norms of *guanxi* relations. According to Potter, "In light of the problems of performance and enforcement in the Chinese legal system, *guanxi* relations play an essential role in providing predictability to legal actors. While the role of *guanxi* can be limited by formal law and legal processes, the formal legal system remains incomplete and would have little effect at all were it not for informal mediating mechanisms such as *guanxi* relations." Thus, somewhat ironically, *guanxi* plays the role of providing stability and predictability to a legal system that is very new and still very much in flux. Wilson takes us into the growing suburbs of Shanghai, arguing that the cash nexus and economic development have changed the character of the gifts individuals exchange in China. For example, individuals are more likely to give cash gifts and they are more likely to develop extra-village ties (as opposed to lineage-based intra-village ties). However, Wilson is very clear on the position that gift economy exchanges are still alive and well in rural China, and they still play a significant role in shaping the nature of norms and social life there. Wilson also points out that studies that distinguish between instrumental and sentimental ties are far too firm in the distinction they draw between these two concepts. To Wilson, *guanxi* is a fluid concept, and even those investing in the gift economy are often not sure whether they are going to call in a debt at some point in the future. Ties that begin as *renqing* exchanges may become instrumental at some point down the line, and vice versa. Farrer examines another way that *guanxi* relates to the norms that serve as the glue holding the social worlds of Chinese society together. Farrer takes on the interesting topic of gossip in an urban neighborhood – where he conducted a two-year ethnography – showing the ways that social norms are structured through the social interaction of community members. As the central form by which normative behavioral codes are maintained (particularly regarding sexual behavior), gossip plays a central role in the structure of Farrer's Shanghai community. However, it is also a means of exchange, a means of expressing sentiment, a way of establishing reciprocal obligation; in short, it is a currency through which the gift economy operates in reform era China.

Finally, we believe that research on *guanxi* will be advanced through work that takes seriously the advancement of social network analysis, of which there is a considerable body of literature outside of the China field. It is in this context that Barry Wellman's chapter adds a generalist perspective to a volume that is heavily focused on a particular area of the world. Arguing that social network analysis does not assume that groups are the "normal" building blocks of social systems, and that group structure and dynamics are to be "discovered" (as opposed to assumed), Wellman presents us with a taste for how rigorous social network analysis would proceed. This is useful for research on *guanxi*, because scholarship in this area has a tendency to begin with an assumption that the phenomenon is important in Chinese life and then proceeds to study its dynamics. As Wellman points out, China's experience in the transition era is far from unique among developing societies, and he makes the case that research in this area should be part of research on general social processes rather than on Chinese society per se. The important issues, from Wellman's perspective, become how we should think about analyzing this phenomenon and the tools we should use in this process.

1

PRACTICES OF *GUANXI* PRODUCTION AND PRACTICES OF *GANQING* AVOIDANCE

Andrew Kipnis

The problem of defining *guanxi* is one that I have dismissed and come back to many times. One can approach it from many angles. Is a definition of *guanxi* meant to distinguish something Chinese from something non-Chinese? Or is it meant to distinguish one sort of Chinese thing from another sort of Chinese thing? Is *guanxi* a "thing" at all, or is it just a sort of linguistic abstraction? If the latter, what sort of abstraction is it – a conceptual tool of (English language or Chinese language) social science, or a "native" one? The pairings implied in these questions all oversimplify. What we today call China has interacted with other parts of the world for so long that it is not possible to strictly differentiate the Chinese from the non-Chinese; linguistic abstractions are "things" that have extra-linguistic effects; "native" and social scientific conceptual abstractions usually interact dialectically. I list these questions at the start to point out that discussions of what *guanxi* are, or about how to approach the study of *guanxi*, often falter because those involved focus on different combinations of those questions. One person discusses the uses of *guanxi* as a theoretical tool in the social sciences (e.g., Hwang 1987), while another discusses whether Chinese *guanxi* and American business networks really differ that sharply (e.g., Guthrie 1998a).

Reviewing my own writings on *guanxi* (Kipnis 1994a, 1996, 1997), I find that I have mostly tried to avoid these questions, precisely because I do find them oversimplistic. Yet, at times, answers emerge in spite of my intentions. In this chapter I set out three tasks. First, I review the theoretical and methodological assumptions that informed my earlier work on *guanxi* (including my strategies for avoiding the aforementioned questions). Second, I observe how answers to some of those questions emerged anyway. And finally I revisit and revise some of my earlier findings.

PRACTICES OF *GUANXI* PRODUCTION

Almost from the very beginning of my stay in rural China, I defined the object of
my research as "practices of *guanxi* production" rather than *guanxi* themselves. By
practices of *guanxi* production, I meant all of those social actions, such as banqueting, gift-giving, visiting, helping out, by which people created, manipulated, and
at times eradicated human relationships. I defined my topic in this way for several
practical and theoretical reasons. First, these activities were easily observed, while
guanxi could only be discussed in conversations, or intuited from the observation
of behavior. This ease of observation was political as well as phenomenological. As
with much research in China during the late 1980s, mine was overseen in various
ways by the Chinese Communist Party (CCP). Consequently, I never felt comfortable prying into those aspects of people's *guanxi* that were not public to begin
with. I thought that verbal requests for private truths were likely to lead to either
lies, political trouble for both me and those I talked to, or perhaps both. Instead
of asking people what the "true nature" of their *guanxi* was, I found it easier to
focus on the public aspects of *guanxi* production. Indeed, much *guanxi* production
was purposefully public. People displayed their gifts, took pride in well-attended
banquets, and banged gongs at their weddings to attract the crowds. Other aspects
of *guanxi* production, such as terms of address and etiquette, were matters of daily
social interaction. For all of these practices, not only could I observe them easily,
but I also had the opportunity – indeed, was compelled – to participate myself.
I gave and received gifts, went to banquets, used various terms of address, and so
on. With so much *guanxi* production going on right under my nose, why go after
secrets?

Additionally, I found it convenient to hide my own interest in the sensitive politics of gender, age, and state regulation behind the innocuous label of "customs and
habits" (*fengsu xiguan*). When I had to explain my research interests to officials in
the Foreign Affairs Office, the police, or anyone who seemed vaguely threatening,
especially in the earliest stages of my research, I always muttered something
about the cross-cultural understanding of customs and habits. Such a description
of my research was not entirely untruthful – banqueting and gift-giving were often
discussed in locally authored Chinese-language books on customs and habits
(e.g., Fang et al., 1988) and I was interested in a cultural understanding of them.
But this description also masked my assumption that the study of these customs
and habits would illuminate village politics and economics in innumerable ways.

Theoretically, I hoped that a focus on practices would enable me to avoid some
of the dualisms implied by the questions at the beginning of the chapter. Rather than
looking at a thing that could be clearly delineated from other things, I thought that
practices could be seen as a series of endless variations, making reifying definitions
supercilious. I could avoid the trap of making *guanxi* either "an orientalist gloss
for networking,"[26] or an acultural, universal human necessity. Second, rather than

---

26   This quote comes from a series of questions posed by Thomas Gold at the conference at which
     this book was conceived. The conference was held in Berkeley, California, October 1998.

consider *guanxi* as either a (signifying) concept or a (signified) thing, I hoped that a focus on practice would enable me to conceive of linguistic and extra-linguistic worlds together. Finally, I hoped that the rather awkward phrase "practices of *guanxi* production" could bridge the conceptual divide between "native" categories (where it was obvious that actions such as banqueting and gift-giving had something to do with *guanxi*) and anthropological ones (where "practice" had become a key word). Further explanation requires a closer examination of my theoretical roots.

THEORIES OF COMMUNICATIVE PRACTICE

For many anthropology graduate students in the 1980s, the seeming demise of the culture concept posed a significant dilemma. On the one hand, Geertzian symbolic anthropology provided rich reading for those interested in the role of meaning in social life. On the other hand, critiques of the culture concept as being too holistic, ideational, and ahistorical, and as implying unreflective, unitary, shared knowledges neatly contained within particular societies seemed to render Geertz's approach irrelevant (see Brightman 1995 for an excellent summary of these issues). A parallel problem plagued linguistic anthropology. The concept of "speech community" – a group of people who share norms (and indeed values) of language use as well as a language itself – likewise came under attack for its presumptions of knowledge systems evenly shared among members of well-bounded groups (Hanks 1996, Bonvillain 1997). The problem with these critiques was that they left linguistically oriented cultural anthropologists with few concepts to approach the problem of intersubjectivity – those shared assumptions, orientations, and linguistic and extra-linguistic knowledges, both conscious and unconscious, that enable human communication.[27] One solution was to try to find a conceptual language with which to describe intersubjectivity without implying that it was ahistorical, evenly shared, unreflective, unitary, or neatly bounded.

For many, including myself, Bourdieu's (1977, 1990) practice theory provided the basis for such a language (Ortner 1984; Brightman 1996). Applied to symbolic action, as in William Hanks's (1996) synthesis, *Language and Communicative Practices*, Bourdieu's theory eases the unrealistic assumptions of too bounded a notion of intersubjectivity. It allows for the manipulation, reproduction, and even creation of those assumptions, knowledges, and orientations that constitute intersubjectivity.[28] The result is that historical, geographical, and social variation in communicative practices are givens. Attention to such variation leads away from

27 Cultural model theorists such as Quinn and Holland (1987) and Gadamer (1975, 1976) provide some of the classic theorization of the role of unspoken knowledges, assumptions, and orientations in human social life.

28 Though I read Hanks (1996) after completing my own book, it draws on almost all of the theorists I took seriously, and explicitly explores many of the theoretical tensions implicit in both my own thinking and that of much linguistic and cultural anthropology of the 1980s and early 1990s. From the start, I attempted to understand "practices of *guanxi* production" as what Hanks calls communicative practice.

both simple essentialisms (the Chinese practice *guanxi* but no one else does) and acultural universalism. In my previous theorization of *guanxi* production, I did my best to speak in terms of communicative practice instead of culture, and to focus on both the strategic manipulation of practices of *guanxi* production and the numerous variations of those practices. However, I also tried to describe some relatively stable cultural grounds for practices of *guanxi* production both in Fengjia village (central Shandong province), where I carried out my ethnographic fieldwork, and in China as whole.

For example, at a concrete level I noted patterns of social interaction in Fengjia – the ways in which village residents categorized relationships (dividing friendly relations into family members, relatives, friends, and fellow villagers), how they negotiated seating, eating, and drinking at banquets, the types of gifts they gave on various occasions and the etiquette involved in giving and receiving them, the manner in which they arranged life cycle rituals, and so on. When possible I compared these patterns with those in other Chinese contexts, and analyzed the assumptions, knowledges, and strategies they entailed. I noted, for example, how gifts of cloth were made exclusively by women to women, how trust was built through drinking, how women were excluded from drinking with men, how equivalencies between the size of cash gifts and feelings of attachment were asserted on gift-giving occasions, and how grooms were ritually forced to place relations with male fellow villagers over their relationship with their brides during their wedding. At the most general level, I argued that all practices of *guanxi* production either presumed or asserted an equivalence between material obligation (the obligation to assist with favors, labor, money, or other material goods at a future date) and human feeling (*ganqing*). Unlike economic contracts, which specify material obligations without necessarily involving human feelings, practices of *guanxi* production invoke a world where depth of feeling and material debt go together.

Because practices of *guanxi* production involve more than one person, they necessitate communication. For *guanxi* to be effective, their existence and their contents must be communicated, both to the parties involved in the relationship and to a wider audience of those who might be affected by a given relationship. Indeed, it is precisely the need for communication that makes practices of *guanxi* production so public. What good is a "marriage" if neither your "spouse" nor the wider public acknowledges its existence? Manipulating relationships involves manipulating the definition of a given relationship in both the eyes of one's partner and various publics.

A final dimension of my understanding of practices of *guanxi* production as a type of communicative practice involves the role I attribute to *ganqing* within them. I take *ganqing* – human feelings – to be simultaneously an internal state that helps constitute the subjectivities of individual people and a medium of communication. Here I rely on the interpretations of Sun Lung-kee, an anthropologist writing in Chinese, who used the metaphor of "a magnetic field of human feelings" (*renqing de cilichang*) reconstituting individual "heart/mind" (*xin*) to describe the psychological aspects of *guanxi* production (Sun 1987). Through practices of *guanxi* production, people not only communicate about their relationships, they also manipulate magnetic fields of human feelings and, if successful, thereby reconstitute the heart/minds of the targets of their practice.

In addition to observing its descriptive power, I find Sun's formulation useful in bridging some of the dualisms posited at the beginning of this essay. Because it is both an abstract model of social psychological reality and a native Chinese-language conception of social relations implicit in many practices of *guanxi* production, Sun's formulation breaks down the division between "analytical" and "native" categories. It also transcends the language/reality dualism by pointing to a mechanism by which communicative acts reconstitute things in the world – namely, human heart/minds. In part to emphasize this reconstituitive power, I use the phrase "generation (or materialization) of *ganqing*" rather than "expression of feelings" to describe the mechanisms by which social actions like giving a gift work. For *ganqing* to be effective, both on the level of communication and on the level of emotional manipulation, it has to be made discernable or concrete, to be materialized in some way. But this materialization is not simply a matter of making previously hidden feelings visible – that is, "expressing" them. Rather, it creates something not previously present. When effective, the *ganqing* generated by one person spreads to others.[29]

WHAT IS *GUANXI*?

Despite my emphasis on practice and variation, definitions of *guanxi* emerge at several points in my 1997 book *Producing Guanxi: Sentiment, Self, and Subculture in a North China Village*. I am aware of three factors that contributed to my need to define. First was my focus on intersubjectivity in general, and on what I now view as too rigid a conception of intersubjectivity in particular. In the continual search for shared presumptions that provided the intersubjective ground for the practices, I neglected a consideration of how these practices might have been possible without such a ground, or at least a ground conceived more flexibly. Second was a desire to avoid the ethnocentric trap of seeing "culture" (in the form of not necessarily conscious intersubjective assumptions) as something Chinese, but not Western – that is to say, to see the West as rational and the Chinese as cultural. To avoid this trap, I sometimes contrasted a Chinese logic with a "Western" one, emphasizing that the "Western" logic was every bit as arbitrary as the Chinese one. Such contrasts always reify, though they serve the textual purpose of making assumptions explicit. I remain ambivalent about my usage of them. Third was

---

29 My conceptualization of *ganqing* also drew on anthropological studies of emotions (e.g., Rosaldo 1984 and Lutz 1987), linguistic anthropology that emphasizes the multimodal nature of human communication (i.e., that communication involves the brain functions of imagery, bodily orientation, and emotion in addition to those of speech – see Gumperz and Levinson 1996), and historical studies of Confucian ritual that transcend language/reality dualisms by emphasizing the ability of "symbolic" ritual acts to effect material transformations in the world (e.g., Hall and Ames 1987, Hevia 1995, Zito 1984, 1997).

my own dissatisfaction with a view of practices of *guanxi* production that simply emphasized their endless variability. If practices of *guanxi* production could take any form whatsoever, and were quickly evolving, then writing about practices that occurred in one village during the late 1980s would have little relevance to what happened elsewhere. The genre in which I wrote seemed to dictate a search for continuities as well as variation. I stick with the importance of looking for continuities with the caveat that I reject the assumption that the continuities somehow underlie the variation.

My definitions of *guanxi* took many forms, all of which involved some sort of congruence between material obligation and human feeling. My first use of this congruence was as a contrast to "Western social relationships," which, I suggested, implicitly opposed amoral commodity exchange to moral kinship. Here I relied on theorists like Mauss and Polanyi, who describe Euro-American history as involving the separation of economic relationships from the rest of social life. In general terms, I see this separation both as a matter of complex institutional histories, in which spheres of commoditization (the reification of economic activity) have continually expanded, and as an evolving moral myth about the extent to which these spheres are and should be separate. In Fengjia during the late 1980s (and China more generally), I often ran into situations that contrasted with my experiences of living this separation in the United States. These situations sometimes involved institutional arrangements, such as the channels of distribution of train tickets that made their purchase (during the 1980s) difficult without reliance on *guanxi*. Other times they revolved around moral predilections, such as the willingness of people to discuss the monetary value of gifts, a social taboo in many American contexts. In short, I partially defined *guanxi* in terms of a contrast with Western social relations.

In addition to a generalized contrast based on the work of Polanyi and Mauss, I presented specific ethnographic evidence of the relations between *ganqing* and material obligations in practices of *guanxi* production. Examination of gift-giving in Fengjia over a wide range of situations demonstrated a consistent relationship between the monetary value of a gift, the closeness of a relationship, and the expressed depth of *ganqing* within a relationship. When queried, Fengjia residents explained that spending a lot of money on a gift or putting considerable work into helping someone were mechanisms for deepening their *ganqing* for a particular person. I also witnessed the collective generation of "magnetic fields of human feeling" in ritual and other collective actions. For example, at the *naofang* (the "stirring up the bridal chamber" ritual at the end of a wedding), village teenage boys extorted candy, money, cookies, and cigarettes from the bride by threatening to and actually painfully twisting her arms and fingers. While this harassment continued for hours, grooms were pressured to play the role of gracious hosts to these boys. Forced to ignore any obligation they might feel to help their wives out of a difficult situation, the grooms at least momentarily participate in a magnetic field of human feeling in which husband/wife relations are less important than relations between village men. If this ritual was effective at all, it worked by the ability of a one-time, public orchestration of concrete behavior to structure sentiment over the long haul. As a result of both such observations and the explanations of Fengjia villagers, I came to see giving gifts, banqueting, ritual, etiquette, and even the use of various forms of address as ways of generating *ganqing*.

A final version of my take on the relation between feeling and obligation in *guanxi* comes from my critique of the work of Sulamith Heins Potter and Jack M. Potter (1990, p. 180) on Chinese cultural models of emotion. The Potters contrast a Western ethic of emotional expression that focuses on sincerity with a Chinese ethic in which emotions are simply irrelevant to social relations. I accept the Potters' argument that Western moralities of sincerity are not crucial to practices of *guanxi* production. Generating *ganqing* does not involve the accurate representation of inner states of feeling (i.e., sincerity), but the remaking of social relationships. However, I cannot accept the Potters' view of the unimportance of emotions in Chinese social relationships. They argue that since emotions "are thought of as lacking the power to create, maintain, injure, or destroy social relationships" (1990, p. 183), rural Chinese people feel "how I feel doesn't matter" (1990, p. 183). They give examples of daughters who choose to affirm their relationships with their parents by working hard rather than through verbal expression, and of women screaming at birth control officials. For them, the daughters' lack of verbal expression of emotion reveals emotion's unimportance (if it were important they would say so), while the women's willingness to display anger in front of officials proves the same (if emotion were important they wouldn't dare express it in front of the powerful). I argue that both examples could be interpreted in the opposite manner. The hard work of daughters is a way of generating *ganqing*, indeed one that goes right to the heart of a presumed connection between emotional connection and material sacrifice (in the form of gifts or labor), while the women's displays of anger could be interpreted as displays of solidarity with those who may have been injured by the birth control policy. The expression "how I feel doesn't matter," I would argue, is better interpreted as an expression of individual powerlessness than a statement about the lack of importance of human feelings for social relationships.

The definition of *guanxi* that emerged from my book is one in which *ganqing* and material obligation are linked together through the generation of *ganqing* in practices of *guanxi* production. Though I also emphasized that variations in practices of *guanxi* production were endless, the versions that I explored all entailed some relationship between *ganqing* and material obligation. In my presentation of recent Fengjia history, for example, who creates *guanxi* with whom, what the significance of those relations is, and where, why, when and how they were formed varied in many ways. All of the examples, however, invoke a linkage between feeling and obligation. In my discussions of producing *guanxi* outside of Fengjia, I include practices as diverse as the CCP's attempts to generate class *ganqing* with "speak bitterness" sessions and a petty entrepreneur's attempt to become friends with a ticket seller by giving a ten-yuan note for a two-yuan ticket. Again, however, at the core of these examples is some attempt to generate *ganqing*, to link material obligation with human feeling. In the rest of this chapter, I go beyond my 1997 book by exploring more seriously the production of relationships without *ganqing*.

What is not Guanxi, *or rather, practices of* Ganqing *avoidance*

My book includes a couple of examples of relationships that are not *guanxi*, though it does not explore the practices of their production. These include business partners for whom maximizing capital return is the only consideration, and CCP comrades whose only concern is with the abstract ideals of the Communist Party. I emphasized that the line between friendship and business or comradeship was difficult to police and define, and necessarily evolved in practice. To reassert my emphasis on practice, I return here to a focus on the practices that produce different types of relationships rather than the type of relationships produced.

To say that *guanxi* always involves *ganqing* and material obligation is a form of idealization; more accurate would be the statement that practices of *guanxi* production rely on strategic and more and less successful attempts to generate *ganqing* and manipulate obligations. There are, however, ways of manipulating relationships that do not rely on the generation of *ganqing* including, to give the most obvious example, drawing up contracts. I call such activities "practices of *ganqing* avoidance" to contrast them with the reliance on *ganqing* in practices of *guanxi* production. I must emphasize, however, that in this usage, "practices of *ganqing* avoidance" do form some sort of relationship, some structure of human obligation. Actions taken to avoid any sort of relationship do not count as practices of *ganqing* avoidance.

There are many possible reasons for wanting to create relationships without generating *ganqing*. As many chapters in this volume argue, the economic costs of generating *ganqing* are in some contexts higher than those of, say, drawing up contracts. Sometimes it is not just the economic cost, but the mutuality and open-endedness implied in *ganqing* manipulation that motivates practices of *ganqing* avoidance. Reliance on *ganqing* opens avenues for the person targeted by one's practice to make unspecified demands at a future date. That a given actor deploys practices of *ganqing* avoidance, however, does not prevent practices of *guanxi* production from being used in the same relationship. Often an actor will want to construct relationships based on both *ganqing* and something else, or one party will deploy practices of *guanxi* production in reaction to the other's use of practices of *ganqing* avoidance. This conceptualization of practices of *ganqing* avoidance enables a reconsideration of the Potters' argument that some Chinese farmers believe human relationships are a matter about which "how I feel doesn't matter." In my earlier critique, I suggested that this statement might best be interpreted as a claim of powerlessness rather than an argument about the place of human feelings in social relationships. Though such a statement is clearly quite vague, I now see how it could be both a claim of powerlessness and an argument about the place of human feelings in social relationships. Here a consideration of the market in people in late imperial China is illuminating.

In his study of Chinese slavery, focused primarily on Hong Kong and south China, James Watson (1980) notes that pre-1949 China had one of the most comprehensive and complex markets for the exchange and sale of human beings anywhere in the world. There were male slaves, females who were purchased as maid servants, females who were purchased as prostitutes, concubines, or secondary wives, and several types of marriage transactions that approached in varying degrees the outright "buying and selling of women." The very notion of buying and selling slaves implies that slave owners must have a means of establishing the obligations of slaves to their masters other than generating *ganqing*, including, first and foremost, effective recourse to physical violence. A consideration of slavery makes clear the inverse relationship between a certain type of powerlessness and the ability to be involved in practices of *guanxi* production. If a powerful person has the ability to compel a given relationship by the threat of physical force, then the feelings of the powerless are of little import for social relations. Conversely, practices of *guanxi* production become more important in relationships that are not necessarily equal, but in which neither party has non-*ganqing* related means to compel the desired social obligation.

In practice, complete one-sidedness in the formation of relationships is impossible. If a slave is willing to suffer death, then the owner/slave relationship will end. Thus, there is room for practices of *guanxi* production (the generation of *ganqing*) even in owner/slave relationships. Watson (1980), for example, describes cases of male slaves whose hard labor on behalf of their owner (a form of *ganqing* materialization) led to better treatment, including the owner's purchase of a wife for his slave. Despite the possibility of such practice, however, the institution of slavery was designed to limit the need of owners to resort to, or be influenced by, such reciprocity. It relied upon an entire series of practices of *ganqing* avoidance. These included the denial of food, actual physical punishment, threats of punishment, legal and quasi-legal contractual guarantees of the rights of owners to punish, forms of physical segregation that limited social interaction (slave quarters), and status-marking practices that restricted the generation of *ganqing* within social interactions such as dress codes, the use of certain terms of address, and the structures of social interaction and ritual (non)participation. All of these actions are meant to inhibit the production of *ganqing* between owner and slave while keeping the owner/slave relationship intact.

A standard contract for the purchase of a male slave in late nineteenth-century Hong Kong illustrates further:

An Absolute Bill of Sale for a Boy made by XX, A Native of XX Village: Whereas, on account of daily maintenance being difficult to obtain, I and my spouse agree to sell our own son, aged 8 years, born in [astrological computations follow]. I at first offered him to my relatives but they did not accept. Through the intervention of Lo Shap-yeung, acting as an intermediary, a stranger [of another surname] agreed to buy my son and in the presence of the intermediary I was paid the sum of XX taels of silver and a bill of sale was immediately handed over to the buyer. The boy has not been kidnapped or anything of the kind. Should anything be found wrong with him the buyer will not be responsible. The seller and the intermediary will clear up the difficulties. The buyer is at liberty to take the boy home and change his surname, and to rear him for posterity. If accidents befall him hereafter these will be regarded as the will of heaven and no questions will be raised about the boy. To prevent any misunderstandings which might hereafter arise from an oral agreement this bill of sale is made out in writing and handed to the buyer to be retained by him as proof hereof. Signed, in the presence of the intermediary XXX, May 20th, 1879 (abridgements and translation by Watson 1980, pp. 234–235).

This bill of sale manipulates two sets of relationships. First, it suppresses the need for any ongoing relation between the buyer and the sellers of the boy except in the case when "anything be found wrong with" the boy. Second, it both legitimates a relationship between the buyer and the boy (the buyer may take the boy home, change his surname, and raise him) and suppresses the need for *ganqing* in the owner/slave relation by legitimizing owner violence ("if accidents befall him hereafter these will be regarded as the will of heaven"). It is the latter of these manipulations – the attempt to simultaneously create a relationship and suppress opportunities for the generation of *ganqing* – that count as a practice of *ganqing* avoidance.

Not all transactions in people would handle the first set of relations in the same way. For example, as occurs in Ba Jin's famous novel *Family*, wealthy men sometimes exchanged concubines as gifts. Such exchanges, like all gift exchanges, generated *ganqing* and deepened friendship. However, from the point of view of the slave boy or the concubine the transfers appear quite similar. Both would have to involve practices of *ganqing* avoidance. In either case, the party that is exchanged could only feel that social relations were a matter about which "how I feel doesn't matter." I suspect that all cases of buying and selling people involve practices of *ganqing* avoidance, and that whoever is bought would feel that way.

All of these gruesome examples may seem rather distant from the practices of *guanxi* production that I described in Fengjia during the late 1980s. Yet, they contain an important lesson for my earlier analysis: that of the intimate comingling of practices of *guanxi* production and practices of *ganqing* avoidance. If even the limiting case of an owner/slave relationship has room for the generation of *ganqing*, might not even the most intimate relations be subject to practices of *ganqing* avoidance? I believe so, and now fault my earlier analysis for not making this side of the coin explicit.

My fault was not so much that I ignored the ways in which *ganqing* was suppressed. I discussed the outright bans on participation in practices of *guanxi* production by bad-class villagers during the Cultural Revolution, discussed how etiquette could be used as a distancing technique, and, as introduced earlier, analyzed the *naofang* portion of the wedding ceremony as a technique of limiting *ganqing* between husband and wife. Rather, my fault was failing to conceptualize these cases in relation to my more generalized arguments about the relationship of *ganqing* to material obligations in practices of *guanxi* production. The suppression of *ganqing* does not necessarily mean a reduction of material obligations if there are other means to compel the obligations. Thus, practices of *ganqing* avoidance act on an entirely different basis than what I have called practices of *guanxi* production. Practices of *guanxi* production manipulate relationships by presuming a congruence between *ganqing* and material obligation. This congruence does not imply that practices of *guanxi* production can only work to deepen relationships. Diminishing both *ganqing* and material obligation, by giving a smaller than expected gift for example, can still be considered a practice of *guanxi* production because of the presumed or asserted correlation between feeling and obligation. In contrast, practices of *ganqing* avoidance work to limit *ganqing* without diminishing the obligations associated with the relationship. Practices of *ganqing* avoidance attempt to produce the situation in which feelings are irrelevant to social relations.

Examining Fengjia within this new framework, some of the most interesting comingling of practices of *guanxi* production with practices of *ganqing* avoidance occurred within families that lived together as single households. This comingling took place both during the marriage process, including the wedding ceremony itself, and thereafter. Significantly, marriage and the family relationships that arise from marriage are subject to both legal regulation and community oversight. Wives, husbands, children, and parents may not simply abandon each other without risking legal, as well as community, sanctions. Indeed, one common definition of *guanxi* within China involves only social relations *outside* of the family. Such a definition points to the fact that family relations are not solely dependent on mutual *ganqing* to hold them together, as can be the case for non-family relations. Consider further that certain practices of *guanxi* production are more common between rather than within families. Some forms of etiquette, such as saying thank you, are not considered proper between close family members (Bi 1990). Likewise, gifts are more often exchanged between rather than within households. In part, this reflects the reality that households share a common budget, so gifts cannot be easily given from one member to another. However, I also would call the habitual avoidance of certain everyday forms of *guanxi* production within a household a practice of *ganqing* avoidance. As communicative acts, practices of *ganqing* avoidance focus attention on the forces that compel the relationships in the absence of *ganqing*. My point here is not to deny the existence of many subtle forms of *ganqing* generation within households. I stand by my earlier contention that the continual exchange of favors between household members serves to generate *ganqing*. Rather, as in the case of owner/slave relations, the point is that these practices of *guanxi* production take place alongside practices of *ganqing* avoidance.

Weddings and marriages proceed on similar principles. Though the marriage process can involve hundreds of gift exchanges, very little passes directly between the bride and groom. Wedding ceremonies involve many practices of *ganqing* avoidance. First is the bridal procession itself. Martin Yang (1945) argues that riding a sedan chair gave pre-1949 marriages legitimacy precisely because it implied that the marriage was the result of parental arrangement rather than the bride's feelings. In this case, the suppression of the bride's *ganqing* is directly tied to the legitimacy that compels the relationship. Though Fengjia marriages of the 1980s were not arranged as strictly as those discussed by Martin Yang, they still involved a predominance of parental manipulation. As Elisabeth Croll (1981) argues, the continued existence of bridal processions with bikes or motorized vehicles as sedan chair substitutes most probably indexes this parental involvement, and thus is what compels the relationship in the absence of *ganqing*.

Second is the marriage ceremony itself. In late 1980s Fengjia, the bride and groom are asked to *bai* ("to embody respect for," which can take the form of bowing) heaven and earth, the ancestors, father and mother, friends and relatives, and finally each other. In the Fengjia version of this ceremony, the bride rarely bows, while in depictions of other weddings in rural post-Mao China the bride is either forced to perform a kneeling bow and/or bows only to the ancestors of the groom. I interpret those versions of this ceremony where the bride is forced to *bai* only the groom's ancestors as orchestrated practices of *ganqing* avoidance. In bowing to the ancestors, the bride is forced to generate *ganqing* with a set of people other than her husband. It is the social relations formed with those people, and not her *ganqing* for her husband, that compels the relationship. The absence of any chance for the bride and groom to *bai* each other underscores this construction of reality.[30] A final example of *ganqing* avoidance in wedding ceremonies is the orchestrated suppression of the husband's *ganqing* for his wife in the *naofang*, as discussed earlier. To sum up, rural Chinese weddings, in Fengjia and elsewhere, ritually structure husband/wife relations so that their obligations depend on and are mediated through third parties, rather than mutual *ganqing*. As such, they involve practices of *ganqing* avoidance.

These observations on the role of *ganqing* avoidance in marriage suggest two further hypotheses, the first of which is that practices of *ganqing* avoidance will surface most prominently in fully arranged marriages. Most marriages in Fengjia during the late 1980s could still be called arranged, in that parents and matchmakers took most of the initiative. However, unlike many pre-1949 marriages, couples did meet both before agreeing to the match (under heavy pressure to consent from parents) and on both formal and informal occasions between engagement and the wedding. I suspect that the extent to which marriage gift-giving arrangements and wedding rituals involved practices of *guanxi* production between husband and wife covaried with the extent to which a given marriage was a matter of parental arrangement. The fact that husband and wife *bai* each other in the late 1980s Fengjia wedding ceremony is a nod toward the increasing importance of *ganqing* in husband-wife relations.[31]

The second hypothesis involves the link of *guanxi* production to gender outside of the institution of arranged marriage itself. Though arranged marriages are equally arranged for both wife and husband, men tend to have a wider range of non-marital social relations than women. In most of rural China, it is predominantly

30 In my earlier (1994b, 1997) analysis of this ceremony in Fengjia, I emphasized the multiple directions in which *guanxi* production was directed. I would now add that relationship construction in weddings involves both practices of *guanxi* production and those of *ganqing* avoidance.

31 This is both a matter of law and practice. The marriage manual, "A Course in the Marriage Law," states "the basis of matrimony ... is feelings of love between man and woman" (Wang 1987, p. 76) and "if *ganqing* breaks down ... then divorce should be permitted" (Wang 1987, p. 129). Yan (1997) argues that conjugality has surpassed the importance of other family relationships in at least some parts of rural China.

the job of men to undertake the practices of *guanxi* production that establish links between households (see Kipnis 1997, Judd 1994). A look at the banqueting rooms of restaurants in rural towns, for example, usually reveals an almost exclusively male clientele. Though women clearly participate in female gift-giving and banqueting networks, these often do not reach beyond their extended families. Thus, the second hypothesis is that those most likely to say that feelings have no import for social relations are women whose lives and networks are dominated by relationships established through arranged marriages.

CONCLUSIONS

Realizing that what I have called practices of *guanxi* production and practices of *ganqing* avoidance are both important for the creation and manipulation of relationships in China (if not everywhere) allows some refinement of the theoretical assumptions I presented in the first part of this chapter. First, it allows the adoption of a more flexible view of intersubjectivity. As Hanks puts it,

In order for two or more people to communicate, at whatever level of effectiveness, it is neither sufficient nor necessary that they "share" the same grammar. What they must share, to a variable degree, is the ability to orient themselves verbally, perceptually, and physically to each other and to their social world. This implies that they have commensurate but not identical categories, plus commensurate ways of locating themselves in relation to them ... Overlapping, merely comparable, or semishared categories may suffice to enable communication (1996, p. 229).

Completely shared categories are not necessary for many of these practices to be successful. Indeed, insofar as they involve force or the manipulation of *ganqing* rather than the sharing of ideas, a certain lack of expertise on the finer points of manipulating relationships may make one's target easier to manage. One might posit that practices of *guanxi* production and practices of *ganqing* avoidance rely on different sorts of multimodal intersubjectivity, but that would be a different project. Here let me simply note that a more flexible view of intersubjectivity allows release from some of the more dichotomous essentialisms that my invocations of Mauss and Polanyi might have implied. The history of capitalism in the West has had an impact on the way relationships are imagined and moralized, but not in any simplistic fashion that causes all Westerners across all contexts to assume that sentiment and economics are separate spheres, while all Chinese always put them together.

In terms of the questions that I posed at the beginning of the chapter, I find that the dual conception of practices of *guanxi* production and practices of *ganqing* avoidance provides both new answers and new ways of avoiding answering. First, it renders the question of defining *guanxi* as one particular type of Chinese relationship, or as the Chinese form of relationships, moot. Owner/slave relationships, husband/wife relationships, or business partner relationships all involve both practices of *guanxi* production and practices of *ganqing* avoidance. At the same time, however, this conception places tighter borders on the definition of practices of *guanxi* production. Many ways of manipulating relationships do not count as practices of *guanxi* production. Only those that presume or assert congruence between *ganqing* and material obligation do.

Thus defined, it would be tempting to suggest "practices of *guanxi* production" and "practices of *ganqing* avoidance" as concepts for a universal social science. One could probably find among all societies both examples of practices designed to manipulate people through their sentiments and practices designed to manipulate people despite their sentiments. However, I suspect that this formulation will derive whatever utility it has because of its basis in the conceptions and actions of modern Chinese people. The tensions around the uses of the word *guanxi* in Chinese society – that it can refer both to the type of extra-family relationships established through "gifts, favors, and banquets" (Yang 1994), as well as any sort of relationship (Kipnis 1996), that the practices that create *guanxi* in the former sense exist within families as well – inform my formulations as much as any abstract theoretical goals. This theory is one of a particular, historically grounded practice. If it is useful it is because it acts as a bridge between a set of "emic" conceptions and the conceptions of contemporary social theory. As such, its utility is dependent on a degree of continuity both within Chinese society and English language social science. If either changes too much, it will become a bridge to nowhere.

METHODOLOGICAL AND CONCEPTUAL CONSIDERATIONS

INFORMATION ASYMMETRIES AND THE PROBLEM OF PERCEPTION: THE SIGNIFICANCE OF STRUCTURAL POSITION IN ASSESSING THE IMPORTANCE OF *GUANXI* IN CHINA

Doug Guthrie

In earlier work, I have taken the position that the importance of *guanxi* in China's transitional economy depends on the institutional environment in which economic and social action are embedded (Guthrie 1998a, 1999). I have also argued that there is nothing fundamentally Chinese about the concept of *guanxi*, as it is dependent on the structure of distributions systems, the structure of opportunities in the market, and the formality and stability of market institutions themselves. In weak institutional environments, where the formal rules of economic interaction are vague or non-existent, where economic and social structures are built on particularistic relationships, it is not surprising to find that *guanxi* carries the day. Such was the type of structure and rules that constituted Chinese society at the dawn of the economic reforms.[32] However, these economic reforms in China have unleashed fundamental changes on the structure, rules, and norms of the economy in China, and as the institutional structure of society has changed in China, so have the rules and practices of the market and economy. This natural experiment has, in my view, been the best test of the *guanxi* question: As institutional and economic structure change, what is the fate of *guanxi* in the midst of these changes? Does *guanxi* remain a fundamental part of economic and social action even in the face of major institutional change? Does it become less important as formal structures become more routinized? In either case, what do the changes (or lack thereof) tell us about the nature of connections in Chinese society?

32 Yang argues that the art of *guanxi* [*guanxi xue*] has its roots in the Cultural Revolution, and that the lack of social order led to a norm of relying on connections to "secure everyday survival." In the Cultural Revolution, an era in which individuals controlled the distribution and allocation of all kinds of goods (including the favor that allowed former Red Guards to avoid the fate of being "sent down" for long periods of time), particularistic relations became the norm of political and social action in China. Similarly, as local bureaucrats controlled distribution systems within the industrial economy, personal networks came to play a critical role in virtually all economic negotiations and decisions.

As one part of the answer to these questions, I have focused on the views and perceptions of general managers in China's urban industrial economy. In the early stages of the economic reforms, the extent to which *guanxi* played a central role in social and economic life in urban China was very different from the situation in the late 1980s and the 1990s. As the state has systematically constructed rational legal systems to control different parts of the economy and society, the rules of exchange have become more clearly defined and routinized. Firms have constructed their own internal bureaucratic structures and systems, and the trend toward a rationalization of economic practices at the firm level is also now in full swing (Guthrie 1999). As economic responsibilities have been placed squarely on the shoulders of individual firms, the push toward competition and profitability within firms has taken on greater meaning for managers. And as distribution channels have been slowly extricated from the control of bureaucrats, the need to curry favor with officials for economic and social goods has given way to the notions of competition, quality, and profitability. All this is to say that the extent to which *guanxi* matters in China's transforming economy depends in crucial ways on the institutions that define economic and social action, and these institutions are changing in dramatic ways. At least with respect to the urban industrial economy, a declining significance of *guanxi* is the clear result.

Some studies, however, do seem to marshall support for the claim that *guanxi* matters in very significant ways. Indeed, recent scholarship has offered compelling accounts of the specific ways that *guanxi* influences labor markets, international investment, and the decisions of entrepreneurs, and while I have been a strong critic of some of that work, it is not my position to argue that all of these studies are wrong; nor is it my position to argue that *guanxi* is an unimportant part of Chinese society. While I maintain the view that *guanxi* is a product of the institutional structure of society more than anything else, this position does not discount the possibility that *guanxi* plays a very significant role in some parts of the economy. In this chapter, I attempt to reconcile my own view of *guanxi* as a system whose role is diminishing in China – as the institutions on which it depends are changing – with those who view *guanxi* as occupying a more central role in the structure of Chinese society. I argue that a positional notion of *guanxi* is crucial to understanding the extent to which a given set of findings tells us something about reform-era China on a general level. I argue that a good deal of what we observe in China, especially with regard to *guanxi*, depends on where we are looking. To state my thesis clearly: The structural position of individuals and firms within Chinese society is one of the central variables figuring into our assessment of the importance of *guanxi* in China's transforming economy.

The purpose of this chapter is three-fold. First, as an entry into my discussion on the structural-position view of *guanxi*, I examine the work of Yanjie Bian. Bian's work is among the most important in the study of *guanxi*, yet I argue that the methodological approach raises some important questions that relate to the thesis I would like to advance here. Second, I present the argument that evidence on the importance of *guanxi* depends heavily on the structural position of the research subjects. Third, I illustrate this theoretical position through an analysis of data gathered in my own research on industrial Shanghai. I show that social position matters for *perceptions* of the importance of *guanxi* in fundamental ways. With regard to the general view of the importance of *guanxi* in the industrial economy, I argue that a firm's position vis-à-vis the state has a tremendous influence over managerial assumptions about the importance of *guanxi*. With regard to hiring, I show that organizations in China, at least according to the general managers that run them, were overall unlikely to allow *guanxi* to be part of the hiring equation in 1995. There are organizational reasons for this that are tied to the economics of the organization, but more importantly to the construction of new bureaucracies in the reform era. I also argue, however, that conclusions are significantly influenced by whether researchers talk to those seeking employment versus those doing the hiring, as these are structurally very different positions that inevitably lead to differences in perceptions over the importance of *guanxi* in a crucial social process such as hiring. Through these two cases, I argue that the social position of actors in the economy, which informs their access to decision-making powers, is perhaps *the* crucial factor to which we can attribute variation in perceptions of the importance of *guanxi* in reform-era China.

THEORETICAL AND METHODOLOGICAL PROBLEMS IN THE ANALYSIS OF *GUANXI*

There are a number of theoretical and methodological problems with research on *guanxi*.[33] The importance of *guanxi* in the allocation of jobs and the general

---

33 In an earlier article on the fate of *guanxi* in China's transitional economy (Guthrie 1998a), I conducted an extensive review of Mayfair Yang's seminal book on *guanxi, Gifts, Favors, and Banquets: The Art of Social Relationships in China*. I will not reconstruct that review here, but it is useful to recount the three central issues I raised in that review, as they provide the backdrop for the discussion that follows. First, I argued that Yang's ethnographic data do not support the argument that the importance of *guanxi* practice (often referred to as *guanxi xue*) has "increased at an accelerated rate" for "all types of commercial transactions" (see Yang 1994, p. 147 and 167). Second, I argued that despite the fact that she distinguishes between *guanxi* and *guanxi xue* early on in her analysis, her argument about the growing importance in *guanxi xue* can only be accomplished by blurring the distinction between the two concepts. Her examples of *guanxi xue* in the economic transition often come across as nothing more than friendships and the cultivation of business relations. But the cultivation of friendships and business relations is nothing particular to the Chinese economy, as a number of scholars have pointed to the fact that social relations influence economic relations and decisions in many societies (see, e.g., Schultz 1990; Whitley et al. 1996; Granovetter 1985; Uzzi 1996). In blurring the distinction between *guanxi* and *guanxi xue*, we lose the sense of what is particularly Chinese – or what is particularly interesting – about the institution in question. As the economic transition progresses, there seems to be less and less of the complex web of obligations and debt – at least in the commercial economy – that China aficionados have come to know so well. Finally, in a related vein, I argued that Yang's discussion makes the mistake of comparing ideal typical notions of market economies with empirical observations of the Chinese economy (Burawoy and Lukacs 1985, p. 723). Of course social relationships are important in Chinese society. But does the presence of these social relationships in economic decision-making distinguish Chinese society from other market

structure of labor markets has been an important empirical site in which to observe the relevance of *guanxi* in reform era China. A number of important articles have given us insight into the institutional conditions under which *guanxi* plays a significant role in social and economic processes (see, e.g., Bian 1994, 1997, 1999; Bian and Ang 1997). This literature is extremely useful as it draws on comparative analytical strategies for assessing the conditions under which *guanxi* matters in significant ways. The typical strategy here is to assess the importance of *guanxi* by asking a sample of individuals whether *guanxi* played a role in helping them obtain their current (or past) job. This literature, however, like others in this field, is problematic in a number of ways.

In the discussion that follows, I focus my analysis on the work of Yanjie Bian, as his work has been the most influential in the study of *guanxi* in the realm of employment practices. I argue that while Bian's commitment to systematic empirical research is impressive, the data employed suffer many pitfalls, and thus the conclusions drawn are questionable. I focus here on three problems. First, survey data on workers' assessments of the use of *guanxi* in job searches are fundamentally flawed because they contain no information on whether the *guanxi* tie actually influenced the employment transaction. Workers may attempt to use *guanxi* to get a job and they may successfully make the desired contact in the process, but they have no way of assessing whether that contact actually influenced the hiring process. Thus, it is problematic to draw conclusions from the use of survey data on workers' experiences. Second, in this area of research, there is an inevitable slippage between the theoretical notions of *guanxi* and the empirical operationalization of this concept, as the empirical observations always include more broadly defined notions of *guanxi* than is defined theoretically. Third, the vast majority of research that has been done in this area captures the experiences of workers under the labor allocation system, and thus is not appropriate for drawing conclusions about the reform era, let alone about the future of *guanxi* in China.

Inappropriate data

Bian's work has relied on two types of survey data to assess the changing nature of *guanxi* in the reform era – large-scale survey research data, gathered from a representative sample of 1,008 households in Tianjin in 1988 (yielding a sample of 938 men and women, Bian 1994, 1997) – and retrospective employment histories of 100 individuals in Beijing in 1996–97 (Bian, this volume). In general, Bian's argument is that as the state has abandoned the practice of job allocation in the reform era, individuals have increasingly relied on social networks to find employment. Positioning himself against Granovetter's (1973) theory of

economies? Only the strictest neoclassical economist would argue that social relations do not play a role in economic decision-making. The question for the China case is whether social relations play a significantly different role in the Chinese economy than they do in advanced capitalist economies.

weak ties, Bian (1997) argues that individuals in reform era China use networks as "bridges" – strong ties – to cross the organizational void in the structure of urban labor markets. He argues that as the state has receded in the allocation of urban jobs, *guanxi* has become increasingly important in the allocation of urban jobs in the reform era.

The first problem with analyses over job allocation that begin with data gathered from individual-level survey research and individuals' employment histories is that while the research begins with a question about decisions occurring at the organizational level (how hiring decisions are made), the data reveal nothing about this. In other words, in the survey research on which analyses of *guanxi* are based, we have no information on how the hiring decision was actually made at the organizational level. This is a huge problem in this genre of research because we are using an individual's perception of the importance of *guanxi* in the hiring practice as a stand-in for an unobservable (from the individual level) empirical process. When an individual reports that *guanxi* was important in obtaining a given job, all we actually know is the individual *attempted* to use *guanxi* in seeking employment or *perceived* that *guanxi* was important in this process. Yet, *we have no information on the actual impact of that connection in the hiring decision itself*. Even if a powerful official puts in a good word for a candidate, we have no information on whether this actually influenced the hiring decision.

Further, and perhaps more importantly, while human-capital variables often make their way into these models, we have no information on *relative* qualifications (i.e., the qualifications of others competing for a given job) – or relative *guanxi* capital, for that matter – so we have no way of assessing the importance of *guanxi* in this process. Whether the individual had the best set of qualifications in the pool or whether other individuals in the pool also had *guanxi* ties are essential pieces of the puzzle to understanding the importance of *guanxi* in the allocation of urban jobs. For example, if an individual reports having used a *guanxi* tie to obtain a given job, whether this individual had superior, equal, or lesser, qualifications than his or her competitors has radical implications for how we assess the importance of *guanxi* in this equation. Given that an individual has qualifications equal to other candidates in the applicant pool, it would not be a surprise to learn that connections were influential in the hiring decision, and this is especially true for the watered-down conception of *guanxi* that is actually used in empirical analyses. It is only in cases when *guanxi* actually overrides the vector of qualification parameters that the importance of *guanxi* tells an interesting story. However, we never have information on the relative measure of a given applicant's qualifications (or *guanxi* capital), so we have no way of even beginning to assess the relative importance of this factor.

Consider the following hypothetical examples, all of which would be perceived to be the same from the point of view of an individual survey respondent but are very different at the organizational level – the level of the employment transaction – and therefore have very different implications for the study of *guanxi*:

1. Two individuals, Wang and Chen, each unknown to the other, are seeking employment at a state-owned enterprise. Both individuals are equally qualified. Wang attempts to use a contact, a team leader in the organization with whom Wang's family has cultivated a relationship of reciprocal obligation, to help his chances in the hiring decision. This team leader puts in a good word for Wang. Chen makes no such attempt. Wang gets the job.
2. Two individuals, Wang and Chen, each unknown to the other, are seeking employment at a state-owned enterprise. Both individuals are equally qualified. Wang attempts to use a contact, a team leader in the organization with whom Wang's family has cultivated a relationship of reciprocal obligation, to help Wang's chances in the hiring decision. This team leader puts in a good word for Wang. However, the organization has a formal policy against the use of *guanxi* in the hiring process (which many organizations in the reform era do), though Wang, Wang's family, and the team leader in the organization still think it cannot hurt to try to influence the hiring manager. The hiring manager thanks the team leader for his input, but it does not factor into his decision. Chen accepts another job and drops out of the job search. Wang gets the job.
3. Two individuals, Wang and Chen, each unknown to the other, are seeking employment at a state-owned enterprise. *Wang has significantly better qualifications than Chen.* Wang attempts to use a contact, a team leader in the organization with whom Wang's family has cultivated a relationship of reciprocal obligation, to help his chances in the hiring decision. This team leader puts in a good word for Wang. The hiring manager thanks the team leader for his input, knowing, however, that he was planning on offering Wang the job anyway. Chen makes no such attempt. Wang gets the job on the basis of his better qualifications.

In each of these examples, Wang, if interviewed as a survey respondent, would report that *guanxi* was a factor in acquiring the job; each of these organizational situations would yield an identical result in the survey research, as Wang has the same information and acts in the same way with the same outcome in each case. Yet, the actual situation at the organizational level – at the level of the hiring transaction – is quite different in each case. In the first example, it appears that *guanxi* was important in the hiring decision (though the only real evidence of this would come from an interview with the manager making the hiring decision). In the second example, it appears that *guanxi* was not important in the hiring decision as there is an organizational prohibition against this (though the individual attempting to use *guanxi* would likely have no knowledge of this). The third example is ambiguous: *guanxi* may have been important in the hiring process, but we have no way of knowing, because Wang was better qualified anyway.

These are obviously simplified cases, but the comparison of the cases raises the fundamental point that because of the information asymmetry that exists between individuals and managers in the employment transaction, individuals are simply ill-equipped to assess the importance of *guanxi* in this process. Thus, in the survey research on which Bian builds his case regarding the importance of *guanxi* in reform era China, all of the cases described here (and likely many more) are treated the same, while the empirical reality of whether *guanxi* actually matters in the hiring process may be very different. In the end, perceptions from below, which lack adequate information on the hiring process at the organizational level, cannot serve as evidence that *guanxi* is an important part of the hiring process.

Difficulties in operationalizing theory

The second problem is also crucial, as it relates to the definition (and significance) of what this literature attempts to examine. Elsewhere (Guthrie 1998a), I have argued that Yang's (1994) empirical examples of *guanxi* do not fit with her own more rigorous definition of *guanxi*, which specifies obligation and indebtedness as part of the *guanxi* equation. The basic idea here is that while the definitions of *guanxi* usually refer to the reciprocal obligation inherent in a gift economy, the empirical examples are more often simple friendships and acquaintances that have no evidence of obligation and indebtedness. In one example, one of Yang's interviewees receives a discount from a manager who runs a small shop. I argued that this and other watered-down examples of *guanxi* not only fail to meet Yang's own definition of *guanxi*, but they also fail to illuminate how *guanxi* in reform era China is any different (or anymore important) from connections and networks in any other market economies. The research on labor markets runs into the same problem. For example, in an instance of *guanxi* that Bian recounts from an individual he interviews, the individual explains (Bian 1994b, p. 977):

I was an outstanding student, but not so by the political standards of that time. My classroom teacher, with whom I had a close relationship, told me how to fill in a questionnaire of "personal desires" for areas and workplaces I would be willing to work in. She also told me to take the first assignment offered to me . . .

Bian uses this individual's story to illuminate the different forms that *guanxi* can take. But is there anything at all particular, in terms of networks or connections, about this type of action? It is difficult to see how good relations with a classroom teacher, who helps a student fill out an employment form, can in any way be stretched to imply the importance of connections in the job allocation process in China. This certainly does not meet the criterion of "reciprocal obligation," which is a central tenet of Bian's own definition of *guanxi* (see Bian 1997, p. 369). If anything, the obligation is one-way and is a part of the job of a teacher or mentor. Would not a teacher in any society, who has a good relationship with a given student, do exactly the same? How does a teacher helping a student fill out an employment form serve as an example of using *guanxi* to get a job? How then is *guanxi* any different from simple acts like seeking and receiving advice from a friend? A deeper problem with this example of *guanxi* is that *it tells us nothing about the actual use of guanxi in the hiring process*. As far as I can tell, this circumstance implies absolutely no link between the *guanxi* contact and those making the employment decisions, which would seem to me to be a necessary part of pulling *guanxi* strings in the hiring process, yet Bian uses it as an example of the role of connections in the hiring process. This individual, who is an example of a *guanxi* contact, is not even connected to the hiring process.

Unfortunately, Bian's research is fraught with this problem. Bian's 1988 Tianjin survey asks respondents if "someone" helped them get their first urban jobs (see Bian 1994b, p. 984; 1997, pp. 373–74). The ambiguity of this question is a critical problem as this "someone" could include in the same category a teacher helping a student fill out employment forms and a powerful person making a call to a potential employer to put in a good word, two very different categories of "connections" (the former I would not consider the use of connections in any context). Thus, in broadening the definition of *guanxi*, we have lost the attributes of *guanxi* as it has been defined, and we have lost the specificity of when and how *guanxi* actually matters.[34] The ambiguity actually runs even deeper, as Bian's survey does not ask individuals about *guanxi* per se: Bian (1994b, p. 984) notes that "Party policies opposed the use of *guanxi* or back door practices in job assignments," and given these inhibitions, discussions of *guanxi* are sensitive topics in China. Accordingly, Bian chose not to use the term *guanxi* in his survey, phrasing the question in the following way: "We would like to learn about someone who provided the greatest help or influence for you to get a job when you first entered the work force" (p. 984). Bian notes in the same footnote that while use of the term *guanxi* "is fine in personal interviews," it is "inappropriate to use the word *guanxi* in a questionnaire." This is a reasonable position, especially for the time of the survey. Unfortunately, however, *guanxi* has a specific enough meaning in the Chinese language that not using the term creates serious problems for the research, above all given that Bian's definition of *guanxi* indicates the special meaning of the term that includes reciprocal obligation. In my interviews with managers in industrial Shanghai, I often encountered this distinction, as managers almost always sought to clarify whether they were talking about *guanxi* as general social relations or the *guanxi* that referred to the system of reciprocal obligation (*guanxi xue*). Given that the term *guanxi* was not used in Bian's interviews, it seems plausible, if not likely, that Bian's respondents answered the question as one of general contacts or social relations, which does not fit with Bian's definition of *guanxi* networks in China.

Predicting the future

A third problem with research in this area has to do with the timing of the research and predictions of social change. If we are going to employ analyses to predict trends of the importance of *guanxi* in China's reform era, we must be very careful to specify the reasons that certain findings give us analytical leverage to look into the future. Bian's data are again problematic here. Bian (1994, p. 999) predicts, "In the years to come, *guanxi* will prevail in manipulating job placement and job mobility processes." Yet, virtually all of Bian's (1994, 1997; Bian and Ang 1997) research captures situations that were primarily, if not wholly, grounded in the era of state job assignments. For the large-scale survey data, the information on an individual's first job placement was collected in 1988, a year that sits at the end of the state job allocation system. Without exception, therefore, these data tell us about the era before the end of state job assignments, and in many cases, because

---

34 By asking whether "someone" helped in acquiring a job, we have completely lost the notion of reciprocal obligation, which is, to my mind, one of the most interesting things about *guanxi*.

the data cover first jobs, the data capture the situation before the economic reforms even began. According to Bian's own argument, *guanxi* is most relevant for study of China's state allocation system, and Bian himself (1997, p. 370) notes that the job allocation system was abolished in the 1990s, which makes the analytical projection that *guanxi* will prevail "in years to come" strange.

Even Bian's current research (this volume) is at best ambiguous on the point of predicting the future of *guanxi*. In 1996–97, Bian interviewed 100 workers about the processes undertaken in all of the jobs they have held throughout their careers; in other words, these are employment histories, with some hiring transactions dating to before the end of the state job assignment, in some cases to the pre-reform era. Bian found that according to his respondents, 69 percent of jobs were obtained through some type of personal contact. However, without the timing of these job events, we are still at a loss as to what proportion of these employment processes occurred in the 1990s, after the end of the state job assignment system (I suspect the proportion is small). We can be certain that some significant proportion of these job attainments occurred in the period of state allocation, meaning that this portion of job processes occurred before reforms reshaped urban labor markets and during the period in which *guanxi* defined labor processes. Not only does this overestimate the importance of *guanxi* in 1996–97, but it also gives us uncertain information on which to base the current (let alone future) situation of *guanxi* in the reform era.

In the end, Bian's research, which employs individual-level survey data to analyze the importance of *guanxi* in reform-era China, raises more questions than it answers. It builds an argument about the nature of the hiring transaction in reform-era China without any way of observing the nature of this transaction itself. We are given individuals' perceptions of the transaction – based on whether or not they have attempted to use *guanxi* to influence the process – but individuals' attempts at influencing the transaction through social connections cannot be taken as evidence that *guanxi* actually does influence the process. From the individual-level data we have no information on the actual criteria that enter into the decisions of this transaction, and this information is crucial for analyses of this social outcome. In addition, problems in the operationalization of the research questions abound in this area of research. The survey questions fail to specify that the *guanxi* in question includes reciprocal obligation, which is central to the definition in all of the research discussed here. The research also generally treats observations from the past as representative of the current situation in China.

STRUCTURAL POSITION AND PERCEPTIONS OF *GUANXI*

The research just discussed raises three central issues regarding social scientific analyses of connections in a rapidly transforming society, such as China's. The first issue is one of misinterpretation of data. It is clear in the examples presented that the empirical data do not conclusively point to the resilience of a network-based society, at least not to the extent that the authors intend them to; at best the data are ambiguous. The fate of *guanxi* in China's economic transition is an issue that is crucial to our understanding of the course of China's reforms, but it is also crucial that our research on this issue not overstep the boundaries of what our data are equipped to reveal. Further, it is important in our analyses of *guanxi* that we have a rigorous bar for evidence – one that adheres to a scholar's own definition of the phenomenon we are observing, one that actually looks for empirical evidence of "reciprocal obligation," given that this notion is central to the definition of *guanxi* in the conceptual framework. It is also important to keep track of the time period to which a given set of data refers: If we are going to make assessments of the fate of *guanxi* in the reform era, we need to be clear that analyses of job attainment processes in the era of state allocation of jobs simply will not illuminate these trends.

Finally, and perhaps most importantly, we must be sensitive to the social position of actors reporting on *guanxi* vis-à-vis decision-making processes. Often times, research in this area generalizes about the importance of *guanxi* in China's econ-omy from cases that are highly sensitive to the social position and specific social and economic context in which they are embedded. For example, based on the discussion here, I would argue that the employment transaction is the appropriate unit of analysis for understanding the role of *guanxi* in hiring practices, and I would question whether individuals' *perceptions* of this process are adequate stand-ins for this information. Whether an actor in the economy is in a powerful or weak position with respect to decision-making processes has significant influence over the individual's perception of the extent to which *guanxi* plays an important role in social processes. This is true for two reasons. First, as I have argued earlier, it is problematic to gather information about the importance of *guanxi* from the weak side of an information asymmetry. Individuals who are not privy to the criteria on which a given decision is based are poor sources of the importance of *guanxi*; it makes little sense to ask individuals who are not part of a decision-making process about the criteria on which that process was based. If individuals *attempt* to use *guanxi* to get a job and they are successful in obtaining that job, they are likely to assume that *guanxi* matters in this process, yet whether this is true is an empirical question that cannot be answered through their perception of the process. Asking a job applicant whether he or she employed *guanxi* to find a job may yield a very different outcome than asking an employer about the same job search.

Second, social position influences the extent to which individuals perceive that they need to cultivate *guanxi* ties. Individuals who are positioned in *guanxi* net-works of powerful individuals are unlikely to see a need to cultivate *guanxi* ties, as they already know and have relationships with the individuals in positions of power. Individuals embedded in powerful social networks may see no need to pull social strings (*la guanxi*), but the social networks in which they are embedded (along with the social position with which they are endowed) may accomplish as much or more than the strings that individuals in lesser positions pull. Consider the hypothetical example of two firms seeking approval for a joint venture con-tract from a municipal bureau, which is the head of both firms' sector; one firm is located directly under the jurisdiction of the bureau, the other under the jurisdiction of a district company (a lower level of the administrative hierarchy of the former command economy). As my own research revealed (Guthrie 1998), the district company firm is significantly more likely to perceive that *guanxi* is a part of this bureaucratic process; the bureau firm is likely to make no attempt to pull *guanxi* strings, and it is likely to report that *guanxi* is not a part of the process. Yet, the fact that the bureau firm is a known quantity to the cadres (and probably also favored by them) in the bureau office and that the managers of this firm are likely to be personal acquaintances of those cadres cannot be lost in the analysis. This situation is analogous to that of employment raised earlier: Individuals at or near the strong side of a power asymmetry will have a different perception of the importance of *guanxi*, regardless of the empirical reality of the extent to which *guanxi* actually matters in the processes of hiring or bureaucratic approvals.

Note that the empirical problems of resolving the perception confusion in both of these circumstances hinge on the *general* definition of *guanxi* as social relations. I have argued here that while Bian *begins* with an appropriately narrow definition of *guanxi* – one that involves reciprocal obligation – his empirical observations rest mainly in the realm of a much more general definition of social relations (see also Guthrie 1998). Sticking to the narrow definition of *guanxi* allows us to empirically distinguish between cases where *guanxi* is actually invoked (cases where a debt of obligation accrues) and those in which social relations simply help grease the wheels of a social or economic process. It also forces the research onto ground that is empirically distinguishable from the general phenomenon of social networks that exists across societies. The interesting thing about *guanxi* networks is that they are structured around an institutionalized system of reciprocal obligation that is distinct from the general importance of social relationships in other parts of the world, and research on *guanxi* must be careful to examine this social institution in precise ways.

TWO EMPIRICAL EXAMPLES

The importance of guanxi *in hiring practices:*
The view from the other side

As I noted earlier, Bian's research on employment practices in reform era China depicts a view in which *guanxi* seems to matter a great deal. Based on his analysis of 1988 Tianjin data, Bian (1994b, p. 999) predicts that *guanxi* will dominate employment processes as China's reform era progresses. Based on more recent research, Bian (this volume) has argued that *guanxi* networks play an "increasingly important" role in the allocation of urban jobs. Despite the fact that Bian's work occasionally slips into the cultural view of the importance of *guanxi* in China (in particular, where he argues that Chinese society is structured around "web[s] of social relationships" [Bian 1994b, p. 972]), his work is primarily institutional in that he is examining the structural circumstances under which individuals will attempt to use *guanxi* capital in seeking employment. As I have also argued earlier, however, there are irresolvable problems with analyzing the importance of *guanxi* through reports from individuals who are on the weak side of the information asymmetry inherent in the hiring process. As an answer to this problem, where most analyses of *guanxi* in employment practices focus on the use of *guanxi* at the individual level (see, e.g., Bian, Hanser, this volume), I begin with the organizational level: Under what circumstances do organizations allow *guanxi* to enter the hiring equation. This perspective is not only important because it helps flesh out a fuller picture of *guanxi* in Chinese labor markets, but also because it allows us to examine the conditions under which the role of *guanxi* is eroding in the hiring equation. Where individuals suffer from a lack of information about how hiring decisions are made, managers within organizations suffer from no such information imbalance. In fact, where individuals can only guess as to whether or the extent to which *guanxi* influences the hiring practices, managers can reveal this information directly.

The evidence I present here suggests that the emergence of formal rational bureaucratic structures at the firm level has significant implications for the rationalization of hiring decisions in reform era China. During the early and mid-1980s, the state was setting in place a number of broad institutional changes that were pushing administrative and economic responsibilities down the hierarchy of the former command economy, putting these responsibilities in the hands of firms themselves and, in some cases, the administrative companies that presided over them (Guthrie 1999). As these institutional changes were new in the mid-1980s, and especially given that there were no other organizational bureaucracies and hiring procedures to replace state control in this area, it is not surprising that organizations relied on institutional systems that were familiar to them – namely, connections. However, with the new autonomy afforded industrial organizations by the receding state and the new more formalized institutional policies forged at the state level, organizations (and the administrative companies presiding over some of these newly independent organizations) have begun to build their own bureaucracies. And these bureaucracies are based, at least on a symbolic level, on formalized rational processes. The empirical question for the reforms is the extent to which these formalized rational structures in organizations have implications for Bian's prediction that connections will continue to dominate in manipulating job placement and hiring processes.

Bian's (1994) argument is basically that the use of connections in hiring decisions varies with the bureaucratic strength of the state: When state bureaucratic control was strong, the use of connections to secure jobs was at its lowest; as direct state bureaucratic control has withered in the period of reform, the use of connections to secure jobs has increased. While the evidence and analysis presented in Bian's study are convincing, the study assumes that government bureaucracy is the only type of bureaucracy that will possibly control hiring practices in urban China. It is true that the receding state bureaucracy coincided with a rise in the use of connections to secure jobs in urban China (as Bian shows), but does not necessarily follow that state bureaucracies are the only bureaucracies that will inhibit the use of connections in hiring practices. Even if state bureaucracies continue to recede, it does not necessarily follow from the evidence that the use of connections will continue to be the dominant system in job allocation and hiring practices. If a new type of bureaucratic system were to arise in China – for example, a formal rational bureaucratic system within organizations – it may very well be that this new bureaucratic system would reduce the importance of connections in hiring decisions and job allocations. In fact, Bian does note that his findings are not only connected to the receding state bureaucracy but also to the lack of formalized internal organizational bureaucracies. According to Bian (1994b, p. 979, emphasis added), "By the late 1980s, *because of a lack of* advertising and *formal hiring procedures*, *guanxi* became the predominant means of channeling individuals to work units." The implication of this statement is that emerging formal hiring procedures would, like government bureaucracies did in the past, alter the prevalence of connections in hiring practices and labor market processes. In fact, this is exactly what is occurring in urban industrial China today.

In earlier work on organizations in urban industrial China, I have shown that formal hiring procedures are dependent primarily on whether or not an organization has a joint venture relationship with a foreign company and the background of the organization's general manager. More important than what determines whether or not an organization will have formalized hiring procedures, however, is whether or not these procedures matter for how organizations actually engage in hiring practices. In my discussions with Chinese managers about the formal structures and practices of their organizations, I discussed the ways that organizations make hiring decisions. Table 2.1 presents the determinants of whether or not organizations allow individuals to be hired through connections [*guanxi*].[35] In the model presented in the table, the presence of a formalized hiring procedure is viewed as an independent variable with respect to hiring practices.

The results of this analysis show the organizational characteristics that influence the use of *guanxi* in hiring decisions, and it is clear from the model that both an organization's economic strength and its internal structure influence the extent to which *guanxi* plays a role in hiring decisions in Chinese industrial organizations. Organizations in the electronics sector are significantly less likely than

35 Data were gathered through in-depth interviews with general managers of a random sample of eighty-one industrial organizations in Shanghai (see Guthrie 1999 for fuller discussion of data collection, sampling, and methodology). The model in Table 2.1 is based on a reduced sample of organizations for the following reason: In the survey, I asked whether the organization is still allocated labor by the Labor Bureau; thirty-six organizations indicated that they are still under some form of state control in the allocation of labor. For these organizations, the institutionalization of formal hiring procedures is somewhat irrelevant. Therefore, I have reduced the sample to the forty-five organizations that are not under any type of state control with respect to hiring decisions.

Table 2.1

Logistic coefficients for the determinants of the use of connections [*guanxi*] in
hiring decisions in four industrial sectors, Shanghai, 1995

Independent Variables	B	S.E.
Organizational variables[a]		
Chemicals	2.32	1.64
Foods	.85	.68
Electronics	−2.33*	1.38
Active employees (ln)	1.16	1.07
Organizational health	−1.73**	.81
Employee ratio	1.13**	.19
Losses 1994	−.36	.58
Joint venture	−.54	.62
Formal hiring procedures	−3.57**	1.61
Governance variables		
GM w/bus./econ. backgrnd.	1.19	.74
Municipal bureau	1.89	1.18
Constant	−2.19	5.57
χ^2	33.94***	
Number of cases	45	

*$p < .1$ *** $p < .01$ *** $p < .01$(2-tailed tests).
Note: See Appendix at end of Chapter 4 for discussion of variables. B is the effect of the
coefficient, S.E. is the standard error.
[a]Reference category for sector is garments.

organizations in other sectors to allow connections to affect a hiring decision.[36]
Although organizations in this sector are no more likely than other organizations to
have institutionalized formalized hiring procedures (see Guthrie 1999, Table 3.1),
they are nevertheless significantly less likely to allow workers to enter the organization through connections. Organizational health is negatively associated with
the use of connections in hiring decisions, meaning that the stronger an organization is economically, the less likely it is to allow *guanxi* to be part of the
hiring equation. Most important for this model, however, is the effect of formal
hiring procedures on whether or not an organization will consider connections in
a hiring decision: There is a strong negative effect of formal hiring procedures
on the likelihood that an organization will allow connections to be considered as
part of the hiring decision. In other words, the formalized hiring practices that
organizations adopt do matter in the overall rationalization of the labor hiring
process.

To place these findings in the context of the debate over network-based views
of Chinese society: A new type of intra-organizational bureaucracy is emerging

36   To test the robustness of the sector effects, I have rerun this model with electronics as the only
      sector in the equation (all other sectors as the left out category). Results show that the effect is
      statistically significant at the p < .05 level ($\beta = −2.827$).

in China. This bureaucracy is arising for a number of reasons, and it has real implications for the rationalization of labor relations and labor market processes. One part of this intra-organizational bureaucracy is the formalized hiring procedures being adopted by firms that have increasing autonomy over labor market decisions. These procedures are more than just symbolic, since the formal hiring procedures of intra-organizational bureaucracies, specifically, inhibit the use of connections in hiring practices in industrial organizations in Shanghai today. Thus, where Bian predicts that connections will dominate labor processes in the future, I argue that the extent to which this is true depends at the very least on the new types of organizational forms that emerge over the course of China's economic transition. If current trends are any indication, contrary to Bian's predictions, formal rational bureaucratic systems within organizations may diminish the power of connections in China's labor market processes.

How can we explain the seemingly irreconcilable views that emerge from Bian's research and my own? One major difference is that our data come from 1988 (for all of Bian's work but that presented in this volume) and 1995, respectively, a span of time that was a critical period with regard to the changes occurring in economic processes in China. With urban industrial reforms essentially beginning in 1984, the period of the late 1980s represented an early stage in the transition from a command to market economy. Organizations had for but a few short years been experimenting with how to organize hiring practices (among many other organizational decisions), and many were struggling, at this early stage, with the construction of new bureaucracies at the firm level. It would not be at all surprising that personal networks would fill this institutional void, but that circumstance would by no means merit a prediction that *guanxi* would "prevail in manipulating" job placement processes. By 1995, organizations had been through more than a decade of reform, and new bureaucratic structures were beginning to settle into place. So, in accordance with Bian's own argument that a lack of formal hiring procedures was the structural opening that allowed *guanxi* to dominate in manipulating labor markets, many organizations by 1995 were beginning to solve the problem of a lack of formal structure. It could only be a matter of time before formal structure took over the importance of *guanxi* in the allocation of urban jobs at a level no different from that experienced in other market economies, and my own arguments, in their more extreme forms, suggest this position.

However, the difference in the timing of the research, while important, is only part of the story. A second issue, which is equally if not more crucial, is the structural position of actors entering the negotiations over jobs in urban China. That we are dealing with employers in one set of analyses and potential employees in another is not inconsequential. My contention is that individuals on the poor end of an information asymmetry are disproportionately likely to attribute success and failure to *guanxi*: If they do get a contract or a job, it is often, they assume, because they made the right connections. If they networked to any degree, which is natural in a market economy, it is likely that they will assume that the networking was the cause for success, *with no knowledge of the level of networking attributed to competing bodies or the extent to which networking figured into the decision among those making the decisions.*

Conflicting reports on the importance of guanxi in a rationalizing economy

That China's economy is undergoing a dramatic rationalization is indisputable. In my own research, I have examined the ways this is occurring at both state and work unit levels (Guthrie 1999) and the ways that managers' perceptions of these changes are affecting the significance of *guanxi* in the industrial economy (Guthrie 1998). The National People's Congress has passed literally thousands of laws, regulations, and resolutions, and these changes have radically transformed the rules under which organizations and individuals function in Chinese society. From the Criminal Procedure Law (1979) and the Prison Law (1994) to the Labor Law (1994) and the Company Law (1994), as well as other institutions, such as the Labor Arbitration Commissions and the revamped Chinese International Economics Arbitration and Trade Commission, the state has moved the economy and society away from the particularistic systems that characterized the command economy. And as the state constructs a rational-legal system of new laws and institutions, industrial organizations are constructing internal bureaucracies that reflect these new institutions. As a result, managerial behavior and attitudes toward informal systems and *guanxi*'s pull toward reciprocal obligation and "backdoor" practices are changing in radical ways.

Yet, some research convincingly shows that *guanxi* plays a significant role in the decisions of economic actors in China's transforming economy. David Wank's (1998a) research presents a picture in which *guanxi* plays a central role: "Business strategies and competition are patterned by the different accumulations of personal ties through social background and skill in the 'art of social relations' (*guanxixue*) of specific firm operators" (pp. 4–5). Wank's argument is that as a new private economy emerges, the patron-client ties of the pre-reform era are not abandoned; rather they are transformed and "commodified." While this picture contrasts with the findings of my own research, Wank's research is both extensive and deep: Wank's conclusions come out of two years of ethnographic field research that included multiple interviews with entrepreneurs from 100 private companies in Xiamen. This research does not suffer from the strange interpretations of data that are found in the work of Yang; thus, Wank's findings must be taken seriously.

Similarly, You-Tien Hsing's work (1998) on investment in Southern China also presents a picture in which *guanxi* ties are a central organizing factor of the economy. Based on 221 interviews with Chinese officials, Taiwanese investors, and Chinese managers and workers along with visits to 40 factories in Southern China (and extended work on the assembly line in two additional factories), Hsing has compiled an impressive battery of support for her thesis. Essentially, Hsing argues that just as industry in Taiwan is heavily organized around industrial and social networks, especially among medium- and small-scale firms, Taiwanese investors have relied heavily on the common language and their knowledge of the nuances of gift exchange in China to advance investment in Southern China. While I have argued here and elsewhere (Guthrie 1998) that some research on *guanxi* suffers from poor research and questionable interpretations of data, this is decidedly *not* the case with the research of Wank and Hsing.

In general, my own research presents a strong contrast to the circumstances presented in Wank's and Hsing's work. What is going on here? Is this simply a case of geographical and methodological particularity, such that my own study of eighty industrial firms in Shanghai and my findings on the rationalization of the Chinese economy cannot be squared with the research of Wank and Hsing? Instead, I think, the difference lies in the structural position of the actors under scrutiny. What is common to the studies of Wank and Hsing is that we are observing economic actors who are outside of the central power structure. In Wank's study, the subject is the private economy, and the structural position of entrepreneurs vis-à-vis the state matters tremendously for their perceptions of the extent to which it is necessary to curry favor with local officials. In other words, Wank's findings and argument about the importance of connections in "commodifying communism" are directly linked to the fact that he is studying the role and experiences of entrepreneurs in this process. In Hsing's study, the subject matter is small-scale investment, and size (not to mention the particularity of investment with Taiwanese investors) becomes a central part of this story. Local officials, who are under economic pressure, are willing to trade the flexible implementation of laws and policies for the gifts and favors that Taiwanese investors bring to the negotiating table. But they are only willing to do so as long as the investments stay local and therefore off the radar screen of higher-level governments. The Taiwanese investors, like Wank's entrepreneurs, are structurally outside of the decision-making realm, and they perceive the need to curry favor with officials to develop the extra advantages needed in a rapidly changing economy such as China's.

Contrast the structural location of these subjects with that of the managers of medium and large-scale industrial firms in my own research, who see the importance of *guanxi* declining significantly in China's economic transition: In general, the managers of these large-scale organizations have close connections with and are closely monitored by the state. A crucial difference between these managers and the entrepreneurs in Wank's study (as well as the investors in Hsing's study) is that the managers in my study are structurally close to the state: They are overseen by a state office [*zhuguan bumen*], which essentially serves as their lifeline to the state. With a state official from their governing office to represent their needs, the managers of these firms perceive little necessity in pulling *guanxi* strings. Yet, even within my own data there is evidence for the argument that structural position determines perceptions of the importance of *guanxi*. As Figure 2.1 shows, *within*

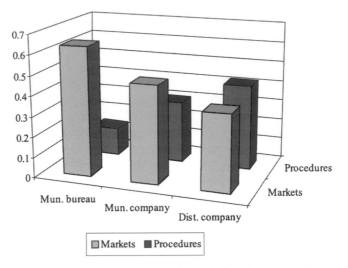

Figure 2.1   Proportion of firms by administrative rank that rely on *guanxi* (in markets) and *guanxi xue* (in official procedures) in four sectors in industrial Shanghai, 1995.

the industrial hierarchy of the former command economy, a similar relationship exists: The closer an organization is to the central government (those governed by bureaus), the less likely the general manager of that organization is to see *guanxi* as continuing to be important in the reform era. Organizations under the jurisdiction of the upper-level government offices are embedded in networks of powerful individuals, and they see little need to emphasize the importance of influencing those officials through creating circumstances of reciprocal obligation.[37] Organizations at lower levels of the industrial hierarchy (those under the jurisdiction of district companies) are not embedded in the same power networks within the state bureaucracy and thus see the need to develop relations and pull *guanxi* strings with state officials.

The central point here is that where a firm is positioned with respect to the state has a significant impact on the extent to which the managers of that firm will perceive *guanxi* as being an important part of successful economic negotiations. Firms further removed from the central power structure see greater need to develop social ties than those embedded in powerful networks. Firms situated outside of the state bureaucracy (i.e., those in the private economy) see an even greater need to develop relations with state officials to achieve ends. Thus, the structural position of a firm in the organizational power structure is a central determinate of the extent to which *guanxi* is viewed as being important by the managers that operate the firm.

---

37   Here again, it should be noted here that being embedded in powerful social and political networks is not the same as employing the system of reciprocal obligation (i.e., employing *guanxi*) to achieve a given end.

CONCLUSION

Whether we are talking about entrepreneurs, Taiwanese businessmen, job seekers, or managers of state-owned organizations, the structural position of interview respondents plays a significant role in the extent to which the respondents perceive the importance of *guanxi* in accomplishing tasks. Individuals embedded in the center of power structures are likely to do little work to exert social influence (and thus report that *guanxi* plays little if any role in the reform era); yet their social positions themselves are significant assets in China's emerging markets. Individuals excluded from central power structures are likely to perceive the need to develop ties to individuals within those power structures (and thus report that *guanxi* plays a significant role in the reform era). In both cases, the perception of the importance of *guanxi* in the reform era is highly contingent on the structural position of the respondent providing the information. Also in both cases, it is important to note that perceptions of the importance of *guanxi* cannot be taken as evidence of the "manufacturing of obligation and indebtedness," the central notion that defines *guanxi* as a system analytically distinct from a general view that social relations are an important part of any social and economic process. Analyses of the importance of *guanxi* must rely on evidence of the actual role that pulling *guanxi* strings has on the evaluation process of a given social outcome.

3

BEYOND DYADIC SOCIAL EXCHANGE: *GUANXI* AND THIRD-PARTY EFFECTS[38]

Yi-min Lin

Guanxi is one of the most noted phenomena in contemporary China. Three related issues figure prominently in the research on *guanxi*: its pervasiveness, the reasons for its pervasiveness, and its role in socioeconomic activities. This chapter attempts to take a further examination of the third issue.[39] In particular, I explore the forces that shape the process and outcome of *guanxi*-mediated social exchange. My investigation is motivated by the fact that despite wide recognition of *guanxi* as the nexus of *multilateral* social networks, *dyadic* interaction remains the focus of analytic attention. Much has yet to be said about how the rules and results of an exchange between two parties connected through *guanxi* are affected by the interactions of either or both of them with other parties in their respective social networks. I call the effects of such interactions on dyadic social exchange "third-party effects."

My analysis of this issue starts from two related views about an essential role that *guanxi* can play in socioeconomic activities – that is, facilitating the exchange of favors.[40] Because of the varying degrees of expressive and normative considerations involved, *guanxi*-mediated favor exchange may have some advantages over pure market transaction. It may, for example, help contain risk and uncertainty, sustain cooperation, and provide a reciprocal lever for opportunities. According to a widely shared view (e.g., Bian 1997), the strength of the ties between the parties involved holds a key to understanding how and to what extent the role of *guanxi* in this regard is played out. Its rationale is straightforward: The "return" on a personal

---

38 This chapter is partly based on Chapter 6 in Lin (2001).

39 For an overview of the literature and discussions on other aspects of *guanxi*, see the Introduction and other chapters of this volume.

40 Although gift exchange is often intertwined with favor exchange (Yang 1994), the *guanxi*-mediated favor exchange that I discuss in this chapter does not fully overlap with the flow of gifts discussed by Yan (1996a). First, the seeker of a favor is always motivated by instrumental concerns, whereas neither side in a gift exchange may have such motivation. Second, reciprocity is an important feature of favor exchange, but it may not appear in the main current of gift flow under certain conditions.

tie is a function of the closeness of the social bonds between the parties involved. After all, blood is thicker than water, and it is a commonly observed fact that people with a strong sense of mutual trust and obligation tend to be more forthcoming than strangers in offering assistance to each other. Another view emphasizes what has been extensively discussed by Yang (1994) – that is, the tactics of weaving personal networks and cultivating indebtedness (see also Wank 1999a). It suggests that whether one can understand well the intricacies and subtleties of complex interpersonal relations and master the skills and etiquette of communication and relationship building is likely to have a direct effect on one's ability to make use of *guanxi*.

An important extension of these views is that the exchange tie between two weakly connected parties may be significantly strengthened with the help or mediation of a third party (e.g., a mutual friend) to whom both are strongly connected (e.g., Bian 1997; Yang 1994). This is a major step toward bringing multilateral interactions into the picture of dyadic exchange. Its focus, however, needs to be expanded so as to enhance the explanatory power of both theses, as third-party effects often come from those who are not commonly connected to the two sides of a social exchange. Consider the following.

A common finding reported in studies of *guanxi* is that in China's reform era it has become increasingly instrumentalized, and the "cash nexus" has assumed growing significance in social exchange (e.g., Bian 1994; Gold 1985; Yan 1996; Yang 1994).[41] This raises two related questions. First, if and where this finding is true, the role of tie strength and networking skills must have been reduced and tilted toward initiating social exchange rather than determining its outcomes,[42] as what dominates the process and outcome of *guanxi*-mediated exchange is the narrow cost-benefit calculus used by the parties involved. Second, given the prevalence of such calculus, the role of third-party intermediation is likely subject to the same rules governing dyadic interaction and therefore confined mainly to connection-making. While neither situation contradicts the tie strength thesis and the networking skill thesis, they do suggest a need to look for further explanations about the composite rules of *guanxi*-mediated social exchange and the forces that have reshaped such rules in the reform era.

41 An example of this is a widely reported phenomenon known as *shashu* or killing friendship (for quick gains) (e.g., He Qinglian 1998; *RMRB*, February 12, 1999). It refers to various forms of egocentric behavior that promote self-interest by sacrificing or taking advantage of friends (e.g., recruitment of friends or even relatives into pyramid schemes of direct marketing).

42 This brings up the issue of what is meant by "strong ties." It seems that most scholars focus on the social bonds between the parties involved. While this appears to be what Bian (1997) focuses on, his definition of "strong tie" includes "the time spent in interaction, emotional intensity, intimacy, or reciprocal services characterizing the tie." The last element in this definition, however, bears no consistent correlation with the other elements (e.g., two persons without significant reciprocal services may have strong affection for each other). Its inclusion may not only decrease conceptual clarity but run the risk of leading to a tautological explanation, where the same factor (i.e., reciprocal service) constitutes both the cause and the effect of "strong tie." In the following discussion, I modify Bian's notion of "strong ties" to include only close ties based on social bonding.

Another important finding is that the abilities to make use of *guanxi* vary among the participants of social exchange (ibid.). A basic proposition of the tie strength thesis and the networking skill thesis is that, other things being equal, those with strong ties and shrewd tactics are likely to achieve better results. This is an empirically and analytically useful argument. It helps bring to light what affects the process and outcome of social exchange where similar structural conditions exist. But the fact remains that participants in social exchange often do not act in similar organizational and institutional settings. So the other side of the coin also needs to be examined to account for variations under different structural conditions. The question to be addressed is: Given similarly strong ties and adequate networking skills, why are some actors more capable of making effective use of *guanxi* than others?

The main point I seek to elaborate in the following discussion is that these underexplored aspects of *guanxi* are subject to the impact of multilateral interactions, especially third-party effects rendered by those without common ties to the two sides of dyadic social exchange. A close examination of such effects helps discern the mechanisms whereby *guanxi* has been instrumentalized in the reform era. It also offers a wide-angle view of how different structural conditions may be translated through multilateral interactions into varying relational constraints that shape the decision-making in dyadic social exchange.

INSTRUMENTALIZATION OF *GUANXI*: MECHANISMS AT WORK

Literally, the term *guanxi* means relationship. In ordinary usage, it refers to a person's nexus of private and particularistic social relationships that have the potential to serve, but do not necessarily exist solely for, instrumental purposes. In a theoretical discussion of *guanxi* in Chinese societies, Hwang (1987) makes a useful distinction among three different rules governing *guanxi*-mediated social exchange: the "need rule," the "*renqing* rule," and the "equity rule." The need rule applies to "expressive ties," where the need of the favor receiver is perceived empathically by the favor-giver as his or her own need. Its basis is affection. The *renqing* rule predominates in "mixed ties," where favor-giving is compelled by considerations of mutual obligation.[43] The main orienting force is social norms. The equity rule is a central feature of "instrumental ties," where the present and/or future use value of what the parties concerned can offer to each other serves as the main yardstick to determine whether and how favors would be extended. It is based on symmetric reciprocity.[44]

---

43 Literally, the term *renqing* means human feelings. It also has the connotations of reasonableness or empathy, as used in the expression of *jin renqing* (being reasonable or empathic). When *renqing* is used in contexts where private social exchanges are referred to, the closest meaning is mutual personal obligation (King 1991).

44 It should be noted that reciprocity is a common feature of *guanxi*-mediated social exchange under all three rules. The giving and return of favors in such exchange may take place at the same time or sequentially. Under the need rule, however, reciprocity is a corollary rather than a precondition of

Apparently, decision-making in favor exchange may involve simultaneous consideration of all three rules, which nevertheless carry different weight.[45] What then determines which rule will be the predominant one? In particular, why has the equity rule gained increasing significance in the reform era – if what is reported in existing studies is true? To address this issue, it is important to consider the consistency between values and the rules of social exchange, the scope of *guanxi* networks, the substitutability of interdependent relationships, and the clarity of the opportunity cost of social exchange.

Cultural and relational factors

Values cast an important shadow over preference formation and choice-making in social interaction (Taylor 1982). The influence of values on social action is often manifested in two dimensions that are different but not totally independent of each other: symbolism and instrumental rationality. The former has to do with the meaningfulness of action itself – especially the process of action.[46] The latter concerns the usefulness of the outcome of action, and spans a spectrum between collective and individual instrumental rationality. Different values attach different importance to these dimensions. Those focusing on symbolism help cement expressive social exchange. Those seeking a balance between symbolism and instrumental rationality inform and sanction norms on mutual obligation.[47] Those emphasizing instrumental rationality (especially individual

favor exchange. Under the *renqing* rule, it looms large in the expectations of the parties involved. What matters, though, is not a precise match of favors in terms of their net worth, but the act of returning favors in iterated interactions. The time frame for returning favors tends to be flexible. Under the equity rule, the net worth of favors is taken as the basis of reciprocity, which resembles "conditional cooperation" (Axelrod 1984) that can be brought to an end by a single failure to reciprocate. To maintain an effective time frame in which to "cash in" a favor owed or contain opportunism through withholding of delivery or even retaliation, a high discount rate is often used in decision-making with regard to favor exchange. Despite their seeming similarity, there are two major differences between *guanxi*-mediated exchange under the equity rule and pure market exchange: The parties involved in the former do not assume anonymity, and their "transactions" are often times not governed or sanctioned by formal contractual institutions ex ante. In other words, the social relationship between the parties forms the main bridge for their exchange.

45 Since the favor seeker is always motivated by instrumental concerns, what matters in this regard is the factors influencing the decision-making of the favor-giver at any given time.

46 Generosity, sensitivity, decency, competence, loyalty, and self-esteem, for example, may be among the virtues that a favor-giver deeply appreciates and wants to demonstrate in social exchange. These qualities may contribute to one's reputation and thereby increases the potential of one's social influence and relational stability with exchange partners. But they can hardly be reduced to instrumental rationality, as what matters most to the person concerned may be the gratification from the meaningful process of demonstrating these qualities by giving favors, rather than the potentially useful consequence of the behavior, which the person may not even exploit in future interaction.

47 In reality, though, a precise balance may be rare. Normative ties that are more heavily influenced by values emphasizing symbolism tend to be more stable and less prone to opportunism than those tilted toward collective instrumental rationality.

instrumental rationality) provide justification for the equity rule. Given people's inclination to minimize what psychologists call "cognitive dissonance" – disagreement between attitude (partly shaped by values) and behavior – the more consistent the values held by a person with a particular type of exchange rule, the more likely that rule is seriously considered and reinforced in decision-making. On the other hand, the more ambiguous one's attitude toward the value(s) underlying an exchange rule, the weaker one's resolve to stay with that rule.

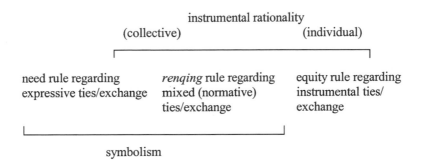

The predominance of an exchange rule means the existence of a critical mass of exchange participants who follow it and likely embrace the underlying value(s). While values influence the orientation of people's behavior in social exchange, the configuration of their *guanxi* networks also plays an important role in this regard. An essential feature of such networks is that they are avenues of multilateral interaction. This has implications for understanding the mechanisms of critical mass formation under different exchange rules.

First the scope of a person's *guanxi* networks has a direct bearing on the composition of his or her exchange ties. The greater such scope, the weaker the person's ability to cultivate and maintain strong social bonds – expressive and/or normative – with all the ties lodged in the networks, resulting in a high degree of relative significance assumed by instrumental ties and the exchange rule governing them. It follows that an increase of instrumental ties in a person's *guanxi* networks may have a diluting effect on his or her efforts to cultivate and sustain non-instrumental ties.

Relatedly, the scope of a person's *guanxi* networks is often associated with the availability of alternative sources of assistance, especially those through instrumental ties. The more available such sources, the more substitutable the mutual commitment between interdependent parties. Moreover, the less exclusive a person's dependency relationships, the less effective the social sanction mechanisms associated with closed social groups or communities (Taylor 1982), such as gossip, peer pressure, reputation, ostracization, and so on.[48] It follows that the greater the reach and resourcefulness of one's *guanxi* networks, the greater the difficulty for the enforcement of social norms that sustain mutual obligations based on

48   For a useful discussion of this issue in the context of agrarian societies, see Little (1989, ch. 2).

collective instrumental rationality, and the stronger the appeal of opportunism.[49] Here, interactions with third parties affect dyadic exchange by cementing or undermining mutual commitment.

Furthermore, there is often an opportunity cost for dyadic favor exchange in the context of multilateral *guanxi* networks – for example, what A returns to B for a favor may be "worth" less than what C could return to B for the same favor should it be extended to C. Such cost is likely to be clarified when the behavior of most parties involved in favor exchange is perceived to be short-term oriented, as it is often difficult to value and compare the favors to be returned over a long period of time. The higher and the clearer such cost, the more pressure on the person concerned to override non-instrumental concerns and attach greater importance to the equity rule in decision-making. In other words, when the majority of one's social exchange partners are long-term players, one tends to deemphasize short-term opportunity costs. When short-term maximizers make up the bulk of one's *guanxi* networks, however, one is likely compelled, consciously or subconsciously, to carefully weigh the opportunity costs with reference to all exchange partners.

The milieu of social exchange under Mao

To see how these factors combine to shape *guanxi*-mediated social exchange in contemporary China, it is important to look at the changing milieu of social interaction. After 1949, Maoism was the dominant force in the moral space of the society. Mao advocated asceticism and altruism as the cornerstones of "socialist culture" (Madsen 1984; Walder 1986), and sought to structure the society around these values by homogenizing the social distance in interpersonal relations under a universalistic banner known as "comradeship" (Vogel 1965). This cast a constraining shadow over open pursuit of self-interest through private social exchange. But there were inconsistencies and contradictions.

The attempt at building a universalistic order of social relations was compromised by the political particularism practised in organizations for behavioral control and mobilization (Walder 1986), which led to differential treatment of individuals in the allocation of opportunities and benefits. Also, policies pursued by pragmatic leaders (e.g., Liu Shaoqi and Deng Xiaoping) assigned greater weight to material rewards and incentives (Madsen 1984), hence diluting Mao's emphasis on the pursuit of spiritual virtues. Before the Cultural Revolution (1966–76),

---

49 Opportunism in favor exchange under the normative rule involves two forms. First, A makes B return favors that are always "worth" more than the favors from A to B, whereas A does not accommodate (e.g., by citing various excuses) B's requests for favors that exceed the "worth" of the favors from B to A. If B is heavily influenced by instrumental considerations, future exchanges between A and B are likely to be shifted, through a "tit-for-tat" mechanism, toward the equity rule. If B is heavily influenced by symbolic considerations, however, A may be able to continue to take advantage of B. Second, A may choose not to return any favors to B. This is likely to break up the exchange tie between them, even if B is heavily influenced by symbolic considerations.

Confucian particularistic values were tolerated to a certain extent,[50] and lingered on to have an impact on social interaction. In the remaining years of the Mao era, the cultural products, relics, and institutions (e.g., ancestral worship) that embodied Confucian values were severely attacked under the radicalist policies enforced by political activists throughout the state bureaucracy and socioeconomic organizations. But the polarization of the society along political lines in fact had the largely unintended effect of distancing the majority of the population (the "non-activists") from the core of Maoist values and pushing them toward other values (Madsen 1984; see also Walder 1986). In addition, the extreme scarcity of opportunities and resources created ground on which to justify a survival ethic that endorsed the provision of private mutual aid to overcome obstacles in the adverse environment.[51] As a result, the containing effect of Maoism on private social exchange was limited.

On the other hand, however, despite the divergent orientations of the moral currents just noted, they all shared with Mao a condemnation of egocentric values, thereby perpetuating a widely shared ambivalence toward extreme forms of instrumentalism in social exchange. Moreover, the rules governing persistent private (i.e., *guanxi*-mediated) social exchange were also subject to the impact of the structural conditions of social interaction in the Mao era, which tended to dilute or limit the significance of purely instrumental considerations.

First, the reach of personal networks and hence the scope of social exchange were limited. Under the central planning system, occupational and spatial mobility was seriously constrained by a number of institutional arrangements, such as the *hukou* (household registration) system (Cheng and Selden 1994), the *danwei* (work unit) system (Walder 1986), the *renshi dangan* (personnel dossier) system (Lee 1990), and the rationing coupon system (Whyte and Parish 1984). Consequently, a person's *guanxi* networks tended to be confined to a circle of limited contacts located within short spatial distance, making it possible and likely to intensify the social interaction among members of this small community.[52] The stronger the resultant social bonds, the firmer the foundation on which to sustain the role of non-instrumental considerations in social exchange.

---

50 Simplistically put, the value system of Confucianism covers a span between two poles: (1) the familist value that places the nuclear family at the center of a person's social network differentiated according to the closeness of kinship ties and the degree of mutual affection and maintained through internalization and various forms of expressive reciprocities, and (2) the communal value that places "public" or "communal" interests above those of the family. A balance between the two poles and between relationships within the private or public sphere of social life is suggested by the principle of *zhongyong* (the doctrine of the mean emphasizing relational harmony and non-excessiveness). Yet, where the pendulum of moral discourse points is situational, depending on the context of value judgment and the specific relationship(s) being judged. For more in-depth discussions, see Fei (1985), King (1991), Madsen (1984), and Yu (1984).

51 Yang (1994) further argues that such attempts also represented a form of resistance to totalitarian state power.

52 It should be noted that the boundaries of such a community were different from those of the organization-based communities shaped by the socioeconomic structure, as its membership was self-selected by those who were involved in it but did not necessarily have the same organizational affiliation.

Second, given low mobility and a total dependence on the work unit for employment, career advancement, and related benefits that could not be provided through alternative sources, one could hardly afford not to cultivate and maintain *guanxi* with those who allocated opportunities and benefits, with those who could help gain access to the allocators, and even with potential spoilers who could otherwise ruin one's career chances in the highly politicized workplace. As a result, there was a high degree of non-substitutability for a large part of one's *guanxi* networks. The difficulty of one's exiting from this closed community cast a heavy shadow over opportunistic behavior in social exchange.

Third, because of the limited scope of *guanxi* networks and the non-substitutability of most contacts in such networks, people tended to use a low time discount rate in decision-making with regard to favor exchange. The low presence of short-term maximizers made it difficult to ascertain the opportunity costs of favors in multilateral exchange over distant time horizons. This in turn reinforced the relational constraints on extreme forms of instrumentalism.

In short, under the political and institutional conditions of the pre-reform system, egocentric values faced strong cultural constraints, and third-party effects were structurally directed toward constraining narrow instrumental considerations in *guanxi*-mediated social exchange. As a result, "strong ties" mattered, both to the initiation and the outcome of *guanxi*-mediated exchange.

Changes in the reform era

The reform era has ushered in many changes. Maoist ideology has declined, and the social practice it guided has been largely discredited. Once an under-current, the economic pragmatism advocated by Deng to justify individual material interests within certain limits has become the official ideology. As Madsen (1984) points out, nevertheless, it lacks a firm moral core, and thus is unable to hold coherent ground in face of competing values. Confucian values have managed to resurface, but the fast changing social environment poses major obstacles to the spread of their influence. They neither have the official endorsement and sponsorship that existed in imperial China and, to a lesser extent, the Republican period (1912–1949); nor do they have a broad base of social relations in autarkic communities with a low degree of commercialization, which was sustained under the pre-reform central planning system. Moreover, they face strong challenge from egocentric and hedonistic values (Ci 1994), which have made significant inroads into the moral space as official censorship is relaxed and as profit-making becomes the focal concern in socioeconomic activities. As a result, the ambivalence toward open pursuit of self-interest has faded (Link et al. 1989; Schell 1989) and the previously strong cultural constraints on pure instrumentalism in social interaction are seriously weakened.

Cultural change, however, is only part of the story. With the gradual marketization of the economy, many traditional behavioral control mechanisms associated with the command economy, such as the household registration system, the *danwei* system, the rationing coupon system, and the personnel dossier system, have fallen apart. The concurrent increase of spatial and occupational mobility has broadened the avenues for people's exchange networks to expand. The central driving force for such expansion stems from profit-making. Consequently, instrumental ties make up the mainstay of the expanded part (and increasingly the full spectrum) of *guanxi* networks. A ripple effect is that as the attention to networking widens, the intensity with which to cultivate and maintain existing ties tends to decrease. If we define "strong ties" solely on the basis of social bonding, then their relative significance in a person's *guanxi* networks also tends to decline.[53] These changes may combine to contribute to the prevalent perception, reported in existing studies, that *guanxi* has become increasingly instrumentalized. But there is more to it.

The decline of the command economy means that people no longer totally depend on the work unit system and are increasingly free to explore alternative partners of social exchange for securing opportunities and resources. The result is a decrease of the non-substitutability of the *guanxi* networks developed within the relatively small, closed communities where they used to seek mutual aid. This does not necessarily diminish the importance of old ties. But it does open the way for mutual commitment to weaken and for opportunism to grow in social exchange. The main contributing factor is the weakening of traditional mechanisms to enforce mutual obligation, especially long-term mutual commitment, in social exchange. The growing availability of alternatives reduces the importance of continued cooperation, assistance, and even censure from certain network members, thus alleviating or even offsetting the effects of communal penalty for failing to fulfil reciprocal obligations to these members. Also, the greater the availability of alternatives, the less stable the status of "essential" contacts in one's *guanxi* networks.

As the presence of instrumental ties gains relative significance in people's *guanxi* networks, as both old and new ties become more substitutable and thus prone to the effect of opportunism, the focus of attention in social exchange gravitates toward short-term reciprocity. The use of high discount rates in decision-making creates an increasingly clear frame of reference in which to make calculations about the opportunity costs of social exchange. This in turn brings pressures to bear on ties that traditionally were governed by predominantly non-instrumental considerations when short-term opportunity costs were given much less weight in view of a long-term time horizon for social exchange. Consequently, more and more people begin to weigh whether they should forgo immediate gain

---

53 This, of course, does not mean that "weak ties" necessarily lead to poorer results in social exchange. It only indicates the likelihood that there are relatively more weak ties than strong ties in a person's *guanxi* networks. Also, some instrumental ties, including newly formed ones, may be turned into mixed (hence "stronger") ties as continued efforts are made to cultivate them over time, even though their number is likely to be limited and their stability may be in question (see the discussion that follows).

(from other parties) or incur short-term costs (that could be better compensated by other parties) to help friends whose abilities to return favors soon and fully are uncertain.

If this account is correct, then we can expect to find not only a decline of the relative significance of "strong ties" (based on social bonding) in people's *guanxi* networks, but an erosion of their role in determining the outcome of favor exchange.[54] Their main role instead gravitates toward connection making, either directly or through third-party intermediation. It should be noted that these changes are by no means even among different social groups across the country. Economically most active members of the society (e.g., enterprise leaders) and holders of political power tend to be the frontrunners, as their social interactions are most susceptible to the effects discussed here. People who have relatively low exposure to egocentric values and continue to live in relatively closed communities are likely to be slow in deviating from the old patterns of behavior in social exchange (e.g., Yan 1996).

UNEVEN STRUCTURAL CONSTRAINTS: A FURTHER ILLUSTRATION

To further illustrate the effects of multilateral interaction on *guanxi*-mediated social exchange, I now turn from the predominant rules to the variations in the outcome of such exchange. The central question is why, assuming similar networking skills and tie strength, some actors are able to use *guanxi* more effectively than others. I focus on the interactions between economic actors and state agents, which are at the center of analytic attention and hold a key to understanding the driving forces of China's recent economic transformation. The premise of this discussion is that the state has become increasingly unable to monitor and contain the self-seeking behavior of its agents, whose discretionary use of power can significantly influence the competitive advantage of economic actors through differential treatment in the allocation of resources, opportunities, and state-engendered liabilities.[55]

Moreover, the level of my analysis is the enterprise, which is the basic unit of economic activities outside the farming sector. What I seek to explain is a finding that I have reported elsewhere: leaders of state-owned enterprises (SOEs hereafter) are generally more constrained than leaders of non-SOEs in making use of their *guanxi* with state agents to help their enterprises compete in the increasingly marketized economy.[56] My basic argument is that to address this issue it is

54 Other things being equal, a "strong tie" may still hold an edge over a "weak tie." But such an edge can be more easily offset than before by substantial instrumental gains from a weak tie. Therefore the role of "strong tie" has turned from a necessary condition to a sufficient condition for successful favor exchange.

55 Such scope of using *guanxi* to manipulate action is greater than that discussed by Guthrie (1998, 1999), which focuses only on procedures. See Lin (2001) for a more elaborate discussion on this.

56 During 1988–1996, I interviewed 168 industrial enterprise leaders in China: 35 SOE managers and 129 non-SOE managers regarded failing to cultivate close *guanxi* with officials as having a significant negative impact on enterprise performance, 35 SOE managers and 126 non-SOE

important to consider the interplay between three types of third-party effects and the path-dependent structural conditions faced by different enterprises.[57]

First, a favor-giver tends to be hesitant if the vested interests embedded in his or her existing relationships with other parties are at odds with what a favor-seeker asks for. Second, a favor-giver faces strong inducement to disregard expressive and normative concerns for individual instrumental gains if the same favor is intensely sought by multiple favor-seekers. Third, a favor-seeker has to take extra precaution if knowledge about such acts can be easily turned into a means to advance the interest of a third party (e.g., a personal rival) at the cost of the favor-seeker.

For historical reasons, SOEs are located in urban areas and face multiple-level regulators with divergent interests. Non-SOEs, in contrast, are mostly under the purview of grassroots jurisdictions where there is a higher degree of consolidation of interests among local officials. Also, the majority of SOEs face highly crowded political markets lodged in open communities of *guanxi* networks, whereas the majority of non-SOEs face less crowded political markets lodged in largely closed communities of *guanxi* networks. Internally, SOEs face more complex organizational politics than non-SOEs, which constrains the use of organizational resources for *guanxi*-mediated favor-seeking. Together, these factors combine to make SOEs more extensively exposed to the downside of the just mentioned third-party effects.

Favor-seeking and state agents' vested interests

A major legacy of the central planning system implemented in the pre-reform era is that SOEs are virtually all located in what the government defines as "urban" places. Because of the varying importance attached to different SOEs in resource allocation, they are "owned" by different levels of government, ranging from the central government to provincial governments to city governments to district (of large cities) and county governments.[58] None of China's SOEs are "owned" by township governments. Other than the township government that has exclusive jurisdiction over an area (the town proper), however, each and every higher-level urban jurisdiction in China is a multilayer administrative center. In other words, the central government, provincial governments, city

managers indicated that direct or indirect personal benefits were needed to gain through *guanxi* favorable treatment from officials, 32 SOE managers and 124 non-SOE managers agreed with the view that SOE managers had greater difficulty in offering personal benefits to officials in *guanxi*-mediated favor exchange. See Lin (2001) for more details about the interviews.

57 The distinction between SOEs and non-SOEs is based on two factors: The former group has had a much slower pace of marketization than the latter, and possesses some rather distinctive structural characteristics (to be discussed later). It does not imply a distinction between public and private enterprises, as many in the latter category are local government controlled entities in the "collective sector." Nor is it intended to paint a black-and-white picture. Rather, its purpose is to identify structural features that condition the manifestation of third-party effects. Non-SOEs that are structurally similar to SOEs in certain aspects are likely to be subject to the same effects in those aspects.

58 My discussion of local government ownership of public enterprises draws on Granick's regional property rights perspective on SOEs in China (1990). For a similar view, see Walder (1992a).

governments, and county governments all share with at least one lower-level government administration the space where their administrative headquarters are located, and the direct administrative authority over such space resides in the lowest level government, which is called township in the countryside or district in the cities.[59]

Because of these spatial features, SOEs are all "enclave enterprises" that fall into two categories. The first category consists of SOEs that are "owned" by a particular level of government and located in a locality where both its owner and at least one lower level government are located. A provincially "owned" enterprise, for example, may be located in a district of the provincial capital, which houses the provincial government, the municipal government, and the district government. The second category includes SOEs that are located in a jurisdiction where the command center of their owner(s) is not located.[60] Instead of being located in Beijing, for example, a centrally "owned" enterprise may be located in an urban district in the city of Guangzhou.

Under China's fiscal regulation, the main stream of tax revenue (i.e., income tax and a large part of turnover taxes) from an enterprise belongs to the administrative level where its principal supervising authority is situated. This seriously limits the financial contribution of "enclave enterprises" to the lower level government(s) in the locales where they are situated. But these enterprises have to deal with or rely on the local government for a variety of matters, including employment of labor, land use, supply of utilities and other infrastructural facilities, licensing, and provision of social services such as health care and education of employees' children. Such an asymmetric interdependence between the local government and the economic enclaves within its territories tends to dilute local state agents' interests in the latter's well-being. This, coupled with the fact that many enclave enterprises often do not have local state agencies as administrative patrons to provide protection through inter-agency ties,[61] makes them easy and vulnerable targets for predatory local state action (e.g., excessive fees and ad hoc levies), which has intensified in the reform era.[62]

59 In the countryside, each township governs dozens of villages. According to China's public ad-ministration laws, villages do not constitute a separate level of government administration. But they do perform many governmental functions, such as provision of public goods and services, enforcement of land lease contracts, and extraction of revenue (mainly on behalf of higher level authorities). Like township governments, they own and regulate enterprises within an exclusive space that has no presence of a higher level government administration. My discussion of the struc-tural conditions faced by township governments and township enterprises therefore also applies to those at the village level.

60 In 1992, 34.4 percent of state-owned industrial enterprises were in this category. The figure is estimated on the basis of an analysis of firms' postal codes recorded in a national industrial firm data set. See Appendix 1 in Lin (2001) for details of the data set.

61 Fiscal decentralization in the reform has had the effect of drastically reducing the resource de-pendence of local governments on higher level authorities (Wong et al., 1995), which used to constitute a major lever for the latter to shape local state action. As a result, the ability of higher level supervising bodies to act on behalf of the enterprises under their control to pressure local governments for favorable treatment has been seriously weakened.

62 See Lin (2001) for a discussion of this issue.

Another important feature of the urban economic space where SOEs cluster is that since the mid-1980s there has been a proliferation of what I call "backyard profit centers" (Lin and Zhang 1999; Lin 2001). They are front organizations set up, run or sponsored by state agencies to derive private profits for agency members. They are major destinations to which state-allocated resources have been diverted away from the central planning system. Their "owners" are dispersed in different niches of the urban state bureaucracy, and there is no coordination of action among them. In fact, they compete both with ordinary enterprises and among themselves. The diversion of plan-allocated industrial materials, capital, and other resources by or through backyard profit centers means that the designated receivers are deprived of their necessary supplies and consequently have to pay an extra price for obtaining them. SOEs have been hardest hit in this regard, as they have been the main destination of plan-allocated resources. Furthermore, their spatial proximity to backyard profit centers makes them easy targets for coerced transactions with backyard profit centers – selling output to and buying input from the latter at disadvantageous prices that they otherwise would not pay (Lin 2001).

In contrast, non-SOEs are somewhat structurally buffered from the adverse effects of these direct and indirect predatory state actions. A majority of them are located in rural jurisdictions,[63] and thus are not constantly exposed to multiple regulators.[64] Backyard profit centers are few and far between in townships (Lin and Zhang 1999). The collective interests of the relatively smaller number of local officials in such jurisdictions are more consolidated than those of officials in urban jurisdictions. They tend to refrain from imposing excessive demands on the enterprises that are under their exclusive purview. These "cash cows" help them fulfil their revenue obligations to higher level authorities and provide them with a pool of resources that they can make discretionary use of.

For enterprises (especially SOEs) that bear the brunt of predatory state action, the implication of such structural variation is two-fold. On the one hand, approaching local officials through *guanxi* and asking them to contain or reverse their predatory actions directly affect the vested interests (i.e., the proceeds from predatory action) that they share with each other and with their backyard profit centers. On the other hand, there are large numbers of predators to deal with, and neutralizing the actions of a few has no ripple effect on the actions of the remaining crowd. Neither condition makes it impossible to defuse (e.g., with the help of certain officials induced to override shared collective interests) these adverse effects from local officials and then some. But such effort is likely to be very costly, particularly in comparison with favor-seeking efforts in contexts where the structural conditions for these forms of predation are limited.

63 According to the 1995 industrial census, 84 percent of "collective enterprises" in 1995 were township and village enterprises (TVEs), and 92 percent of those were classified as "other" (vs. state and collective) enterprises based in the countryside (GYPCBGS 1997, p. 4).

64 Of the non-SOEs situated in urban jurisdictions, most are directly regulated by grassroots jurisdictions. All the urban private enterprises (including *getihu* or self-employed individuals), which accounted for the majority of non-SOEs in urban areas, are under the jurisdiction of grassroots-level urban governments, which also "own" the majority of urban collective enterprises.

Crowded political market

The urban state bureaucracy not only features more divergent interests but is crowded with more favor-seekers. As the centers of market-oriented economic activities and the loci of allocative and regulatory decisions of the government, urban places tend to attract more outside favor-seekers than townships in the countryside. Furthermore, the dispersion of the loci of urban state authorities, the divergence of interests among government agencies, and the resultant inconsistency in decision-making leave open broader avenues for favor-seekers, both local and non-local, to approach local officials for resources, regulatory flexibilities, and market access, which, under a more coherent political authority structure, tend to be granted according to a more consistently prioritized order. There is also a historical factor that facilitates the concentration of favor-seeking in urban places. That is, there have been broad and diverse avenues to the urban social space because of changes resulting from revolution, industrialization, and urbanization.

Unlike the Russian Bolshevik Revolution, where urban proletarians played a central role, the Chinese Communist revolution was based in the countryside. The millions of peasants who had joined the rank and file of the revolutionary army became the main source of cadres for the state bureaucracy after the victory of the revolution in 1949 (Song 1994). They have worked, lived, and developed personal networks in urban administrative centers while maintaining social ties with their relatives in rural areas. Such ties provide a potential bridge for the latter to explore access to opportunities and resources outside their local social spaces.

The massive absorption of rural laborers into the urban work force in the 1950s further increased the social networks between urban and rural areas. A survey conducted by the Policy Research Office of the CCP's Secretariat in 1982 revealed that 70 percent of those who joined the urban workforce before 1957 were recruited from the countryside (SJCYJS 1982, pp. 172–73). The local personal contacts that they have accumulated over time also provide a major stepping stone for their relatives in the countryside to explore access to the loci of state authority in urban areas.[65] With the deepening of the reform process, such interaction has been further facilitated by the relaxation and eventual removal of stringent travel restrictions and by the improvement in telecommunication facilities and services, such as telephones, pagers, faxes, and mobile phones.

The flocking of favor-seekers to urban places adds a complicating factor to favor exchange with officials. It extends the reach of *guanxi* networks that crisscross the

---

65 In-depth case studies of rural industrialization during the reform era clearly show that social networks of rural entrepreneurs and officials have been a most important avenue for them to tap urban financial and human resources and input supplies, promote sales, acquire information and technology, develop business connections, and facilitate deal-making (Byrd and Lin 1990; Ma et al. 1994). 72 of the 168 factory managers I interviewed during 1988 and 1996 were based in rural areas. They all indicated that their primary contacts in urban areas were mostly people with family ties in their locales. It was through these contacts that they approached different levels of urban state authorities for various forms of help and assistance.

urban political economy, increases the substitutability of pre-existing network ties, and clarifies the frame of reference for officials to evaluate the opportunity cost of favor-giving. As discussed earlier, these conditions contribute to the instrumentalization of *guanxi*. An implication of this is that in the face of large numbers of favor-seekers in increasingly open communities of social exchange, close personal relationship with officials is often not enough for securing special favors. Concrete material benefits are not only indispensable but need to be offered on terms that are more favorable than those of rival favor-seekers, as the prize tends to go to the highest bidder. Since multilateral interaction in favor exchange with officials frequently shifts the balance of benefits and costs with regard to each of the dyadic relationships centered around a particular favor-giver, stable commitment is difficult to sustain and opportunism is likely to result and spread.

To be sure, doing business in a crowded political market is likely to be as costly for outside favor-seekers as for their local counterparts. The difference, however, is that the former only partially and selectively count on the outcome from exchange in such market, but the latter's competitive positions are overwhelmingly dependent on it, as most basic aspects of their operations are under the influence of local state actions.

On the home front of enterprises operating under rural administration, the degree of crowding in favor-seeking tends to be lower. Outside favor-seekers are few and far between. More importantly, the clustering of local officials' interests under an integrated authority structure leads to the formation of a pecking order for prioritizing the allocation of special favors. It also deters opportunistic behavior in favor-granting, especially that on a large scale. This, of course, does not mean that those at the lower end of the pecking order are deterred from seeking favors from local officials. The distribution of some favors, such as bending rules on environmental protection and labor rights protection, may not result in a "winner-takes-all" outcome. They tend to be more actively sought than favors that are in limited supply, such as low-interest loans. But those that do not see the prospect of forming a close tie between their enterprises and local officials' shared interests tend to refrain from competing directly with those that have established such a tie. Also, an important trend in rural social change during the reform is the revival of kinship networks. In some locales, the authority relations embedded in such networks have interlocked with those of the local state, turning the local state into a de facto clan organization (e.g., Chen 1999; Lin 1995; Lin and Chen 1999). This poses a further constraint on the attempts of those on the fringe to compete with those in the "inner circle" for the same kind of special favors.

Collusion and whistle-blowing

Favor-seekers often need to make unauthorized use of organizational resources to pave the way for obtaining favors, and the officials granting special favors in exchange for private gains can hardly do so without making inappropriate or illicit diversion of state-controlled resources and opportunities. Hence, *guanxi*-mediated favor exchange with officials is in large part a collusive act that breaks existing rules and thus involves a risk. Violation of the code of conduct for enterprise leaders and public office holders can lead to adverse consequences, ranging from disciplinary action to legal punishment.[66] In order to reduce risk and protect their mutual interests, colluding parties need to restrict outside parties' access to the information concerning their private dealings. In the process of doing so, they have to confront the constraints posed by the organizational environments in which they operate.

Neither state agencies nor economic organizations are devoid of internal politics, which spawns power struggle and interpersonal rivalry among key decision-makers. Organizational politics is especially likely to be complex when the degree of relational stability and congeniality among key decision-makers is low, making it difficult for them to trust each other and form a solid informal basis of common interests. In such a situation, any information on the trespass of existing rules by a decision-maker can jeopardize his or her career if it falls into the hands of personal rivals. It follows that a decision-making group of small size and stable and self-selected membership may be more effective for containing the risk in collusion than a group of large size and unstable and externally appointed membership, because the former may be more conducive to fostering group cohesion, developing consensus, and sustaining cooperation. Assuming individuals are risk-averse, therefore, collusive behavior is likely to be most active and fruitful between officials and their "clients" who both face weak constraints from their respective organizational processes.[67]

In China's reform era, this condition is most widely available in the interface between grassroots (i.e., township) level governments and the enterprises under their jurisdiction. Small in size, township governments are mostly run by a circle of closely linked officials. Unlike decision-making power in governments at higher levels, here it is less diffused and more concentrated in the hands of a few key figures in charge of limited numbers of administrative units overseeing a rather wide range of combined and integrated functions. Although the township director and party secretary are rotated periodically between different localities, their deputies and subordinates are all locals who know each other well and expect to stay where their roots are.

Other than township enterprises, many private enterprises, foreign capital enterprises, and joint ownership enterprises also operate under the purview of township

---

66 This is particularly likely to be the case in a political process where the policy orientation zig-zags between different ideological and factional agendas and thereby creates opportunities for some decision-makers to use evidence of "inappropriate" conduct to launch attacks on their personal rivals at the height of a change in the political climate. Lei Yu and Liang Xiang, for example, were both former governors of Hainan province who attempted bold reform measures. They were forced out of office by their political opponents on charges of inappropriate use of authority for personal gains (*RMRB* August 1, 1985, September 15, 1989).

67 Olson (1965, 1982) also emphasizes the importance of small group size to the success of collusive collective action. But his analysis is primarily focused on the "free rider" problem and incentives for commitment rather than on the risk factor.

governments. Most township enterprises and all the other non-SOEs operating under the purview of grassroots governments were established in the reform era. Their leaders, especially private owners, have the authority to fill their management teams with loyalists and conduct their business in an autocratic fashion. Major decisions are often made and monopolized by the enterprise leader who is also able to keep virtually all the information on any external transactions to himself.

In contrast, authority relations in SOEs, especially large and medium ones, tend to be more complicated. Few of them are under the sole purview of grassroots government, as the county is the lowest level of SOEs' supervising authority. They are monitored by a number of agencies (e.g., the industry-specific department, the fiscal authority, the planning authority, among others) whose actions are often not coordinated. Information concerning the interaction between an SOE and a supervising agency is likely to be known to other relevant agencies. The majority of SOEs have been in existence for a long time,[68] and many still bear the scars of wounds in interpersonal relations left over from the highly politicized and divided workplace life (Walder 1986) under Maoist radicalism during the Cultural Revolution. The top leaders are appointed by their supervising bodies and transferred periodically; few of them have full authority to handpick their deputies.[69] These institutional features may foster latent and manifest factional conflicts between political functionaries and non-political managers, between "old timers" and new appointees from outside, and between personal rivals, making it difficult for the top leader to engage in extensive informal transactions through private ties and cut deals with outsiders while keeping all the information to himself.[70]

The consequence of the variations described here across different organizational settings is obvious. Enterprise leaders who are less constrained by internal politics can be more aggressive in using concrete benefits to enhance the effectiveness of their personal connections with officials in exchange for special treatment, especially where officials also face weaker relational constraints. Likewise, officials tend to be more forthcoming in favor exchange when they are capable of doing it in a clandestine fashion and transact through informal channels with parties that have the same capability in information control. The tendency to collude between firm leaders and officials is likely to be weakened if one of the two conditions (weak constraints on both parties involved) is not present, and seriously constrained

68 For example, only 28.2 percent of the state industrial enterprises that were in operation in 1992 were established after 1978 (Lin 2001, ch. 6).

69 According to a 1992 survey conducted by the World Bank and the Chinese Academy of Social Sciences on 1,663 urban and rural industrial enterprises, the average tenure was four years for SOEs and urban collectives (n = 1,270) and eight years for large township enterprises (n = 281); the percentages for enterprises directors who claimed to have the authority to pick their deputies are 20 percent (n = 1,265) and 40 percent (n = 285) for the two groups, respectively. See Lin (2001).

70 This, of course, does not mean the structural constraints are insurmountable obstacles. Where and when they are overcome, we would expect to see more effective use of *guanxi* by enterprise leaders.

if both conditions are absent.[71] Since this last situation is what most SOEs have faced in the reform, it imposes a major constraint on their effective use of personal networks for favor-seeking.

SUMMARY

This chapter addresses two central issues in the study of *guanxi* in China's reform era: why it has become increasingly instrumentalized, and why some people are better able to make use of *guanxi* than others. The analysis presented provides explanations that complement the tie strength thesis and the networking skill thesis. More important, it shows that a look beyond dyadic interaction may lead to further insights into the forces that shape the process and outcome of *guanxi*-mediated social exchange. While the findings are preliminary and by no means exhaustive, they do indicate that to discern the impact of multilateral interaction on dyadic social exchange, it is important to pay close attention to the milieu of such interaction. In particular, the path-dependent structural conditions – relational patterns defined by institutions and organizations – faced by different actors appear to hold a key to understanding the mechanisms at work.

Theoretically, this account points to a direction where more fruitful analyses can be developed to narrow the gap between social exchange theory and social network theory. The former focuses on dyadic interaction (Blau 1986; Cook 1987; Coleman 1988), whereas the latter emphasizes multilateral interconnectedness among individuals and groups (Burt 1982; Granovetter 1985; Wellman and Berkowitz 1997). But there remains considerable open ground where the analytic thrusts derived from the two can inform and reinforce one another to produce more powerful explanations about social action.[72] Tapping this potential, as I have shown, requires closer attention to the interdependent nature of decision-making.

71   A precondition for such a pattern of effects has of course to be that there remains a certain degree of potency in the state's legal and regulatory power to enforce, at least superficially, its formal claim of neutrality despite the significant and continuing slippage of state action toward informal and particularistic agendas.
72   Burt (1992) represents a fruitful effort in this direction.

NEW SUBSTANTIVE STUDIES
OF *GUANXI*

4

GUANXI IN BUSINESS GROUPS: SOCIAL TIES AND THE FORMATION OF ECONOMIC RELATIONS

Lisa A. Keister

INTRODUCTION

The role that *guanxi* plays in organizing social and economic interactions in China has been the subject of considerable debate among scholars, particularly since the beginning of reform (Bian 1997, 1999; Gold 1985; Guthrie 1998a; Kipnis 1997; Yan 1996a; Yang 1994). In this chapter, I examine the role that *guanxi* played in the emergence of firm-to-firm lending and trade relations in the early stages of reform. The structure of lending and trade relations is one of the fundamental defining features of any economic system. The nature of relations among buyers and sellers of commercial goods and the borrowers and lenders of financial resources determines a great deal not only about flows of resources in an economy but also about the financial performance of firms and entire regions (Cool and Schendel 1987; Haveman 1992; Lincoln, Gerlach, and Ahmadjian 1996), the economic and political influence of organizations (Lincoln, Gerlach, and Takahashi 1992; Mizruchi 1989, 1992), power and dependence relations among firms (Mintz and Schwartz 1985; Pfeffer and Salancik 1978; Scott 1991), and the relative economic and social advantages enjoyed by workers in those firms (Mizruchi 1992; Pfeffer 1981).

From the beginning of China's economic reform, lending and trade relations among firms were dismantled and rebuilt. As the state decreased central planning and reduced its role in the management of firms, managers became responsible for finding productive inputs, for acquiring capital, and for finding markets for finished products for the first time in decades. As organizational decision-makers sought out goods and capital, they established relations with other firms, and many of these relations quickly became ongoing trade or finance ties of the sort that define the structure of an economy. Some of these relations mimicked relations that were imposed by the state prior to reform, while others developed where no tie existed previously. To a large extent, the nature of China's economy in coming years will reflect the structure of lending and trade relations that developed in the early stages of reform.

A large portion of the lending and trade relations that developed in China formed within the country's emerging business groups, the *qiye jituan*. Starting in the mid-1980s, reformers encouraged firms to become members of business groups to protect them from the shock of reform, and for the next few years, most firms developed lending and trade relations within these groups (Keister 1998). Like business groups in other parts of the world, China's *qiye jituan* are groups of related firms that are legally and socially connected and that conduct business together over long periods of time (Granovetter 1995a). The member firms in business groups typically operate in a diverse set of industries, and there is usually a central firm or family that oversees some aspects of group activities.[72] By the early 1990s, there were more than 7,000 known business groups in China (Reform 1993), and these groups were infused with elaborate intercorporate ties, similar to those found in Japan's *keiretsu* and Korea's *chaebol*.[73] In the early stages of reform, little exchange occurred across group boundaries, and the business groups accounted for a large fraction of the nation's total industrial assets (Li 1995). In fact, the total 1993 assets of state-owned *qiye jituan* was 1.12 trillion yuan ($135.70 billion), one-quarter of all state-owned assets (Kan 1996).

In this chapter, I examine the role that *guanxi* played in the development of lending and trade relations in the business groups. Where David Wank (in this volume) finds that *guanxi* is an important factor for small scale entrepreneurs in reform-era China, I find that it influences decision-making in member firms in China's largest business groups. Specifically, I ask four questions: Did managers in the business groups cultivate social indebtedness in order to gain advantage in lending and trade? Did managers use social relations to avoid complying with laws regarding the development of lending and trade relations? Did managers use social relations as they decided with whom they would establish lending and trade relations? And did managers avoid dependent economic relations with those with whom they were socially connected? I first discuss theoretical literature on the role of social relations in the emergence and structure of economic relations. I then draw on data that I gathered in in-depth interviews between 1995 and 1997 with managers throughout China to address these questions. I also use 1988 and 1990 quantitative panel data that I collected on the country's 40 largest business groups and their 535 member firms to analyze the factors that influence the formation

72 The core firm's role in the management of firms typically varies with its ownership stake in the firms. A core firm that owns a large proportion of a firm is generally more active in its operations, while a core firm whose ownership stake is smaller will likely minimize its management role as well. Chinese business groups did have core firms in the early stages of their development. Unlike Korea's *chaebol*, however, it was unusual for family connections to play a central role in the organization of China's business groups.

73 There were two types of business groups in China in the early stages of the development of the groups: groups of small, often private firms that resemble Taiwan's *guanxi qiye* (Fields 1995), and *qiye jituan*, groups of large, primarily state-owned firms that resemble Japan's *keiretsu*. I focus on the second type because they predominated. Estimates of the proportion of state-owned firms that are members of *qiye jituan* vary with definitions of ownership; 1990 estimates range from 20 percent to more than 50 percent (Li 1995).

of lending and trade relations. The quantitative data include information about intra-group lending and trade relations, business group structure, firm financial performance, manager characteristics, and the costs of goods traded. Using the quantitative data, I model 16,306 ordered pairs of intra-group dyadic lending and trade relations as a function of firm, dyad, and regional covariates. These analyses allow me to isolate the effects of one manifestation of *guanxi* – school ties among managers – in firm-to-firm lending and trade ties, and to discuss the role that these social ties played in the development of economic relations.

THEORETICAL ISSUES

Manufacturing social indebtedness

In all economies, social relations affect the development, structure, and mainte-nance of economic relations. Research on the development of markets in the United States and Europe indicates that social ties directed much of the early financial and other economic exchange that occurred during development and industrialization in the United States, Scotland, England, Germany, France, and other economies that are now considered developed, market economies (Cottrell 1980; Lamoreaux 1994; Leff 1976; Munn 1981; Smelser 1959). There is also evidence that social re-lations formed the basis of the industrialization and development of the economies of many Latin American countries (Balmori, Voss, and Wortman 1984; Haber 1991; Strachan 1979). However, the role that social relations play in the creation and maintenance of economic exchange has received perhaps the greatest attention in Asia, where the *keiretsu*, *chaebol*, *guanxi qiye*, and similar organizational forms in Japan, Korea, Taiwan, Hong Kong, Malaysia, Singapore, and other countries have attracted for decades the attention of both social sciences researchers and those with more practical concerns (Amsden 1989; Gerlach 1992; Hamilton 1991; Lincoln, Gerlach and Takahashi 1992).

Even within Asia, the effect of social relations on economic exchange has at-tracted perhaps the greatest attention in China. In China, economic actors are often characterized as not simply recognizing and using social relations to their benefit in economic exchange, but researchers and practitioners alike quite often portray the Chinese as deliberately and strategically manufacturing social relations for the purpose of economic gain. In her ethnographic study of social relations in China, for instance, Mayfair Yang used extensive interviews conducted over a decade to conclude that *guanxi* and *guanxi* practice (*guanxi xue*) are key to understanding all manner of social relations, including economic relations, in China. Yang made the key distinction between *guanxi* and *guanxi* practice. *Guanxi*, or social relations, are the personal relations and other social ties that people develop through their lives through normal interactions. Family ties, strong ties with close friends, and weak ties with acquaintances would all be considered *guanxi*. In contrast, *guanxi* practice (literally "the study of *guanxi*"), refers to the deliberate and strategic cul-tivation and use of social relations. Yang agreed with other scholars and observers of Chinese society when she argued that an understanding of Chinese society, including economic relations, must include a conception of *guanxi*. Yang, however, was much stronger in her argument about the role that *guanxi* played in organizing life in China in the first decade of reform. In particular, she contended that *guanxi practice*, not simply *guanxi*, became increasingly important during that decade (see also Guthrie 1998a for an excellent discussion of Yang's work).

Yang argued that job scarcity and the scarcity of other necessities encouraged actors – both individual and corporate – to rely increasingly heavily on both *guanxi* and *guanxi* practice during the Cultural Revolution and particularly during the first decade of economic transition (Yang 1994). One result was that it became acceptable to use *guanxi* practice to circumvent laws and other regulations. She characterized economic actors as deliberately and strategically manufacturing social ties for the purpose of skirting policies with which they did not agree or that were not in their interest. While few other scholars have made such strong arguments about the deliberate creation and use of social ties in China, there is considerable agreement that *guanxi* matters (Bian 1999; Blau, Ruan, and Ardelt 1991; Gold 1985; Hwang 1987; King 1991; Ruan 1993). There are those who disagree, including Guthrie, who argued that while *guanxi* remained important during the first decade of reform, *guanxi* practice and the use of *guanxi* to circumvent laws and regulations was not common practice (Guthrie 1998a). However, on the whole, if we look at this literature we would conclude that actors were strategic and deliberate in their cultivation of social ties for economic gain and for the purpose of circumventing laws, policies, and regulations with which they did not agree.

Taking these observations and discussions of the importance of social relations as guidelines, it follows that managers are likely to have cultivated social ties that they could then exploit for gain in the formation of lending and trade relations in the early business groups. We would expect that managers would have cultivated social ties with those who made strategic economic partners and then used those relations to manufacture advantageous lending and trade relations. That is, we would expect findings that affirm my first two questions: Did managers manufacture social ties for economic gain? And did managers use social ties to circumvent laws and regulations?

Social relations and economic exchange

Although most research in organization theory has primarily been conducted in Western countries in the past, this literature can nonetheless also be useful in understanding the role of *guanxi* in the development of lending and trade relations in China. Ideas from transaction cost economics, social exchange theory, and resource dependence theory are all useful in understanding how firms exchange resources and the role that social relations play in the creation, maintenance, and structure of economic ties. These approaches share the assumption that managers seek to reduce uncertainty and avoid opportunism in lending and trade. Transaction cost economics emphasizes the tendency of firms to create boundaries that separate them from markets and market failure. Mergers, acquisitions, vertical integration, and the formation of multidivisional forms are all strategies used by corporate decision makers to reduce uncertainty and the transaction costs that result from uncertainty (Lincoln, Gerlach and Takahashi 1992; Williamson 1975). "Hybrid" forms of organizing, between arms-length market transactions and the hierarchies that develop when firms merge completely, develop when managers do not trust market forces alone to coordinate exchange (Williamson 1985). Similarly, social exchange theory argues that uncertainty regarding the availability of productive inputs and markets for finished goods leads firms to develop ongoing lending and trade relations (Cook and Emerson 1984; Emerson 1976). Research in this tradition has found that firms are often willing to forgo the cost advantages of market exchange for the safety and certainty of a negotiated environment. Resource dependence theory emphasizes the tendency of firms to coopt the sources of uncertainty or to create bridges to increase control over their environments (Lincoln, Gerlach and Ahmadjian 1996; Pfeffer and Salancik 1978). Again, the result is ongoing lending or trade that falls short of hierarchy but that joins firms in lasting ties that avoid the pitfalls accompanying market exchange.

During China's economic transition, emerging markets and managers' lack of experience transacting on these markets increased levels of uncertainty and the risk of opportunism in lending and trade. Equity markets were rudimentary: Most of the nation's large domestic banks operated under the aegis of the Central Bank and engaged primarily in government-directed credit extension. State funds were limited, and social and political factors were often more important than firm performance or other determinants of creditworthiness in borrowing (Goldie-Scott 1995b; Yi 1994). Private and foreign banks were only permitted to operate under highly constrained conditions (Goldie-Scott 1995a), and while Chinese stock markets had begun to develop, stock trading was limited and provided little capital to firms (Goldie-Scott 1995b; Gong 1995).

Product markets were also in the initial stages of development. Firm access to inputs and markets for finished goods was limited, and infrastructure constraints and a scarcity of reliable firms specializing in transportation often precluded the national distribution of products. Finally, labor markets began to develop early in reform, but national labor markets did not exist even in the late 1990s and local markets were seldom reliable sources of personnel (Naughton 1992, 1995). Changes in administrative control also contributed to uncertainty during transition (Guthrie 1997, p. 1261), but this source of uncertainty had little effect on the development of lending and trade relations in the business groups. Managers in the groups had considerable autonomy in establishing these ties. Moreover, while the core firm did influence exchange relations, the web of lending and trade ties that developed quickly became extremely complex, and as a result, core firm managers typically had little control over or even influence on the development or nature of a particular tie (Keister 1998).

Yet there were obstacles that discouraged mergers and integration in favor of long-term lending and trade relations between firms that remained legally independent. Because property rights were not well defined, managers and reformers alike were uncertain about the legal implications of ownership. The state had reduced its role to that of a shareholder in most major corporations, and private property slowly developed. However, China did not have laws governing private ownership and the transfer of ownership, and Chinese courts were ill-equipped to handle disputes over property rights. Thus, rather than risk losing control to an outside entity, particularly since firms were just beginning to acquire control of their operations, managers fostered close exchange relations that did not involve complete integration.

The structure of the lending and trade relations that emerged in China's business groups reflected the various strategies managers used to reduce uncertainty and opportunism and to avoid dependence as the groups emerged. A particularly common strategy was to develop new lending and trade relations where prior social ties existed. It is possible that habit explained some of the persistence of prior social connections, but habit was only part of the explanation. If a firm regularly obtained certain unfinished goods, particularly specialized goods, from another firm prior to reform, habit and ease might make it more likely to continue to trade with the pre-reform supplier. However, because firms in transition economies faced exacerbated levels of uncertainty, transaction costs involved in finding suitable trade partners were also higher. As a result, familiarity with trade partners was even more important than it might be in a more stable economy. Managers preferred to trade with those they trusted, not just those with whom they traded in the past. Thus, firms were willing to forgo opportunities for objectively more lucrative exchange relations to maintain relations with those they knew socially in the past. For this reason, I would expect to find confirmation for my third question: Did managers manufacture social ties for economic gain?

While there are various social relations that might have affected the formation of economic ties, I focus on the effects of school ties (whether they were *tongxue*) between managers. It was not uncommon for managers to develop lending and trade relations with friends from college. I argue that these relations developed more than we would expect by chance, indicating that managers relied on these ties when making lending and trade decisions. In particular, I argue that if managers had school ties prior to reform, we would expect their firms to be more likely to have established lending and trade relations in the early stages of reform.

Social relations and economic dependence

Ideas from resource dependence theory predict another outcome of uncertainty: the formation of dependent economic relations in which the partner that faces less uncertainty is able to cultivate dependent relations with others in more uncertain conditions. Research in this tradition also emphasizes the importance of uncertainty in the development of exchange ties: Task specialization and resource scarcity create uncertainty regarding the availability of both inputs and markets for finished goods. This uncertainty leads to the formation of stable exchange relations among organizations that are willing to forgo the advantages of trade across pure markets for the security of a negotiated environment (Cook 1977). Moreover, resource dependence theory posits that an organization's power in the negotiated environment is directly related to its need for the resource it receives in the exchange and inversely related to the availability of the resource from other sources (Thompson 1967, pp. 29–30). Resource dependence theory would predict that Chinese managers would cultivate dependent economic relations, relations in which less powerful firms are dependent on more powerful ones. It is likely, however, that the presence of a prior social tie between the two firms would mitigate this effect. That is, where a social tie existed between two firms, the social tie would override the desire for dependence and the dependent relationship would be less likely to develop.

Because access to resources is a primary source of uncertainty, uncertainty can be extreme where markets are not developed. Firms that appear to have secure, long-term access to resources make more attractive trading partners because the potential future cost of not having the resource at all or having to pay a much higher price for the resource makes a dependable source attractive. Added to this is the cost of searching for new trade partners. Such costs are particularly high in developing markets, where potential partners are scarce and information about their track records is limited. In fact (as the manager quoted earlier suggested), estimates of the cost of leaving the current exchange relation may appear so great that firms will be willing to pay a higher price to maintain an ongoing exchange than to take advantage of lower current prices available from other potential partners. For these reasons, I would expect to find confirmation for my fourth question: Did managers avoid cultivating dependent economic relations with those with whom they had prior social ties?

GUANXI IN THE FORMATION OF EXCHANGE TIES IN CHINA

In order to examine the role that social relations played in the development of lending and trade ties in China's business groups, I first draw on interviews that I conducted with managers in China's 40 largest business groups (by total 1990 assets) and their 535 firms. I also use interviews that I conducted in a random sample of 40 small, medium, and large groups in Shanghai, and in additional groups in 8 cities and several underrepresented industries. I conducted the interviews between 1995 and 1997.

Contrary to many previous arguments and findings on the importance of *guanxi*, the managers I interviewed were quite consistent in denying that they manufactured indebtedness in the development of lending and trade ties. The managers clearly distinguished between *guanxi* (the social relations) and *guanxi* practice (cultivating social relations for strategic purposes). As others, such as Guthrie (1998a), have argued is becoming increasingly common, particularly in urban China, the managers in the business groups distinguished between developing good business relations (*gaohao shangye guanxi*) and using social ties to take care of matters (*kao guanxi xue ban shouxu*). A manager in an automobile manufacturing plant said:

I do not think managers in China are really that much different than managers in the United States or Japan, or in Europe either. We want our companies to do well, we need for them to do well. Sometimes it is good practice to do business with a friend. You can call that using *guanxi* if you want, but it is no different than what western managers do. Do we go out and look for social relations that will help us in business? No. Definitely not. Sure there might be some [Chinese managers] who are dishonest in this way, but they are rare. I would guess that there are as many business people in the west who are dishonest in this way as there are in China (personal interview, 1996).

The finance manager in a pharmaceutical company concurred:

To know who your friends are and even to call on those friends when you need help is one thing. But making sure you know the right people in the right places so that you can get rules passed that benefit you or so that you can get things done. Well, that is very different. It used to be that people in China tried to work this way, but they discovered that everything takes much too long to get done if you do it like this. My sense is that now people follow rules more. If they want to get things done, they do what the rules tell them to do. You know what? I think most of them would agree that this way of working is much more efficient (personal interview, 1995).

Far from being anomalies among the managers I interviewed, these sentiments characterized much of what I learned in my interviews about the way business was done in China in the decade following reform and into the 1990s. Indeed, none of the managers I interviewed agreed that *guanxi* practice continued to be a viable or common way of doing business in transition China. As I will discuss later, they acknowledged (with considerable conviction that it was justified) that they turned to friends and other social relations when they were in need. But the managers with whom I spoke consistently and repeatedly denied that *guanxi* practice was increasingly important in China during the 1980s and 1990s.

As the two earlier quotes indicate, the managers with whom I spoke recognized that managers in market economies also rely on social ties to get business done, but they consistently claimed that they did not attempt to cultivate social relations for economic gain. These findings are consistent with Guthrie's (1998a) findings that the distinction between *guanxi* (social relations) and *guanxi* practice (the deliberate and strategic use of social relations) is important. Guthrie used interviews with managers and officials in Shanghai to argue that in the early 1990s, managers were concerned with obeying laws and regulations. The managers whom Guthrie interviewed agreed that *guanxi* practice is not only distasteful but that it actually became less common, rather than more common, in the years following reform. Practices in the business groups during the 1980s and 1990s were similar to what Guthrie found. In fact, more than denying that they, or those they knew, engaged in *guanxi* practice, the managers agreed that relying on *guanxi* to get things done (*kao guanxi xue ban shouxu*) was dishonest.

The managers I interviewed used words such as dangerous and corrupt to describe the practice and expressed their distaste not only for the practice but also for those who continued to engage in it. Occasionally, those who were less actively opposed to the practice would smile and acknowledge that this is the way business was done in the past, but even these managers were quick to point out that since reform, things had changed. They would point out that dishonest people had not disappeared but that dishonest practices had become unacceptable. Frequently, the managers would also make the point that while *guanxi* practice might help you get ahead in the short run, there were few long-term benefits. The managers pointed to the time it takes to try to use *guanxi* to circumvent rules and regulations as being inefficient and producing less benefit than doing business honestly. Moreover, many of the managers argued that *guanxi* practice would make them look bad to actual or potential foreign business partners. A manager in a company that produced various important oils and food products told of the temptation to revert to practices that were common in the past but being discouraged because it would have made him look bad to his foreign partners:

There was a time in about 1990 when I wanted to import some soybean oil from Argentina. There are lots of restrictions on the importation of edible oils, particularly soybean oil, because someone once replaced edible oils coming from, I think it was Malaysia, with non-edible oils. It could have made lots of people sick. Anyway, when I tried to import the oil from Argentina, I found that the quota for my area had already been filled. It was tempting to use the old methods [rely on *guanxi* practice] to get this changed, but how would that have looked to the Argentines? We [the Chinese people] need foreign trade partners. Why would we want to make them think that China is a dishonest, corrupt place to do business? It would be bad for us. Besides, it would have taken too long to get things changed. I just convinced the Argentines to get involved in another deal with me (personal interview, 1995).

In short, I found that in China's business groups in the 1980s and 1990s, the answer to each of my first two questions was an overwhelming "no." Managers did not appear to view *guanxi* practice as a viable way to do business, they did not manufacture social relations for economic gain, nor did they use social relations to change or circumvent laws or practices. I did, however, find evidence in my interviews that my expectations for my third and fourth questions were upheld in the business groups. Managers admitted that they took advantage of the social ties they had – primarily ties through school and former political activities – to reduce uncertainty in finding lending and trade partners. The managers I interviewed admitted that they also tried to take advantage of the resources to which they had access by cultivating dependent economic relations. That is, the managers realized that not all firms were going to survive through the next decade, and that those who were in powerful positions economically (i.e., those on whom others were dependent for resources) would be more likely to survive. The managers willingly admitted that they cultivated relations in which they were powerful, taking advantage of their strengths. They acknowledged, however, that they were very reluctant to cultivate dependent economic relations with those to whom they were socially connected. As a manager in a coal mining equipment manufacturer explained:

It is difficult to manage trade relations in China since the beginning of reform. It is difficult to find suppliers and customers. It is also difficult to find capital. In another ten years, markets in China will be more developed, and these things will be less of a problem. For now, though, I'm not afraid to say that there are times when I look to my friends to find the supplies I need. I have also loaned money to friends. I do not look for these types of relations. It is just that I trust my friends to repay the loan. This is just sensible (personal interview, 1996).

Another manager, this time from a company that made automotive electrical parts, summarized the arguments that I outlined earlier regarding the cultivation of dependent lending and trade relations:

It is good for our company if we create a group of companies throughout China who need our products. This will guarantee demand for what we are producing not just for a year or two, but for a long time down the road. It is good to have guaranteed customers. Do I try to create relations such as these with my friends? No. There is something dishonest about that. I would not want my personal friends to treat me so instrumentally, so I will not do it to them. Even if I just think about it strategically, it is better for me to have friends who are powerful and competitive. Why would I want to make my friends dependent or less competitive? It would be bad financial and social practice in many ways (personal interview, 1997).

EMPIRICAL EVALUATION OF LENDING AND TRADE IN BUSINESS GROUPS

Data

In addition to the qualitative data I used here, I also collected quantitative data on the social and economic relations among members of China's early business groups. In this section, I use the quantitative data to further examine my third and fourth questions (Did managers use social connections as they formed lending and trade relations? Did managers avoid cultivating dependent lending and trade relations with those with whom they had prior social ties?). I do not investigate my first and second questions (Did managers manufacture social ties for economic gain? Did managers use social ties to circumvent laws and regulations?) because the lack of qualitative support and my initial investigations of the questions using the quantitative data suggests that quantitative analysis would be futile. Moreover, preliminary investigation suggested that the quantitative findings corroborated the qualitative results.

Specifically, I collected 1988–90 panel data on resource exchange relations among the 535 firms that were members of China's 40 largest business groups (by total 1990 assets).[74] I used basic 1990 firm statistics from the Chinese Economic and Trade Commission in Beijing to identify and locate the largest groups and their constituent firms.[75] I then interviewed business group managers to obtain detailed 1988 and 1990 information about intercorporate exchange relations within the

74   These groups accounted for 68 percent of the total assets of state-owned business groups in 1990.
75   Gary Hamilton and Robert Feenstra obtained the basic 1990 data.

group as well as firm, dyad, and group characteristics.[76] I collected the majority of the data during 1995 and 1996 in interviews with the managers of the groups' core firms. To maximize accuracy, I personally copied data from the firms' financial statements, spoke with managers formally and informally (out of the plant), and validated the data against other published sources.

The business groups in this sample were headquartered in fifteen of China's twenty-nine provinces and in Beijing, Tianjin, and Shanghai (municipalities that are under the direct jurisdiction of the central government), and their member firms are located in all provinces, autonomous regions, and independent municipalities. Most of the firms are former state-owned enterprises, although joint ventures and collective enterprises are also included.[77] These groups represent a variety of industries, including manufacturing and services as well as China's central, or pillar, industries (energy, transportation, and communications). For two reasons, I exclude firms whose business is related to national security, defense, advanced proprietary technologies, and scarce mineral mining. First, access to the accounts of these firms is highly restricted. Second, firms in these industries are treated differently in the formation of business groups (i.e., formerly state-owned enterprises in these industries may be sold, but the state always maintains a majority share), suggesting that the processes underlying the formation of resource exchange ties in these industries might be dramatically different from processes that prevail in other industries (Bureau 1995; Dong and Hu 1995).

Methods of analysis

To explore the formation of lending and trade relations in the business groups using the quantitative data, I use logistic regression analysis (I explain the details of the methods and variable creation in the Appendix). The outcome I examine in this analysis is whether a firm had a lending or trade tie with another firm in 1990. That is, I explore the factors that influenced two dependent variables: whether pairs of firms (1) loaned capital to each other, or (2) bought or sold products from each other. In the models, I include independent variables that assess the importance of various potential influences on the presence of these two lending and trade ties. For example, I include a variable that allows me to evaluate the importance of personal histories between managers on the likelihood that firms traded. Specifically, I evaluate whether school ties between managers affected lending and trade. If this variable is positive and significant in the model, it will

---

76 The data include information on ties among levels of the groups' hierarchy (e.g., between the head office and constituent companies) as well as ties within a single stratum of a level (e.g., between factories).

77 A collective is jointly owned by a "guardian" organization (another firm, a social organization, or a government agency) and a rural township or urban municipality. Collectives existed prior to 1978, but were often ignored by the state planning system. Since reform, they have thrived because of their flexible management systems, low labor costs, and ability to retain profits (Oi 1990; Walder 1995a).

lend support to the argument that personal ties play a role in the development of lending and trade relations (question three).

I also include two variables that allow me to assess whether levels of market development influence the development of lending and trade relations. One variable indicates the level of market development where the lender/seller is located. The other variable indicates the level of market development where the borrower/buyer is located. If the first variable is positive and significant in the model *and* the second variable is negative and significant, this lends support to the idea that managers cultivated dependent lending and trade relations. However, if we multiply the school ties variable and the market development variables together and we find a negative and significant effect, we can conclude that managers avoid cultivating dependent relations with those with whom they have social ties (question four).

In both cases, I also include a variable that indicates the effect of cost on the development of lending and trade relations. If we were to espouse a standard economic argument, we would expect cost to be the dominant, if not the only, influence on whether firms buy and sell resources. That is, we would expect managers to buy their goods at the lowest possible cost. The variable I include is the difference between the cost the firm actually pays (for example, the price for the good or the interest for the loan) and the cost it expects it would pay from the next most likely source. We would expect to find a negative and significant effect of this variable on the likelihood that the firm actually bought the good or borrowed the money. Intuitively, we would expect that if the price were cheaper somewhere else, the firm would go to that source.

To fully understand these empirical analyses, we need to consider these variables together. Consider, for example, the implications of finding that the effect of cost is negative and significant *and* the effect of having a school tie is positive and significant. This suggests that even if the firm can find the resource cheaper somewhere else, it still gets it from the firm with which it has a school tie. Similarly, if the effect of cost is negative and significant *and* the effect of the market development variables are significant in the directions we anticipated, we would conclude that there is reason to believe that market development affected lending and trade even when the firms had better price options elsewhere.

In short, to conclude that there is evidence to answer yes to question three, we would expect to find that the indicator of school ties (labeled school tie$_{ij}$) is positive and significant. To conclude that there is evidence to answer yes to question four, we would expect to find that the indicator of school ties and market development together (labeled school tie$_{ij}$* market development$_j$) is negative and significant.

Results

What do these analyses indicate about the role that social relations played in the development of lending and trade relations in China's business groups? First, they support the idea that firms did avoid arms-length transactions when environmental uncertainty was high. That is, the firms tended to develop lending and trade relations with their friends when uncertainty was high. Second, the results provide support for the idea that firms sought to foster dependence on the resources they controlled when conditions were relatively certain, but that they avoided cultivating dependence if the other firm was managed by a friend. In other words, I find that firms opted to minimize long-term cost rather than current price by choosing to trade with those that would be reliable partners in ongoing relations and those with whom they had *guanxi*.

Table 4.1 presents the results of the logistic regression analyses. The coefficient estimate for the variable indicating school ties between the firms was indeed positive and significant in both models. Moreover, the results indicate that environmental uncertainty was a strong positive predictor that a firm would be a sender of a resource and a strong negative predictor that the firm would be a receiver. That is, the coefficient estimates for both market development variables were significant and in the anticipated direction, suggesting that uncertainty leads to the development of dependent exchange relations. The interaction between the market development variable and the indicator of school ties, however, suggests that these relations were less likely to develop between friends. Again, the coefficient estimate for this variable was significant and in the anticipated direction. Each of these findings persists even though I control for the availability of cheaper alternatives, providing support for the idea that processes other than pure economic rationality influenced the formation of lending and trade relations among the firms I studied.

I argued that resource dependence ideas predicted that organizations that are not subject to as much uncertainty would seek out dependent relations. The uncertainty evidence in the table provides support for these ideas. The mechanism by which uncertainty leads a firm to become a receiver is made clear by the cost coefficients (the firms continued to receive from stable suppliers even when resources were available cheaper elsewhere – see Table 4.1). Alternatively, the mechanism by which uncertainty affected the propensity of a firm to send resources is less clear from the regression results. While it might simply be that resource access leads firms to be senders (rather than a desire to cultivate dependence), my interviews suggested otherwise. Specifically, managers in firms that were predominantly senders overwhelmingly acknowledged awareness that trade partners might have been dependent on them, and nearly always argued that this was desirable.

The notion that the managers were concerned with more than immediate economic gains, particularly under uncertain conditions, is evident in the cost results. Not only did firms opt to trade with seemingly stable partners, but they were also willing to forgo less expensive alternatives for these relations. The negative effect of the single cost variable included in the first model for each tie indicates, as we would expect, firms were less willing to be involved in the repeated exchange tie if the resource was available cheaper elsewhere. Interpreted together with the uncertainty coefficients, this result provides evidence that uncertainty is a significant predictor of the presence of a tie despite cost. The

Table 4.1

Guanxi in lending and trade relations: Logistic regression results

	Financial Tie$_{ij1990}$	Commercial Tie$_{ij1990}$
Tie$_{ij1988}$(lagged DV)	2.38**	2.32**
	(1.43)	(1.37)
Reciprocity (tie$_{ji1990}$)	−.159***	2.84
	(.005)	(1.80)
School tie$_{ij}$	.522***	.406***
	(.107)	(.198)
Market development$_i$	.700***	.122***
	(.082)	(.050)
Market development$_j$	−.244***	−.191***
	(.019)	(.101)
Financial tie$_{ij1988}$	—	.121***
		(.001)
School tie$_{ij}$* market development$_j$	−.012**	−.111***
	(.007)	(.055)
Cost of resource		
Cost − cost elsewhere$_j$	−.045*	−.099**
	(.039)	(.072)
(Cost − cost elsewhere$_j$)	.001**	.006**
	(.000)	(.004)
(Cost − cost elsewhere$_j$)	−.0007**	−.0001**
	(.005)	(.001)
Firm characteristics		
Core firm$_i$	.009***	.260***
	(.001)	(.100)
Core firm$_j$	−161*	.280***
	(.120)	(.200)
Finance company$_i$	.225***	.122
	(.050)	(.550)
Finance company$_j$	−230***	−.151**
	(.070)	(.080)
(Profits/assets)* same prior bureau$_{ij}$	.225***	.005**
	(.042)	(.002)
(Profits/assets)* school tie$_{ij}$	.095*	.110**
	(.035)	(.000)
Control variables		
Two or more sources available$_i$	.143***	.461***
	(.071)	(.120)
Two or more sources available$_j$	.013	−.014**
	(.111)	(.009)
Administrative rank$_i$	1.20***	.832
	(.179)	(1.39)
Administrative rank$_j$	−.092***	−.089***
	(.019)	(.013)
Market$_i$* two or more sources$_i$	.001	.100
	(.001)	(.100)

Table 4.1 (*cont.*)

	Financial Tie$_{ij1990}$	Commercial Tie$_{ij1990}$
Dyad autoregressive term	.202***	.005***
	(.002)	(.002)
N	15,917	15,941
Pearson χ^2	978.89	911.12

*$p < .05$ **$p < .01$ ***$p < .001$.

Notes: Entries are coefficient estimates; standard errors are in parentheses. "Market development" and "market" indicators are equivalent. In models predicting a lending relation, the market variables refer to *financial* market development and the lagged dependent variable is the presence of a *lending* tie in 1988. Likewise, in models predicting a trade relation, the market variables refer to *commodity* market development and the lagged dependent variable is the presence of a *trade* tie in 1988. Included in the regression (but not displayed) are dummy variables for each of the forty business groups, the independent indicator of profits/assets, and indicators of ownership structure, industry, percent of profits remitted to the state (for each firm), geographic proximity to Beijing, geographic distance between the firms, and total assets.

uncertainty results are particularly strong given that the definition of uncertainty is resource-specific.

Research on market transition has been accumulating in recent years, most evidence about how transition occurs is derived from research on individuals or economic aggregates (Bian 1997; Nee 1996; Xie and Hannum 1996; Zhou, Tuma, and Moen 1997). Important exceptions exist (Guthrie 1997; Nee 1992), but direct observations of the economic choices made by actors during transition are rare (Oberschall 1996). My results concern one of the most fundamental economic decisions made during transition – the decision to trade, not just once but repeatedly, with another actor. The results suggest that while cost is an important determinant of exchange, environmental uncertainty matters even more. Specifically, to minimize long-term cost rather than minimizing current price, firms opted to trade with others that would be stable trading partners, those with whom they had *guanxi*. This indicates much about the decision-making of organizational decision makers and also implies that firms located in relatively developed areas will enjoy advantages in exchange that are likely to persist post-transition. One strategy used repeatedly by the Chinese government to gradually introduce reform has been the introduction of a change in a limited number of areas (test areas), followed by the universal introduction of the policy if the test is successful. Reformers have used this strategy in introducing various reforms, including the manager responsibility system, financial reform, labor reform, and housing reform. When the gradualism of Chinese reforms has clear advantages over the shock therapy that characterizes other transition efforts, the exchange advantages enjoyed by those in the early-developing regions might create long-term inequities.

CONCLUSIONS

In this chapter, I asked four questions about the role that *guanxi* and *guanxi* practice played in the formation of lending and trade relations in China's business groups in the first decade of reform. I asked: Did managers in the business groups cultivate social indebtedness in order to gain advantage in lending and trade? Did managers use social relations to avoid complying with laws regarding the development of lending and trade relations? Did managers use social relations as they decided with whom they would establish lending and trade relations? And did managers avoid dependent economic relations with those with whom they were socially connected? I argued that the structure of lending and trade relations is a fundamental defining characteristic of any economic system, one that affects a great deal about the organization and impact of other aspects of economic and social life. Because economic ties tend to demonstrate a fair amount of path dependence, the structure of China's economy will likely come to reflect, in future years, the nature of exchange relations in the early stages of reform.

I drew on research on the nature and impact of *guanxi* in China to anticipate that the answers to the first two questions would be affirmative. Research in this tradition has distinguished between *guanxi* (social relations) and *guanxi* practice (the cultivation and strategic use of social relations), and researchers have argued that the importance of both increased in the decade following reform. I then drew on literature from organization theory from the West to anticipate that the answers to the third and fourth questions would also be positive. This research acknowledges the importance of social relations in the creation and maintenance of economic ties, and lends support to the idea that actors would rely on social connections in the development of economic exchange, particularly given the high levels of uncertainty that characterized China's economy during the 1980s and early 1990s. Ideas from resource dependence theory also predict that organizations cultivate dependent lending and trade relations, but it follows from this literature that prior social ties would likely mitigate this process.

Qualitative evidence failed to lend support for the expectation that the answer to the first two questions would be positive. Both the qualitative and quantitative analyses provided support for my expectation that the answer to the third and fourth questions would also be affirmative. Indeed, the evidence suggested that managers in the business groups were highly resistant to either the deliberate creation and use of social ties for economic gain or the use of social ties to circumvent laws and regulations.[78] In contrast, the qualitative evidence provided considerable support for the third and fourth questions. I then used quantitative data on China's forty largest business groups to examine the third and fourth questions more systematically, and again found considerable support. I did not continue to explore the first two questions, given the qualitative findings. In short, my findings suggested that

---

78 Preliminary investigation of the quantitative data suggested that the qualitative data were corroborated by quantitative analyses: There was little support in either type of analysis to suggest positive answers to either of the first two questions.

managers did not manufacture social relations for the purpose of economic gain, nor did they use their social ties to avoid complying with laws and regulations. I did find, however, that the qualitative evidence supported the idea that managers relied on the social ties they already had to reduce the uncertainty that characterized China's economy in the early stages of reform. I also found support in the qualitative data for the idea that while managers cultivated dependent lending and trade relations with less powerful others, they avoided cultivating these relations with others with whom they had prior social ties.

These findings speak to two broad questions. First, they speak to the debate about the role of *guanxi* during China's economic transition. Second, they speak to the role of social relations in the development of China's economy. The findings indicate that *guanxi*, or social relations, were indeed important during transition. However, these results indicate that while managers were willing to use social ties to their advantage, they did not deliberately cultivate these relations for this purpose. Thus, these findings support the notion that *guanxi* was important during transition, but that *guanxi* practice was likely becoming a less important feature of exchange during that time. In addition, these findings indicate that social relations did indeed play an important part in the formation of early lending and trade relations and will likely affect the structure of these ties in the future. Environmental uncertainty is present in all economies, but it is much more apparent in transforming economies. The influence that uncertainty had on the formation of exchange ties among the firms in this study suggests that the distribution of uncertainty is likely to affect the distribution of power and privilege post-transition. Firms that are located in experimental regions of China, for example, where market reforms are tested and where development has proceeded at a much more rapid pace have access to scarce resources needed by firms in other locations. Resource access has given firms the means to establish dependent exchange relations that have the potential to persist.

APPENDIX

Logistic regression models

The unit of analysis for this study is the intercorporate dyad – that is, the

$$ n = \sum_{i=1}^{40} n_i \, (n_{i-1}) = 16{,}306 $$

ordered pairs of the 535 member firms within the 40 largest business groups with every other firm in the same group.[79] Following Lincoln (1984) and Lincoln, Gerlach and Takahashi (1992), I focus on the off-diagonal cells in a matrix

79 This can also be thought of as the $n(n-1) = 285{,}690$ total dyads among each of the 535 firms, minus any dyads containing firms not in the same business group. I did not collect data on between-group ties because these ties were rare in the early stages of reform.

representation of the 40 networks, or each of 40 (n × n) matrices where the rows $(i = 1, \ldots n)$ are senders in a relationship and the columns $(j = 1, \ldots n)$ are receivers. These are arrayed as a column vector (p) such that

$$p = \{1, 2; 1, 3; \ldots 1, n; 2, 1; 2, 3; \ldots 2, n; \ldots n - 1, 1; n - 1, 2; \ldots n - 1, n\}$$

An (i, j) pair and (j, i) are separate observations because a resource exchange tie, such as a loan, from firm i to firm j is different from a tie from firm j to firm i.

I model the presence (yes/no) of a particular tie as a function of characteristics of the firms, the dyad, and the region:

$$y_{ij1990} = \beta y_{ji1990} + \alpha y_{ij1988} + \lambda_i' P_i + \lambda_j' P_j + \pi_{ij}' R_{ij} + \gamma_i' X_i + \gamma_j' X_j$$
$$+ \rho W y_{ij} + u_{ijk} + \varepsilon_{ij}$$

where y_{ij1990} is a relation from firm i to firm j; y_{ji1990} is a reciprocal relation from firm j to firm i; and y_{ij1988} is a lagged relation from firm i to firm j. The dependent variable is a dichotomous indicator that firm i sends a resource to firm j. P_i is a column vector of variables at the province level, for the k provinces in which the firms are located; P_j is a column vector of variables at the province level, for the province in which firm j is located. R_{ij} is a column vector of variables at the dyad level; X_i is a column vector of variables describing firm i; and X_j is a column vector of variables describing firm j.[80] β, α, λ', π_{ij}', γ_i', γ_j', and ρ are regression coefficients to be estimated. $W y_{ij}$ is a dyad autoregressive term included to control bias that might occur because some dyads contain the same firms.[81] I use region-specific variables and error components models to account for regional effects; u_{ij}, and ε_{ij} are the stochastic error terms, with u_{ijk} representing the error that is region-specific and ε_{ij} representing dyad-specific error. I use fixed effects to control for group-level variation – that is, include $(n - 1) = 39$ dummy variables for each group. For both types of equations, I estimate generalized linear mixed (pseudo-likelihood) equations that allow the decomposition of the error term into its fixed and random components (Wolfinger 1993).[82]

80 Because all firms are represented the same number of times in the set of all dyads, the mean of X_i is always equal to the mean of X_j. Because the presence of directional relations from firm i to firm j vary across dyads, the mean of X_{ij} is not always equal to the mean of X_{ji}.

81 $W y_{ij} = \Sigma_p W_{pq} y_q$ where p and q are dyads and $p \neq q$. $W_{pq} = 1/n_p$ if dyad p and q share a common firm and 0 otherwise. $W y_{ij}$ is the mean of the dependent variable over all dyads that include firm i or firm j (excluding ij). This method is similar to the spatial autoregressive model used in contagion models (Doreian 1980; Land and Deane 1992; Lincoln, Gerlach, and Takahashi 1992; Tolnay, Deane, and Beck 1996).

82 The equations do not include group effects in addition to the fixed effects (dummy variables) that control for the group-specific effects and the dummy variables indicating group control of production and administrative decisions. Because the groups are not nested in regions (i.e., group members are not all located in a single region), it is not possible to do random effects and control for the contextual effects of group and region. In addition, because both members of each dyad under observation are in the same business group, only a limited number of group characteristics

The dependent variables are dichotomous indicators of the presence of lending and trade (specific to the firms trading) ties in 1990. Financial tie$_{ij1990}$ is a dummy variable coded 1 if firm i loaned funds to firm j three or more times in 1990, and 0 otherwise. Commercial tie$_{ij1990}$ is a dummy variable coded 1 if firm i sent commercial goods (finished products or intermediate goods) to firm j three or more times in 1990, and 0 otherwise. The lagged dependent variable, y_{ij1988}, is equivalent to the dependent variable but is measured in 1988 (e.g., it is coded 1 if the ordered pair of firms exchanged the resource more than three times). A significant positive estimate of the α coefficient indicates that if firm i sent the resource to firm j in 1988, it was more likely to send that resource in 1990. The reciprocal term, y_{ji1990}, indicates whether firm j also sent the resource to firm i in 1990. A positive estimate of the β coefficient indicates that the resource exchange relationship was reciprocal. I also control for the presence of an ij financial tie in 1988 in equations predicting the presence of 1990 commercial ties to capture the interrelatedness of the exchange ties. If one firm lends capital to another, it is likely to take an active interest in the survival of the borrower and lend other resources as well.

Firm characteristics enter the regression equations as both a characteristic of firm i and a characteristic of firm j. A significant positive estimate of γ_i', the coefficient associated with $\mathbf{X}_i$, indicates that the greater the value of $\mathbf{X}_i$ the more likely firm i was to be the sender in the dyadic tie. A positive γ_j' indicates that the stronger the value of $\mathbf{X}_j$ the more likely firm j was to be the receiver. Regional characteristics also enter the regression equations as both characteristics of firm i and firm j. A positive estimate of λ_i', the coefficient associated with $\mathbf{P}_i$, indicates that as the value of $\mathbf{P}_i$ (e.g., the level of labor market development) increases, i was more likely to be the sender. Likewise, a positive estimate of λ_j', the coefficient associated with $\mathbf{P}_j$, indicates that as the value of $\mathbf{P}_j$ increases, j was more likely to be the receiver. A positive estimate of π_{ij}', the coefficient associated with $\mathbf{R}_{ij}$, indicates that attributes of this pairing make a tie more likely.

Variables

I use resource-specific, provincial indicators of market development to test ideas about environmental uncertainty. The measures are resource-specific (vary with the dependent variable) because uncertainty in finding one input may not be related to uncertainty in finding other inputs. Commodity market development (indicating uncertainty in the commercial exchange equations) is the number of private and collective firms as a percentage of the number of state-owned firms, and financial market development (indicating uncertainty in the financial exchange equations) is the deposits of foreign banks as a percentage of total bank deposits. I use a

would have any meaning in these analyses. I removed the regional effects and tested various group-level influences (e.g., the geographic spread of the group's member firms, the presence of a specialized financial firm, the presence and extent of interlocking directorates) in random effects models. I found no consistent group-level effects on the formation of dyadic exchange relations. In addition, including the group-level effects did not materially affect the other results.

dummy variable indicating that members of the firm's upper-level management were classmates in college to test the effects of school ties. I collected the school ties data in interviews with the managers. Using matrices that listed company names and manager names with titles, I asked the managers to indicate which of the managers were their classmates (*tongxue*) in college. I also include an interaction between market development and the presence of school ties to test whether firms cultivated dependent relations with those with whom they had social connections.

The variable cost – cost elsewhere$_i$ – indicates whether the resource was available cheaper elsewhere. This variable is based on managers' accounts of the cost of the resource (the interest rate for financial exchange) and the cost the organization would pay for the resource if it were to buy it from the next most likely alternative source. The alternative cost is widely known because most exchange was conducted within the business group. If the two firms do not trade, the cost is coded as the cost if the trade were to exist (again, this figure is widely known as all exchange considered here occurs within the same business group). I include the squared and cubed version of this variable to capture the more complex relationship between cost and the likelihood of an exchange relationship that emerges when indicators of interorganizational familiarity are introduced.

5

BUSINESS-STATE CLIENTELISM IN CHINA: DECLINE OR EVOLUTION?

David Wank

How has China's emerging market economy affected popular reliance on networks to bypass state administrative procedures in pursuing ends? Debate on this question has focused on the consequences for *guanxi* practice – the manipulation of normative obligations in personal ties – which became a widespread strategy in the prior planned economy for citizens to cope with its shortages and inequalities by influencing officials' allocation decisions. One view, expressed by Mayfair Yang (1994), sees *guanxi practice* as adapting to and expanding in the market economy by the intermingling of normative obligations with new monetary values. A competing perspective is advanced by Doug Guthrie (1998a). He first criticizes Yang's argument by noting that among other things, her claim that *guanxi practice* expands through commodification contradicts her definition of *guanxi practice* as the production of obligated indebtedness because the quid pro quo character of monetary transactions erases indebtedness (Guthrie 1998a, p. 261).[83] He then argues that the emerging institutions of the market transition erode *guanxi*'s significance as intensifying market competition values efficiency over obligations while legal norms delegitimate personal ties to subvert procedures.

This chapter reflects on the debate over *guanxi practice* in the evolving market economy. I concur with Guthrie that new market players are coming to rely less on *guanxi practice* as efficiency considerations become increasingly important and new laws alter perceptions. But I take issue with Guthrie's claim that this indicates the declining utility of networks to maneuver around standard state procedures at local levels. Based on fieldwork in a private business community, I show that even as entrepreneurs rely less on *guanxi practice* to forge supportive relations with local officialdom, new types of clientelist networks emerge to achieve similar ends. These new networks are named in the business community as reputation (*mingyu*),

---

83   He also argues that her claims are based on data that seem to indicate the opposite. Thus, data comments by persons that Yang says show the heightened importance of *guanxi* practice in the market economy can also be interpreted to mean new perceptions of price and legality are reducing reliance on *guanxi practice*.

embodying perceptions of status and norms of respect, and place (*difang*), invoking perceptions of locality and values of expediency.[84] Inasmuch as they invoke particularistic identities to link private firms and local governments in non-standard administrative practices for mutual benefit, these networks do not conform to a market transition. Instead, they suggest a process of pluralizing power in which new types of networks are forged as a response to new constraints faced by local officials and new monetary resources of entrepreneurs in the emerging market economy.

Debate over *guanxi practice* also highlights theoretical issues in explaining changes in state power and social structure in China that have accompanied the two-decades-old shift from a plan to a market economy. Guthrie's explanation appears consistent with the widely used concept of a market transition. This concept sees change as a shift from an ideal – typical and logically opposing plan to market, the inevitability of the state project of a legal system, and the market as trade relations of efficiency and equality. Adherents of this concept generally lack direct observations of *guanxi practice* and deduce its decline from the definition of the market transition (i.e. Nee 1989).[85] Guthrie eschews this tautology and marshals empirical data on *guanxi practice* to support his argument. This a noteworthy advance of the market transition concept, and deserves careful consideration. But as I will show in the first section, key assumptions of the market transition concept guide Guthrie's analysis to conclusions that do not necessarily follow from his data. Building on this critique, the second section presents the perceptions of private entrepreneurs on *guanxi practice* relative to other networks in influencing officials. The third section weaves these perceptions into accounts of competition and clientelism in the business process. The data stem from fieldwork, including interviews and limited participant observation, on non-state wholesale trading companies (*maoyi gongsi*) in Xiamen City, Fujian province, in 1988–90 and 1995 (see Wank 1999a, pp. 244–251), and news accounts in 1999–2000.

THEORETICAL ISSUES

Three mutually reinforcing assumptions undergird Guthrie's claim about the declining significance of *guanxi practice*. The first is a framework of institutional change that positions *guanxi practice* and legal norms in inverse correspondence, thereby precluding other possible changes that might be accompanying reduced reliance on the former. The second is the assumption of the inevitability of central state projects, which overlooks popular innovations that respond to, without

---

84   This argument is a more focused version of a thesis I proposed in *Commodifying Communism* (Wank 1999a). I used the term the "pluralization of power" (Wank 1999a, p. 202) and described the kinds of networks mentioned in this chapter.

85   I discuss this point at length elsewhere (Wank 2001). Nee bases his claims about changing transaction modes from the individuated income. But income is the outcome of a transaction that offers no insight into the kind of transaction mode that it derives from. Therefore, Nee's data actually say nothing about networks. Instead, his conclusions on changing allocation systems are derived from his broader assumptions about a change from a logically opposing ideal-typical plan to a market economy.

necessarily conforming to, these projects. The third is the definition of the market economy as buying and selling relations, a narrow definition that overlooks other market processes that contain new utilities for particularistic access to state power. These assumptions are problematic because their premises are debatable, and a different premise could lead to different explanations of the declining significance of *guanxi practice*.

The first problematic is the assumption of change as the inverse interaction of two mutually exclusive institutions, *guanxi practice* and legal norms (i.e., an increase in one diminishes the other). " . . . [T]he major force in the diminishing importance of *guanxi practice* is the rational-legal system being constructed at the state level" (Guthrie 1998a, p. 273). This statement renders it a foregone conclusion that the direction of behavioral change signified by a decline of *guanxi practice* is toward legal rationalization. The possible emergence of other types of networks for access to state power is precluded by definitional fiat. The persuasiveness of this conclusion is enhanced by the analytic conflation of *guanxi practice* with irregular actions and evasions of the state's standard administrative procedure. Conflation renders declining reliance on *guanxi practice* logically coterminous with the decline of particularistic strategies to influence officialdom. However, eschewing this conflation would make *guanxi practice* only one possible strategy to influence local officialdom, opening the possibility that other means are increasingly used to achieve similar ends. In other words, the decline of *guanxi practice* might be accompanied by the rise of other networks to subvert administrative procedures, a change that would not conform to a market transition.[86]

Furthermore, Guthrie's own data do not necessarily support his claim that reduced reliance on *guanxi practice* corresponds to the rise of rational-legal decisions and behavior. These data are comments by state enterprise managers obtained in formal interviews that laws are becoming more "important" relative to *guanxi practice*. They say: "In the future *guanxi* will be less and less important, laws will be more and more important" (Guthrie 1998a, p. 271); "Relying on connections to get things done (*kao guanxi ban shouxu*) is . . . a situation that is changing, becoming less and less important. Laws have become a more important part of doing things in China today, especially in organizing the market" (Guthrie 1998a, p. 272); "For official procedure, *guanxi* is less important today than it ever has been. Mostly this is because laws are more important now than ever before" (Guthrie 1998a, p. 273). Clearly managers are saying that laws are becoming more important than *guanxi practice*. But what do they mean by this? Are laws important because they change perceptions of legitimacy (*guanxi practice* is now wrong)? Or are they important because they change perceptions of risk (one is now more likely to be caught and punished for using *guanxi practice*)?

The issue of meaning is central to Guthrie's assumption of how change occurs because he uses "meaning" to link changing macro-institutions to micro-level changes in the thought and behavior of persons. " . . . I assume that the creation

---

86   Nor would they conform to Yang's claim of commodified *guanxi practice*.

of new institutional environments (primarily in the form of laws and new eco-nomic policies) have an impact on the ways in which economic actors perceive their environments (yet I also believe that these changes become tangible in an incremental way, as economic actors become familiar with the meaning of new institutions and policies over time)" (Guthrie 1998a, p. 266, ftn. 38). In other words, the meaning that actors acquire from the proliferation of laws is crucial for the gradual changes in perceptions and behavior that follow. If managers acquire the meaning that laws are universal judgments about right and wrong, they might be coming to view *guanxi practice* as illegitimate and its use to subvert standard procedures as wrong. But if they acquire the meaning that the proliferation of new laws makes use of *guanxi practice* in administrative matters more dangerous, they might simply switch to different means in order to achieve the same end, if they still see utility in bypassing standard procedures (this is considered later in the discussion of the third problematic). So there are at least two possible meanings that actors could attach to laws, but Guthrie's data do not clearly point to either one. His data clearly show a step *away* from reliance on *guanxi practice* but not what it is a step *toward*. Without knowing the meaning that actors attach to new laws, the way in which the proliferation of laws changes perceptions and behavior is ambiguous.

The second problematic is the assumption that central state policies embody the main direction of change. "The state is implementing broad-based institutional changes that define the transition away from personal power and the use of par-ticularistic relations to accomplish procedural and official tasks" (Guthrie 1998a, p. 271). This problematic is intertwined with the first one because the meaning that Guthrie assumes that managers attach to laws reflects the laws' ostensible purpose and the state's intention in their promulgation. What is debatable here is whether the meanings that actors attach to state-promulgated institutions ever fully accord with the intentions of the state. Scholarly explanations for the original rise of *guanxi practice* are that it was an unintended consequences of the state initiative to erect a planned economy in the 1950s and 1960s (Gold 1985, Walder 1986, Yang 1994). This was arguably as far reaching an initiative at economy and administra-tion building as the market promotion efforts since 1979. And just as clientelist ties of *guanxi practice* were an unintended response to this earlier initiative, it seems reasonable to hypothesize that unintended consequences might also be occurring among the populace under the new market building efforts. At the very least, there is no reason to a priori dismiss this possibility.[87]

An analytic possibility for seeing unintended consequences in market reform policies can be opened up by challenging the assumption that legal rationali-zation is the key behavioral constraint on actors in the market economy. Arguably, the decentralization of government authority over the past two decades (Wang 1995; Yang 1994) is as least as consequential a central state project of

---

87   Furthermore, the position voiced by some scholars that the impetus for market-oriented policies has been popular pressure that compelled the state to adopt new policies (Kelliher 1992; Zhou 1996) also attenuates the assumption of the central state as the main agent of change.

instituting a market economy. At the level of local government, this enhances autonomy in administration, control over revenue production, and responsibility for fiscal funding. Governments now have more responsibilities, less centrally allocated resources to achieve them, and greater autonomy to devise solutions. Increasingly they have turned to their regulatory powers in the market economy to derive income in such myriad ways as ad hoc levies of taxes and fines and various kinds of relations with private entrepreneurs. The logic of this behavior is independent from the state project of legal rationalization, although the proliferation of laws means that these local government actions and relations with business can increasingly be labeled as illegal. The broader point is that the distinct state initiatives of administrative decentralization and legal rationalization that help constitute the market building efforts do not necessarily proceed in tandem to further a market transition. They can also proceed according to discrete logics that can even work at cross purposes.

The third problematic is the thin or reductionist assumption of the market economy. The market economy is defined purely as trade transactions of efficiency and equality. This deflects from analytic purview other kinds of decisions and reduces the possibility for discerning new utilities for networks to gain particularistic favors from officialdom. To illustrate this, let me cite at length Guthrie's description of the kind of market economy that is emerging in the transition.

In China today, emerging markets and the transition from a command to market economy allows businesses the freedom to make economic choices in an open market. If one element of *guanxi practice* for industrial managers under the command economy was the necessity of gaining access to distribution channels (input and output) which were controlled by state officials under that system, officials in China's transitional economy have no such control over the distribution of resources and products. In many sectors, an open market increasingly controls the flow of goods. This change has profound implications for the transition away from a focus on *guanxi practice* to a more general focus on *guanxi* as business relationships. Industrial managers no longer need to curry favor with state officials to overcome bottlenecks or gain access to resources. As a result, they do not view *guanxi practice* as an important part of decision-making in China's industrial economy. They do, however, view general relationships forged with potential business associates (suppliers and customers) as an important part of gaining a competitive advantage in the markets of the transitional economy (Guthrie 1998a, pp. 267–268).

This view of the market economy as an arena of transactions between buyers and sellers omits such key processes as market entry and contractual enforcement. This is a critical omission because it places decisions and behavior by economic actors that are not buy-and-sell decisions outside the definition of the market economy and therefore not subject to analysis. Yet it is precisely in these other processes that state power is most likely to have utility and influence is most likely to be sought. For example, it is possible to have "open" access for established traders in a market sector but not for new entrants. Entering a sector might require different types of networks than for maintaining trade relations. For example, *guanxi practice* might be necessary for entry because the relevant licenses and business sites are controlled by local government although its utility is rapidly discounted after entry because the trade relations that are forged after entry hinge on quality and price. In other words, the significance of *guanxi practice* for a firm might change over time as it goes from being a new to an established player. But without initially resorting to *guanxi practice*, the firm would have been unable (or at least far less likely) to enter the business field. As long as subsequent entrants to the business field also have to rely on *guanxi practice*, the need for it can be considered an enduring competitive structure in the market economy for entry but a variable competitive resource for a specific firm because its utility diminishes after the firm has entered the business and sets about maintaining established trade relations.[88]

The crucial issue therefore is the definition of the market economy. If one accepts the thin definition of a market economy as trade transactions then its depiction as an "open" arena of "economic decisions" based on efficiency and equality could appear more plausible. But a thicker or more substantive definition that includes business entry and contractual enforcement renders such a depiction implausible by highlighting new utilities of ties with officialdom in such administrative matters as licensing and taxation. The notion of open market in which resource allocation is based solely on economic criteria (i.e. price and quality) is also attenuated by the continuation of dual pricing policies in key raw materials and energy sources. Also, one of the basic commodities of a market economy – land – is owned by the state and under the control of local governments and so any significant undertaking tends to involve local government support to obtain business sites.

Guthrie's own data reveals ongoing inequalities in access to key administrative resources that appear to contradict the idea of an "open" market but that are explained away by the thin definition of a market economy as not part of the transition.

Irrespective of whether or not firms at the upper levels of the administrative hierarchy actually resort to measures of *guanxi practice*, their social and political connections (their *guanxi*) to state actors who really matter in the decision-making processes are much better than those of firms at lower levels of the hierarchy. These firms are positioned directly under the jurisdiction of the government organizational units that make decisions surrounding project and product approvals and the like.... [T]he bureaucrats in these offices tend to favor these firms and, even without any kind of explicit *guanxi practice* at work, they are likely to speed approvals along for them (Guthrie 1998a, p. 275).

This passage asserts the declining relevance of *guanxi practice* in subverting standard procedure.[89] But it also reveals that state managers continue to benefit mightily from their high bureaucratic rank, a process that does not suggest an "open" market transition. Higher structural position in the state bureaucracy is

---

88 This difference between the kinds of practices necessary for a business to enter a market field and the practices necessary to its ongoing success once the field has been entered was noted over fifty years ago in William Foote Whyte's ethnography of racketeering in Boston's North End. To enter a field, a businessman can rely on racketeers for investment capital and coercing customers into purchasing his product. But once the field has been entered, the coercive techniques are abandoned as customers' relations rely on price and quality (Whyte 1993 [1943], p. 145).

89 Guthrie emphasizes the distinction between *guanxi*, which is personal relations between people who know each other, and *guanxi practice*, which is the manipulation of these ties (by producing obligated indebtedness) to achieve ends. In the market economy, the former is synonymous with the legitimate use of trust, while the latter is illegitimate corruption.

beneficial in administrative matters, which is consequential for resource flows and speed of receiving licenses and permits. State managers do not need to produce obligations in their *guanxi* for favorable administrative support because they already have effective *guanxi* by virtue of their high bureaucratic rank. No doubt those farther down the hierarchy would take exception to the state enterprise manager who told Guthrie, "Everything has been standardized and equalized" (Guthrie 1998a, p. 274).

The persistence of structural inequalities raises the basic question of which market players should be studied to best illustrate the changing significance of *guanxi practice*. As Guthrie notes, the more highly ranked the manager, the less likely he or she is to see *guanxi practice* as relevant to their activities. He attributes this to the greater advance of legal rationalization at the upper levels (because higher-ups are more closely monitored by the central state for compliance). But it could also simply reflect the fact that the managerial elite do not use *guanxi practice* because as the elite they can obtain advantages by other means. This is precisely the import of Guthrie's observation: "Firms at upper levels of the administrative hierarchy have significant advantages over firms at lower levels of the hierarchy – in part because of the inherently close connections to the administrative organs of the state (both organizationally as well as personally) – so there is less necessity for firms in this position to evoke the gift economy" (Guthrie 1998a, p. 276). This observation does not appear to indicate a market transition but rather the importance of hierarchical power in the market economy. It reaffirms the classic insight from community power studies that elites at the top of governing structures exercise power in ways that enhance private advantage but are not blatantly corrupt. Instead, personal familiarity and value convergence facilitates coordination among elites to achieve their preferences (i.e. Hunter 1953). This observation also reaffirms in a roundabout way Mayfair Yang's characterization of *guanxi practice* as a "weapon of the weak" (1993, p. 126), deployed primarily by those far from the seats of power.

To assess the changing significance of *guanxi practice*, it seems more relevant to consider market players at the farther removes from state power. Such players are more likely to pursue active network strategies with officials to compensate for their lack of higher structural position in the state. Private entrepreneurs are such players because, unlike state enterprise managers, they are not officials, are rarely Communist Party members and their firms are not part of the state. They would probably be more likely to use *guanxi practice* in seeking to influence officials than state enterprise managers. Therefore, data that show entrepreneurs view *guanxi* practice links with officials as of declining use would strongly support the "declining significance of *guanxi*" thesis. In contrast, the views of state enterprise managers that *guanxi practice* is less useful must be discounted because they are closer to the pinnacles of power and less likely to use *guanxi practice* to subvert administrative procedures in the first place.

With regard to entrepreneurs' changing perceptions of *guanxi practice*, one could in fact hypothesize the opposite trend from what Guthrie describes. Should private entrepreneurs see that market players at the commanding heights of the state structure are benefiting from positional power, this might stimulate them to redouble efforts to forge networks with local state agents. Thus the perceptions among state enterprise managers higher up the state's economic bureaucracy that *guanxi practice* is declining might be offset by the intensified efforts at cultivating ties with officialdom through *guanxi practice* and other networks by private entrepreneurs who are structurally outside the state.

Ultimately, Guthrie's explanation appears undergirded by the same mutually supportive assumptions that constitute the explanations of other scholars who adhere to the inevitability of a market transition. Interpretations of data appear informed by the assumption of inevitable movement toward legal rationalization and standard business relationships while errant observations tend to be explained out of the analysis. This is aptly illustrated in Victor Nee's interpretation of his finding that entrepreneurs with the best connections to the local state are among the wealthiest in their communities (1991). While this would seem to contradict his broader assertion of a market transition, Nee asserts that this finding actually supports his overall theory. His logic is that the data reveal a pathology of a market transition that is underway but not yet complete (a "partial market transition"). Guthrie carefully avoids such theoretical circularity. He notes that institutional change takes time and that his observations are but of an early stage of the transition. Nevertheless, he sees them as constituting a "first step" in a process of legal rationalization and standard marketization that will presumably only intensify and deepen, despite his data on the continuing importance of political hierarchy that might suggest other processes underway.

Later I will examine the perceptions of power inequality among private entrepreneurs and the kinds of particularistic networks they forge with local officialdom. I do not deny that efficiency considerations are becoming more important and that entrepreneurs increasingly engage in transactions of relative equality. But I maintain that power inequalities still loom large in the perceptions of private entrepreneurs, who see preferential access to administrative advantages as playing a significant role as a competitive advantage. Instead, in the next section I will describe significant changes in the perceptions of private entrepreneurs regarding the utility of access to state power and the kinds of networks most useful to acquire it. The following section then uses these perceptions to explain patterns of competition and clientelism.

ENTREPRENEURIAL PERCEPTIONS

My observations are grounded in the privately operated business community of Xiamen, an old port city and one of China's five special economic zones. As Xiamen is relatively small by Chinese standards – with an urban population of under one million – many entrepreneurs knew each other, which was invaluable for me in making contacts for interviews and cross-checking information and hunches. When I began field work in the summer of 1988, my interest in *guanxi* was subordinated to my broader concern for understanding the implications of revived private business for the kinds of patron-client ties that had grown up in the planned economy. I usually began interviews by asking operators questions about the business process so as to gauge changing dependence on local officials, and in ensuing conversations, the issue of *guanxi* and other types of networks with officials came up. Subsequent free-ranging conversations on doing business, conducted at entrepreneurs' residences, offices, and in restaurants and nightclubs over meals and beer, helped me to understand clientelist networks in business.

The perception was widespread among entrepreneurs that maintaining relations with suppliers and customers depends on efficiency considerations of price, quality, and service. This was usually referred to as credit (*xinyong*).[90] Credit ties are seen as involving objective evaluations of price and quality, in contrast to *guanxi,* which is seen as subjective evaluations by two people of the sentiments (*renqing*) and affect (*ganqing*) between them. In the business world, one builds credit by providing quality commodities and service and by making deliveries and payments on time. In other words, credit is produced and enhanced by doing what one promises to do. Also, in contrast to *guanxi*, which is often linked to perceived power asymmetries, credit is considered a relation of equality in that the criteria are objective (i.e., evaluations are independent of the status of the person or firm involved).

However, support from officialdom was seen as crucial in administrative matters and new ventures, and obtaining this support required other kinds of ties. A number of entrepreneurs used the expression that business also "depends on the support of the local government" (*yao kao difang zhengfu de zhichi*) to gain permits and licenses, information on policy stability and loopholes, protection from excessive fines and levies by other government bureaus, and to ensure that public enterprises honored contracts with them. It also referred to access to material resources, often linked to procurement procedures, such as land controlled by local government and public units, equipment at bargain prices, and scarce commodities regulated by the two-tier pricing system (Wank 1995, pp. 160–66). This kind of support was of course not openly available. It required particularistic links with officials for favorable decisions and access. In fact, the more successful entrepreneurs seemed to spend as much if not more time developing these ties than credit relations with suppliers and customers of commodities.

This support was seen as forthcoming in several ways. One was *guanxi practice*, a strategy emphasized by entrepreneurs who emerged at the onset of the reform era from humble backgrounds and initially lacked ties with officialdom. However, by the time that I was doing my fieldwork, *guanxi practice* was coming to be seen as dangerous and inefficient. It was increasingly viewed as dangerous because in light of ongoing state campaigns against corruption and to implement the rule of law, entrepreneurs saw its use as exposing them to charges of economic crimes. It was coming to be seen as inefficient because the time spent choosing gifts, extending invitations, and performing etiquette was something that entrepreneurs could ill afford in a market economy where time is money.

90 Some also referred to it as customer relations (*kehu guanxi*). The term business relations (*shangye guanxi*) used by state enterprise managers in interviews with Guthrie would also seem to fit.

A less dangerous strategy for invoking officialdom's support that was perceived as increasingly widespread in the late 1980s was reputation (*mingsheng, mingyu* and *mingqi*). Reputation is possession of characteristics that are positively valued by society or specific social groups. Unlike *guanxi*, it is linked to public rather than dyadic judgments. For example, being the offspring of a high-ranking national cadre would be a positively valued attribute. Knowledge of the cadre diffused among the population would assure deference to the son in interactions with others. For those lacking such family ties to officialdom, a reputation emphasizing connections to state power could be cultivated through such public displays as hosting parties in which high-ranking officials are invited, employing Communist Party members and former ranking officials, and other manipulative displays of the symbols of state power. Spreading knowledge of these ties and links among the populace through gossip and publicity could enhance perceptions of the entrepreneur's connections to officialdom, eliciting responses of deference and awe in interactions.

Entrepreneurs from humbler backgrounds who lacked officials among their kin offered one explanation for the increasing importance of reputation relative to *guanxi practice* for influencing officials. They perceived *guanxi practice* as a time-consuming strategy that was primarily useful for dealing with street and low-level state agents but not for higher support. They therefore sought to augment their reputations. One way, as previously mentioned, was to hire Communist Party members and former officials and to include current and former officials on their boards of directors. An augmented reputation elicited some deference and better treatment from government agencies. The persons they hired could also lobby officials they knew. For example, several firms had professors from Xiamen University's finance department as board members so that they could lobby former students who were officials in state banks, state foreign trade corporations, and other crucial agencies. These entrepreneurs bragged to me about the number of such people they employed. Another similar strategy of enhancing reputation was to invite officials to lavish parties to mark such auspicious occasions as a company opening, New Year, and weddings. These parties could serve as a visible display of the entrepreneur's ties to officialdom, thereby increasing his reputation of closeness to power.

In the late 1980s, the new wave of entrepreneurs from better social backgrounds (i.e., family, education, occupation) with extensive personal ties in government and the state sector (Wank 1999a, pp. 116–149) suggested another explanation for the rise of reputational strategies. These entrepreneurs used the reputations they had as members of politically powerful families and did not see *guanxi practice* as significant in their business. An example is an entrepreneur whose sister was married to the son of one of the highest cadre families in Guangdong province, a connection that gave her discounts when she purchased goods confiscated from smugglers by the Guangdong province Customs Bureau. She said, "I use their name in doing business and so people know that I belong to this lineage. I don't actually have to use their power in business as people trust me because of the family connection." The view she expressed to me was that officials supported her because of who she was rather than because she influenced them with gifts or bribes. Her statement also suggests that entrepreneurs view reputation as different from *guanxi practice* because it does not involve direct manipulation of personal relations for advantage through calculated gift-giving. A comparable position was expressed to me by the manager of a state trading company in Xiamen that represented an inland province where the manager's father was a provincial vice party secretary. The manager often visited state factories and mines in his home province to seek raw materials for export. He did not view this as *guanxi practice* because he did not obtain meetings with enterprise and mine directors by "pulling" *guanxi*; indeed, in many cases, he did not know the managers beforehand and did not seek third-party introductions. Instead he said that enterprise managers in this land-locked province welcomed his visits and sold him commodities because they were eager for export outlets abroad. He clearly viewed his business as operating in market relations with his role as connecting supply and demand.

However, entrepreneurs from humbler backgrounds scoffed at the claims that such well-connected persons were operating simply through market connections. They saw the business activities of these persons as the blatant exercise of political power, although not via *guanxi practice*. As one entrepreneur said:

There is the so-called Prince's Party. They are the sons and daughters of the officials in Zhongnanhai and they all do business. But they are not real entrepreneurs because they rely entirely on their family name. Everybody will rush to open the front door for the children of Deng Xiaoping or Zhao Ziyang . . . do you think they go in the back door? So the name gives them a big power (*daquan*). They do business on a much larger scale than anything us private bosses in Xiamen can dream of. We are really entrepreneurs because we do business by our own efforts (*zijigan*). We can use *guanxi* to get support from officialdom. But *guanxi* only gives you a little power (*xiaoquan*) to get in the back door. So we can only hope to run a middling (*zhongdeng*) enterprise.

This statement also illustrates an entrepreneurial view emerging in the late 1980s that *guanxi practice* involved small amounts of power and was the hallmark of petty business, a view that was more pronounced during a subsequent visit to Xiamen.

When I returned to Xiamen in 1995 after five years, entrepreneurs were referring to new relations of "locality" (*difang*) between private firms and local state bureaus. Entrepreneurs and officials both spoke of a new aggressiveness on the part of local (city and district) government to cooperate with businesses and a new flexibility by bureaus for actions that deviated from central state policies. This was distinct from *guanxi practice* because it emphasized coordination between private firms and government bureaus as part of the broader agendas and policies of the bureaus rather than as the isolated actions of single officials to circumvent standard procedure on behalf of entrepreneurial clients. Business people attributed the rise of this relationship to the decline of special economic zone policy advantages as many of the original central state policy concessions granted to these locales (including Xiamen) in the 1980s had become generalized throughout China in the

1990s. Both entrepreneurs and officials alike talked about the dangers of Xiamen's being left behind as such local market advantages as size of the consumer market and transportation infrastructure became more important relative to policy concessions. They talked in dark tones of the Pearl River and Yangtze River regions as surging ahead and Xiamen as falling behind. This sense of intensifying market competition seems to have stimulated local bureaus to focus on the few material and administrative monopolies remaining to them in their cooperation with private firms, resulting in a new organizational local network between firms and bureaus.

The key value of this network between firms and government is expediency. Although they used practices that deviate from central state policies and laws, local actors legitimate them by a logic that represents their practices as actually according with state intentions. This logic makes a distinction between the spirit (*jingshen*) and stipulations (*tiaoli*) of a policy. The spirit is the policy's goal or intention, while the stipulations are the state-sanctioned behavior and procedures to attain it. According to this logic, since China is vast and has much regional variation, universal (i.e., national) stipulations often do not fit local conditions and, if rigidly adopted, might work at cross-purposes with the policy's goal. Therefore, local actors justify deviant actions as necessary adaptations of central policies not only to ameliorate the policies' harmful effects but also to achieve their goals. As the state's main goal is economic development, deviant local policies (*tuzhengce*) in economic activities can be justified if they promote economic development more rapidly than what would be likely through strict adherence to the stipulations. This network is expressed idiomatically as "the necessity of adapting to local conditions" (*yao fuhe difang tiaojian*) and by reference to historically enduring traditions (*chuantong*) and styles (*zuofeng*) of locale (*difang*).

PATTERNS OF COMPETITION AND CLIENTELISM

The operation of business can be explained through the aforementioned kinds of networks described by entrepreneurs. Intensifying market competition constrains the evolution of clientelist links between private firms with local officialdom. This section offers several examples of this. The first shows the different dynamics for *guanxi practice in* different processes of the market economy, market entry and maintaining established trade relations. The second shows the discrete types of networks that different scales of business operate through in the same market sector. The third shows the shift from personal to organizational clientelism.

The first two examples are based on the automotive trade as my data on this sector are abundant. Privately operated firms emerged in this sector in 1985 when many foreign cars began to be imported into China. This increase in foreign cars stemmed from the differences between the liberal economic policies in the special economic zones and open cities, and the rest of China. In the former, cars could be imported duty-free and then resold elsewhere at much higher prices. The extreme of this smuggling operation was the Hainan Car Incident of 1984 in which 100,000 Toyota vans were imported to Hainan Island and resold on the Mainland

(Vogel 1989, pp. 291–294). One of my research assistants worked as a claims adjuster in a local branch of the state real estate company. He introduced me to entrepreneurs running private car-body repair garages and wholesale firms dealing in car parts and shared his intimate knowledge of this market sector with me.[91]

Enduring and temporal utilities of guanxi practice

Here I examine the shifting competitive constraints faced by firms over time and the consequences for the kinds of networks they sought to cultivate in the late 1980s. Specifically, I show that the kinds of networks that a firm relies on for entry into a market sector shifts once a firm becomes established and its trading relations stabilize. For any specific firm, the utility of *guanxi practice* is temporal because it varies in significance over the course of a firm's activities. However, as a criterion for entry into a sector, *guanxi practice* is a more enduring structure.

I develop these insights in the car-body repair business. The increased flow of imported cars into China from the mid-1980s also created a market for car-body repair as their light bodies were more easily dented on the crowded roads than the heavy bodies of domestic vehicles. Also many public drivers moonlighted by using their vehicles to transport people and goods for personal profit. In the event of an accident, they needed repairs immediately. Demand was further stoked by the increase of non-governmental transportation firms that lacked their own in-house repair shops; by 1989, there were 20 bus companies operating over 3,000 buses and 30 taxi firms with 1,500 taxis plying Xiamen's roads (Lu et al., 1989, p. 169). In Xiamen prior to the mid-1980s, most body repair was done in-house by public units that had large fleets, and there was only a single state-run body repair shop open for paying customers. Its pace of work was slow, requiring weeks to do jobs. In contrast, the private firms offered much quicker service and better quality. This attracted customers, and by the late 1980s there were, according to my own survey, thirteen body repair shops, including ten private (four legal private *siying* firms and

---

91   The emergence of privately operated firms to fill this demand is in turn linked to policy innovations in the collective sector in the mid-1980s that permitted privately run collective firms
(hereafter referred to as cooperatives). New policies permitted the establishment of cooperative
firms. Formally known as popularly run collectives (*minban jiti*), these were firms that were legally
owned by state and collective public units or through the district level Labor Service Company established to find jobs for unemployed persons, privately managed. According to the regulations, a
minimum of four unemployed persons could establish such a firm using their own financial capital
and making business decisions independently of their sponsoring public agency and subject only
to the stipulation that the shares be traded only among partners and dividends should not exceed
15 percent of the shares' values. This policy enabled private entrepreneurs to bypass the restrictions that limited the scale of private firms under the Individual Business Policy (*getihu*) first
promulgated in the late 1970s. For example, the getihu policy that limited receipts to 100 yuan
did not apply to cooperatives, enabling the latter firms to conduct large-volume trade with public
units. Also, whereas the *getihu* policy limited firm size to seven persons, this restriction did not
apply to cooperatives, facilitating the emergence of cooperative body repair shops that had dozens
of workers.

six privately run cooperative *minban jiti* firms), and three leased collective shops in Xiamen.[92]

The first non-state body repair shop was founded in 1985 by a partnership of four unemployed young men. Previously, two were workers, one an unemployed youth, and one a functionary in the Public Security Bureau. One of the former workers was a tool and die maker whose enterprise was declining in the early 1980s owing to poor product quality. To generate income, its workshops went into the scrap metal salvaging business. In 1985, the worker and a colleague contracted a workshop, giving them control of its site alongside a major road. They invited an unemployed friend who was married to the daughter of a spray painter at a state enterprise to help. The salvage business was profitable, and they sought new ventures. The idea for the car-body repair business came from the third friend. His father-in-law was increasingly busy repainting the imported vans his unit had purchased. He sensed an untapped market, and asked his father-in-law to teach him spray-painting. Thereupon the friends went into the car-body repair business on the site of their salvage business. They realized the importance of political connections when trying to obtain various permits, and invited a former classmate – a functionary in the Public Security Bureau whose father was a vice-bureau chief in the Xiamen City government, to be their partner.

The firm's customers were mostly private taxi drivers and moonlighting public unit drivers. The partners had been hoping to attract business from public units, but no orders were forthcoming because of the bad image of privately operated firms at the time. So the partner whose father was a ranking city government official asked his father to persuade his bureau to send over cars for repair. The bureau did so, and its personnel were so impressed by the quality and speed of the repair work that they sent over more cars. Word of the good work spread, and other bureaus began to send over cars for repair. The *guanxi* relation had clearly been critical for the initial opportunity to deal with the bureau, but subsequent business depended on credit relations expressed as quality of service. But the partners also continued to cultivate their reputation as having good connections in the city government. The official's son represented them at all public functions ranging from policy meetings called by bureaus, visits by officials to the firm, and festival parties organized by the local chamber of commerce. In interviews with me, the other partners disparaged his business acumen but reaffirmed his usefulness as the firm's public face for creating an impression of connections with power.

The success of this and other private firms led to the entrance of new competitors. State and collective enterprises increasingly sent their cars to the cooperative body shops and leased out their inefficient in-house body repair workshops. Barriers to entry were much higher in the late 1980s than only a few years earlier. Car-body repair garages need to have enough land to undertake repairs, park cars, and house employees while being conveniently located for their customers in the urban districts. Real estate prices had increased many times in the second half of the 1980s

---

92   These figures do not include the in-house garages of public units.

(Wank 1995, p. 161), and the best sites were several in-house garages owned by state enterprises in Xiamen's urban districts. According to accounts I heard of the bidding process, leases for these garages were obtained by officials in the enterprises who used their personal ties with enterprise officials to gain insider knowledge on the amount of bids, enabling them to offer the highest bid (Wank 1999b, pp. 261–264). These new competitors also used their bureaucratic connections to get newer equipment, and began to challenge the cooperative firms for orders from public units. The facilities of these new entrants were more professional in appearance than the ramshackle tin roofed wooden structures of the cooperatives, and many of the Taiwanese and Hong Kong businessmen who were investing in Xiamen in increasing numbers preferred doing business with these more modern firms.

This vignette has suggested the changing utility of *guanxi practice* for firms over time. *Guanxi practice* was crucial for entry to a market sector in order to obtain the necessary permits, but then its utility for competitive advantage in business declined rapidly. But *guanxi practice* remained important for subsequent entry into the field of car body repair. This can be seen in the later entry of several leased firms in the late 1980s. They surmounted entry barriers by using *guanxi practice* to obtain choice business sites and facilities from public units, sometimes at below market value. *Guanxi practice* apparently remained crucial to firms entering the field, although it diminished rapidly in importance for firms once they had entered the field and set about cultivating customers. The broader theoretical point is that a market economy is constituted by discrete processes in such a way that the declining utility of *guanxi practice* in one process does not necessarily correspond to its decline in others.

Business scale and differential networks

Here I examine the competitive situations of smaller and larger firms in the car parts trade in the late 1980s and show the very different networks they operate in. Smaller firms relied heavily on credit relations with suppliers and customers, while larger firms increasingly relied on *guanxi practice* and reputational ties. The key point here is that as business scale increases, clientelist networks become more important to the trade relations of the private firms.

To illustrate this, I examine the wholesale trade in car parts. By the late 1980s, there were over 100 firms in Xiamen, mostly cooperative and leased companies that dealt in car parts.[93] The smaller ones were stand-alone firms, while the larger ones were part of diversified business groups consisting of three or more companies. These firms had arisen to meet the burgeoning demand for imported car parts.

---

93 The actual number of firms engaged in this line is impossible to know. This is due to the government practice that requires firms to list the commodities they intend to trade in when they apply for their business licenses. To ensure flexibility, entrepreneurs seek to have as many items as possible included. Thus the number of firms licensed to trade in car parts is larger than the number of firms that actually carry them.

Firms in the special economic zones were at an advantage compared with firms elsewhere because import duties were half the national rate. According to regulations, the remaining 50 percent of the duty had to be paid upon carrying the goods out of the special economic zone, but buyers evaded this by under-reporting the size of their purchases when they shipped them out of the zone. Also, as Xiamen was the northernmost special economic zone, the shipping costs to northern and inland locations could be cheaper than from the other zones farther south in Guangdong province. Buyers came to Xiamen from all over the country. Trade volume in automobile parts was so large that by 1989, automobile parts were a main import in the Xiamen Special Economic Zone (Lu et al. 1989, p. 119).

The different kinds of networks of these firms reflect their different customer base. Let me first consider the small firms. The large volume of customers that flocked to Xiamen for car parts made it a buyers' market and enabled the smaller operators to cooperate to reduce risk. Cooperation centered on the goal of keeping stock to a minimum for several reasons. First, real estate in the urban districts of Xiamen was expensive and the companies were too small to stockpile goods. Entrepreneurs had to borrow from each other to meet orders. Second, entrepreneurs did not want to have large amounts of capital tied up in stock in the event that sudden changes in state policy made their trade difficult or caused harmful changes in the economic environment, such as a state freeze on bank transactions that prevented buyers from obtaining bank checks to pay for purchases. Third was to reduce the perceptions of the Industry and Commerce Bureau and the Tax Bureau about their business scale in order to evade taxes. Fourth was to reduce losses in the event that their goods were confiscated by officials, be it on real or trumped up charges. The capacity to borrow from other entrepreneurs relied on good credit relations. Good credit relations were maintained by reimbursing on time for borrowed stock. After an entrepreneur delivered the parts to a customer, he would immediately visit his colleagues to repay them with the proceeds from the sale.

The larger, more successful firms had a different customer base. They aggressively cultivated customers on regional and national scales as they saw limited opportunities by simply waiting for customers to come to Xiamen. One way was to organize a car parts exhibition in Xiamen and invite purchasing agents from state enterprises who were then wined and dined in the restaurants and hotels that were sometimes part of the entrepreneurs' business groups. For these agents, the chance to visit the famous tourist destination of Xiamen was enticing, and presumably the obligation they incurred by accepting the entrepreneurs' hospitality induced them to place large orders for car parts. In this fashion, the larger firms built up a far-flung customer base of state enterprises that placed large orders. The exclusivity of large firms' customer base and greater trade volumes precluded their participation in the practice of sharing stock and credit relations found in smaller firms. Instead, they had relations with automotive parts companies in Hong Kong. They would then fax orders to Hong Kong, and the parts were immediately shipped.

Due to the character of their trade, the operators of larger firms spent much more time cultivating officials in key agencies. As private firms were prohibited from importing commodities, they relied on good relations with officials in the Customs Bureaus and the staff of state foreign trade corporations to import the car parts. In order to ship the goods to northern customers, good relations with officials in the Railroad Bureau were needed to ensure freight space. Presumably, in order to smuggle the goods out of the special economic zone without paying duties, they also needed support from customs and tax officials. Their more expansive business necessitated new kinds of relations with officialdom that emphasized not only *guanxi practice* but also reputational practices. For managerial positions and for positions on their board of directors, they hired Communist Party members and former officials who had recently retired from prominent positions. Thus, as firms grew, they were more likely to seek links with state power through reputational strategies in order to manage the myriad interactions with local officialdom that stemmed from their more far-flung business activities.[94]

Interestingly, the pattern just described seems somewhat opposite to the perceptions of the utility of *guanxi practice* among the state enterprise managers that Guthrie interviewed. Managers from firms higher up the hierarchy were less likely to see *guanxi* practice to influence administrative officials as important to business. In contrast, among the entrepreneurs, larger scales of trade and capital accumulation appear to correspond to heightened perceptions of the necessity to have ties to influence officialdom through *guanxi practice* and other kinds of network strategies. Guthrie is careful to specify that his data and insights are limited to state industrial enterprises, so our findings are not contradictory. But they do suggest that different structural locations in the market economy are constituted by discrete dynamics and perceptions. These disjunctures in turn belie the more sweeping and all-encompassing imagery conveyed in such terms as "market transition" and "bureaucratic legal rationalization."

From personal to localistic networks

The emergence of localistic networks of place in the mid-1990s suggests evolutionary processes within particularistic strategies to engage state power. Unlike ties of *guanxi* and *mingyu*, which seek to influence individual officials to make non-standard decisions, links of locale are organizational support from bureaus through the routinization of non-standard administrative procedure in bureaus' daily operations. This is not a case of scattered officials supporting entrepreneurs by making deviant decisions to favor them but a case of entire bureaus defining their practical policies and operating procedures to support private firms in ways of varying legality.

One example of such localistic ties is private entrepreneurs' use of the Xiamen Chamber of Commerce to forge connections with officials for favorable administrative decisions. When a 1994 state regulation proscribed the officials

94 Their firms still relied heavily on *guanxi practice* to maintain support from relations with pettier officials, and often had persons in the firm designated to cultivate relations with officials in such agencies as the railway and tax bureaus.

of regulatory and administrative bureaus from serving as advisors for societal groups and associations, entrepreneurs responded by setting up new district-level chambers of commerce beneath the city chamber. These district chambers continued to ensure officials' support by giving them honorariums for speeches at the district chambers and invitations to chamber parties. In return, officials led district chambers on business-finding tours to the Fujian hinterland. On these trips, officials lobbied hinterland governments for special concessions for Xiamen entrepreneurs. Examples included charging entrepreneurs lower rates for land leased from local governments and the authority to trade in gold. Although these concessions were of dubious legality, chamber officers I interviewed justified them and the efforts of government officials to secure them as being in accord with the spirit of the central policies to encourage investment from richer coastal regions to the hinterland (Wank 1999a, pp. 213–215) and as beneficial to both Xiamen's entrepreneurs and the hinterland regions.

Another example shows more integrated coordination between private firms and multiple bureaus and was publicized beginning in 1999 as the largest corruption scandal in China since the founding of the People's Republic. It involved $10 billion worth of imports in cars, oil, rubber, mobile telephones, cigarettes and semiconductors by a private firm called the Fairwell (*Yuanhua*) Group. The support web of the operator of this enterprise extended all the way to the wife of a central Politburo member. Even more remarkable is the degree of routinized support he received from local government bureaus and the Communist Party. This was not a web of *guanxi* networks of a few officials in key bureaus but rather the support by entire bureaus and their apparent coordination with other bureaus. According to reports, most of the leaders of the Xiamen Communist Party branch, Xiamen vice mayor in charge of foreign trade and public security (the police), the heads of Xiamen's customs, public security and telecommunications bureaus, the Xiamen branch managers of China's three largest banks, as well as ranking officials in other Fujian cities and even provincial level officials were alleged to have been on the Fairwell Group's payroll. In addition, the Fairwell Group employed the offspring of many high-ranking officers in the People's Liberation Army stationed in Xiamen (Conachy 2000). These officials gave the entrepreneur a broad range of government support. The Customs Bureau gave him his own private bonded area, while customs and police officials facilitated the movement of foreign goods out of the bonded area without payment of duties for resale in China. The Fairwell Group's extensive real estate activities, including a theme park, a luxury resort, and a proposed eighty-eight story skyscraper and a thirty story international hotel, would have required strong support from the highest levels of the local government, presumably including the mayor's office, leaders of the Communist Party branch, and possibly the People's Liberation Army, to obtain the necessary land for such ambitious projects. The local Public Security Bureau tapped the telephones of an investigative team sent by the central government in an effort to obstruct the investigation (Conachy 2000).

This kind of broad institutionalized support is characteristic of the new localistic networks. New constraints of economic necessity stemming from intensifying competition and hard budget constraints impel administrative and policing organs of the local state to develop strong links with private firms in order to turn a profit on their local state monopoly power. These links also reflect the ongoing entrepreneurial perceptions of the utility of influencing state agents to enhance their firms. The emergence of such links also suggests yet another evolutionary shift in clientelism away from a highly personalistic to an organizational basis. Their emergence underscores the malleability of clientelist strategies and the analytic shortcoming of seeing clientelism only in the personalized terms of *guanxi* practice. Under the prior central planning, state power was strong enough to force all clientelist ties into furtive *guanxi* practice exchanges, but this is no longer so.

CONCLUSION

Guanxi practice first appeared as an analytic category in U.S. social science studies of China as a window for viewing state power. Guthrie is right to maintain that *guanxi practice* should not be reified as an enduring cultural characteristic of China but rather as a reflection of broader institutional changes. But in the market transition concept that he furthers, the issue of state power appears to drop out of analytic purview by assumptions of dichotomous change, legal rationalization, and standard marketization. In this chapter, I have revived this issue by uncoupling the analysis of particularistic strategies and *guanxi practice*. *Guanxi practice*, as a popular strategy of citizens to cope with the scarcities induced by the party-state monopoly over goods and opportunities in the 1960s and 1970s, may indeed be in decline. But the rise of a market economy in the context of an ongoing state monopoly over such basic commodities as land, and the perception that laws, while proliferating, are not impartially enforced, stimulates new clientelist networks to influence officialdom across local state-society borders.

6

INSTITUTIONAL HOLES AND JOB MOBILITY PROCESSES: *GUANXI* MECHANISMS IN CHINA'S EMERGENT LABOR MARKETS

Yanjie Bian

China's economic transition toward a market-oriented system should give rise to a legal-rational logic of resource allocation. A transition of this kind, if occurring, implies that *guanxi* rules, which are commonly understood to be informal and anti-rational, would decline. This hypothesis has been put forward with the attention to decision-making processes at the level of economic enterprises in Chinese cities (Guthrie 1998). In the context of labor markets, Hanser and Guthrie argue in their chapters in this volume that *guanxi* ties may have become less relevant among their interviewees.

I offer a counterobservation about the persistent roles of *guanxi* in China's emergent labor markets in the 1990s. My focus of attention is on the roles of *guanxi* in job changes in the 1990s, and my data come from a diverse sample of 100 individuals whom I interviewed in six Chinese cities in 1996 and 1997. This sample of individuals rejected my pre-study hypothesis about the declining significance of *guanxi* in China's emergent labor markets. Their stories speak in favor of an antithesis: *Guanxi* plays a persistent role in matching individuals to job slots in the 1990s. I will argue this is because China's emergent labor markets are full of "institutional holes" – a state of labor markets in which formal mechanisms are either unavailable or insufficient in connecting job seekers and prospective employers. *Guanxi* networks of intimate and reciprocal relations are the informal mechanisms to fill up these institutional holes, facilitating employment and reemployment processes in Chinese cities.

In the remaining pages, I will first review the sociological literature that led to my pre-study hypothesis about the declining significance of *guanxi* in China's emergent labor markets. Second, the 100 interviews I conducted in 1996 and 1997 will be summarized and presented. Third, several views about China's transition to labor markets will be reviewed. Fourth, I will sketch out an institutional explanation about the persistent significance of *guanxi* in the emergent labor markets, and the job-change experiences of some of my inter-viewees will be used to support this explanation. Finally, I will discuss some implications of this explanation for research on social mobility in China's reform era.

FROM *GUANXI* TO STRONG TIES

There have been different understandings about the nature of *guanxi*. In the early works of the influential Chinese social scientists Liang Shuming ([1949] 1986) and Fei Xiaotung ([1949] 1992), *guanxi* is understood as the web of familial obligations and sentiments, and the core relational bases of *guanxi* are familial and pseudo-familial ties. For students of post-revolutionary China, on the other hand, *guanxi* refers to the informal, particular ties that are maintained and mobilized for instrumental purposes (Jacobs 1979; Gold 1985; Walder 1986; Yang 1994; Wank 1994). In this second understanding, the relational bases of *guanxi* become quite broad in scope, but the essence of *guanxi* as being reciprocal and instrumental is emphasized. Still a third understanding about *guanxi* views it as informal and intimate networks of social exchange. Proponents of this view recognize both the sentimental and instrumental components of *guanxi* (Hwang 1987; Yan 1996; Lin 2001b). To them, the defining characteristics of *guanxi* are that individuals engaged in a *guanxi* connection value their relationship as given and interact accordingly. "It is the relationship that is valued and must be maintained, not the value of the favor transacted per se," thus "instrumental action becomes the means and *guanxi* [building] becomes the end" (Lin 2001b, p. 22). Lin conceptualizes this feature of *guanxi* to be "relational rationality."

This last understanding about *guanxi* calls for an attention to individuals' perceptions about the strength of their ties with others. "Strong ties" may result from a combination of frequent interaction and reciprocal exchanges for expressive and instrumental purposes, high intimacy and mutual trust to each other, and strong "we-group" feelings toward each other. Strong ties can thus be recognized in popular discourse as *guanxi* among Chinese people. Although not all strong ties are *guanxi* as understood by the individuals who are connected by strong ties, *guanxi* must be strong ties. "Weak ties," in contrast, cannot meet many of these requirements, and thus are not considered as *guanxi*. Ethnographic studies about networking activities in Chinese cities (Yang 1994) and villages (Yan 1996) support the characterization of *guanxi* as strong ties.

To characterize *guanxi* as strong ties gives us the benefit of linking to the sociological literature on the roles of social networks in employment processes. Sociologists generally agree that strong and weak ties play different roles in job mobility processes in market and planned economies. In a market economy, profit-driven employers intend to hire labor with low cost and high productivity. Thus, at a fixed market level of labor cost, workers who have high potential (i.e., human capital) to deliver quality products should enjoy great opportunity for upward job mobility. However, this neoclassical economic view is only partially correct because job seekers are constrained by their interpersonal social networks from which they obtain information about jobs (Granovetter 1973,

1974). Because weak ties of low intimacy are wide ranging and can transmit non-redundant job information more frequently than strong ties, Granovetter's "strength of weak ties" hypothesis predicts that those using weak ties to collect employment information are more likely to move into desirable jobs than those using strong ties. This prediction was confirmed in Granovetter's and other researchers' empirical studies in Western capitalist countries (see Granovetter 1995 for a review).

In a socialist planned economy, jobs are hierarchically controlled and assigned by government labor agencies. In China under the system of job assignments through the 1980s, state-owned enterprises operated with "soft budget constraints" (Kornai 1986) and were not concerned about labor costs. Instead, they had to hire all workers assigned to help achieve the government's goal of full employment. At the individual level, although almost everyone was guaranteed work, job seekers did not wait for assignments, but mobilized their social networks in order to have good jobs (Bian 1994b). The role of social networks in this system was not to collect employment information, because even when they had information, job seekers could not apply for jobs. Instead, social networks were used by job seekers to influence job-assigning authorities through intimate and reciprocal relationships of trust and obligation – or *guanxi* – so jobs could be assigned as favors to someone who was strongly connected, either directly or indirectly, to the authorities. Earlier I proposed and tested this "strong tie" hypothesis with a case study of job assignments in Tianjin (Bian 1997; also see Bian 1994a, 1999; Bian and Ang 1997).

In short, the sociological literature reviewed here indicates that in market economies, the role of social networks is to collect employment information through weak ties, and that in planned economies, its role is to influence job assigning authorities through strong ties. Logically, when an economy is transformed from a planned economy to a market economy, one would expect changes in the relative efficacy of strong ties and weak ties in job matching processes. One hypothesis is that *influence networks* of strong ties may be giving way to *information networks* of weak ties in matching individuals to jobs in China's emergent labor markets. This would imply the decline of *guanxi* in job mobility processes in the 1990s.

PERSISTENCE OF *GUANXI* EFFECTS: OBSERVATION
FROM 100 JOB CHANGERS

I had this hypothesis in mind when I began interviewing a diverse sample of 100 individuals in 1996 and 1997 in six cities: Beijing, Shanghai, Tianjin, Shenzhen, Haikou, and Wuxi (see Table 6.1 for characteristics of this sample). Because my objective was to learn about a wide range of job mobility experiences, I used a combination of purposive and network sampling methods to select interviewees who worked in different economic sectors and who had changed jobs in recent years. Although my interviewees are not statistically representative of China's urban

Table 6.1

Basic characteristics of a sample of 100 interviewees

Characteristic	Number of interviewees	Characteristic	Number of interviewees
City		**Sector**	
Beijing	10	*Reforming public sectors*	
Tianjin	45	Government agency	6
Shanghai	17	State nonprofit organization	7
Shenzhen	20	State enterprise	10
Wuxi	8	Collective enterprise	10
Haikou	10		
		Emergent labor markets	
Sex		Subsidiary establishment	23
Male	63	International joint venture	10
Female	37	Foreign firm	12
		Domestic private business	4
Age		Mixed property entity	8
Younger than 30	12		
30–40	21	*Floating population*	
40–50	50	Migrant peasant labor	10
Older than 50	17		
		Occupation	
Number of job changes		Party/administrative leaders	7
Never changed	3	Managers, owners	28
Once	5	Professionals and technicians	25
Twice	9	Clerical workers	10
Three times	21	Manual workers	30
Four times	39		
Five times and more	25		

workers, on the whole their job searching and job changing experiences generally rejected my hypothesis. Table 6.2 summarizes the results of the interviews.

Of first interest in Table 6.2 is the distribution of methods used by my interviewees to search for and change jobs. Theories of labor market economics suggest a tripartite classification of job-change methods into "hierarchy," "market," and "networks" (Granovetter 1995). In reality, when they searched for jobs, my interviewees tried many different methods simultaneously to collect employment information and to secure job opportunities. With my research interest in mind, I have summarized their job-searching methods into four categories: (1) hierarchical allocation/reallocation by state or work-unit authorities that give little personal freedom to search for jobs; (2) use of predominantly strong ties; (3) use of predominantly weak ties; and (4) some kinds of more open, "market"-driven methods, such as direct application, use of mass media, use of formal employment services, etc. This last category was described by my interviewees as a method of "all by myself." Of the 392 jobs obtained by the 100 interviewees in

Table 6.2
Job changes experienced by a sample of 100 interviewees

Sector of job destination	Number of jobs	Job-Search and Job-Change Methods (percentage)			
		1	2	3	4
Total	392	15	52	17	16
Reforming public sectors					
Government agency	25	28	48	8	16
State nonprofit organization	48	13	42	21	24
State enterprise	66	6	66	17	11
Collective enterprise	33	6	45	30	19
Emerging market sectors					
Subsidiary establishment	53	38	49	13	0
International joint ventures	37	54	27	0	19
Foreign firms	25	0	44	24	32
Domestic private firms	26	0	35	31	35
Mixed property entities	32	0	69	10	21
Floating population					
Migrant peasant labor	47	0	72	17	11

1 = Hierarchical allocation/reallocation by state or work-unit authority
2 = Use of predominantly strong ties
3 = Use of predominantly weak ties
4 = Direct application/formal procedure/"all by myself"

the period of 1992 to 1997, 15 percent were by way of hierarchical assignments, 52 percent by way of predominantly strong ties, 17 percent by way of predominantly weak ties, and 16 percent by way of "all by myself." The method of strong ties was more frequently used than any other method.

Would strong ties be frequently used to secure job opportunities in public sectors? This is true. The four public sectors under reform are government agencies, state non-profit organizations, state enterprises, and collective enterprises; the use of predominantly strong ties accounted for 48, 42, 66, and 45 percent of the jobs that were obtained by my interviewees in these sectors, respectively. In the late 1970s and early 1980s, these four sectors, comprised 98 percent of urban jobs in the country and state assignment, was the predominant mode of job allocation then (Walder 1986; Bian 1994a). Under state assignments, strong ties were used to influence authorities for securing good jobs for someone. Since 1992, state assignments have been replaced by the policy of "bilateral choices" (job seekers and employers choose each other). Under this new policy, state labor bureaus can no longer control and assign jobs, however; administrators and managers of organizations in the public sectors gain much of the authority to hire employees. As indicated by my interviewees, they used strong ties mostly for influencing these new decision-makers in order to work in the reforming public sectors.

Would strong ties be less useful than weak ties in getting jobs in emergent labor markets? No. On the contrary, strong ties were far more frequently used to obtain jobs in each of the emergent labor markets than were weak ties. The emergent labor markets include: (1) subsidiary establishments that grow out of and are affiliated with the reforming public organizations; (2) international joint ventures, formed mostly between foreign investors and Chinese state enterprises; (3) foreign firms; (4) domestic private businesses, including family businesses and private companies; and (5) businesses with ambiguous or mixed property forms. In addition, there is the emergent labor market for migrant peasant labor, or the so-called "floating population." These six types of emerging economic organizations have grown rapidly since 1992, and in 1998 at least half of China's urban labor worked in them (Watson 1998). I describe labor market processes and the role of *guanxi* in each of them in turn.

Subsidiary establishments

Subsidiary establishments grew out of "parent" organizations in the reforming public sectors in light of two central policies. The first, implemented in 1979, was the policy to allow public-sector organizations to establish "labor service companies" to hire their employees' children who needed jobs. Some of them were sent to the countryside during the Cultural Revolution but returned to their home cities during 1978–80; others were urban youths waiting for job assignments after graduation from high schools. These youths brought employment pressure to the cities, and their long-term unemployment would be a potential cause of economic poverty and social instability. The central policy was a response to the fear of these consequences. Thus, parent-child relations were the mechanism through which jobless youths could work in labor service companies. Some of these labor service companies were successful in business and consequently expanded. The expanded companies were no longer restrained by the central policy of hiring employees' children, and thus opened their job slots to a broader pool of applicants. Since relatives and friends were important mechanisms to hire people, strong ties of kin and friendship have been the main method of employment in labor service companies.

The second policy was the policy to allow public organizations to establish "tertiary sector" businesses – that is, the businesses in commercial and service sectors. This policy was implemented in the 1980s but became popular in the 1990s when a growing number of state enterprises were on the verge of bankruptcy. The tertiary sector businesses established this way would generate extra-budgetary income for and hire surplus labor of the parent public organizations. Much of the surplus labor was assigned by the parent organizations to the tertiary sector businesses. Others used their *guanxi* to authorities of their organizations to reallocate. Still others used both strong ties and weak ties to get jobs in the tertiary sector businesses established by their friends' work organizations.

I call these two kinds of economic entities "subsidiary establishments" because they were subsidized by parent organizations when they were established. All of the subsidiary establishments were recognized as "collective enterprises," which were subjected to tax exemption and tax benefits; fiscally they are under less control by the state and thus are more flexible to engage in income-generating businesses than their parent organizations. For these reasons, subsidiary establishments have provided an institution for labor governments and their public organizations to generate extra-budgetary income, escape state taxes, and engage in rent-seeking or corrupt activities. Under Zhu Rongji's administration since 1998, government agencies and military organizations are required to disconnect from their subsidiary establishments.

Of the fifty-three jobs that were obtained by my interviewees in various subsidiary establishments, 38 percent were found through hierarchical allocation, 49 percent through the use of predominantly strong ties, 13 percent through the use of predominantly weak ties, and none through the method of "all by myself." This percentage distribution makes it clear that the emerging labor markets in subsidiary establishments are not at all market-driven.

International joint ventures

International joint ventures are businesses established by foreign investors and their Chinese partner organizations. The latter are frequently state-owned firms, which provide the joint ventures with infrastructures and labor. This means that job slots in international joint ventures are not open to external labor markets but instead are filled internally by the Chinese partner organizations. This is why the jobs obtained by my interviewees in international joint ventures were mostly found by way of hierarchical allocation (54 percent). While they are on the payroll of the joint ventures, the workers' personnel relationships are officially with the Chinese partner organizations from which they get reallocated, so they can continue to have housing and other benefits from the latter. This is an excellent deal for the workers, and accordingly many want to be reallocated to the joint ventures. This motivation increased the use of strong ties in order to work in international joint ventures; 27 percent of the jobs obtained by my interviewees in the joint ventures were found by way of predominantly strong ties, compared with none by way of predominantly weak ties. International joint ventures have some flexibility to open their job slots to external labor markets; 19 percent of my sample found jobs by way of "all by myself."

Foreign firms

Foreign firms differ significantly from international joint ventures in the operation of labor recruitment. Because they do not have Chinese partner organizations, they need not hire anyone officially reallocated by authorities. This is true among my interviewees. Of the twenty-five jobs that my interviewees had in foreign firms, none was found through hierarchical allocation. However, foreign firms cannot hire people through entirely market-oriented methods either. Such methods as newspaper ads, street posts, employment services, and walk-in application are inefficient in spreading information or ineffective in generating a desired pool of applicants. For example, not many Chinese people are used to newspaper ads and street posts to collect employment information. Employment services, on the other hand, are affiliated with a governmental labor bureau, and in most cases only undesirable jobs would be registered in these services. Use of network ties, in contrast, has been an effective method to search for jobs in foreign firms. Among my interviewees, 44 percent of the jobs in foreign firms were found through the use of predominantly strong ties, 24 percent through the use of predominantly weak ties, and 32 percent through the method of "all by myself." The last two methods combined account for 56 percent of jobs in foreign firms, implying that the labor market in foreign firms is largely market-driven.

How do we explain the 44 percent of jobs that were found through strong ties in foreign firms? My interviewees told me of two kinds of strong ties they used to search for jobs in foreign firms. The first is kin and friends (neighbors, former classmates, etc.) who somehow obtained information about job openings and spread to my interviewees. The second is a tie to Chinese managers of the foreign firm to which they intend to find a job. In many cases, this is a strong tie of high intimacy. If the tie is not strong enough, strong-tie intermediaries would be used to influence the Chinese managers. Usually the Chinese managers cannot influence the decision-makers of foreign firms for hiring someone of their *guanxi*, but they can effectively assist my interviewees by applying "on time" and "in a right way," which increased the chances of getting a face-to-face interview.

Domestic private businesses

Like foreign firms, domestic private businesses – family businesses, partnerships, and private firms that are established by Chinese nationals – do not need to hire anyone through hierarchical allocation. Being a private investor, the domestic private business relies on "external labor markets" for labor supply. Of the twenty-six jobs that were obtained by my interviewees in domestic private businesses, none was found through hierarchical allocation by authority, 35 percent through the use of predominantly strong ties, 31 percent through the use of predominantly weak ties, and 35 percent through the method of "all by myself." This distribution is about the same as that for foreign firms.

Economic entities with ambiguous or mixed-property forms

The percentage distribution of job-change methods differs in economic entities with ambiguous or mixed property forms. Here, jobs were found by interviewees mostly by using strong ties (69 percent), some by weak ties (10 percent), "all by myself" (21 percent), and none by hierarchical allocation. This probably testifies to the nature of these entities as being embedded in social networks.

The economic entities I classify in this category are mostly registered as enterprises of collective ownership. This is quite misleading, because the investment capital, both for initiation and operation, is from the individuals who establish them. By the private nature of capital investment, these entities should have been recognized as household businesses or private companies. However, the government has had regulations to limit private ownership to a certain size and industry. Private-owned businesses are also not given any consideration in loan applications to state banks. These various limitations would be minimized when private investors get a local government agency or a public organization to be its affiliation, recognized either as "*gua kao danwei*" (literally, an organization to "hook and lean on") or as "*shangji jiguan*" (jurisdictional agency). This affiliation provides two forms of capital to the affiliated economic entities. First, it provides symbolic capital, so that the established entities can market their products in the name of the affiliated government or public organization, which is more reliable than the name of private entities in the Chinese context. Second, it provides network capital, so that the established entities can benefit from the formal and informal connections of the affiliated government or public organization in developing their businesses.

These entities do not operate as collective enterprises, nor are they intended as collectively owned. The affiliated government or public organization requires a yearly "management charge" from the entities and leaves everything else to be operated solely by the private investors of the entities themselves. What is essentially important for the business development, though, are the connections between the entities and the significant *guanxi* persons in its affiliated government or public organizations. If the connections were maintained, the *guanxi* persons in the affiliated government or public organizations would work in the interest of the entities by providing business opportunities and social-political influences. The entities, in turn, would definitely pay the services provided by the *guanxi* persons in tangible ways; hiring workers recommended by these *guanxi* persons is one of the tangible ways. Most of my interviewees who worked in the entities with mixed or ambiguous property forms got jobs this way.

Migrant peasant labor in the cities

Since 1992, migrant peasants have become a main source of cheap labor supply in the cities. While no accurate statistics are available, one official estimate is that there were eighty million as of 1996 (State Labor Department 1996). This is about one-third of China's urban labor force. A large number of them "float" between cities and their home villages, and many in fact have returned home after gaining working experience and non-agricultural skills in the cities (Ma 1999). Researchers so far have emphasized the role of village-city kin networks through which peasant labor can migrate to work in the cities. My interviews with ten migrant workers confirm this finding. As shown in Table 6.2, of the forty-Seven jobs obtained by the migrant peasant workers I interviewed, none was found through hierarchical allocation, 72 percent were found through the use of predominantly strong ties (mainly kin ties and community-based friends), 17 percent were found through the use of predominantly weak ties (work-related ties developed in the cities), and 11 percent were found through the more market-driven method of "all by myself."

VIEWS OF CHINA'S TRANSITION TO LABOR MARKETS

How do we account for the significant proportions of strong ties used to facilitate job changes in China's emergent labor markets? Why would *guanxi* be persistently significant during the transition from job assignments to labor markets?

One view from recent China research is that the country does not yet have labor markets in their own right (Xie and Hannum 1996). This view assumes that jobs in Chinese cities are still hierarchically controlled in one way or another and that workers are given neither the right nor the freedom to exchange their labor power for rewards in the marketplace. Accordingly, it is understandable that job seekers would use their *guanxi* networks of strong ties to influence authorities in job searches and job mobility processes.

The lack of labor markets was indeed the case for pre-reform China, and for the first decade of reforms when the program of state job assignments was in effect in major Chinese cities (Davis 1990; Bian 1994a). Since 1992, however, the program of job assignments has largely been abolished (Bian and Logan 1996). In the new system, although the state still monitors labor supply and labor demand on a macro-economic level and speaks for the socialist goal of full employment, government labor bureaus in the cities consider their employment services (in place of job assignments) as a supplement to the "market allocation of labor." In the Chinese context, this term means that employers in the state and non-state sectors carry out their recruitment plans independently, that youths entering the labor force can search for jobs by themselves, and that employees are given the right and the freedom to move between employers. Consequently, only a small proportion of new jobs (about 10–15 percent in Tianjin) are allocated through the employment services of government labor bureaus (and jobs available from these services are usually undesirable ones). All of these changes mean that labor markets actually emerged in their own right and grew rapidly in Chinese cities in the 1990s.

A second view of China's labor markets is that of "partial reform" (Nee 1991). The assumption behind the term is that hierarchy and markets are competing economic institutions and the transition from hierarchy to markets presents a zero-sum scenario: In the allocation of economic resources, reduction of hierarchical arrangements means growth of market-driven arrangements. This tendency was seen by Naughton (1995) as the result of the Chinese economy's being gradually "out of the plan," and the resulting economic environment is one in which rationalization grows and anti-rational *guanxi* rules decline (Guthrie 1998a). According to these views, China's reforms in the labor sphere are gradual and incomplete, and the persistent effects of *guanxi* networks are a signal for further reforms.

The view of partial reform appears to be empirically grounded, but the problem with this conceptualization is that hypotheses derived from it are not falsifiable. Indeed, any research findings from China that are at variance with the expectations of the ideal-typical concept of "market" are interpretable from the viewpoints of partial reform (see Nee and Mathews 1996). More importantly, partial reform assumes unidimensional transformation from a total non-market system to a partial market system to a total market system, incorrectly ignoring multiple paths of economic developments that are necessitated by countries' diverse histories and social, political, and cultural backgrounds (for critiques of partial reform, see Parish and Michaelson 1996; Walder 1996).

The third view that may help explain the persistence of *guanxi* networks in job mobility processes emphasizes the influence of Confucianism in Chinese cultures. Individuals *normatively* build and maintain intimate and reciprocal relationships with significant others in their families, kinships, communities, and friendship circles, and rely on these *guanxi* networks to exchange favors, trust, and information with closely connected others (Liang 1949; Fei [1949] 1992; Hwang 1987; Yang 1994; Yan 1996). Because of this cultural influence, argued by some scholars (e.g., Cheng and Rosett 1991; Smart 1993), *guanxi* networks have been an important principle guiding Chinese people's behaviors and Chinese organizations in both Mainland and Overseas Chinese societies. Thus, *guanxi* is modeled as a contributor to the initiation of small businesses in Taiwan (Luo 1997), to the organizational structure of Hong Kong firms (Wong 1988), to firm performance and efficiency in Chinese societies (Lovett, Simmons, and Kali 1997; Luo and Chen 1997), and to Chinese workers' performance in formal organizations anywhere in the world (Tsui and Farh 1997). Kao (1993, p. 24) has argued that overseas Chinese businesses are "a network of entrepreneurial relationships." In the labor sphere, Bian and Ang (1997) found that in Singapore, where 78 percent of the population are of Chinese origin, strong ties are more frequently used and more effective than weak ties in facilitating job mobility despite the presence of labor markets.

To be sure, cultural explanations are helpful in comparing the East with the West. However, cultural explanations alone are insufficient to explain why the effects of *guanxi* were highly persistent in job mobility processes when the institutional contexts of China's labor markets changed rather significantly in the 1990s. The stories of my interviewees have pointed to the specific institutional arrangements in labor markets, making it possible for *guanxi* networks of strong ties to play a persistent role in job matching processes. These stories support an institutional explanation about the roles of *guanxi* networks in transmitting information, building and maintaining trust, and enforcing economic and moral obligations between job seekers and their employers in an economy of institutional holes.

INSTITUTIONAL HOLES AND *GUANXI*
IN EMERGENT LABOR MARKETS

I offer an institutional explanation calling for attention to the information, trust, and obligation-binding functions of *guanxi* networks through which job seekers connect to prospective employers and are matched to jobs. This explanation assumes that in any labor market, job seekers and prospective employers must have a necessary amount of information about each other before they can approach each other, must achieve a minimal level of trust in each other's accountability before they sign a contract, and must be subject to obligation-binding measures to ensure that contracted terms are fulfilled. I argue that these processes would have been facilitated through formal institutional arrangements if they were available and effective. In reality, however, because of fast removal of hierarchical institutions and slow growth of market institutions, emergent labor markets in Chinese cities are full of institutional holes, making formal channels ineffective for transmitting information, building trust, and binding obligations between job seekers and prospective employers. *Guanxi* networks of interpersonal relationships are the informal mechanisms to fill up these holes. I analyze three functions of *guanxi* in turn – information flow, trust bridging, and obligation binding – and use the in-depth interviews to support my analyses.

Information flow

Let us look at planned and market economies first. Both systems have problems in formal channels for diffusing employment information. The problem in the planned economy is the control and distortion of information by government labor agencies. Under the system of job assignments, because job seekers and employers are given no rights to choose each other, they are provided with limited and sometimes distorted information about each other before they are matched by the government agencies. To break free from this control and distortion of information, job seekers and employers have to rely on their *guanxi* connections with job-assigning authorities to gain access to internally circulated information. In the market economy, on the other hand, although job seekers and employers have the right to choose each other, their freedom to do so is limited because formal channels (i.e., employment services, mass media, internet, street posts) are insufficient in diffusing employment information. Under this situation, social networks supplement the formal channels for the flow of employment information.

In China's emergent labor markets, the problem concerning information diffusion is that formal information channels are either restricted or ineffective. The first scenario applies to subsidiary establishments and international joint ventures. Subsidiary establishments are designed to hire the surplus labor of the parent organizations (in the form of "tertiary sector companies") or the children of their employees (in the form of "labor service companies"). International joint ventures, on the other hand, are expected to recruit from the internal labor markets of the Chinese partner organizations. Under these circumstances, information about job positions in subsidiary establishments and international joint ventures is under the control of the authorities of the Chinese parent/partner organizations. *Guanxi* to these authorities therefore becomes important in getting the information and subsequently getting reallocated to the high-paying jobs in these newly emerged economic entities.

The second scenario – ineffective information channels – applies to other emergent labor markets – namely, foreign firms, domestic private businesses, businesses with ambiguous and mixed property forms, and migrant peasant labor in the cities. These businesses do not grow out of existing organizations, and they rely on external labor markets to recruit workers. However, formal information channels such as newspapers and employment services are ineffective in diffusing employment information for two reasons. First, these channels are government-sponsored and lack incentives to take active roles in collecting and diffusing employment information. Second, employers and job seekers are biased toward these channels, believing that only bad, undesirable jobs would be advertised through them. This belief is empirically grounded; jobs that are circulated through employment services are, as a Tianjin employment service director told me, those that "nobody seems to want."

Domestic private businesses and organizations with mixed or ambiguous property forms tend to go through their interorganizational and interpersonal networks to spread job information and recruit workers. Foreign firms, although lacking these networks, get help from their Chinese managers whose interpersonal connections and previous organizational networks are always handy. Foreign firms do use employment services to recruit, however, as one Chinese manager emphasized; foreign executives always make sure that among applicants with similar qualifications, those who have connections with their Chinese managers get jobs. Finally, migrant peasant laborers learn job information mostly through their kin and villager networks. One multi-province study shows that about 80 percent of these migrant workers receive information through these "self-organization" channels (Zhao et al., 1997). In the most marketized southern city of Shenzhen, a study of five manufacturing factories indicates that more than 40 percent of migrant workers came to the city through family or village connections, 10 percent came through other personal or interorganizational connections, 20 percent were hired in their hometowns by Shenzhen companies that have local connections, 10 percent followed official channels, and less than 10 percent came individually without any connections or pre-arrangements (Shi 1997).

Job seekers take an active role in getting job information through *guanxi*. Three groups of twenty-one students I interviewed in Beijing, Tianjin, and Shanghai universities indicated that they were open for all channels of information when they were about to search for jobs. However, in the end they all learned job information through *guanxi* connections and secured jobs that way before they graduated. Two of the twenty-one students secured jobs through their parents back home (not in the three cities), five found jobs through friends in the southern cities of Shenzhen and Haikou where pay scales are significantly higher, and the rest had offers from government agencies or foreign firms in the three cities, and all the offers became available through some sorts of *guanxi* connections.

Going through connections to learn about job openings is almost always the first idea coming to everyone's mind. I asked every interviewee this question, "When you began job searches that led to your present job, how did you start the process? Did you start by looking at newspapers, going through employment services, asking your relatives or *shuren*, or what?" *Shuren* here means someone with whom one is familiar and strongly connected, and thus it is *guanxi*. "Asking relatives and *shuren*" is almost always the answer I received. "Why not going through other means first?" I asked. I was told that these other means are "not as reliable" and "not as useful." Then, they would tell me why relatives and *shuren* are more trustful and why trust matters. One interviewee in Shanghai supplied me with this story:

Working in Japan for two years after receiving a certificate in home interior design from a small Japanese school, I returned to Shanghai in 1995. I did not want to work in the company in which I worked before going to Japan several years ago, because people there would say, 'this guy must have done things wrong in Japan, or otherwise he would not have returned.' I was prepared to search for jobs through all other channels instead. I contacted several employment services, including 'talent centers' (*rencai zhongxin*), but only one center offered me the opportunity to interview for a job at a Chinese-Japanese joint venture. I would not work in that firm because they wanted a Japanese translator, not a professional designer. I read street posts about jobs, but they were all for labor-intensive work, not for me as a professional. I dropped by several employers I thought I would look attractive to; they either had excuses not to hire me or did not want any more people to work for them. I asked my *guanxi*, or relatives and friends, or their relatives and friends, to help. I brought from Japan a lot of small presents and I used them when I asked people to care about [collect and tell] job opportunities for me. I gave larger presents to the persons who connected me to real job opportunities [meaning interviews or job offers]. Over the last two years since I returned home [from Japan], I have worked in five different jobs and all of them came to me through my *guanxi*.

Trust-Bridging

The notion of trust applies to job-matching processes because job seekers and prospective employers must have a minimal level of trust in each other's accountability before they can sign a contract. The greater the mutual trust between job seekers and prospective employers, the greater the confidence they have in their future relationships, and the less the perceived opportunity costs in letting go other job/labor possibilities. However, this kind of trust does not apply to the planned economy, in which job seekers and employers are given no freedom to choose each other. In a market economy, job seekers' trust in prospective employers is largely based on the latter's reputation. Employers' trust in their candidates' accountability, on the other hand, is gained by examining candidates' qualifications and achievements, but recommendations from the candidates' past employers or other respected authorities are an important measure of insurance.

In China's emergent labor markets, the trust issue has become sensitized, for there are great uncertainties as well as plenty of opportunities facing both workers and employers. The greatest uncertainty ever facing Chinese workers since 1949 is the loss of job security; at the same time, those who are active in the emergent labor markets will have plenty of opportunities for new jobs with high prestige, decent pay, or opportunities to move to new and better jobs. The combination of these two societal forces encourages opportunistic behavior, discourages workers' commitment to employers, and increases job turnover. These behavioral outcomes on the part of workers bring about the greatest uncertainty ever facing Chinese employers: Employers no longer have the kind of control they had over workers before economic reforms. This is despite the fact that employers now are given the freedom and opportunity to hire workers in the labor markets at will.

Opportunism can make things go in the wrong direction. For example, job seekers can provide false statements about their qualifications and work experiences in their applications, submit fake school diplomas or certificates for vocational training, and even prepare letters of introduction by themselves in the names of their schools, current employers, or local government offices. These problems are rare in the recruitment processes for subsidiary establishments and international joint ventures, which hire workers mostly within the internal labor markets of the Chinese parent organizations. However, the occurrence of these problems is high in other types of emergent labor markets in which employers recruit workers from external labor markets. In cases of inter-city, inter-region, or inter-industry job changes, these problems are very serious. Consequently, employers would prefer those candidates who have been referred through their personal or organizational connections. Here, *guanxi* networks become a basis for bridging trust.

Not all job seekers with *guanxi* connections to employers are accountable for their words of promise, nor do *guanxi* connections have everlasting effects for the job seekers once they are hired. However, *guanxi* connections do help employers to know job seekers better and increase their level of trust (or distrust) in the latter. Among the 100 individuals I interviewed, there was a tendency for those who used *guanxi* connections to stay in their jobs longer than those who did not use any connections, and those who used strong-tie intermediates to connect to the employers tended to stay in their jobs longest.

Many migrant workers do not have strong-tie or even weak-tie intermediates to help connect to their employers in the cities far from their homes. In Shenzhen and Haikou, the two southern cities where I conducted my interviews, 80 percent of the current labor force came from outside the cities. Many of them came without any prior connections of any kind, and they all suffered from this fact, despite getting jobs in the first days of their arrival. In most cases, they work in temporary jobs, and after they cultivate and maintain good connections with their employers, they can stay in their jobs for long-term contracts. For many others, job hunting is almost an everyday task; this would not be so if they had *guanxi* to help them build trusting relationships with prospective employers. One young man in Shenzhen told me his story:

I am from Jilin [province] and had joined the army. My hometown is very poor and I wanted to come here to make money so I can return home with money needed to get married. [One of] my army comrade[s] (*zhanyou*) is from my home county and came to Shenzhen before me. He helped me a lot in getting the job I have now. When I came, I knew nobody beside him. I lived in his apartment. He took me to his boss [a foreman in a construction company], influencing him to let me work there. His boss kind of trusted him, believing that I would work hard, so [he was happy about] having me in his team. [Many people came to Shenzhen and landed in a job as a springboard to another job with better benefits, and employers do not want to hire these kinds of people unless someone in between would provide strong recommendation.] I liked the work and pay is fair. I still have not changed my job yet [after almost a year].

To some employers, certain positions must be occupied by those in whom they trust. Managerial positions in subsidiary establishments, domestic private companies, and businesses with ambiguous and mixed property forms are such positions, not only because these managers are engaged in decision-making for these organizations, but more importantly because the decision making is usually about illicit transactions and unjustified distributions of earnings. For example, one function of subsidiary establishments is to generate funds to be used by the heads of the parent organization for public and private purposes. Therefore, managers of the subsidiary establishments must necessarily be in good *guanxi* with the heads of the parent organization to be appointed to the position. In these organizations, other trust-sensitive, key positions include financial officers and clerks (accountants and cashiers are knowledgeable about cash flows of the companies) and business development and purchasing agents (who are in control of companies' inter-organizational networks and business opportunities for the companies), and are usually hired from the managers' *guanxi* circles.

Obligation binding

Emergent labor markets in China's transitional economy, as I have indicated, are high in information uncertainty and low in institutional trust. They are also weak in measures that can be used to enforce obligations between workers and employers. For workers, their obligation is to perform to the expectation of labor contracts even when they are not monitored. Examples of violations include laziness, intentional delays of work orders, stealing, and so on. Employers, on the other hand, must fulfill their economic and moral obligations to the workers as specified in labor contracts or promised otherwise. Employers can violate contracted terms or break promises by delaying pay schedules, miscounting work hours, increasing overtime workloads, making no payments to the insured, and so on. Because both workers and employers can violate labor contracts, enforcement measures are necessary.

These measures exist, and are probably effective in both planned economies and market economies. In the planned economy as observed in China before reforms, government hierarchy was effective in regulating and monitoring employers through a system of administrative and political control and monitoring. In disciplining workers, although it was almost impossible to lay workers off, work units had measures to enforce social and political control of workers (Shaw 1996). In the market economy as observed in the United States, on the other hand, legal institutions are available to deal with labor-capital disputes on an individual basis, and worker unions are the means of collective action to help organized workers fight against the capitalist and managerial class (Hodson 1995).

In China's transitional economy, none of these measures is effective. First, the monitoring function of the government hierarchy is much weakened when state firms and organizations are less dependent on government budgets (Wang 1996). Second, such new entities as international joint ventures and foreign firms are almost free of the monitoring of the government because the latter is dependent on the former for foreign investments. Third, legal institutions are so corrupt that workers do not rely on them to solve disputes with their leaders or business owners. Finally, worker unions are non-existent in new economic entities and no organized action can be taken by workers to protect their collective interests. In Shenzhen and Haikou, I heard many stories about employers not fulfilling their obligations. For instance, a two-month delay of wage payments is very common in Hong Kong firms in Shenzhen.

In the absence of effective measures in enforcing the obligations between workers and employers, *guanxi* networks are instead intended by workers to perform the function of obligation binding. One example is that of a woman who worked in her Hong Kong relative's firm in Shanghai. She admitted that because of the kinship tie between her and her employer, she was "obligated to work hard for him no matter what happened to the business." At the same time, she also believed that her employer would "not impose any unreasonable requests" on her because "he would lose face among all relatives in Hong Kong and the Mainland." Another example is the expectation and experience of one of the migrant peasant workers I interviewed in Tianjin. He came to Tianjin with his uncle, who was the head of a construction team. He knew about all problems in the construction industry: no job security, heavy work loads, low hourly wage, no guarantee to pay on time, no promise to be released from work to return home during holidays. But he was not afraid of all of these because "my uncle would not make me the first one or the only one to swallow all these kinds of bitterness." Although they are not the solutions to the problems, *guanxi* connections of mutual trust and reciprocal obligation are useful in reducing anxieties of the workers. This increases the probability of getting jobs through the use of strong ties.

GUANXI CAPITAL IN THE ECONOMY OF INSTITUTIONAL HOLES

I have sketched an institutional explanation to account for the persistence of *guanxi* in occupational processes in China's emergent labor markets. I argued that China's emergent labor markets are full of institutional holes that make formal channels ineffective for transmitting information, building trust, and binding obligations between job seekers and prospective employers. The existence of these institutional holes makes it possible for *guanxi* to play an important role in the emergent labor markets. Although not representative of China's labor force, my 100 interviewees allow us to get a sense of how *guanxi* facilitates occupational attainments in several types of emergent labor markets.

The presence of institutional holes is due, in my observation, to the fast removal of hierarchical mechanisms of labor allocation (e.g., job-assignment programs) and the slow growth of market mechanisms in matching job seekers to prospective employers. The fast removal of job-assignment programs was probably highly desirable because these programs were not effective in allocating labor (see Bian 1994b). But the resulting problem has been the sudden decline of the formal organizational framework consisting of government labor offices, employers, and schools. This organizational framework had functioned, though inefficiently, to flow job information, to certify the trustworthiness of job seekers and employers (through the use of personnel dossiers), and to enforce any misconduct. When this organizational framework was dismantled in the late 1980s or early 1990s, as in the six Chinese cities in which I conducted my interviews, "market" institutions (e.g., employment services, talent centers, mass media, and direct application) did not function effectively. But effective market-oriented institutions never would be born from the designs of policymakers, as China's past reform experiences have shown (Naughton 1995); they would grow out of the practices already operating in labor markets. In this view, the persistent practices of *guanxi* rules in China's emergent labor markets may serve as a transitional mechanism to lead to a set of more market-driven arrangements in regulating labor markets in the cities. It is in this sense that in the economy of institutional holes, the growth of markets would necessarily mean the decline of *guanxi*, or vice versa.

The institutional holes argument implies that individuals who are most active in the emergent labor markets may be those who have high levels of social network capital. With respect to information, trust, and obligation that flow through social networks in job mobility processes, I suggest two composite measures of social network capital. The first measure is a combination of size and diversity of interpersonal networks in which an individual lives. The larger the network *and* the greater the diversity of the network one lives in, the greater the probability that non-redundant job information can be accessed through the network. The second measure is the ability of one's own network to bridge into networks of others. Because the essence of Chinese *guanxi* networks is to exchange favors and resources through strong ties, weak ties are unlikely to serve as bridges in the Chinese context even if they are structurally better able to do so (Granovetter 1973). Also, in industrialized or industrializing societies, even if exchanges of favors are likely to occur among people with similar characteristics, they are most desirable among those who have different resources to trade. This means that in China, the ability of one's network to bridge into the networks of others will increase with the number of strong *and* diverse ties one has in one's own network. The likelihood for relaying trust and transferring obligations will increase when one's network has greater abilities to bridge into the networks of others.

The concept of social network capital should not be confused with human capital and political capital. Human capital and political capital are attributes and resources an individual possesses alone. Social network capital, however, is one's network *accessibility* to the human and political capitals of others. Therefore, social network capital is relational, transactional, and dynamic; social network capital will deteriorate if the individual becomes less active in networking.

The importance of social network capital in occupational attainment processes in transitional societies should be carefully assessed with reference to human capital and political capital. For example, the "market transition debate" (see a special volume of the *American Journal of Sociology* January 1996) raises concerns about the significance of human and political capital in the changing system of social stratification in China. Victor Nee's (1989a, 1991, 1996) market-transition theory predicts that political capital will be giving way to human capital as the most significant mobility path during China's transition toward a market economy. However, other scholars point to the continuation of China's political structure and path dependence of its economic reforms, arguing for the persistence of political capital (Bian and Logan 1996), the conversion of government bureaucracy into economic enterprises (Walder 1995a), and the rise of political markets (Parish and Michaelson 1996). Nonetheless, no one has given systematic analysis to the increasingly important role played by social network capital in occupational and social mobility during market transition.

With American society in mind, James Coleman (1988) has suggested the idea that social [network] capital conditions the development of human capital in a positive manner. The 100 individuals I interviewed suggest that this argument is highly applicable to occupational processes in China. That is, because the emergent labor markets are full of institutional holes, persons with high levels of social network capital are most active in the labor markets and are best able to catch job opportunities. Their high levels of human or political capital will help them maintain and advance quickly in their jobs. Persons with high levels of social network capital but low levels of human and political capital are expected to be active in the labor markets, but they will have a slow pace of career advancement. Persons with low levels of social network capital are less active and less able to catch job opportunities in the emergent labor markets of institutional holes, even if they have high levels of human and political capital. Finally, persons who are low on any of these three forms of capital are least able to catch job opportunities and are the last to succeed in their careers.

7

YOUTH JOB SEARCHES IN URBAN CHINA: THE USE OF SOCIAL CONNECTIONS IN A CHANGING LABOR MARKET

Amy Hanser

GUANXI AND FINDING A JOB

Guanxi is often characterized as a notion rooted in the specificity and uniqueness of Chinese culture, and for this reason, studying how Chinese people use and think about their social relationships with others provides an interesting standpoint from which to observe and analyze social change. In this chapter, I will consider the use of *guanxi* in the job searches of urban youths and explore how perceptions and practices of *guanxi* might be shifting with broader social and economic changes. To this end, I will make some broad conjectures about how urban youths find work in China's cities in the late 1990s and consider some of the implications changing labor market conditions have for *guanxi* and youth job searches. I hope to demonstrate that with respect to *guanxi* and finding a job, individuals consider their options within a culturally and institutionally situated context. With change, people react and adjust accordingly. My findings suggest some interesting and fairly radical changes might be afoot regarding the ways young urbanites, at least, think about *guanxi* in relation to job searches. In contrast with Bian's findings (this volume) but similar to Guthrie's findings (this volume), the importance of *guanxi* in urban employment appears to be in decline.

Rather than seeking statistical or numerical generalizations, what I examine here is the place of *guanxi* in the way young urbanites conceptualize job searches.[95] In this respect, my subjects' responses were clear: *Guanxi* is often not perceived as the best, most effective, or even most common way of procuring employment. The many possible reasons for this are explored in detail. However, my reasoning can be briefly summed up as follows:

---

95 In Yanjie Bian's 1988 data on employment patterns in the northern Chinese city of Tianjin, he found that over 45 percent of respondents used some form of social ties to find their first jobs (1997); at the same time, that means that almost 55 percent *did not* use a helper, or *guanxi*, to find their first job. The evidence I present here is no basis on which to argue that that number has changed in any significant way.

- *Labor market reform and employer demands*: Labor market reforms have brought
  about new job search avenues. Work units and employers also have more discretion
  over whom they hire, and at the same time shoulder more economic responsibility, encouraging merit-based hiring. My data reflect only indirectly on this second assertion,
  but evidence from other studies provides considerable basis for this claim (e.g. Wang
  1998; Guthrie 1997, 1998b, this volume). These broader changes to China's urban labor
  markets serve as partial preconditions for the assertions that follow.
- *Workplace and regional mobility*: Individuals in cities are increasingly able to travel
  to different cities and regions for work, and they are able and willing to make numerous job changes. Moves may be facilitated by *guanxi*, but particularly if individuals
  are highly employable, they may be better off *not* relying on *guanxi*. (This is especially true given young people's limited social networks generally and particularly in
  distant locales.)
- *Job specificity and skill marketability*: Young people in urban areas increasingly seek
  specific types of work (as opposed to specific work units) and jobs related to their
  specific skills, to which their networks of strong social ties provide limited access.
  Reliance (or not) on *guanxi* may also be reflective of an individual's relative position
  within the job market, where the more marketable the skills (generally speaking, the
  higher the level of education), the less the reliance on *guanxi*.
- Guanxi *or Ties*? When social connections are used in job searches, they may only involve
  word-of-mouth information exchanges about job openings (which are not so different
  from formal job search methods). In other words, what people now expect of social ties
  is perhaps different from past expectations. With changes to the labor market, different
  degrees of social ties and *guanxi* may arise.

I do not want to suggest that *guanxi* have become irrelevant to finding work
in China. Indeed, as one informant told me, a lot of people *do* use *guanxi*, or
social connections, to find work. "It will never disappear," he said of this method.
However, while interviewees did speak of *guanxi,* it was rarely in connection with
their own job searches. Even when people had relied on a friend or relative – a
strong tie – to find a job, they saw this as unrelated to their ability to keep their
jobs. In short, in terms of finding work, *guanxi* did not play a primary role for the
subjects of my study. Rather, social ties, when used at all, were usually limited to
an introduction of limited influence or simply a job tip.

The rise (and fall?) of guanxi

The term *guanxi* itself literally means "relationship" in Chinese, and is often used
to refer to social relations between and among people. In academic circles, the
specific connotations of the term, and particularly the role of *guanxi* (the rise or
fall of its significance in daily life) in reform-era China, have come under debate.
While it is not my intention to resolve these issues, some definition or understanding of *guanxi* is indispensable to a meaningful discussion of job search methods in
China.

The most extensive study on *guanxi* is Mayfair Yang's monograph *Gifts, Favors
and Banquets* (1994). *Guanxi*, Yang contends, is a cultural constant common to
Chinese everywhere: It represents a belief in the "primacy and binding power of
personal relationships" (6). She argues that *guanxi* also entails "the sense of 'social

connections,' dyadic relationships that are based implicitly (rather than explicitly) on mutual interest and benefit. Once guanxi is established between two people, each can ask a favor of the other with the expectation that the debt incurred will be repaid sometime in the future" (1–2).

Yang then considers the phenomenon of *guanxixue*, or "the art of *guanxi*," a set of social practices related to, but neither limited to nor entirely coextensive with, *guanxi*. *Guanxixue* differs from *guanxi*, both as a practice and in terms of symbolic content. *Guanxixue* places greater emphasis on instrumentality (though affectual elements remain strong [123]).[96] And in contrast to *guanxi*, *guanxixue* is a product of socialist China's state distributive economy (7, 189), where *guanxi* plays a symbolic role by providing an alternative, subversive domain of power opposing state bureaucratic institutions – a "gift economy" that redistributes power and material wealth counter to the state-controlled distributive economy (178–9).[97]

Guanxixue, then, is a term that describes the instrumental use of social connections (*guanxi*) on the basis of an accompanying system of personalistic ethics, in the context of (and often in opposition to) a socialist, redistributive state and the universalistic ethics it advocates. Yang gives two reasons why the influence of *guanxixue* in Chinese society will increase with economic reforms: first, as long as the state redistributive apparatus continues to play a role in society, *guanxixue* will also be present (310). Second, even within a commodity economy the practices of *guanxixue* are able to graft onto market-oriented behaviors (167, 171).

Douglas Guthrie (1998a; this volume) has taken issue with claims that the salience of *guanxixue* is on the rise in urban China. Guthrie contends that economic reforms have resulted in the "bifurcation of *guanxi* and *guanxi* practice [*guanxixue*] in the urban industrial economy" (1998a, p. 262) such that the two concepts "are increasingly viewed as distinguishable in the economic transition" (256). The notion of *guanxi*, Guthrie argues, often involves simple maintenance of good business relations, social connections between business people for which market demands and priorities supercede (though do not obliterate) personal or relational ones. At the same time, the Shanghai industrial managers Guthrie interviewed increasingly associated *guanxixue* with the inefficiencies and complexities of a redistributive economic system (256–7). Further, Guthrie (this volume) argues that only employers, not job-seekers, truly know the significance of *guanxi* in hiring

---

96 Yang's definition of *guanxixue* is complex and nuanced but may be simplified to "the exchange of gifts, favors, and banquets; the cultivation of personal relationships and networks of mutual dependence; and the manufacturing of obligation and indebtedness" (6). This definition, however, is almost indistinguishable from the one cited earlier for *guanxi;* the difficulty of disentangling the two terms is further highlighted by the fact that as Yang points out, *guanxixue* "can only be expressed and satisfied *through* various social bonds of affect, obligation and propriety" (123), the hallmarks of *guanxi*. This is also how *guanxixue* remains distinct from, say, simple bribes and money relations (123).

97 A perfect example of this would be the use of social connections to secure a job in a desirable (i.e., state-owned) work unit, a use of *guanxi* involving an exchange of gifts (or favors) of some kind. This would be *guanxixue*.

decisions. His data in this regard provide a basis for questioning the centrality of *guanxi* in China's economic transition.

Guthrie's conclusions also raise two important issues for defining a concept such as *guanxi* in social science research: First, how is *guanxi* distinct from notions of "social relations" in other cultures? He points out (this volume) that a strict definition of *guanxi* is crucial for the term to have any theoretical force. Second, assuming *guanxi* is culturally specific, is it less of a cultural constant than has been suggested? In other words, how can and does *guanxi* change?

Network theory and tie strength

One way to gain leverage on the first question is to consider treatments of "social relations" or "interpersonal relations" in non-Chinese contexts. Research on networks seeks to understand how the structure of social relations influences the flow of information and opportunities (Powell and Smith-Doerr 1994, p. 372). One branch of network theory – that focusing on employment and labor markets – has generated concepts relevant to the study of *guanxi*. Most notably, Mark Granovetter's well-known 1974 study *Getting a Job* explored the use of social connections in job searches in a middle-class American community, where he differentiated social links on the basis of "tie strength."

Tie strength is determined by several factors: "The strength of a tie is a . . . combination of the amount of time, the emotional intensity, the intimacy (mutual confiding), and the reciprocal services which characterize the tie" (1973, p. 1361). Granovetter relies primarily on a measurement of time (amount of contact between individuals) to determine if a tie is strong or weak. Weak contacts are almost entirely work or professional contacts, though some work contacts might be strong ties if the relationship has become one of friendship.[98]

Granovetter discovered that weak ties were more likely than strong ties to serve as bridges between individuals through which information or influence might flow. Granovetter's findings generated a "strength of weak ties" hypothesis, which asserts that individuals are more likely to find jobs through links to acquaintances and business contacts (weak ties) than through close friends and family (strong ties). The logic of the argument is that friends and family move in roughly the same social circles as an individual, while casual acquaintances are more likely to move in different circles and hence provide a wider net for collecting job information, offers, and opportunities (1973; 1995b [1974]).

When juxtaposed with the definitions of *guanxi* discussed earlier, we find that Granovetter's strong and weak ties fail to capture the "primacy of relationships" that Yang highlights. This difference is reflected in Yanjie Bian's research on China's labor markets (1994a, 1994b, 1997, 1999). Bian measures tie strength by utilizing two different parameters – role relation (relatives, friends, and acquaintances) and intimacy (knowing each other "very well," "well," "so-so," "not well," or

---

98   Granovetter found that for the group in his study, the two types of ties (family-social and work) did not often overlap (1995 [1974], p. 41).

"not at all") (1997, p. 373). These parameters grow out of Bian's understanding of *guanxi* (partly based on Yang's definition) as ties constituted by intimacy, trustworthiness, and reciprocity (1997, pp. 369–70) used in an instrumental way.[99] *Guanxi* by this definition are strong ties infused with trust and obligation (1997, p. 381; Bian, this volume). Bian also considers whether a job search using personal ties involved a direct tie (just a helper) or an indirect tie (an intermediary and a helper).

Bian's findings highlight two important corollaries to the process of measuring tie strength not addressed in Granovetter's original work: first, how tie strength (and the relative efficacy of different tie strengths) is related to the institutional and cultural setting in which it is embedded, and second, what flows through a tie – influence or information. The two issues are closely linked, and they perhaps reflect the instability of the concepts of social ties and *guanxi*. Indeed, the core of Bian's critique of the "strength of weak ties" thesis is that "hypotheses about tie strength must be proposed within the *institutional contexts* that condition the use of networks in job searches" (1997, p. 367).[100]

Bian finds that in the 1980s (and earlier), strong ties, as opposed to weak ones, were more important for finding a job in China. Government policies discouraged and even punished the use of personal connections (*guanxi*) to secure employment, and placed extreme restrictions on labor mobility (1994a, 1994b, 1997, 1999). As a result, such *guanxi* arrangements occurred only between parties where substantial mutual trust existed. Bian also argues that *guanxi* networks, combined with the state socialist institution of job assignments, caused influence rather than information flows through ties. In other words, job seekers did not get information about a specific job opening, but rather their helpers used their influence to secure employment in a particular (type of) work unit (1997, pp. 381–2). Bian's most recent work (this volume) argues that despite labor market reforms, imperfections in the market that hinder the flow of information and institutional weaknesses that fail to guarantee bonds of trust and obligation between workers and employers have enhanced the importance of *guanxi* in securing a job, again a consequence of institutional circumstances.

---

99   Given the historical and cultural context (which is virtually the same one that Yang studied), this would in fact be *guanxixue*.

100   Granovetter is not oblivious to these issues. In *Getting a Job*, he writes: "... the questions of my study apply poorly to societies where most individuals do not hold jobs which are clearly differentiated from their other activities, or do not work in organizations created by others" (120). Granovetter goes on to consider work arrangements in pre-industrial settings, but his point might apply equally well to a setting like China, where since the 1950s the work unit, or *danwei*, has played such an overarching role in people's lives that work and private life have not been as distinct and separate as in non-socialist settings like the United States (Lü and Perry 1997; Wang 1998, pp. 113–19). Bian's system of measurement avoids making a division between family-social and work ties, which is important considering the all-encompassing nature of the workplace and the extremely low degrees of labor and workplace mobility that characterized urban China from the 1950s on through the 1980s and into the 1990s (Zhou et al., 1997; Wang 1998, p. 141).

Guanxi *and social ties*

Contrasting the concept of *guanxi* (or even *guanxixue*) with that of tie strength generates two insights: First, there *is* something different about *guanxi* relative to Granovetter's concept of tie strength. There is more reciprocity involved, a greater sense of trust and obligation than is captured in the notion of a simple "social tie." Second, social ties can and do work differently in different contexts – and we can come up with institutional explanations that explain, in part at least, these differences.

This second point lends credence to the assertion that the difference between *guanxi* and *guanxixue* can be seen largely as a consequence of institutional context, as Guthrie suggests. Drawing on both Bian and Yang, we might argue that it was the institutional context of the 1980s, and the consequent instrumental role of *guanxi*, that generated *guanxixue*. Guthrie's data are important here: If, in certain, contexts *guanxi* and *guanxixue* are in fact perceived as distinct and distinguishable, then in such instances perhaps *guanxi* resembles Granovetter's social ties.[101] In other words, in some contexts (here, business/economic), as institutional or other factors change, the actual content of social ties and relationships may also shift.[102]

The distinction between *guanxi*, steeped in notions of obligation and trust, and (strong) social ties provides insights into China's specific employment environment. There is a danger in relying too heavily on the notion of *guanxi* when considering job search behavior, however. Are strong ties *always guanxi* ties? By defining *guanxi* as generally equivalent to strong social ties, distinctions between different types of strong ties are obscured. Granovetter and other researchers often consider strong "family/social" ties as distinct from weak "work" ones. As noted earlier, in the United States, "social" and "work" ties usually do not overlap, and it is the "work" ties that are more fruitful in generating job opportunities. But in China, the nature of the workplace has meant that strong ties are likely to include "work" ties, and as a result overemphasis upon the "*guanxi*"-ness of ties might obscure qualitative differences in what kinds of resources individuals are able to mobilize through different ties.

Likewise, does the use of strong ties in China always mean that trust and obligation are called into play? As Guthrie (this volume) points out, clearly defining behavior that is "*guanxi*" is important because otherwise interesting social and institutional changes might go unnoticed. By labeling all (strong) social ties *guanxi*, we risk creating a false sense of "Chineseness" where other explanations might apply.

---

101 In the examples Guthrie gives, trust appears to remain in business relationships, while sense of obligation is considerably curtailed by market imperatives (1998a).

102 Ambrose Yeo-chi King has also argued that Chinese culture includes "mechanisms to neutralize or to freeze the practice of [*renqing*] or [*guanxi*] in order to carve out room for instrumental rationality that is necessary for the management of economic and (in the Weberian sense) "bureaucratic conduct" (1994, p. 125). King suggests that in economic contexts in particular, market rationality often prevails, and the scope of *guanxi* practices may become circumscribed (125).

This is not to throw out the notion of cultural influences. Perhaps it is best to think of *guanxi* use, and in this case the job searches of young urbanites, as strategies reflecting both institutional conditions as well as cultural knowledge, experience, and skills. I borrow this notion of strategy from Ann Swidler (1986), who defines strategies as "the larger ways of trying to organize a life... within which particular choices make sense, and for which particular culturally shaped skills and habits are useful" (279, note 9). Swidler characterizes culture as a "tool kit" that is used to construct strategies of action (the means, not the ends) (273). In an "unsettled" environment – one characterized by change – new strategies are not built from scratch nor are they determined solely by "tradition" or "common sense" (277).

With respect to *guanxi* and job searches, we might conclude several things. First, we should expect people to continue to rely on *guanxi* to find jobs, since this is most certainly a tool in the "tool kits" of urban Chinese. At the same time, *guanxi* is not some free-floating idea without historical and institutional context, nor should reliance on *guanxi* be seen as an automatic response to economic and institutional changes in China. To this end, the work of Yang, Guthrie, and Bian all depict the use of *guanxi* as strategic, albeit in different contexts. Thomas Gold's "After Comradeship" (1985) also attests to the endurance of *guanxi* as a "tool" in interpersonal relations that is at the same time securely lodged in specific historical contexts, where tradition, history, and institutional change all play a role.

In short, people take context into account, and their understandings of their social relations with others (and what they might reasonably expect out of those relationships) can change as external conditions change. I will try to approach the role of *guanxi* in finding work from this perspective: What is the context in which young urbanites look for work? How effective do they perceive the use of *guanxi* to be when finding work, and what are their expectations regarding *guanxi* in such a context? In addition, to avoid confusion, I will use the term *guanxi* in my discussion to mean the use of a social tie infused with reciprocity and sense of obligation (that is, something more than simple "strong ties"), and return to the question of *guanxi* and ties at the end of the chapter.

Social connections and youth

One additional note on the study of social connections and job searches: There is no reason to believe that the relative importance of social connections in job searches remains constant throughout an individual's career. Specifically, youth job searches (and first-time job searches especially) are generally distinct in this regard. Because they have no work experience, young people have few or no work-related connections on which to draw, and are largely restricted to networks of family, friends, and classmates. Contacts who are friends and classmates, especially contemporaries, equally lack work experience and work-based ties. These factors elevate the importance of both family ties and formal methods

in youth job searches relative to those of older workers.[103] Under such circumstances, strong ties may provide constrained job options for many educated, urban
youths.

Finding a job in urban China: The 1990s

We now need to consider two questions: What is actually changing in the job
search environment? And what are the implications of these changes for the use
of *guanxi*? This calls for a consideration of the practices and expectations young
people have about how to find a job and how *guanxi* fits into this picture.

Empirical data come from interviews conducted with urban young people (ages
nineteen to twenty-nine) during the summer of 1998, when I visited the cities
of Beijing, Shenyang, Harbin and Qingdao (all in north or northeastern China).
Utilizing my own networks of friends, ex-students and acquaintances, I used a
snowball technique to locate potential interview subjects. In addition, I visited
job fairs in Harbin and Beijing, collected articles and books about and for young
people looking for work, and had innumerable shorter conversations with both
friends and strangers I met during my stay. In some cases, conversations extended
over several days, and often turned into group discussions.[104]

In all, I conducted twenty in-depth interviews (ranging from forty-five minutes
to an hour and a half in length) with ten men and twelve women. The educational
backgrounds of respondents were fairly diverse, ranging from high school to three
years of graduate study (a master's degree). Three subjects had graduated from
zkhongzhuan, or technical high schools, five from *dazhuan*, or two-year technical
colleges, and six from *daxue*, or four-year universities. Eight respondents were
working towards master's degrees, heavily skewing my sample toward very highly
educated young people. However, of these eight, only three had never worked
before. Five had looked for jobs on graduating from college, so they fall into both
the college and graduate student categories.

Many of the factors outlined at the beginning of this chapter – such as "job
specificity" and "skill marketability" – reflect an individual's position in the

103 Granovetter's data from the 1970s bear this out in the American context (1974, p. 42). He also
finds that for professionals, the likelihood of netting a job through work-related contacts grows
over the career of an individual. Walter Licht has found a similar trend from survey data gathered
in Philadelphia in 1936, where first jobs were most frequently obtained through direct application
(40 percent), and a sizable minority (25 percent) of first-time job seekers relied on family contacts
(1992, pp. 32–3). Likewise, "personal connections" (work-based ties) grew in importance over
individuals' lifetimes. Licht concludes that "[m]ethods of obtaining work in general, and the role
of family connections specifically, cannot be properly assessed . . . without proper regard to the
stages of occupational life cycle" (33).

104 For better or worse, conversations and interviews were rarely conducted without at least one
listener, often a mutual friend, at times a sibling or classmate. I do not believe this affected the
honesty with which young people spoke about their experiences. Often, the third (or fourth) party
would contribute valuable information to the discussion or make comments that sparked lively
debate.

urban job market, which is very often determined by education.[105] Therefore, in the discussion that follows, I will often divide the individuals I studied into three groups: graduate students, young people with college or *dazhuan* degrees, and those with *zhongzhuan* education. While the paths young urbanites take in finding work and the types of jobs they look for are often linked to differences in educational level, these three groupings should nonetheless be thought of as heuristic points on a continuum rather than as discrete categories in which individuals' education levels inevitably land them.

Labor market reform and employer demands

Since the late 1970s and throughout the '80s and '90s, market reforms have led to a general relaxation of government control over the economy and the labor market more specifically. These changes have opened many new formal routes to employment. At the same time, reforms have given work units and employers more discretion over hiring decisions, while also forcing them to shoulder more economic responsibility for their operations. In this section, I argue that these changes have both direct and indirect implications for the use of *guanxi* by young people when looking for work.

State job assignments, or *guojia fenpei*, gradually instituted in the 1950s, represented a system by which, in principle, the government's labor bureaus served as the sole means for matching urban workers with jobs. As early as the late 1970s, young people were encouraged to seek alternatives to the standard *fenpei* system (Lu et al., 1994, p. 190), and since then expanded laws covering employment have drastically reduced the scope of *fenpei* for new workers (Ikels 1996, p. 191; Davis 1999, p. 2930). Starting in 1983, only graduates of technical schools and four-year colleges were guaranteed state job allocation (Lu et al. 1994, p. 191), and in 1986, even students with higher education could search for work on their own, though use of this option remained limited (Bian 1994, p. 60). By 1998, when I conducted my interviews, the scope of the *fenpei* system had been drastically curtailed, even at the university (four-year) or vocational college (two-year) level.

There is no doubt that changes to the labor market have been profound. In a recent study of China's labor allocation patterns, political scientist Wang Fei-ling contends that "[b]y the late 1990s, a national labor market had become a highly visible presence and significant player in Chinese labor allocation, although it still needed institutionalization and maturing" (1998, p. 244).[106] What currently

---

105 Gender is also a very important element in determining a young person's "marketability." While my interviews yielded insights regarding the relative positions of men and women in China's job markets, I cannot confidently draw any conclusions specifically regarding use of *guanxi* and gender from my interview data. Therefore, while it is probable that gender differences exist within the group I studied, I will treat *guanxi* use among young men and women as a single issue.

106 Characteristics of China's emergent national labor market, Wang suggests, include mobility (both geographical and social), pay determined by supply/demand, "natural" unemployment, worker

exists and continues to emerge is an extremely fluid and changing system of labor allocation. While laws and rules regarding the job assignment or search process are in place, changes are continuous, and enforcement and even awareness of existing rules irregular (see Bian, this volume).

Nonetheless, reforms have had a disproportionately strong effect on young people. Because many new labor market regulations grandfather existing arrangements, new workers (and workers who switch jobs) are often the first to experience the impact of reforms (e.g., Guthrie 1998b; Lu 1994 et al.).[107] As noted earlier, high school graduates (and youths with even less education) were the first urbanites for whom *fenpei* was ended.

Nowadays, at the college and *dazhuan* levels, an interested employer may directly contact a school that is training students in relevant majors. Schools often serve as the link between students and potential employers (as opposed to labor bureaus operating with labor quotas). Here, the school frequently serves as a conduit for information, not a distributor of jobs or an arbiter of opportunities.[108]

For many, however, finding work on one's own is the only option, and it is increasingly the method of choice, even for those with alternatives. Even among college students, some remarked that nowadays *fenpei* is something people only fall back on when they are unable to find work on their own. While many surely rely on their *guanxi* networks to secure employment, among my interviewees only one individual had clearly secured a job in the past through *guanxi* (a strong tie wielding influence and weighty with obligation and reciprocity). What emerged from interviews and more casual conversations were many fairly attractive and oft-utilized formal and semi-formal routes to employment that have emerged in recent years.

Formal methods included directly applying to a work unit, by letter or phone call. One informant noted that large work units may hold regular tests for interested applicants. Young people favoring this approach tended to be very well-educated, often either with graduate-level training or educated at prestigious undergraduate institutions. Graduate students often simply called or otherwise directly contacted a number of desirable or suitable work units to inquire about hiring possibilities. One young man in Harbin with a recent master's degree in medicine told me that was all he did – he made a couple of phone calls, and ended up with a number of job offers, including attractive ones in Beijing and Shenzhen. His friend and

---

performance as the basis for hiring and promotion, and labor contracts protected by the state and accepted by workers and employers alike (238–9). Wang emphasizes that while these elements by no means represent most labor market situations in China, they are becoming increasingly widespread and institutionalized (252, 259).

107   The institution of the labor contract system and the phasing out of "permanent" employees in the mid-1980s is one example; housing reform policies under which newly hired workers no longer receive housing benefits, at state work units especially, also disproportionately affects new hires.

108   For example, two individuals in my sample found employment when a pharmaceutical factory contacted their school in search of new workers. The school simply posted an announcement regarding job openings, and the two young men signed up for interviews and were later hired.

fellow master's student, Xie Gang, followed a similar procedure, writing letters and making phone calls to potential employers.[109]

Despite a number of other job offers, Xie had to work hard to sell himself to his new employer down in the free-wheeling southern city of Shenzhen. The Sino-foreign joint venture told him that his major was not suited to their line of business. Determined to get himself a job in medicine sales, Xie barraged the company with letters and phone calls, insisting that he could and would be right for the job. In the end, they hired him. Indeed, perhaps Xie had proved that he was well-equipped for sales work. The implication was that, for a first job at least, the highly educated seemed comfortable resorting to formal job search methods.

Another formal search method was attendance at job fairs (*zhaopinhui* or *rencai jiaolinhui*), gatherings that ranged greatly in size and scope and even in the groups to which they cater.[110] Applicants scan job listings and sign up for interviews, sometimes first taking written tests. Newspapers have also come to serve as a source of potential job leads, and like job fairs, the targets of job ads range greatly. Interested applicants either call or visit potential employers and workplaces. All of the lesser-educated people I spoke with (high school education) had looked for work by these methods, as had many of the college and *dazhuan* graduates. Newspapers may also carry advertisements about vocational classes organized with a specific employer (usually in the service sector) in mind. Participation guarantees employment on graduation.

The increased control employers exert over hiring is another relevant aspect of labor market reforms, an aspect of economic and enterprise reform often highlighted by domestic employment research as key to enabling enterprises to become productive and profitable (e.g., Yang 1997b, pp. 26–28, 39–40). Guthrie's discussion of *guanxi* practices in Shanghai's industrial sector cites many managers claiming to hire workers on the basis of competence and not connections (1998a). Likewise, Wang outlines the hiring practices of a number of foreign-invested and privately operated businesses that follow a similar logic (1998, p. 252), and

---

109   When I asked how Xie Gang knew which *danwei* to contact, his response was vague. "You go by feeling (*kao ganjue*)," he said, adding that professors and other students also serve as sources of information. In this particular case, Xie's classmate told him about the existence of this company in Shenzhen (7/17/98). Other recent graduates from master's programs noted that work units themselves might direct a job seeker to another, more suitable unit. It is likely, though no one actually said this to me, that professors, as mentors, serve as important job search resources for graduate students, as is often the case in the United States (Brown 1967, cited in Granovetter 1995b [1974]). Whether these are *guanxi*, strong ties, or weak "professional" ones is debatable. This specific set of social connections will not be explored in depth here.

110   In Beijing, the two-day job fair I attended was massive, attracting some 10,000 job seekers and more than 200 employers. Educational standards were quite high, however; it was rare to see a job opening for anyone with less than a *dazhuan* education. By contrast, at the four different job fairs I visited in Harbin, employers rarely demanded anything higher than high school education, and most jobs involved service or sales work. A young woman in Harbin commented on the contrast between job fairs in the two cities, remarking that compared with Beijing, Harbin's job fairs "are not standard" (*bu zhenggui*).

emphasizes the growing popularity of these labor market practices (259).[111] These findings were reflected in the mindsets of many of my interviewees.

In short, with the rise of an admittedly imperfect labor market, there are many possible routes to employment, and both job seekers and employers may be increasingly open to relying on such mechanisms. The old *fenpei* option is almost gone, and many people doubtlessly still use *guanxi* to find work, but young people in China have a lot of other options too. So why might they opt to rely on newspapers, job ads, and other fairly formal job search methods as opposed to using strong *guanxi* ties? Some reasons why *guanxi* may not be perceived as the best option are further explored next.

Workplace and regional mobility

Many recent changes in China, both general and labor market-related, have made regional and workplace mobility much easier for many Chinese. More and more people are looking to leave home and go elsewhere for work, and they are able and willing to make numerous job changes.[112] What I hope to demonstrate is that in the minds of young urbanites, job and regional mobility are both feasible and desirable and that employment-related mobility is not necessarily tied to the use of *guanxi*. For while workplace and regional moves may sometimes be facilitated by *guanxi*, this was not the case for the majority of my interviewees. In fact, an individual who is highly employable might be better off *not* relying on *guanxi*, which for young people are more likely to be strong family/social ties and tightly bounded geographically. Evidence for this was borne out on two levels: how these young people thought about work and mobility, and how they actually moved from one job (or one place) to another.

Regardless of level of education or area of specialization, most young people I interviewed felt that job changes were both possible and likely. One young college graduate from Liaoning province noted that two years out of college she had looked up a handful of classmates at their original work units and found every one of them had already moved on to a new job (7/7/98). A number of legal or organizational arrangements have made this possible, the most obvious being the replacement of life-long employment with renewable contracts, a gradual change since the mid-1980s (Lu et al., 1994, p. 192). Additionally, the existence of a "trial period" or *shangye shiyongqi* before the signing of a binding contract facilitates employees

---

111   Wang is careful to point out, however, that there are many exceptions, and *guanxi* are still often used in hiring decisions. A perfect example of the complex mix of social ties and formal methods that make up hiring practices in many businesses is the following, quoted in Wang (1998, p. 278): "Liu [owner of a hightech company] described a 'rationalization of his hiring practice, drawing less from friends and relatives and more from "the capable."' Still, the two most important company positions were occupied by Liu's relatives..."

112   I am not making a blanket statement about job mobility in the broader urban population, however. Recent research has shown that despite economic reforms, job mobility for most urban Chinese has remained limited, though this is more true for older Chinese than for younger generations (see Zhou et al. 1997; Wang 1998, p. 140).

both leaving and being fired. Even those who have signed long-term contracts (usually three to five years) can leave, though in order to take their personal dossiers with them they must pay a fine for each remaining contract year.[113]

The critical issue for regional mobility is that of *hukou*, or residence permits.[114] Many interviewees argued that the *hukou* system had lost almost all of its original significance, and if you were able to get a job that pays well enough, you could find housing on your own. "*Hukou* is not a barrier to moving some place new," a male college graduate in Harbin forcefully argued (7/12/98). At a job fair, another young man told me the disadvantages of living in Beijing without a residence permit are few. When pressed on the issue, he offered: "*Hukou* is not important unless you have a child you want to send to school. Perhaps that is very expensive in Beijing"(8/8/98).[115] One striking example of this was Zhang Huarong, a twenty-six-year-old woman enrolled in graduate school solely to improve her chances of moving to Beijing, where her long-time boyfriend lives and works. Zhang's main criterion for a job was that it supply her with a Beijing *hukou*, without which her future child would not get immediate access to schools or childcare facilities. Without a local *hukou*, she argued, such services become prohibitively expensive (7/5/98).[116]

For many, however, workplace and/or regional mobility were both feasible and desirable. This reflects a change in how young people think about jobs, employment, and work generally. Most graduate students adhered to certain standards of professionalism that led them to feel that both regional and workplace mobility

---

113 *Dang'an*, or personal dossiers, are records kept in the personnel departments of work units on every permanent employee (except top leaders). *Dang'an* serve as a complete record of an individual's political and family history, including class background, work evaluations, criticisms, warnings, and punishments. A person's *dang'an* follows him through life, its contents largely unknown, but used to determine promotions, punishments, and targeting in political campaigns (Walder 1986, pp. 91–2).

114 A critical complement to the *danwei*, or work unit, is the system of residential registration (*hukou*) in both urban and rural areas. By 1960, the central government had installed a system of resident permits that effectively ended rural migration into urban areas, enabling the state to guarantee jobs, food, and housing for all urban residents. *Hukou* were issued on the basis of households, but in fact it was "the *danwei* or work unit and not the family" that defined a household (Cheng and Selden 1994).

115 I do not want to overstate the case here; one individual I interviewed did cite *hukou* as a concern, and local Beijing residents felt they had an edge over people without a local *hukou* when applying for a job. Wang also notes the continuing effectiveness of the *hukou* system, especially for low-skilled and non-urban workers (250, 262). For the continued importance of *hukou* for employment in Shanghai, see Davis (1999, p. 31). Sally Sargeson (1999) argues that the rural/urban *hukou* divide delineates the boundaries of two distinct labor markets in urban areas (80).

116 Zhang's concern about having the proper *hukou* is a very real one for women of all educational levels, because when a couple has a child, the child's residence permit "follows" the mother's *hukou*. By contrast, many men and younger women I interviewed, of all educational levels, felt strongly that residence permits were of virtually no significance any more. However, as long as children's permits are linked to those of their mothers, and residence permits are the basis for access to schools and childcare, *hukou* will remain a major concern for many of China's urban women and will impact their job choice and mobility.

were critical to finding a job that would provide them with ample opportunities for development and advancement (and money), hence the desire to go to major cities such as Beijing. Many others of differing levels of education and technical specialization were also articulate on this point.[117]

For example, Du Liming, a college graduate, told me he regrets remaining in his hometown after graduation: "I feel like staying here was a mistake. Harbin doesn't have the kind of large foreign or joint venture companies that I'd really like to be working for. I really wish I could have the opportunity to go out (*chuqu*), to Beijing or maybe somewhere down south. But since I'm about to get married, the chances of that now are pretty slim" (7/12/98). He also emphasized the importance of workplace mobility: "I'll probably look for a new job after I get married. It's really important to switch jobs in order to gain new and broader experience."

The belief that changing jobs is an important part of work experience and a crucial aspect of the development of one's professional life was echoed by many. A young *dazhuan* graduate in Beijing, Luo Anda, remarked of his four different workplaces: "I think since graduation [three years ago], every time I've changed jobs, I've felt like da-da-da [moving up steps]. Wait till I have the skills [*nengli*], [then] I'll go to an even better company." He added, "Maybe I'll [spend my life] within a single industry, but not at a single company or in a single place" (6/27/98). Similarly, a young man from Guangdong province, a college graduate, had worked three or four different jobs in the past two years, and planned to spend another two years in Beijing "working on my career" (*ba shiye gaohao*). He had used job fairs to find work since leaving his first job, a position he found through school (8/8/98).

For those less able to compete for jobs – in this case, the high school graduates I interviewed – job changes were viewed with more reticence. However, Ahong, a young female high school graduate in Harbin, reflected: "In the past two years or so, I haven't held a job for more than three months at a stretch. I left those jobs for lots of different reasons – sometimes I was fired because I didn't have the ability (*nengli*) to do the job, and sometimes I left because the wages were too low. Sometimes I'll work a job until I learn pretty much all there is to learn about it, and then it gets to be boring and I quit . . . My future goals are pretty much to find jobs with higher salaries and to try different jobs . . . With all the changes in China now, there are many, many different types of jobs I can try" (7/22/98).

As Ahong's comments suggest, changing jobs was also tied to specific criteria regarding specific jobs: Salary is most often primary, though work environment was frequently mentioned, and people left specific jobs for all sorts of reasons. Regional mobility was also largely a question of finding better job opportunities. For the ambitious, certain regions and cities were most attractive: Beijing, Shenzhen, Guangzhou, Shanghai, "The South." Some individuals sought cities with good climates and pleasant locations (in addition to growing economies) – Qingdao

117   Deborah Davis (1999) also reports that in Shanghai, recent school graduates expected a high degree of job mobility "until they found an 'ideal job'" (27, note 21). On high job mobility among migrant female factory workers in Shenzhen, see Lee (1998, pp. 81 and 110) and Wang (1998, p. 295, note 85).

and Dalian in the north. Others felt their area of specialization required them to look for suitable jobs in large cities.

How is job mobility, both in terms of perception and practice, related to the use of *guanxi* in finding work? In the case of regional moves, interviewees had often moved to regions not where they had *guanxi* but where they felt job opportunities were good. As a result, they had relied on formal methods to find work. This contrasts sharply with the picture of migration and employment based on localistic ties and networks – a kind of chain migration – Ching Kwan Lee describes for the young, mostly female factory workers from China's countryside whom she studied in Shenzhen (1998, pp. 116–132; see also Wang 1998, p. 270, Sargeson 1999, pp. 90–1). Young, well-educated urbanites appear to simply follow a different pattern – a migration of professionals (Granovetter 1973, pp. 42–3).

This was especially true for young people who had never worked before and did not yet have networks of work-related ties. In one instance, a young woman with a *dazhuan* degree in traditional Chinese medicine went to Beijing because finding work in her home city proved impossible. "All the job openings were restricted to men," she noted. She had no *guanxi* in Beijing and so had relied on job fairs to secure a job (6/30/98). The young man from Guangdong quoted earlier, whose parents were farmers, also relied on formal methods to find work in Beijing (8/8/98). This was also true of all the graduate students I interviewed who had made or were planning to make a regional move, and also of all the college and *dazhuan* graduates, with one exception. In that one case, where a tie was an important factor in determining what location (city) a young woman would move to, the social connection (her uncle) merely provided a place to live. The young woman found work on her own.[118]

As for workplace mobility, I can be less certain in arguing that *guanxi* do not play a role in such switches. But from my interview data, career-oriented job changes, especially among young people, were not likely to be *guanxi*-related.[119] This logically makes sense, as I have argued, because younger workers have fewer contacts, especially of the professional kind. Young people with extremely high job turnover rates – like Ahong in Harbin – could quickly exhaust their job options by relying solely on *guanxi*.

Job specificity and skill marketability

Given an institutional setting that allows for greater mobility, and job mobility in particular, two other issues arise that are of increasing importance to young Chinese urbanites' job market behavior: job specificity and job skill marketability. Here

---

118 This young woman did want to make another move, this time to Shanghai, but she planned to do this through the company she currently worked for.

119 I should point out that certain types of work might actually increase the likelihood of making a job change through social connections. For example, several people I spoke to suggested that some forms of sales work, which put an individual in direct contact with many customers and businesses, can net salespeople numerous job offers.

I use the term "job specificity" in two senses: First, individuals with specialized skills tend to look for jobs that match their specific skill base. A second sense of this term refers to choosing a job on the basis of work environment, advancement opportunities, salary, or even something more mundane such as work hours – the specifics of the job itself. The notion of "job specificity" contrasts with earlier employment patterns where urban Chinese were concerned with their job unit and its location in the bureaucratic hierarchy more than the specific job they would hold there (Bian 1997).

Job specificity has a number of implications for *guanxi* and job searches. In the first sense (looking for work in a specific field or of a specific technical nature), young job seekers may find that their own or their families' *guanxi* networks do not gain them access to these specific jobs. Because these ties are based on family or friend connections, overlap with a young job seeker's occupational needs may be limited. This was the case for many of my interviewees who had majored in a specialized field such as Chinese pharmacology, hotel management, or computer engineering as a college or *dazhuan* student. One young man in Harbin (whose parents were factory workers) specialized in computers as a *dazhuan* student, and relied on job fairs, newspaper ads and the advice of classmates to find employment. His sister majored in the more general and less technical field of accounting and was able to find work through a friend.

Such examples provide an interesting contrast to the ways in which Bian reports that *guanxi* in the 1980s served to channel influence over hiring decisions. He found that *guanxi* was used to secure individuals work in specific work units, but the use of *guanxi* was much less tied to landing a specific position (1997). Now, when people seem to be more concerned about the actual specifics of a job, information is of greater importance. This aspect of *guanxi* – the question of influence or information – will be explored in more detail.

Job skill marketability and job specificity are closely linked. Individuals with high job skill marketability feel confident relying on their formal job qualifications when seeking work. In this way, job search methods also often reflect a young person's relative position within the job market, where the more marketable the skills (or educational credentials) are, the less likely the person is to rely upon *guanxi*. For the very well educated – graduate students and often college and even *dazhuan* graduates – the very skills that make them marketable will in part determine the kinds of jobs they look for. When looking for less technically specific or skill-intensive work, as was characteristic of many of the high school and some *dazhuan* interviewees, salary and work-environment became primary and the use of *guanxi* more salient. Sally Sargeson discovered a similar pattern among the Hangzhou workers she interviewed between 1992 and 1993. Graduates from technical schools had clearly been hired on the basis of skill, whereas unskilled workers usually found work through word-of-mouth. Less advantaged job seekers relied more heavily on *guanxi* (1999, pp. 90–2).

These issues of job specificity, job skill marketability, and *guanxi* are perhaps most important among graduate students, simply by virtue of their specialized training. Indeed, graduate students – in this case, young people with master's degrees – are rare commodities in China, and as a result they enjoy a privileged position in the job market.[120] An obvious consequence is that due to their specialized training, graduate students almost always find work related to their field of study.[121]

Li Xiaoping, a master's student from Shandong, intended to find work in her field of study. One of the implications of this was that Xiaoping and those of her classmates to whom I spoke did not plan to use family contacts in finding work. Their areas of specialization and their families' *guanxi* simply did not overlap. Xiaoping emphasized that her farmer parents pretty much leave her to her own devices: "They think, 'How far you're able to get is how far you get' (*neng zou dao nar jiu zou dao nar*)" (7/4/98). And lacking such *guanxi* was not generally perceived as a problem. Graduate student interviewees felt they were in a good position to compete in a rapidly liberalizing job market. As one talented young master's student confidently noted, "Whoever's the strongest is the most successful" (7/5/98). A newly minted medical doctor in Harbin boasted that "there are plenty of jobs; it's a question of finding a satisfying job" (7/11/98).

Very often, college and *dazhuan* graduates, especially those with "hot" (*remen*) or in-demand majors, also expressed great confidence in their job marketability and their willingness to rely on formal job search methods. Zhou Min, a recent college graduate working as a computer programmer in Beijing, was bursting with confidence about his ability to "compete," in his view a combination of personality and skill level (8/7/98). At a Beijing job fair, a recent college graduate was equally confident about his ability to secure work. "I can always get a job in a hotel," he said. "That's my major" (8/8/98).

Even when not blasé about the ease of finding work, the actual job market behavior of college and *dazhuan* graduates seemed to confirm their strong position in China's urban job market. Lin Fangli found her first job by dropping off resumes at relevant work units. When a unit expressed interest, she successfully convinced it to hire her (7/7/98). Likewise, Luo Anda in Beijing suggested that despite his indecision about what career to pursue (his major was "international trade"), his positive experiences finding work on his own have made him keenly aware of his marketability. It was a matter of knowing what it takes to find a job, knowing how to interview, and how to appear marketable, he said (6/26/98).

Specificity was important for college and *dazhuan* graduates as well, and their *guanxi* networks were often likewise unsuited to netting them the jobs they wanted. For a young woman from the Hebei countryside, her fairly specialized major of

---

120 A recent study of earnings and education in China suggests that in contrast with the past, the positive impact of education on earnings is significant and growing. Rong Wang, "Earnings and Education in Urban China in 1991," PhD dissertation, University of California, Berkeley, 1999.

121 Even in cases where they did not feel any strong attraction toward or interest in their field of study – true of a number of interviewees – graduate students still expected to find work within their field. One young woman in Shenyang noted that because she specializes in pharmacology, only a small number of professional options were open to her (7/5/98). A cautionary note: The master's students I interviewed were all in scientific or medical fields. Graduate students specializing in less technical or scientific fields might feel less constrained by their majors.

Chinese medicine determined her job choice, marketing of medicines to Beijing hospitals (6/30/98). A young woman originally from the Heilongjiang countryside specialized in public health, and had found both her previous and current jobs on her own. Her father, who operates a local bank, employed her brother and sister, both of whom have no specialized or advanced education (7/14/98).

Young people also cited issues such as work environment, management-style, and of course salary as reasons for changing or leaving jobs. For example, Luo Anda disliked the management style in a state-owned company he worked for, and his close friend Feng Lei left a state-owned construction company because he tired of the complex personal relationships there (8/9/98).[122] Other criteria given by interviewees included finding "challenging work" that provided opportunity for both self-improvement ("*fazhan ziji*") and professional advancement. If their social networks did not provide them access to such jobs, these young people found that formal methods could do so.

I do not want to suggest that young job seekers would not utilize connections if they had ones that would get them the specific kinds of jobs they were looking for.[123] Resorting to more formal job search methods might simply be seen as a consequence of lacking the right connections. In addition, when individuals perceive themselves to be highly marketable, formal methods are attractive and seen to provide a wide range of options. For this reason, my argument holds less well for those looking for work in less technical areas, or those who cannot afford to be choosy about what kind of job they end up in.

Indeed, young people with less "specialized" majors ("finance," "trade," or even "accounting") and those with lower levels of education (in this case, high school graduates) faced the job market with less certainty. Competition is stiffer among low- and unskilled urban workers, and *guanxi* can serve to differentiate workers and protect them from exploitative employers (the "institutional holes" Bian discusses, this volume; see also Sargeson 1999, p. 86). Observations at job fairs and interview data indicate that youths with less than a *dazhuan* education were often not even considered for a wide range of higher-paying jobs.[124] The actual experiences of young workers also bear this out. In Harbin, Ahong, said: "I had worked for almost three years doing accounting in a joint venture company when it was decided that

---

122 Feng specifically said that he disliked the need to *biaoxian*, or present a false appearance of flattery and supportiveness, to work superiors (see Walder 1986).

123 Wang gives examples where family and privately run businesses hire workers this way (1998, pp. 265, 275–7), as do Sargeson (1999, p. 90) and Lee (1998, pp. 84–88) in the context of unskilled, migrant workers.

124 While this seemed truer of jobs formally advertised in Beijing, a magnet for well-educated talent, than in Harbin, even in Harbin any job with the tag "manager" (*jingli*) required at least a two-year college degree. For young high school graduates with little or no job experience, the types of jobs they seek are generally ones with which they consider their education level commensurate. Most of the high school interviewees, and sometimes the technical school grads, sought low-level service work – that is, low prestige and often fairly low-paying positions. These jobs ranged from store clerks and cashiers to restaurant waiters, "greeters" *jiedai renyuan* (door attendants), and sales positions.

the company would only employ people with a *daxue* (four-year college) degree or higher. So I stepped down. We all felt very badly about it . . . I don't think the new policy was very fair. People should be hired on the basis of ability (*nengli*) and not educational level (*xueli*)" (7/22/98).

Twenty-six-year-old Zhao Jun had worked in a number of low-paying service jobs in Harbin since finishing school, despite his *dazhuan* education. His first job experience was common among young urbanites, especially those with less specialized training. Zhao Jun found his first job through a job fair, a job he thought was going to be computer programming but turned out to be clerking in the company's store. Zhao's boss was highly critical of his performance; what is more, after fifty days of work, Zhao had only been paid 100 yuan of the 300 per month he had been promised. "I didn't understand anything just after college! . . . I was so green (*shengshou*). The 300 yuan per month I was supposed to get is the lowest salary offered by such companies. There are several companies in the computer business that you always see at the job fairs; they are always looking for new workers [because they don't pay wages as they should]. It makes you think those things [job fairs] are just set up to cheat people!" (7/15/98).

For such reasons, job specificity for high school and *zhongzhuan* graduates was largely a question of salary. A couple of interviewees had started out working in factories, but in each case they switched to service work. These jobs paid more and provided a more pleasant environment but invariably required longer hours and had less job security. A number of people in this group expressed mild regret that the government no longer guaranteed them employment.[125] Such sentiment was perhaps in reaction to two things: the vulnerability these young people felt at work, and bad experiences finding work. Zhao Jun, mentioned earlier, described a "good job" as "A stable job. With the job I have now, I could get fired at any time. When my boss gets angry, I get really worried." This is one of the drawbacks of switching from the "iron rice bowl" to a "clay" one, he added (7/15/98).

Consequently, this group of interviewees was more likely than their better-educated or more technically specialized peers to rely on family and friends – strong ties, but not workplace-based – in finding employment. Zhao Hui, for example, found both her first and second jobs through *guanxi*. In the first case, her uncle managed to get her work at a local cement factory, in the factory's "quality control" laboratory. More recently, however, Zhao Hui had found work as an accountant at a small photo shop. This second job she found through a friend who, knowing the shop was in need of an accountant and that Zhao Hui had studied accounting, told her about the job and provided her with an introduction (7/15/98).

Ahong, quoted earlier, also found her first job through a relative, in a clear case of *guanxi* use. But it is interesting to note that her connections were not good enough

125 It should be pointed out, however, that with the exception of lost benefits and the pitfalls of finding work, the old *fenpei* system was not considered superior to the current situation. *Fenpei* jobs are associated with financially troubled state work units, low wages, and dull jobs. Two different women commented that even if they did work for a state *danwei*, they would certainly moonlight on the side (*gao di'er zhiye*).

to preserve her job when the company policy regarding educational requirements changed. Since losing that job, Ahong had relied almost entirely on job fairs and advertisements in local newspapers to find work (7/22/98).[126] By contrast, Zhao Jun had relied on a job fair to find his first job. Since that bad experience, he suggested, he is more likely to rely on friends when looking for work. He found his fourth and current job through a tip from a classmate (7/15/98).

For those well-placed in China's urban job market, formal job search options are often effective, particularly given the high marketability and specific job criteria that highly educated youth bring to their job searches. For young people, especially first-time job seekers, job fairs and directly applying to potential employers can provide a better net for job opportunities than *guanxi*. For other urban youths whose labor and skills are in less demand, however, the effectiveness of using *guanxi* to secure employment relative to formal methods is less clear. As Bian (this volume) suggests, they may need *guanxi* to distinguish themselves from other job seekers and to establish bonds of trust and obligation with an employer. However, their use of *guanxi* to find employment is tempered in two respects. First, as noted, sometimes a friend would simply pass on information about a job opening – would this then be *guanxi*? Second, there was general agreement among my sources that even with *guanxi*, one must still rely on one's own merits to hold on to a job. This brings us to back to the question of *guanxi*, *guanxixue*, and social ties, how they are used and how they are distinct.

Guanxi *or ties?*

Keeping in mind the factors laid out here, some of the theoretical questions regarding *guanxi* raised at the beginning of this chapter bear revisiting. First, I want to consider the question of how interviewees thought about *guanxi* – that is, how useful or effective or even appropriate *guanxi* is for finding a job. Second, I would like to contrast these opinions with the actual use of social connections in job searches, as related to me by young people. Do they, in fact, practice *guanxixue* – that is, an instrumental use of *guanxi*?

Mayfair Yang's treatment of *guanxi* in *Gifts, Favors and Banquets* again provides a useful framework. Yang found popular discourse characterized the instrumental use of social connections in several ways: There were pejorative, mixed, and morally neutral stances (50). Although these categories are not a perfect match for the kinds of attitudes I encountered, most opinions on the use of *guanxi* to find a job fell on a similar continuum. I might add to, or extend, this continuum somewhat to include another position: skepticism, at times bordering on disdain, regarding the use and usefulness of *guanxi*.

126   Ahong's reliance on formal job search methods reflected her relatively good position in Harbin's job market. Many of the jobs advertised in newspapers and job fairs are service work, for which employers wish to hire young women. When I asked her if being female made finding work more difficult (as is the case for highly educated women; see e.g., Honig and Hershatter 1988; Li 1997), Ahong scoffed at the idea.

Yang suggests many conflicting attitudes about *guanxixue* coexist not simply because people occupy different structural positions within society, but also because China "is undergoing specific social changes or a historical shift from one worldview and set of habits and interpretations to another" (49–50), what Swidler would characterize as an "unsettled" period (1986, p. 277). I would like to echo Yang's assertion while emphasizing that structural positions (or social positions, as Guthrie notes, this volume) *do* play an important role in how individuals feel about *guanxi*.

Specifically, individuals who either lacked good *guanxi* resources or did not need such connections to find work were often dismissive or negative about the use of *guanxi*. Luo Anda in Beijing suggested that using *guanxi* to find work is unfair.[127] (He added: "I have no such connections.") Luo continued: "Even if you have connections, [if] you are not the best man for the position, you [won't] get the position, I think . . . unless your dad's the boss – then it doesn't matter!" (6/26/98). Zhao Hui, who was matched up with her employer by a friend, maintained that she was able to keep her job because she is hard working; just that week, her boss had fired two lazy workers. Zhao pointed out that when she considered leaving the job to devote more time to her studies, her boss had made special concessions to her schedule in order to keep her on as an employee (7/15/98).

Young people lacking *guanxi* and disparaging its use nonetheless did not totally discount the effectiveness of *guanxi*. A young office worker in Beijing noted that most of the people in her office were "relatives of the boss"; for this reason, she felt she had little opportunity for advancement, and wanted to move to the company's Shanghai office (8/9/98). Xie Gang, the Harbin graduate student headed to Shenzhen, turned down a potentially attractive job offer at a research institute because he believed the work unit was parochial (and by extension, unprofessional). "Without *guanxi*, I could work a lifetime at that unit and never be promoted very high in the organization," he said (7/17/98). Lin Fangli, a graduate student in Shenyang, spoke of the tiresome nature of *guanxi* in her previous job: "There were some 200 employees at this school, though only about 70 of them were actually teachers. The rest had gotten hired through *guanxi*. You had to be careful not to offend (*dezui*) anyone, especially those people with *guanxi*. Otherwise all sorts of things became difficult, like *baoxiao* (getting reimbursed for work expenses). There was pressure to hang out with these people, to maintain good relations. I was just a young woman . . . I didn't feel like I should have to waste time playing cards and mahjongg with such people" (7/7/98).

Among the well-educated, relying on *guanxi* to find work was often regarded as both unprofessional and indicative of weakness or lack of ability on the part of the *guanxi*-user.[128] For example, on his graduation from college, Du Liming's

127 Sargeson (1999) found that among the workers she studied, use of *guanxi* and localistic favoritism were the key elements of what they perceive to be "unfairness" in the workplace (174). See also Lee 1998.

128 This provides a striking contrast to the popular interpretation of *guanxi* in the 1980s. Gold (1985) reports: "As people see it, *guanxi* is the basis for personal relations because it works; playing by

parents (city government officials) wanted to use their connections to find him a government job. At the time, Du wanted to look for work on his own (which he did), and he still feels this way today, arguing, "It is important to do something on your own" (7/30/98). Tang Xiaoli, a college graduate working in Qingdao, expressed a similar sentiment: "When I was looking for a job, I could have asked my family for help." Her brother-in-law's family operates two stores, and Tang's brother works in one of them as a manager. With her background in accounting, Tang could easily have gotten work there, but instead she decided to go it alone: "Having gone to college [the only one in my family], I ought to have the ability to find a job on my own." So she went to job fairs and asked friends for job leads; someone directed her to the company for whom she now works. Still, finding work was a stressful process, Tang suggested, and "looking back I kind of regret not asking my family for help" (8/1/98).

Again, I do not want to suggest that young people would not utilize their *guanxi* if it were to their advantage to do so. Feng Lei left his job at a state construction company in Beijing only because a friend had already arranged another job for him (8/9/98).[129] What was considered a sign of weakness or incompetence was (when an option at all) the use of one's family's *guanxi*, especially one's parents connections. Many of the young people I interviewed fully expected to develop their own networks of professional connections during their careers. But is this distinctively *guanxi*? Will these ties be strong ones or, with changes to the workplace and the economy in China, weak ones? Granovetter's 1973 study and the job market research it has inspired attest to the importance of personal relationships in facilitating job searches and changes throughout the world. As Guthrie (this volume) notes, using a neoclassical economic ideal type as a point of comparison obscures the fact that *all* economic systems are embedded in social networks, making any sort of social connection appear to be *guanxi* use.

A strict definition of *guanxi* is necessary to fully evaluate the case of Lin Fangli, the woman above who complained about *guanxi*. She said that she lost her first job out of college when someone with *guanxi* managed to take her job, and later found her current work unit (she was sent to graduate school by this unit) through hearing of a job opening from a friend. The friend did not, however, get Lin the job – she had to convince the school that she was just the person it needed – but she would not have known about the position at all without her friend's information (7/7/98).

So was this *guanxi* in the sense Yang (and even Bian) defines it? Is a job tip, which Lin implied this was, instrumental use of *guanxi*, infused with obligation and reciprocity, or just information passed through a social tie? Given the changes in China outlined earlier, might weak ties begin to be of increasing importance to the job trajectories of China's new cohorts of skilled and professional workers?

the rules takes much longer – if it ever bears fruit – and is something only the very naïve or inept would resort to" (662).

129   It seems likely that because Feng Lei was already four years out of school at that point, his friends and old classmates could serve as useful job contacts, unlike most of my other interviewees.

Other examples that people gave of friends trying to help friends find jobs suggest that these information exchanges are not heavily imbued with notions of obligation or reciprocity, partly because information was often transmitted by individuals who had little power over whether the job seeker got hired or not. Friends, just embarking on their own careers, simply did not wield much influence in their own workplaces or were perhaps in the job market themselves. Zhao Jun pointed out the limits to finding work by relying on information passed on by friends: "Friends certainly serve as an important way to find work, but you've got to have the skills to do the job in the first place. Just today I tried to help a friend get a job at a neighboring computer company but he wasn't hired. He didn't have a background in computers, and was unfamiliar with the way computer stores work [so the job introduction wasn't enough] (7/15/98). A young woman in Beijing had a similar experience trying to help a friend find a job. Through her sales work, she knew of a company looking for a secretary, and so introduced her friend to the boss there. Her friend was heavy-set, and as a result not hired (8/9/98).[130]

For the majority of my interviewees, it was connections with friends, passing on information, or advice for a job search that served as important social resources. Luo Anda works for a company he learned about from a friend. He added that when he first started looking for work, he would talk to friends about what interviews were like. He found his father and mother limited sources of help: "Because [they are] older, and couldn't give me good advice, [so] I [would] ask my friends and get some good ideas [that way]." Now he was experienced enough that his friends "ask me." Luo's friend Feng Lei first went to a job fair at Luo's encouraging (6/26/98).

Within the narrow context of finding a job, these particular relationships would appear to be strong ties through which information flows. Exchange of information does not appear to be a heavy, long-term investment, and it is a favor that may or may not produce the desired result. There is reciprocity – after all, these are friendships – but in a labor market full of change and uncertainty, networks of friends serve practical roles within the job search process. Mayfair Yang observed one consequence of economic reforms to be that "impersonal money has begun to replace some of the affectively charged relationships created by gifts and reciprocal favors" (171). Is it not equally possible that market mechanisms could also remove the impetus for the instrumental use of *guanxi*? Is any strong tie in China *guanxi*? The importance of making this distinction is clear: Many of the factors described earlier – the nature of young people's social contacts, institutional changes in employment and the labor market, and changes in where and what kinds of jobs young people desire – have created conditions under which instrumental ties may be no more effective than formal and semi-formal avenues to employment for this group. Under such circumstances, social relationships do not disappear; they just reflect those circumstances and probably should not be labeled "*guanxi*."

---

130   I do not want to overstate my case. Both Zhao Hui and her brother Zhao Jun had bosses with equal or less education than themselves but who, because of their families' economic resources, were able to start their own businesses. Lin Fangli lost her job to someone with *guanxi*, an instance where social connections might have been unfair but effective.

Where circumstances have not changed, the instrumental application of social connections remains strong. Yang predicts: "So long as the state redistributive apparatus predominates, there will be a need for *guanxi* to obtain through political channels what is not available through the market" (310). My data bear this out. Zhang Huarong, the young woman determined to secure herself a Beijing residence permit, said she might have to use *guanxi* (and here she specifically meant *zou houmen*, or "take the back door" – an explicit reference to *guanxixue*) (7/5/98). Zhou Min, the computer technician in Beijing, alluded to the use of "*guanxi*" when switching jobs as a way to avoid payment of the fine for breaking his contract and still holding onto his personal dossier, or *dang'an* (6/27/98). Another, slightly different, example is that of Du Liming, who made a point of *not* using his parents' connections to find a job yet did rely on his parents' connections to secure housing. Du, who worked for a Sino-foreign joint venture company with no housing provisions, was about to be married, and wanted his own apartment (7/12/98). For someone of his economic means, purchasing an apartment without relying on *guanxi* would have been impossible. In all three cases, individuals instrumentally used *guanxi* in contexts similar to those Yang details – opposition to bureaucracy – highlighting the connection between *guanxixue* and state control (in this case, of scarce goods). Housing shortages, residence permits, and personal files all characterize life under Chinese socialism.[131]

CONCLUSION

So in both perception and in practice, *guanxi* did not play a major role in the job searches of my interviewees. In fact, there was significant reliance on formal job search methods and a measured degree of skepticism about the effectiveness, and at times the appropriateness, of using *guanxi*. How are we to understand this change?

I want to suggest that because the instrumental use of *guanxi* is strategic (in the sense that it draws on culturally shaped skills but is historically situated), it is changeable. When individuals go about looking for work in urban China, they take their *guanxi* "tool kits" with them, but that does not mean they find all those tools useful or appropriate. Guthrie provides an institutional and structural argument as to why the importance of *guanxi* in hiring decisions is on the decline. This argument and the picture drawn in my chapter are very different from the one Yanjie Bian describes for the 1990s, but they are not, I believe, inherently contradictory. Whereas Bian has described how labor market and legal imperfections lead to "institutional holes," and *guanxi* patches up those gaps in information, trust, and obligation, the picture I present is one of holes in *guanxi* webs.

---

131   Sargeson argues that "free market" hiring situations characterized by intense competition, such as those encountered by unskilled and semi-skilled workers, also promote the use of *guanxi* as individuals need to distinguish themselves from other potential workers, an argument that parallels Bian's "institutional holes" (Sargeson 1999, p. 86; Bian, this volume).

As I have tried to demonstrate, larger economic and social changes are behind the job search behavior I observed young people practicing in China's cities, and of course young people's stage in life is also important. Market reforms have largely dismantled the old system of centralized job allocation, forcing most young urbanites to find work on their own. And why do they not rely more on *guanxi*? Many of the individuals I spoke to believe employers are increasingly likely to hire workers on the basis of merit. In addition, youths in search of better job opportunities are now able and willing to move (both in terms of work unit and in terms of city) in search of work, and this mobility, I argue, is for young people often less conducive to the use of *guanxi*. What is more, young people, particularly those with specialized training, feel they have a choice in what kind of work they do, and consequently look for specific jobs – jobs to which their *guanxi* might not give them access; other *guanxi* may supply information but little or no influence over their ability to accrue job opportunities. And for those in a particularly strong position in the urban job market (namely, the more educated), their marketability makes them confident about and willing to rely on their merits and qualifications in their job searches.

This is not just a case of exceptionalism, however. If work ties grow in importance for young urbanites as their careers progress, will those ties be *guanxi* in the strict sense of strong ties imbued with the weight of obligation and reciprocity? Will those ties be strong or weak? What is missing here, then, is the "cultural" side of this picture: a more explicit treatment of the notions about the shape a career should take, what appropriate job market behaviors are, and the like. I would locate these at a level of a common sense that is being reconstructed through new labor market practices and institutions. Job fairs, school information sessions on job search tactics, and even informal channels of information among friends and classmates all contribute to changing ideas about what a job should be and how one should acquire it. The skepticism young people often expressed about *guanxi*, both in regard to its effectiveness as a means of securing employment and how its use reflects on their own abilities, are suggestive of broader changes. Though an exploration of these issues is beyond the scope of this chapter, my findings here suggest that the effect of economic, institutional, and broad social change on *guanxi*, or social relationships, in China is a dynamic one. If this exploration into the role of *guanxi* in finding a job does not produce concrete conclusions, it does perhaps serve to evoke a flavor of change.

8

FACE, NORMS, AND INSTRUMENTALITY

Scott Wilson

During the first half of the 1990s, I researched the social and political consequences of the local economic reforms and transformation of two villages in periurban Shanghai. Over the course of two decades since the introduction of Deng's economic reforms in 1978, those villages experienced the reintroduction of a cash economy, the rapid expansion of rural industry, integration into regional labor markets, and encroachment of urban life on village soil. Almost every facet of villagers' social life – daily routines, regular interactions, and the mode of exchange – changed. This chapter traces the social changes wrought by economic reforms and the attendant transformation of local economic practice. In particular, I will analyze the changing contours of Chinese particularistic ties, *guanxi*. To preview my findings, I will argue that the economic reforms significantly recast *guanxi* in two ways: (1) *guanxi* became increasingly imbued with a commercial quality, and (2) the geographical distance of *guanxi* increased as a result of integration into the regional economy. Both of these developments would seem to lead to a greater emphasis on instrumentalism in social relations. However, I find that the development of cash-based exchange and long-distance *guanxi* are not inherently more instrumental than labor-based and proximate *guanxi*.

The chapter analyzes the mutual aid and money-based exchanges that occur during the agricultural busy season (*nongmang*) and during house construction. After local decollectivization in 1983, the pre-revolutionary practice in agriculture reemerged. I account for the reappearance and later decline in agricultural mutual aid. When building a new or refurbishing an old house, villagers engage in numerous forms of social exchange including lending money, offering gifts, and practicing mutual aid. The reemergence of the cash nexus eroded some types of social exchange while enhancing others. A comparison of the social exchanges for these two matters reveals some of the significant changes in village social relations. These two cases are particularly important because both are sensitive to economic changes. Shifts in household labor allocation and regional labor markets can undermine a family's ability to engage in mutual aid and hire workers for agriculture. Improved living standards contribute to the building of new and the improvement of old houses. In other words, the expanding cash nexus and rising incomes imperil fundamental social exchanges within villagers' social networks. Furthermore, the shifts in social exchanges will be used to indicate the transformation of *guanxi*.

THEORETICAL ISSUES

Over the last decade, Chinese particularistic ties, or *guanxi*, have attracted increasing scholarly attention. Since Fei Xiaotong's study of rural China in the 1940s (trans. 1992), scholars have believed such ties form (at least one of) the main building blocks of that society. Throughout the Maoist and early Deng eras, *guanxi* persisted, and often took a patron-client form (Walder 1985 and Oi 1989), which resulted from state centralization of economic resources and politically charged mass campaigns. Yet the Deng era witnessed a rapid set of economic reforms that altered the resources controlled by the state. More recently, the impact of these economic reforms (usually described in "marketization" terms) on *guanxi* has received scholarly attention. At the heart of this debate are two matters: (1) Have the economic reforms undermined the basis of and reliance upon *guanxi* (Guthrie 1998a), and (2) have the economic reforms made *guanxi* more instrumental. Elsewhere, I have summarized many of these changes as the reemergence of a "cash nexus" in the countryside (Wilson 1997). This chapter builds on my earlier work on the cash nexus and social relations and extends the discussion to examine the issue of instrumentalism.

According to many preeminent social theorists such as Simmel, Weber, and Marx, the introduction of markets and a cash economy erode particularistic attachments such as *guanxi*. Max Weber wrote,

Money is the most abstract and impersonal element that exists in human life. The more the world of the modern capitalist economy follows its immanent laws, the less accessible it is to any imaginable relationship with a religious ethic of brotherliness . . . no personal bonds of any sort exist. (1946, p. 331.)

Similarly, Georg Simmel linked money to objectivity and lack of emotion, calling it a "prostitute." "The indifference as to its use, the lack of attachment to any individual because it is unrelated to any of them, the objectivity inherent in money as a mere means which excludes any emotional relationship – all this produces an ominous analogy between money and prostitution" (1990, p. 377). To both Weber and Simmel, the rise of capitalism and its attendant reliance on money undermines social relations.[132]

132   For an excellent discussion of the grand theorists' views of money and social relations, see Zelizer (1994, pp. 6–30). Zelizer challenges the notion that money is perfectly fungible by documenting the way people "earmark" money and variously handle different types of money. Bloch and Parry (1998) suggest that the handling of money is embedded in local cultures and cosmologies, which implies that money is not a universal medium of exchange that breaks down social bonds.

More recently, Anthony Giddens has linked the use of money with modernity. Giddens calls money one of the two "disembedding mechanisms" of modernity (1990, p. 22). "By disembedding [Giddens] mean[s] the 'lifting out' of social relations from local contexts of interaction and their restructuring across indefinite spans of time-space" (1990, p. 21). According to Giddens, the transition to modernity encompasses a shift from kinship relations orienting social ties to "personal relationships of friendship or sexual intimacy" becoming the basis of social relations (1990, p. 102). Yunxiang Yan's contrast of social relations at the "inner core" of social networks (composed of close kin) to the more instrumental relations outside of the village parallels aspects of Giddens' analysis of space and intimacy.

Studies of Chinese social ties trace similar social transformations as those depicted by Simmel and Weber. Authors describe village social relations in terms of "sentiment" (*renqing*) and affection (*ganqing*). Rural social relations are considered to be so because of the strong sense of community within villages and, in part, based on a moral economy that characterizes village life rather than a fully marketized economy. Fei Xiaotong distinguishes intra-village relations from market relations outside the village, which he said are "without human feelings (*wuqing*)" (1992, p. 126). Following Fei, Yunxiang Yan characterizes gift exchanges that extend beyond the village as "indirect payments," "flattery gifts," and "lubricating gifts" (1996a, p. 101). More directly, Yan writes, "a clear line can be drawn between the village community and the outside world, paralleling the distinction between expressive and instrumental gift-giving activities. . . . [A]ll instrumental gift-giving relations go beyond the village boundary" (1996a, p. 102). According to Yan, such instrumental exchanges differ from intra-village gift exchanges, which follow *renqing* (ethical) practices. Similarly, Mayfair Yang compared urban and rural gift exchanges and found that in the latter, *renqing* outweighed instrumentalism (1994, p. 312).[133]

Studies of urban *guanxi* have emphasized its instrumental uses and corrupting influence. For example, Wong Siu-lun found Hong Kong entrepreneurs of Chinese origin relied on personal ties to get bank loans and to get business orders (1991, p. 20). Barbara Ward observed that Hong Kong factory managers used personal ties to recruit scarce skilled laborers (1972, p. 364). In a study of Tianjin's labor market, Bian Yanjie (1994) asserted that social ties were important in securing favorable employment. David Wank's study of recent political economy in Xiamen reveals that private entrepreneurs use *guanxi* with local officials to gain licenses and protection (1996).

Typically, authors have described urban and rural social relations (*guanxi*) in dichotomous terms. For example, Mayfair Yang "found *renqing* to be preponderant in discursive practice over the more instrumental *guanxi*" (1994, p. 312).

---

133 Douglas Guthrie's distinction between *guanxi* and *guanxixue*, a term that he borrows from Mayfair Yang, I believe, implies a similar dichotomization of *renqing* and instrumentalism (1998). My own work has focused on such a dichotomy of exchanges (1997).

Elsewhere, Yang calls the "urban art of *guanxi* . . . a particular instrumentalized and politicized form of a more traditional body of *renqing* principles and rural gift economy" (1994, p. 320). Similarly, Godwin Chu and Yanan Ju surveyed urban and rural citizens in the Shanghai area and found a distinction between the two groups' attitudes toward social relations.

Generally, relations with others appear to be much less intimate than those with relatives; they tend to be superficial. Money seems to become increasingly important as a factor influencing social relations. . . . However, the traditional value of repaying kindness, a very important cornerstone of social relations in China, is still largely honored, although *there are clear signs of erosion in urban areas.* (1993, p. 101, emphasis added.)

Recast in Yunxiang Yan's terms, *renqing* is declining in relations, and instrumentalism and the use of money are being inserted in social relations. In sum, most studies of Chinese *guanxi* posit that the urban-rural dichotomy roughly aligns with an ethical-instrumental dichotomy.

In this chapter, I challenge such a strict dichotomy of norm-based and instrumental social relations and social exchanges.[134] I will show that villagers rely on proximate social relations to derive utilities. Moreover, even gifts and other social exchanges that outwardly appear expressive influence how other villagers view a person's standing, or face (*mianzi*) (see also Smart 1993, p. 402). David Ho defines face as "the respectability and/or deference which a person can claim for himself from others, by virtue of the relative position he occupies in his social network and the degree to which he is judged to have functioned adequately in that position as well as acceptably in his general conduct . . ." (1976, p. 883). Following norms in social exchanges adds to one's face, a form of social capital (Hwang 1987, pp. 953–957).[135] Earlier studies of business practice in Chinese social milieux assert that one's reputation, which is almost analogous to face, shapes one's ability to succeed in business. Applied to the villages analyzed here, maintaining one's face is a prerequisite for acquiring capital and material goods through social relations.[136]

I conducted the research for this chapter in peri-urban Shanghai, in villages that previously engaged in agricultural production but in the 1990s were slowly engulfed by factories and urban sprawl. The location of the research is significant

---

134   Alan Smart implicitly challenges such a dichotomy by rejecting a strict distinction between gifts and bribes (1993, pp. 401–402). Thomas Gold notes that "[t]he pre-eminent characteristic of personal relations in China today is instrumentalism. . . . It is not a cold exchange but is intertwined with *renqing* . . . and may also be based on a degree of *ganqing* (affect)" (1985, pp. 659–660). However Gold observes more "comradeship" with its emphasis on equality than "friendship," which is rooted in unequal relations, in China's countryside (1985, p. 666). Similarly, Wong Siu-lun notes that Chinese entrepreneurs in Hong Kong mix instrumental and expressive social relations (1991, p. 21). Finally, Andrew Kipnis asserts that gift relations in Fengjia village, Shandong province, combine aspects of instrumentality and affection (1996, pp. 285–314).

135   Alan Smart (1993) also analyzes bribery and gift exchange in terms of social capital, a term he borrows from Pierre Bourdieu.

136   This point echoes the work of Robert H. Silin, who describes the importance of reputation and trust in gaining credit (1972, p. 338).

for two reasons: (1) The locale stands in the middle of the dichotomy of isolated villages and urban anomie, and (2) since 1978, the locale has been in the process of rapid industrialization and urbanization caused by spillover from Shanghai municipal development. The proximity to a major metropolitan center and the growing number of linkages to the urban economy has shaped villagers' social networks. In the context of the Chinese villages under study, how have the rapid social, political, and cultural transformations that accompanied the Deng era economic reforms altered the importance and formation of *guanxi*?

In the research site, villagers who extended their networks beyond the village, especially those engaged in commerce or industrial production, had opportunities to establish ties to people in urban Shanghai. The incorporation of urban social ties holds out the possibility of a radical restructuring of social relations in village networks. Has such an extension of ties outside the core of village social relations diminished the importance of *renqing* and substituted instrumentalism? This chapter concludes that the line between instrumentality and *renqing* ethics is a fine and, sometimes, indistinguishable one.

VILLAGE LEVEL CHANGES

Changes in the local economy

Since 1978, the local political economy has fundamentally changed in at least three ways. First, rural industry has rapidly expanded and encroached upon agricultural fields. In 1978, the beginning of the reform period, local agricultural production only contributed 27 percent of the township income (*Local Township Economic Documents*, 1983, p. 28). By 1990, agriculture, despite steady increases in aggregate production, contributed a scant 5 percent to the township income (*Local Township Economic Documents*, 1990, p. 2).[137] The contribution of rural industry grew from 54 percent of township income in 1978 to 78 percent in 1990 (*Local Township Economic Documents*, 1983, p. 28 and 1990, p. 2). The remaining share was contributed by the tertiary sector.

Village industrial employment kept pace with this major economic shift. In the aggregate, village industrial employment expanded from 124 workers in 1980 to 608 in 1990 (*Local Township Economic Documents*). Interviewed families had all placed at least one (and many families several) family member into non-agricultural work. About half of the interviewees worked in village-run factories; most of the other half labored in township-run factories, and a small but growing number found work beyond the township.

Second, villagers have made the transition from a remuneration system based primarily on barter to a cash economy. This transition and the positive results of the rural economic reforms have left villagers with much more cash in their hands. Factory employment has significantly raised the income levels of villagers. During

---

137 Such figures underestimate the importance of agriculture in the villages' economy. The township includes a large number of residents who own no land and therefore are not engaged in farming.

the period 1977–1995, workers in village factories increased their income from 279 *yuan* per year to 5000–6000 *yuan* (1750–2100 in 1977 *yuan*), a seven-fold increase in real terms.[138]

Third, villagers slowly have been integrated into regional labor markets. In Shanghai, the reinvigoration of local commerce and the rapid expansion of industry offered villagers opportunities to find employment up the regional hierarchy and outside of their production team, village, township, and even county. Most villagers work in village- or township-run factories, but a few have found employment in units outside of the county (now, Minhang District) or municipal levels. Similarly, workers from outside Shanghai and mainly from poorer provinces entered the village to seek out employment. Many of these "outsiders" sought itinerant work in the fields, either helping with transplanting or harvesting crops. Other outside workers found longer-term employment in construction[139] or, more rarely, in factories.

Changes in village guanxi networks

These fundamental economic changes directly and indirectly reshaped villagers' social networks and exchanges, eroding the cellular wall around villages. The transition to industrial employment brought villagers into contact with new people and restructured the workday. Prior to the takeoff of industrialization after 1978, villagers worked together in the agricultural fields.[140] Cooperation was instituted in the form of agricultural production brigades (administrative villages) and production teams (natural villages or "small groups," *xiaozu*). The latter groups were formed around clusters of families, many of whom were related by kinship or lineage ties, which Yunxiang Yan calls the "inner core" and the "reliable zone" (composed of friends and relatives) of rural social networks (Yan 1996a, pp. 99–100).[141] Such social networks and the social exchanges that took place within them were limited in geographical scope.

Rural industrialization broke down these isolated production brigades and teams. In the early wave of village industrialization, village officials claimed eminent domain on teams' agricultural land in order to build factories. In turn, affected team

138   These figures come from estimates by local officials. The income figures were deflated using the rural retail price indexes in the State Statistical Bureau of the People's Republic of China (1993); Joint Publication Research Service, China Report (94-058); and Bennett (1995).

139   During the 1980s, rural China experienced a housing boom due to expanding income and loosened restrictions on consumerism. Shanghai was at the forefront of this house construction wave, which continued locally through the mid-1990s. For an excellent discussion of the rural house construction "rage," see Zhang (1991).

140   In fact, officials divided the local collective fields for the household responsibility system in 1983, much later than most villages. The relative success of collective agriculture in the lower Yangzi (Sunan) region and the high level of anti-capitalist rhetoric and campaigns in Shanghai help account for the late division of the local fields. For a discussion of this topic, see Jiang (1991).

141   As Yunxiang Yan notes, the boundary between the "inner core" and the "reliable zone" is a fluid one. Best friends may be closer, in terms of affection, than relatives, and therefore belong in the inner core.

members were usually compensated with factory jobs. This process transferred team members together into the same factories. Factories that came on line roughly after 1989, and especially those above the village level, brought production team members into factories with workers from outside their teams, villages, and even township. The construction of work-related social relations (*tongshi guanxi*) in the factories thus geographically extended villagers' social networks. Village-run industries were important in another respect. Through industrial employment, villagers gained access to resources such as trucks that factories had under their control. Villagers drew on their co-worker ties with those who drove vehicles to move corpses at funerals and transport building materials for house construction.

Rural industrialization also reordered the rhythm of village life. Agricultural life is punctuated by busy seasons such as the period for transplanting rice and harvesting crops. In between these peaks, villagers experienced slower periods of work or intervals of no agricultural production. During such times, villagers could engage in non-agricultural sideline production or work that did not generate income such as refurbishing houses. Rural industrialization reordered villagers' workdays. Villagers worked in factories for eight or more hours, six days a week, most weeks of the year. The factory work schedule left few unaccounted hours for non-productive activities, and limited the casual daily encounters among villagers. Even more importantly, regimented factory work limited villagers' ability to engage in mutual aid exchanges.

Shifts in village social exchange

The reemergence of the cash nexus altered both the frequency of exchange and the medium of exchange within social networks. Under the Maoist political economy, villagers did not engage in many social exchanges for three reasons (see also Wilson 1997). First, campaigns against "the four olds" (*sijiu*) and other traditional celebrations suppressed such ritualized activities and the social exchanges that accompanied them. Second, villagers received most of their remuneration for work in the form of material goods rather than cash (Zweig 1989). As a result, villagers had little money to offer as gifts or loans to their social relations. Finally, villagers had few things to celebrate. Villagers rarely had sufficient resources to build new houses or even to host banquets.

During the Mao era, villagers exchanged the factor of production that they had in abundance – their labor. Mutual aid, an informal exchange of labor days, was institutionalized in agricultural production teams. Villagers would also help one another with small house construction projects. For wedding celebrations, villagers offered gifts such as quilts, clothes, and shoulder poles that embodied family labor inputs. Concomitantly, villagers conserved the factor of production that was most dear – capital.[142]

---

142 The third factor of production – land – was under state control, and anyway, villagers would not easily or willingly have exchanged it.

After 1978, the rapid shift of economic organization and the concomitant rise in village living standards altered the relative scarcity of the factors of production. With the shift to a factory work schedule, villagers' labor became dear. Rising and steady factory wages, however, increased the relative abundance of family capital. This shift in the balance of labor and capital caused villagers to alter their social exchanges. Village mutual aid diminished as labor grew scarcer, and villagers began to substitute cash gifts for the pre-reform material gifts that embodied villagers' labor.

The substitution of cash-based exchanges for labor-based exchanges led villagers to reintroduce ledger books for recording cash gifts. At any celebratory event where cash gifts were offered, host families dutifully recorded the amount of cash gifts, called *renqing* ("sentiment"). Later, when it came to reciprocate, villagers consulted their gift ledgers to determine the appropriate amount of cash gift to offer. Villagers called these obligations to give a cash gift *renqingzhai* ("a debt of sentiment" or "a debt of past gifts"). These ledger books thus recorded the balance sheet of human affairs within village social networks. The substitution of cash for material gifts allowed villagers easily to assign quantitative measures to gifts, and indirectly, to the value placed on *guanxi*.[143]

Finally, improved villager incomes gave rise to a status contest that took the form of cash gifts. In other settings in China, villagers have been obligated to reciprocate with a gift of the same amount of cash that they received (Kipnis 1996, p. 302). In the Shanghai suburbs, local norms dictate that villagers reciprocate with greater gifts than they received. Failure to do so would reduce a villager's reputation. One villager noted, "We all want face (*mianzi*). If someone gives me sentiment (*renqing*), then I will return more" (China Interview; also cited in Wilson 1997). Another villager graphically revealed the consequences of disobeying this norm of one-upmanship: "If you do not give more than you receive, then you will have a bad reputation [literally, an 'ugly face']" (China Interview; also cited in Wilson 1997). Such pressure to raise the amount of a reciprocated gift caused a rapid inflation of cash gift amounts.

House construction and shifting forms of aid

During the 1980s, villagers rebuilt rural China. In the period 1980-1991, rural housing (measured in floor space) throughout China nearly doubled from 11.59 to 21.88 square meters per person. In particular, rural residents in periurban Shanghai led the way in house construction; they nearly tripled their per capita floor space from 16.56 square meters in 1980 to 44.64 in 1991. To undertake such large-scale construction projects, villagers had to rely on numerous forms of aid such as labor exchanges, loans, and cash gifts from their social networks. The various social exchanges around house construction projects illuminate some of these general transformations of *guanxi* and social exchanges.

---

143   Yunxiang Yan draws a related conclusion on the use of gift ledgers and especially the size of cash gifts and the degree of closeness of social relations (1996a, p. 111).

When constructing a new house, villagers frequently engage in mutual aid. Prior to the break up of the collective in 1983, villagers formed a construction team that helped to build houses, which was supplemented by informal but extensive mutual aid. Villagers rarely had enough capital to build new houses or even refurbish old ones, but these informal labor-pooling techniques helped to minimize the costs for the fortunate few who could afford such endeavors.

Since 1983, villagers have shifted to hiring construction teams from outside the Shanghai area. Again, mutual aid has supplemented the hired workers. Mutual aid helped to reduce the cost of constructing new houses, but after 1983 these labor exchanges began to diminish in importance. Industrialization and the revived cash nexus undermined such mutual aid in three ways.

First, villagers had difficulty mobilizing workers through their social networks for house building. Many tasks related to house construction require several days of labor from a social network. Rural factory schedules did not afford villagers the opportunity to make such extensive time commitments. Increasingly, villagers were forced to rely on hired outside construction teams to complete the work formerly done within the production team. Prior to 1976, all village house construction projects relied on mutual aid, and none was built by hiring outside construction teams. During the period 1976–1983, villagers still received mutual aid donations in 91 percent of the cases of house construction, but villagers also hired construction teams in 77 percent of the cases. From 1988 until my last round of interviews in 1995, villagers who built houses received mutual aid donations in just 61 percent of the cases and hired construction teams for 95 percent of the projects.

After 1976, these data evince a precipitous drop in mutual aid and a rapid integration into regional markets for construction workers. Yet they also hide a qualitative shift in mutual aid for house construction. Prior to 1976, villagers helped each other with all aspects of house construction, even the most onerous work. After 1976, villagers reduced their mutual aid commitments and especially dropped the more physically demanding work.[144]

To counter the drop in mutual aid, villagers increased their cash-based exchanges. For example, villagers give cash gifts at house-warming banquets to help with construction costs. In the late 1970s, villagers typically offered gifts of 10–30 *yuan*. By 1991, villagers had increased their cash gift amounts to 60–200 *yuan* (30–100 in 1977 *yuan*). The total amount of cash gifts received covered approximately 7–8 percent of the house construction costs. During the post-1978 period, villagers' living standards improved enough that cash gifts were becoming less important for covering housing costs.

By the early 1990s, villagers spent approximately as much on their house-warming banquets as they received in cash gifts. Such lavish banquets helped

144 A change in tastes contributed to villagers' decreased reliance on mutual aid for house construction. Specifically, villagers wanted more elaborate and finer houses, which only hired construction teams could guarantee to build. Villagers felt awkward complaining about the poor craftsmanship of their network's freely donated labor (Wilson 1996).

villagers to garner prestige and to thank their social networks for the various forms of aid received during the house construction.[145]

Interest-free loans covered a much larger share of house construction costs than cash gifts. As village houses increased in size and construction costs soared, villagers borrowed ever-larger amounts of money. Around 1980, villagers borrowed 1000–3000 *yuan* to build new houses. In 1990, the average amount borrowed increased to 14,000 *yuan* (7200 in 1977 *yuan*). Based on just two cases of construction in 1994, villagers borrowed 40,000 *yuan* (14,000 in 1977 *yuan*). The figures show a clear escalation of the amounts borrowed, even in real terms. Interest-free loans covered approximately 40 percent of total construction costs.

Villagers who lent out money without charging interest incurred a real cost. Typically, villagers required three to six years to repay such loans. In the meantime, the money repaid to the lenders lost part of its value due to inflation. Periods of high inflation during the 1980s made such interest-free lending a potentially very significant social burden. Villagers refused to charge each other interest on loans because, in villagers' terms, such conduct would be "impolite." Although villagers adamantly denied the calculation of interest on loans, villagers offered gifts to those who lent them money in a form of in-kind interest payment.

At the beginning of the reform period, both rich and poor villagers borrowed sums of money from several families in their social networks. Generally speaking, wealthier families could afford to build larger houses and borrow more money than middle-income or poor families. If wealthy families borrowed more money or more frequently than poor families, interest-free borrowing could effectively transfer resources to wealthier families. By the early 1990s, members of the nascent village elite felt pressure not to accept interest-free loans. The comments of a village head demonstrate a high degree of consciousness not to accept loans: "Our redecorating of the old house was paid for by ourselves – we didn't have to borrow any money. Last year, I probably made the most money in the village. It wouldn't look good if I borrowed money" (China Interview; also cited in Wilson 1997). Average villagers viewed the elite stratum of families, especially those of officials, as too wealthy to borrow money.

Similarly, villagers who undertook construction projects to refurbish their houses several times felt pressure not to borrow money or to receive cash gifts. One team leader said, "We did not tell anyone about our new house. They gave us money when we built our old house, so we did not want to notify others about our new house. It would be embarrassing to get cash gifts again" (China Interview; also cited in Wilson 1997). Such comments underscore the embarrassment of riches felt by the village wealthy, who could construct large and elaborately decorated houses that were beyond the economic reach of other villagers.

---

145   Over the same period, villagers received less mutual aid from their social networks. Thus, the house-warming banquets, ostensibly thrown to receive cash gifts and to thank social networks for labor donations, were more likely a vehicle to improve one's face in the community.

Agricultural mutual aid

Prior to local decollectivization in 1983,[146] agricultural cooperation was instituted in production teams.[147] During the period 1983–1988, agricultural mutual aid reemerged to fill a gap left by collective agricultural work after local authorities implemented the contract household responsibility system. Certain crops, rice in particular, required timely transplanting and harvesting. Local agricultural fields were small by Chinese standards,[148] but family labor supplies proved inadequate to transplant or bring in crops in a timely fashion.

In the mid-1980s, villagers informally pooled labor to overcome household labor shortages during agricultural peak seasons. Typically, when its fields were ready to be transplanted or harvested, a household would seek out help from a handful of its friends, relatives, or lineage members for a day's work. At the end of the day, villagers compensated these workers with a free meal rather than wages. Such reciprocal exchanges allowed for the timely and efficient agricultural work during the peak seasons.

Agricultural mutual aid was undermined by two economic shifts in the village– rising incomes and a more rigid work schedule. The steady daytime work schedule of village factories limited villagers' ability to devote even a full day's work in their fields. Moreover, interviewees simply noted that it became impossible to find workers with free time for mutual aid in the fields.

In addition, rising village incomes indirectly undermined agricultural mutual aid. As village living standards rose, workers who donated time for mutual aid expected improved banquets at the end of the day. In 1991, one villager noted:

> The first one or two years after the land was divided [in 1984], people still practiced mutual aid ... But from an economic standpoint it simply does not pay (*bu hesuan*), so people don't exchange labor as often. For example, if people help me during the agricultural busy season, I have to invite them for dinner. A month's salary is about 150 *yuan*, but the cost of having guests is about fifty to sixty *yuan*. It doesn't pay – in fact, you could lose money that way. (China Interview; quoted in Wilson 1997, p. 108.)

In fact, the cost of hiring outside itinerant workers in 1991 was 50 *yuan*,[149] or the same cost as hosting a dinner for the mutual aid donors. Mutual aid and hiring outside laborers were roughly equal in quality and price, yet villagers were not randomly distributed between these two options. Rather, the vast majority of villagers engaged in mutual aid or hiring outsiders, shifting from one method of gathering labor to another within a year's time. I believe that the reason for the shift

146 The villages under study made a late transition to the agricultural household responsibility system.
147 During periods of Maoist radicalism such as the Cultural Revolution, wealthy production teams, production brigades, and communes were forced to donate labor to poorer work units (Nickum 1978 and Zweig 1989).
148 In the mid-1980s, each villager received approximately 0.8 *mu* of agricultural land for cultivation.
149 The cost of hiring outside workers is based on the average household landholding of a little more than two *mu*.

away from mutual aid was a growing distaste for heavy manual labor, especially that required in the agricultural fields.

About 1995, agricultural labor practice took another twist. In that year, newly developed rice seeds that could be sown by casting them about and without need of transplanting were introduced. This technological development greatly reduced the agricultural labor requirement during one of the busy seasons. For the crucial transplanting stage of rice cultivation, villagers required neither mutual aid nor hiring itinerant workers. Unfortunately, I left the field in 1995 before the rice harvest, so I do not know if villagers hired workers to bring in the crop that year.

In sum, economic reforms altered social exchanges and social relations. Cash-based exchanges grew in importance while labor-based exchanges declined. The reasons for these shifts are complex and reveal subtle shifts in local *guanxi*; however, they do not reveal a decline in the importance of *guanxi* in managing local affairs.

Cash, geography, and instrumentality

A question remains: Have the shifting lines of *guanxi* and the reermergence of a cash economy caused social relations to become instrumental? The grand German theorists of economy and society – Simmel, Marx, and Weber – assert that the arrival of capitalism and a cash economy undermine intimate social relations. Instead, the profit motive of capitalism and the advent of money as a universal mode of exchange and valuation inculcate an instrumental mode of conduct. Additionally, one might expect that urbanization, with its greater sense of anomie and with the extension of the cash nexus social relations, would cause *guanxi* to take on an instrumental quality.

First we must define what we mean by instrumenality in social relations. In his discussion of gift exchange, Yunxiang Yan defines "expressive gifts" as those that "are ends in themselves and often reflect a long-term relationship between a giver and a recipient"; in contrast, "instrumental gifts are means to some utilitarian end and ordinarily indicate a short-term relationship" (1996a, p. 45).[150] More generally, instrumental relations entail the use of social ties to achieve some personal utility. These distinctions, though useful in theory, are problematic in practice. As mentioned, Yunxiang Yan and Mayfair Yang both assert that more distant relations are more instrumental than core relations in social networks. Yet, can we assume that social relations, even at the core, do not have an instrumental character?

At the heart of such theorizing is a distinction between *renqing* (sentiment) and instrumentality. As Yunxiang Yan correctly asserts, *renqing* has several meanings including "sentiment" and a "code of ethics" (1996a, pp. 128–46; see also Hwang 1987, pp. 953–954). Norm-guided action may appear to be other-regarding,

---

150   Mayfair Yang makes a similar distinction between "emotional friendship" and "instrumental friendship" (1994, p. 117).

and therefore expressive; however, I assert that even norm-guided exchanges are imbued with self-interest.

Many *guanxi* that I encountered comingled instrumental and expressive relations. Certainly, villagers felt little compunction when turning to friends, relatives, lineage members, and co-workers for highly utilitarian favors such as help in their agricultural fields, moving construction materials, or preparing food for weddings. These examples imply that intra-village social relations mixed instrumentality with expressiveness.

More fundamentally, do villagers give gifts as "ends in themselves"? Interview data suggest that villagers do not. Villagers give gifts and engage in mutual aid based on a "sense of indebtedness" (*renqingzhai*). Gift records are kept to recall to whom one owes a gift and to determine how large a gift to reciprocate. Such a practice undermines the notion of intimacy that Allan Silver suggests is at the heart of close personal relations and friendship. According to Silver, "friendship is diminished in moral quality if friends consciously monitor the balance of exchanges between them, for this implies that the utilities friends offer each other constitute their relationship, rather than being valued as expressions of personal commitment" (1990, p. 1477). In the Chinese setting, a profound fear of losing face drives the keeping of records about gift and aid exchanges. Failure appropriately to reciprocate a gift would generate gossip within the village and a loss of face for the villager who did not follow etiquette.

The emphasis on maintaining or adding to one's face through gift exchange implies three limits to villagers' altruism. First, villagers do not offer a gift or aid as an end in itself but, at least secondarily, to help themselves. Villagers aggressively pursue prestige through their social exchanges. Our interview data demonstrate that villagers are highly conscious of their level of face and that they use gifts to negotiate their prestige. Second, maintaining face with gifts assures fellow villagers that one is trustworthy (*xinyong*), which villagers take into account when extending interest-free loans, engaging in mutual aid, and offering other forms of help. Potentially, the stakes in mishandling gifts and social relations are high: loss of future interest-free loans, fewer gifts received, and diminishing mutual aid. Third, villagers never expect their gift to be the final one in a history of exchanges. Villagers do not just give a gift as an end in itself but as a means to future gifts. In sum, a villager's gift has an other-regarding quality, but it also contributes to a broader process of negotiating one's place in the community and one's ability to gain access to resources.

Importantly, all members of a social network, even the closest of friends and relatives, have their gift amounts recorded at celebrations. Indeed, villagers at the core of social networks have the greatest obligation and feel the most pressure to give the largest amounts of cash at weddings and other celebratory banquets. Interviewees conveyed a high degree of consciousness about their gift amounts, especially for their geographically and emotionally closest relatives. Thus, the "inner core" of social networks, to use Yunxiang Yan's term, mixes elements of reciprocity and *renqing* with instrumentality.

Moreover, villagers' return to cash-based gift exchange has caused an alienation of the gift from the giver. Cash is usually devoid of intimacy. Villagers try to maintain a notion of intimacy within cash-based gift exchanges by calling such money, "sentiment" (*renqing*). Nevertheless, the fungibility of cash limits its particularity and intimate quality. Indeed, Georg Simmel declared that cash was an inappropriate form of gift because cash does not embody a personal element (cited in Zelizer 1994, pp. 82–83).

If Yunxiang Yan and Mayfair Yang are correct in their assertion that geographically distant social relations are instrumental, one might expect the villagers' new social relations with municipal residents to be rooted in instrumental exchange. Interviews reveal that villagers' long-distance ties fell into two types. First, villagers' long-distance relations that revolved around business transactions were primarily instrumental. Local officials' ties to higher-level officials often involved some type of "friendship" but were clearly built around instrumental exchanges. For example, village officials threw banquets to cultivate ties to township and county officials in land management offices. Such relations help village officials to receive quick approval for projects that required confiscating land from villagers.

In contrast, other long-distance *guanxi* were more expressive than instrumental. Most interactions with urban residents in villagers' social networks took place at informal dinners and gatherings rather than as an exchange of gift for favor. One interviewee recalled how he did not have a house-warming banquet for lineage members and relatives from the village when he moved into a new flat. Instead, he hosted two tables of good friends, which included people from Shanghai municipality. The (mostly younger) villagers who had built ties to Shanghai municipal citizens discussed their *guanxi* with pride. Indeed, villagers viewed such relations as a positive reflection on their social power or face.

I would suggest that villagers regarded such urban citizens, like urban style of dress and construction detail, as part of the modern world they so desired. Villagers' attitudes toward Shanghai urban residents contrasted sharply to their views of itinerant workers from surrounding provinces; villagers often derided the latter group. The difference between the two groups of "outsiders" was the groups' place in the geographic status hierarchy. Social ties up the status hierarchy (to people in Shanghai municipality) raised villagers' face, but ties to people down the status hierarchy (from outlying provinces) lowered villagers' face. If this line of analysis is accurate, villagers enjoyed just one utility from their social ties to urban residents: face, a non-material benefit. Indeed, villagers may have had to expend their material resources to cultivate such ties without gaining much material benefit in return. In contrast, villagers derived greater material utility from their core social relations, who extended interest-free loans, gave large cash gifts, and offered mutual aid. Both intra-village and extra-village social relations affect a villager's face, but intra-village relations also contain an element of instrumentality that ties to urban residents sometimes lack.

CONCLUSION

The post-1978 reforms have reshaped the economic and social life of villagers in at least three ways: (1) factory work has restructured villagers' daily lives and limited opportunities to engage in mutual aid; (2) the improvement and steadiness of incomes – a product of industrial employment – has led to the substitution of cash-based exchanges for labor-based exchanges; and (3) factory work has extended the geographic scope of social networks by changing the people with whom villagers come into contact. We might have expected these grand socioeconomic transformations to have caused social relations to diminish in importance and/or to have become more instrumental. This research problematizes both of these assumptions.

Certainly, the cash nexus has reshaped social relations, but it has also had a positive effect on certain aspects of social exchanges. Cash gift amounts have escalated in real terms. Moreover, rising incomes and a politically relaxed atmosphere have afforded villagers more occasions to celebrate and exchange gifts. Since 1978, villagers have given more often and in larger amounts. Too, intra-village relations, which were constructed around lineages, have decreased in importance, but extra-village relations have offered access to new resources and new ties to co-workers and friends. More accurately, village networks have been transformed rather than eroded by market reforms and the reemergence of the cash nexus.

Authors have drawn too strict a dichotomy between norm-based (*renqing*) exchanges and instrumental exchanges (*guanxixue*) (Yang 1994; Yan 1996a; Wilson 1997; Guthrie 1998). Gifts and mutual aid are means of gaining face and an indirect method to gain access to capital in the form of gifts and loans, labor through mutual aid, and material resources such as trucks and construction materials. Stated otherwise, norm-based exchanges are long-term investments in social capital that may produce delayed material benefits. Thus the boundary between *renqing* and instrumental exchanges is as fluid as the boundary between urban and rural social life in the villages under study.

9

GUANXI AND THE PRC LEGAL SYSTEM: FROM CONTRADICTION TO COMPLEMENTARITY

Pitman B. Potter

INTRODUCTION

Discussions of the role of "*guanxi*" in Chinese society are commonplace. Whether in economics, politics, or social relations, *guanxi* is frequently posited as a fundamental dynamic that determines the process and outcomes of behavior.[151] *guanxi* has also been examined as a critical element in business relationships.[152] While the importance of personal relationships and networks is widely acknowledged as a universal, albeit socially embedded, phenomenon, analysis of *guanxi* in China represents an effort to contextualize these practices to local conditions.[153] This chapter will examine the role of *guanxi* in the Chinese legal system in the context of legal culture and by reference to the attitudes and behavior of Chinese legal actors.

Preparing a chapter on the role of *guanxi* in the Chinese legal system might appear at first blush as the equivalent of introducing Star Trek's Borg to the Red Queen of Alice and Wonderland. Like the Red Queen the Chinese legal system appears as a puzzling series of contradictions, where formal (often formalistic and draconian) rules and procedures are often interpreted and applied according to arbitrary held views of powerful officials yielding a variety of unintended results, or else ignored altogether.[154] Conventional wisdom on *guanxi* relations in Chinese society often portrays this dynamic in ways emblematic of Borg, as an all-encompassing

151 See Luo Yadong, "Guanxi": Principles, philosophies, and implications," in *Human Systems Management* vol. 16 (1997), pp. 43–51.

152 See Farh Jing-lih, M.S. Tsue, Katherine R. Xin, and Cheng Bor Shiuan, "The Influence of Relational Demography and *Guanxi*: The Chinese Case," in *Organization Science* vol. 9 no. 4 (July-August 1998), pp. 471–488; Kiongtuong Chee, Keeyong Pit, "*Guanxi* Bases, Xinyong and Chinese Business Networks," *British Journal of Sociology* vol. 49 no. 1 (March 1998), pp. 75–96.

153 See Udo Staber and Howard E. Aldrich "Cross-National Similarities in the Personal Networks of Small Business Owners, " in *Canadian Journal of Sociology* vol. 20 no. 4 (fall 1995), pp. 441–467; Huang, Kwang-kuo, "Face and Favour: The Chinese Power Game," in *American Journal of Sociology* vol. 92 no. 4 (January, 1987), pp. 994–74.

154 See generally, *China's Legal Reforms* (Special Issue), *The China Quarterly* no. 141 (March 1995).

set of norms that all members of the assimilated community understand and to which they all subscribe. Moreover, as with both the Red Queen and Borg, direct engagement is discouraged. The closely held notion that formal law and legal institutions operate in contradistinction to the role of *guanxi* means that anyone who attempts to relate the two to each other runs the risk of professional beheading or conceptual assimilation to one or another established viewpoint. Nonetheless, I shall attempt the task, armed with what I hope is a healthy scepticism for both the lawyer's confidence in formal rules and processes and the social scientist's loyalty to culturally and socially specific explanations for behavior.

GUANXI AND CHINESE LEGAL CULTURE

The role of *guanxi* in China is often seen as operating in juxtaposition to the role of law and legal institutions.[155] The importance of *guanxi* in China is attributed to the weakness of institutions for managing social, economic, and political relations, and allocating resources.[156] Thus, *guanxi* is seen as a coping mechanism that substitutes for the norms and processes associated with formal institutions. The continued dominance of the state in Chinese society and the relative absence of formal institutional limits on state power continued to militate in favor of *guanxi* relations. As the state takes on the attributes of the industrial firm[157] *guanxi* relations become increasingly important in economic relationships. The prevalence of clientelism in market relations is another aspect of this phenomenon,[158] while the importance of building *guanxi* relations as a strategy for pursuing group interests in the absence of formal institution structures is evident in the emergence of "civil associations" (*minjian xiehui*).[159]

The juxtaposition of relational *guanxi* and formal institutions is illustrated by the aphorism that contracts are agreements between people who don't trust each other – hence law becomes necessary only where relationships cannot be driven by trust. Rather than viewing *guanxi* as an antipole to law, however, it might be more useful to examine the role of *guanxi* in the legal system as a matter of legal culture. The efforts of numerous scholars to apply definitional precision to the concept of legal culture have succeeded mainly in underscoring its elusiveness.

155 See Jose Tomas and Gomez Arias, "A Relationship Marketing Approach to *Guanxi*," in *European Journal of Marketing* vol. 32 no. 1/2 (1998) p.145; Hui Chin and George Graen, "*Guanxi* and Professional Leadership in Contemporary Sino-American Joint Ventures in Mainland China," in *Leadership Quarterly* vol. 8 no. 4 (winter 1997), pp. 451–465.

156 See Katherine R. Xin, Jone L. Pearce, "*Guanxi*: Connections as Substitutes for Formal Institutional Support," in *Academy of Management Journal* vol. 39 no. 6 (December 1996) pp. 1641–1658

157 See Andrew Walder "Local Governments as Industrial Firms: An Organizational Analysis of China's Transitional Economy," in *American Journal of Sociology* vol. 101 no. 2 (September 1995), pp. 263–301.

158 See David C. Wank, "The Institutional Process of Market Clientelism: *Guanxi* and Private Business in a South China City," in *The China Quarterly* no. 147 (September 1996), pp. 820–38.

159 See Jonathan Unger, "'Bridges': Private Business, The Chinese Government and the Rise of New Associations," in *The China Quarterly* no. 147 (September 1996) pp. 795–819.

Drawing on the interplay of sociology and political science, Friedman defined legal culture in terms of customs and opinions, and ways of thinking and doing about the law.[160] Ehrmann's review of Friedman's initial explorations views legal culture essentially as a variant on political culture but in the realm of law.[161] Lubman has applied the Friedman approach more specifically to the study of law and legal culture in the PRC and juxaposed it to functional approaches,[162] while Glendon takes Ehrmann and Friedman a step farther still in an effort to identify specific bases for comparison among different legal systems.[163] More recently, Varga has explored the term by reference to a challenge/response paradigm in the context of comparative perspectives ranging from the legal anthropology of Gluckman and Diamond to the civil/common law dichotomy and ultimately the Marxist revolutionary rejection of legal culture.[164] If we conceive of legal culture as entailing a pattern of reciprocal influences between parallel phenomena of law and society,[165] the concept offers a vehicle for examining the responses to law reform in China and the interplay with traditional social practices such as *guanxi*.

As the Chinese experience with law building throughout the PRC's history has involved borrowing from legal systems of Europe and North America,[166] social responses to law reform in China involve essentially reactions to imported legal norms. These imported forms of law may be seen to reflect changing economic[167] and philosophical[168] conditions of their places of origin, whereas legal conduct in China and the responses of Chinese society to the imported legal regime are dictated by local culture.[169] In an important sense, law in the European/North

---

160 See Lawrence M. Friedman, *The Legal System: A Social Science Perspective*, (Englewood Cliffs, N.J.: Prentice-Hall, 1975), p. 15.

161 See Henry W. Ehrmann, *Comparative Legal Cultures* (Englewood Cliffs, N.J., Prentice-Hall; 1976), pp. 6, et seq.

162 See Stanley Lubman, "Studying Contemporary Chinese Law: Limits, Possibilities and Strategy", in 39 *Am. J. Comp. Law* 293–341 (1991), p. 333.

163 See Mary Anne Glendon, *Comparative Legal Systems* (St. Paul: West, 1985).

164 See Csaba Varga, ed., *Comparative Legal Cultures* (NY: NYU Press, 1992). Interestingly, Paul Bohannon's seminal work on "double institutionalization" in the anthropology of law is included in Varba's collection only as the focus of Diamond's critique.

165 Cf. Lauren Nader, *Law in Culture and Society*, Chicago: Aldine Press (1969), p. 8.

166 See Pitman B. Potter, "The Chinese Legal System: Continuing Commitment to the Primacy of State Power," in *The China Quarterly* No. 159 (1999), pp. 673–683.

167 See A. S. Diamond, *Primitive Law, Past and Present*, London: Methuen (1971), reprinted in J. C. Smith and David N. Weisstub, *The Western Idea of Law*, London and Toronto: Butterworths (1983), p. 19.

168 See DeLloyd Guth, "The Age of Debt, The Reformation and English Law," in D. J. Guth and J. W. McKenna, eds., *Tudor Rule and Revolution: Essays for G. R. Elton From His American Friends*, Cambridge: Cambridge University Press (1982), reprinted in Smith, J. C. and David N. Weisstub, *The Western Idea of Law*, London and Toronto: Butterworths (1983), p. 28.

169 See J. C. Smith and David N. Weisstub, *The Western Idea of Law*, London and Toronto: Butterworths (1983), pp. 1–3; also See Felix Cohen, "The Relativity of Philosophical Systems and the Method of Systematic Relativism," in *The Legal Conscience: Selected Papers of Felix S. Cohen* (ed. Lucy Kramer Cohen), Shoe String Press (1970), reprinted in J. C. Smith and David N. Weisstub, *The Western Idea of Law*, London and Toronto: Butterworths (1983), p. 16.

American tradition itself may be viewed as a belief system, which having been imported into China must operate in the context of local belief systems.[170]

The effect of imported law norms on behavior and attitudes in China may be identified by reference to compliance,[171] which depends in part on the extent to which the norms of the legal regime comport with those of received tradition. The survival of customary norms despite new institutional arrangements is a salient factor in political culture of modernizing societies, and is no less evident in the area of legal culture.[172] The influence of tradition on cultural responses to law is a key element in interaction of law and custom. Whereas indigenous legal norms may emerge gradually through a process of formalization of customary norms,[173] where law norms are imported, compliance requires that these imported norms accommodate local norms and practices.

Compliance may also depend on the extent to which legal forms respond to social and economic needs. Where traditional relational norms are ineffective to manage changing social and economic conditions, new norms may emerge as an ideological response to changing conditions.[174] This local acceptance of imported law norms may depend on a process by which traditional norms that are unresponsive to new realities are discarded ("delegitimization") and replaced by new norms as part of an evolving belief system ("transvaluation").[175] With social complexity comes alienation of individuals, as the personal trust relationship among members of society is replaced by institutionalized trust among social groups and individuals without kinship or other personalist ties.[176] As increased complexity of society permits creation of increasingly diverse and broad relationships beyond those of kinship and community, informal and subjective relational norms may be required to give way to formality and objectivity.[177] Systems of formal jural rules, particularly regarding procedure, become desirable when social

170 See Clifford Geertz, *Local Knowledge: Further Essays in Interpretive Anthropology*, New York: Basic Books (1983), ch. 8.

171 See generally, Barrington Moore, *Injustice: The Social Bases of Obedience and Revolt*, White Plains, N. Y.: M.E. Sharpe (1978).

172 See Mary McAuley, "Political Culture and Communist Politics: One Step Forward Two Steps Back," in Archie Brown, ed., *Political Culture and Communist Studies*, Hampshire and London: Macmillan Press (1984), p. 31.

173 See Paul Bohannon, "The Differing Realms of Law," in *American Anthropologist*, Vol. 67, No. 6, Dec. 1965, p. 33. Also See Stanley Diamond, "The Rule of Law Versus the Order of Custom," in Donald Black and Maureen Mileski, eds., *The Social Organization of Law*, New York and London: Seminar Press (1973), p. 318; Harold J. Berman, *Law and Revolution: The Formation of the Western Legal Tradition*, Cambridge, Mass. and London: Harvard University Press (1983), p. 79.

174 See Clifford Geertz, "Ideology as a Cultural System," in David E. Apter, ed., *Ideology and Discontent*, New York: The Free Press, London: Collier-Macmillan (1964), p. 64.

175 See Ofira Seliktar, "Identifying a Society's Belief Systems," in Margaret Herman, ed., *Political Psychology*, San Francisco and London: Jossey-Bass (1986), pp. 321–22.

176 See generally, S. W. Eisenstadt and L. Roniger, *Patrons, Clients and Friends: Interpersonal Relations and the Structure of Trust in Society*, Cambridge: Cambridge University Press (1984).

177 See Henry S. Maine, *Ancient Law*, London: Oxford University Press (reprinted, 1959, copyright 1861). Also See Robert Redfield, "Maine's Ancient Law in the Light of Primitive Societies," in

relationships (including economic and political relationships) become complex to the degree that shared norms, values, and language cannot be assumed, and distrust within society requires that subjectivity and informalism give way to objectivity and formal rules.[178] Thus, in China, compliance with imported law norms may depend not only on their accommodation of traditional norms and practices, but paradoxically on their displacing traditional relational norms with norms of formality and objectivity in response to new socioeconomic conditions and the perceived needs of members of society that result.

In the context of the effort to build a legal system in China, *guanxi* relations and formal institutional relations can be seen to work together. The traditional *guanxi* system retains its importance, but must operate alongside an increasingly formal set of largely imported rules and processes made necessary by the increased complexity of social, economic, and political relations, Thus, *guanxi* becomes an asset, which can be banked or deployed as needed to serve the interests of the holder in the context of a larger institutional system.[179] As an expression of social capital, *guanxi* operates along with other mechanisms of economic or symbolic capital for regulating social, economic, and political relationships.[180] In the course of China's ongoing legal reforms, the role of *guanxi* may increasingly be seen to operate as a complement to rather than a substitute for the role of formal institutions.

THE ROLE OF *GUANXI* IN LEGAL ATTITUDES AND BEHAVIOR

The complementary relationship between *guanxi* and formal legal institutions is borne out by the results of research on legal culture in Chinese urban communities, as well through analysis of case reporting on disputes between foreign and Chinese companies. Finally, a series of informal conversations held with Chinese lawyers and arbitrators during 1997 to 1999 and the review of documents related to business negotiations and dispute resolution over the same period suggest as well the close interplay between *guanxi* relations and the role of formal institutions.

Attitudes about guanxi *in domestic legal relations*

My survey of the *getihu* in the Jingan District of Shanghai was completed in 1994, with the expectation that *guanxi* dynamics would operate in juxtaposition to

3 *Western Political Quarterly* 586 (1950), as cited in J. C. Smith and David N. Weisstub, *The Western Idea of Law*, London and Toronto: Butterworths (1983), p. 81.

178 See Robert K. Merton, *Social Theory and Social Structure* (revised and enlarged edition), New York: Free Press (1965), reprinted in Robert M. Cover and Owen M. Fiss, *The Structure of Procedure*, Mineola, N.Y.: Foundation Press (1979), p. 377.

179 See David C. Wank, "The Institutional Process of Market Clientelism: *Guanxi* and Private Business in a South China City," in *The China Quarterly* no. 147 (September 1996), pp. 820–38.

180 See Alan Smart, "Gifts, Bribes and *Guanxi*: A Reconsideration of Bourdieu's Social Capital," in *Cutural Anthropology* vol. 8 no. 3 (August 1993), pp. 388–408.

reliance on formal rules.[181] However, responses of *getihu* operators to questions about enforcement of private law relations revealed the extent to which respondents remained wedded to informal mechanisms. Responses of *getihu* operators to questions about private law relations revealed growing acceptance of formal law requirements on formation and enforcement, while the effects of traditional norms of informality also remained in evidence.

In response to questions about the formation of loan obligations, a sizable proportion (58 percent) of the *getihu* respondents indicated that the loan was more important if the agreement were in writing, while 51 percent of the respondents from the general Jingan population held that the importance of the loan was unaffected by the presence of a written agreement. On the one hand, this reflects increased compliance with official PRC doctrine on formation of contracts, which generally requires contracts to be in writing.[182] However, compliance was not complete, and as between friends and family members resistance to the requirements of formal rules was greater. Indeed a majority of *getihu* (56 percent) and general population (65 percent) respondents indicated they would attach less importance to the obligation if the loan were made to a friend or family member. The views of *getihu* respondents that the formal legal relationship derived from a loan agreement was less important when it concerned family members or friends also indicated the limits to which the law should be expected to intrude in private relationships. This view contrasts with the conclusion of the majority (66 percent) of *getihu* respondents that the law should be permitted to intrude into family matters. One interpretation of this inconsistency might be that support for the law's intrusion is confined to the realm of the abstract, but fades when specific cases arise involving personal relationships.

While there was evident acceptance of formal law norms on formation of civil law relations, the respondents appeared to remain wedded to informal mechanisms in the area of performance and enforcement. On the matter of debt, the *getihu* respondents appeared to express a broader mix of human and institutional reasons for performance of obligations. In response to questions concerning enforcement of a loan agreement, the most common response (50 percent) to the debtor's refusal to pay was to seek a mutual friend to remind the debtor to perform. When asked under what circumstances would they go to court to enforce the loan agreement, the most common response (19/50) was that judicial action would be sought only after a mutual friend or family member had tried and failed to persuade the debtor to perform. The preference for this response over that indicating that formal recourse would be sought only after the respondent had personally failed to persuade the debtor to perform suggests a lingering willingness to continue to use relational dynamics such as *guanxi* to resolve disputes before resorting to formal action.

Yet there were also indications of increased support for the role of formal judicial mechanisms in dispute resolution. For example, a sizable minority (41 percent)

---

181   See Pitman B. Potter, "Civil Obligations and Legal Culture in Shanghai: A Survey of the *Getihu*, *Canadian Journal of Law and Society* vol. 9, no. 2 (Fall 1994), pp. 41–72.
182   See Economic Contract Law of the PRC, Article 3.

of the *getihu* respondents indicated they would ask a lawyer to arrange matters in the case of non-payment of the loan. While respondents from the general Jingan population respondents indicated similar views (38 percent indicated a willingness to seek a lawyer), when asked about the possibility of court action, nearly twice the proportion from the general Jingan populace indicated a strict aversion to litigation. Thus, there was evident an emerging willingness among the *getihu* respondents to use judicial institutions, its still embryonic nature explained perhaps by the fact that only six of the respondents had any actual experience with actual disputes, and these all concerned housing-related matters. And yet even of these, one had actually gone to court. Thus, the experience of the respondents with resolving disputes through friends and family contracts or through the work unit undoubtedly informed their responses, yet also permitted an emerging capacity to view formal judicial institutions as a way to resolve disputes.

The attitudes of the *getihu* respondents that formal law norms should be considered along with traditional informal *guanxi* relations in civil law relations was indicated as well in part by responses to a question about repayment of debt. While the vast majority of *getihu* respondents indicated that they would repay a debt in order to protect their reputation (71 percent), a significant minority (14 percent) indicated that legal duty would be the reason for repayment. Repayment by reason of moral duty also elicited 14 percent of responses. By comparison, respondents from the general Jingan population indicated that repayment would be for reasons of reputation (76 percent), legal duty (10 percent), and moral duty (14 percent). Here again, the elements of social capital that involve *guanxi* are seen to operate as a complement to formal law.

Behavior: Guanxi *and foreign-related dispute resolution*[183]

The role of *guanxi* in legal relations has also been evident in disputes between Chinese and foreign parties.[184] In a number of these cases, the contractual agreement between the parties operates within a context of a continually evolving relationship involving constant changes or requests for changes in legal obligations. In a case involving the shipment of galvanized plates, for example, the parties

---

183 See Pitman B. Potter and Michael Donnelly, "Cultural Aspects of Trade Dispute Resolution in Japan and China," *Asia Pacific Foundation*, 1996.
184 See Arbitral decisions by CIETAC are available in Cheng Dejun, (ed.), *Shewai zhongcai yu falu* (foreign-related arbitration and law) (Beijing: Chinese People's University Press, 1992) and Civil Law Office of the NPC Standing Committee on Legal Affairs and CCPIT Secretariat, (ed.), *Zhonghua renmin gongheguo zhongcai fa quanshu* (Encyclopedia of arbitration law of the PRC) (Beijing: Law Publishers, 1995). Case decisions by Chinese courts and arbitral agencies appear in Qi Tianchang, (ed.), *Hetong anli pingxi* (Discussion of contract cases) (Beijing: Chinese University of Politics and Law Press, 1991); Wang Cunxue, *Zhongguo jingji zhongcai he susong shiyong shouce* (Practical handbook of Chinese economic arbitration and litigation) (Beijing: Development Press, 1993); Zhang Huilong, *Shewai jingji fa anli jiexi* (Analysis of Sino-foreign economic law cases) (Beijing: Youth Publishers, 1990); and *New Selections of the Foreign-Related Economic Cases in China* (Shanghai: Economic Information Agency, 1992).

agreed to change the addressee for delivery after conclusion of the contract but before delivery.[185] Problems arise when requests for change occur later in the transactions, such as when changes are sought in the quality and quantity of goods ordered well after the contract was concluded.[186] In a similar case, the seller of aluminum ingots requested a change in the price and delivery terms well after the letter of credit paying for the goods had already been opened.[187] While Chinese requests to modify agreed contract terms have been viewed by foreign businesses as evidence of lack of good faith,[188] in many instances they reflect an expectation on the Chinese side that the parties to the transaction ought to help one another respond to volatile (and to the Chinese possibly unknowable) market conditions. Requests for changes in contract terms do not always signify expectations of a close relationship, however, as in one case involving a leather production invest-ment project, changed contract terms were the basis for a claim (later accepted by the arbitral tribunal) that the contract had never been formed.[189]

In several cases, fundamental differences of expectations were at the root of the conflict. A typical concern touches on the nature of the obligation relation-ship between the parties.[190] For example, a transaction involving a technology and equipment sale and compensation trade agreement gave rise to a dispute over whether the equipment and technology met the contract specifications.[191] The basic issue in dispute seemed to be whether the obligation of the foreign party was limited solely to the contract terms or should be measured by the broader expectations of the Chinese party. Thus, while the foreign seller/licensor made several attempts to correct perceived inadequacies in the equipment and techno-logy, the Chinese purchaser/licensee remained dissatisfied–not because the terms of the contract were not fulfilled but because the Chinese were unable to reach what they considered to be the ultimate goal of the project. In the view of the Chinese side, the relationship between the contracting parties required a mutual commitment to achieving project goals. Assumptions that the Chinese contracting party's special relationship with its counterpart transcends the contract terms were also evident where the Chinese party discovered that the foreign party did not view the relationship as particularly special. In a case involving the sale of bread preservatives, the Chinese party agreed to a revise the contract payment terms, then reneged when they concluded that the foreign seller was seeking merely to avoid

185   See Cheng Dejun, supra, Case No. 1.   186   See Cheng Dejun, supra, Case No. 2.
187   See Wang Cunxue, supra, Case No. 3.
188   See generally, Lynn Chu, "The Chimera of the China Market," *Atlantic Monthly*, October 1990 at 56.
189   See e.g., *Zhongcai fa quanshu*, supra, Case No. 3. Also see Si Xiaotan, "CIETAC Arbitration: Joint Venture Case Studies No. 1," in China Law & Practice (ed.), *Dispute Resolution in the PRC: A Practical Guide to Litigation and Arbitration in China* (Hong Kong, China Law & Practice, 1995), 139; and Wang Cunxue, supra, Case No. 6.
190   For discussion of this concern in the context of the Sino-Japanese Fujian Television JV, see "Zhong wai hezi jingying qiye ruhe 'hezi'?" in Zhang Huilong, *Shewai jingji fa anli jiexi* (Analysis of Sino-foreign economic law cases) (Beijing: Youth Publishers, 1990) at 239.
191   See *Zhongcai fa quanshu*, supra, Case No. 5.

Chinese customs duties.[192] The Chinese party's response seemed motivated not by the desire to enrich the Chinese Customs Service, but apparently was due to disappointment that the foreign partner would subordinate its relations with the Chinese seller to concerns about avoiding import duties. A Chinese purchaser of packaging materials and equipment revealed a similar level of disappointment in attempting to resist payment of a performance bond insisted upon by the foreign seller.[193]

The importance of the *guanxi* relationship can also affect the conduct of disputes, as Chinese norms of collective responsibility for management of conflict are evident in expectations about mediation and conciliation.[194] In a dispute between a Chinese and a Thai company, the issue concerned conformity of documents with the requirements of a letter of credit.[195] The Chinese bank insisted on "strict compliance," while the Thai seller and its negotiating bank claimed that the documentary differences were inconsequential. In this case, both parties engaged in a lengthy process of negotiation, political intercession, and litigation before settling on mediation under the auspices of the Chinese International Economic and Trade Arbitration Commission (CIETAC). After negotiations were unavailing, the Thai seller sought a political solution through the local bureau of the State Administration for Industry and Commerce (SAIC) and appealed for a court judgment before pursuing resolution through CIETAC. CIETAC oversaw a mediated solution by which the Thai seller was largely made whole. The Thai company then wrote a lengthy missive extolling the virtues of mediation.

In this case, there was no direct dispute between the parties over performance of the terms of the contractual agreement. Rather the matter was conformity of the documents necessary to secure payment on the letter of credit. Normally this would be a matter for discussion between the negotiating and confirming banks.[196] In this case, however, although the contract parties were unable to negotiate a mutually (agreeable) conclusion to the matter, they revealed a clear willingness to participate in a managed solution. It would appear that their willingness to engage in successful mediation was helped by the fact that as between them there was no substantial disagreement on performance of the contract. Thus, the willingness to engage in voluntary dispute settlement in this case depended not on the extent of economic interest, but rather in part at least on the fact that the relationship was not undermined by either party's contract performance.

In some instances, however, negotiated solutions do not solve the dispute but only serve to sharpen the parties' differences. In a case involving the sale of steel

192 See *Zhongcai fa quanshu*, supra, Case No. 10.
193 See *Zhongcai fa quanshu*, supra, Case No. 12.
194 See e.g., Johannes Trappe, "Conciliation in the Far East," 5(2) *International Arbitration*, vol. 5 no. 2 (1989), pp. 173–198; Greg Vickery, "International Commercial Arbitration in China," 5 *Australian Dispute Resolution Journal* 75 (1994); and Anne Judith Farina, "'Talking Disputes into Harmony;' China Approaches International Commercial Arbitration," 4 *American University Journal of International Law and Policy*, 137 (1989).
195 See Cheng Dejun, supra, Case No. 7. Also see *Zhongcai fa quanshu*, supra, Case No. 8.
196 See generally, J.G. Castel, A.L.C. de Mestral, and W.C. Graham, *The Canadian Law and Practice of International Trade* (Toronto: Emond Montgomery, 1991).

plate for use in a hydroelectric project, for example, a dispute over alleged failure of timely delivery was settled, and the seller agreed to pay a negotiated measure of compensation.[197] The Chinese importer, however, still filed for arbitration claiming additional compensation. Communications difficulties during the course of settling a dispute have in some cases served to exacerbate tensions between the parties, contributing to a breakdown in the transaction.[198] This helps explain the increased willingness of Chinese parties to turn disputes over to lawyers and other professionals, so that the relationship between the principals in the disputing companies can be preserved – while the lawyers may bicker and negotiate, the principals remain above the fray and attend to maintaining the *guanxi* tie.

Guanxi *and judicial behavior*

The emerging complementarity between the dynamics of *guanxi* and the role of formal law and legal institutions is also evident in the behavior of lawyers and legal officials. On the one hand, widespread statistical and anecdotal evidence of corruption among the judiciary suggests that the requirements of formal law and legal institutions remain contingent on political arrangements and *guanxi* relations, while the commonplace offenses of taking bribes suggests that the requirements of formal law and institutions may be disregarded altogether for monetary reward.[199] However, many instances of alleged judicial misconduct involve not bribery but the use of *guanxi* to influence judicial and regulatory decision-making and conversely the willingness of judges and administrative regulators to base decisions on requirements of personal networks rather than requirements of law.[200] *Guanxi* thus serves as a "gap-filler" by which litigants and their counsel can make the best use of the limited requirements of formal law.

The dilemma of corruption in the judiciary and in the administrative bureaucracy, however, is not merely a matter of suspending moral or legal values. Rather it reflects uncertainties and tensions as to the permissible parameters for *guanxi* behavior and the parameters for formal institutional behavior – in other words, where legal requirements and processes end and where informal relations may legitimately be permitted to have influence. Whereas effective formal rules provide officials with legitimate justification for denying requests for favoritism based

---

197 See *Zhongcai fa quanshu*, supra, Case No. 11.
198 See *Zhongcai fa quanshu*, supra, Case No. 12 (sale of fax machine packing materials and equipment) and No. 13 (sale of parts and equipment for use on Jacquard looms).
199 See "China: Supreme Court, Procuratorate Report Work," Beijing *Xinhua* Domestic Service 14 Sept. 1998, in FBIS-CHI-98-260, 17 Sept. 1998; Han Zhubin Stresses Need to Better Handle Appearls, Tips," Beijing *Xinhua* Domestic Service Sept. 25, 1998, in FBIS-CHI-98-271, 28 Sept. 1998. Also See Shao Chongzhu, ed., *Zhong gong fan tan da an zhong an* (Big cases and serious cases on the Chinese communists fight against corruption) (Hong Kong: So far (xiafeier) publishers, 1998), pp. 337 (Hebei High Level People's Court), p. 339 (Wuxi Procuracy) and p. 346 (Nanjing Middle Level People's Court).
200 See generally, Susan Finder, "Litigation in the Chinese courts: A new frontier for foreign business," in *China Law & Practice* Feb. 1996, pp. 18–19.

on *guanxi* ties, thus protecting officials from the demands of *guanxi* networks, the absence of official rules permits *guanxi* relations to drive official decision-making. Thus, where judges are expected personally to investigate the circumstances of disputes before them, this is generally seen to require judges to meet with litigants and their counsel to collect evidence and hear argument – not necessarily in the presence of the opposing party or its counsel. In the context of Chinese social practices, this investigation process is very likely to involve banquets, individual meetings, and other part social, part professional encounters.[201] During the course of such investigations, the temptation for one party or another to attempt to influence judicial decision-making through improper inducements is high. Yet there is a fine line, and one that is not well understood, between a litigant hosting an investigating judge or judicial official to a series of banquets and meetings at which the litigant puts its case in a most favorable light, and the direct offering of economic inducements. The uncertainty in the relationship between the permitted scope of investigatory behavior and the prohibited scope of taking bribes and engaging in corrupt conduct is heightened by the formalism that pervades Chinese legal culture.

Official norms about justice in post-Mao China are characterized by legal formalism as the criterion for findings of justice.[202] This has led to judicial decisions in the area of economic regulation that elevate slavish reliance on formal rules and procedures over concerns with substantive fairness.[203] Such an approach permits judges and legal and administrative officials to confine their decision-making processes to formalistic references to statutory provisions without the requirement of detailed fact *cum* law analysis. Such a circumstance then permits decisions to be made with little explanation, and insulates them from challenge. Whether driven by improper economic inducements or skilled persuasion, the legal or administrative decision need not be explained in detail and the decision-maker need not address how the balance of interest and argument between the disputants was handled. This, in effect, insulates from scrutiny the judicial investigatory and

---

201   See Alan Smart, "Gifts, Bribes and *Guanxi*: A Reconsideration of Bourdieu's Social Capital," in *Cutural Anthropology* vol. 8 no. 3 (August 1993), pp. 388–408; Mayfair Yang, *Gifts, Favors, and Banquets: The Art of Social Relationships in China* (Ithaca: Cornell University Press, 1994). I have personally observed the practice of judges meeting over dinner with one of the disputants and / or their counsel to investigate the circumstances of the case and to hear one side's arguments informally. In most jurisdictions of Europe and North America, these ex parte meetings would be considered a violation of the judge's duty of disinterestedness, but in China they often are not considered improper.

202   Legal formalism may be conceived of as an approach that emphasizes doctrinal consistency and gives absolute precedence to objective performance of legal rules, institutions, and processes, regardless of the subjectively unjust results that ensue. For discussion of the origins and pitfalls of legal formalism, see Thomas C. Grey, "Langdell's Orthodoxy," in *University of Pittsburgh Law Review*, Vol. 45, No. 1 (Fall, 1983), p. 1.

203   See Pitman B. Potter, "Riding the Tiger – Legitimacy and Legal Culture in Post-Mao China," in *The China Quarterly* no. 138 (1994), pp. 325–358. Chinese and foreign lawyers practicing in China interviewed during 1997–98 underscored that judicial decision-making continues to exhibit the characteristics of formalism described in this article.

analytical processes, and expands the possibilities for decisions to be based on *guanxi* relations.

Anecdotal discussions with Chinese and foreign lawyers involved in litigation and arbitration in China suggest that the inadequacy of formal rules controlling the behavior of counsel and their clients permits *guanxi* relations with judicial and arbitral decision-makers to distort dispute settlement processes. The general absence in Chinese civil procedure law of provisions on abuse of process have been seen to permit Chinese counsel to use extremely aggressive procedural tactics to delay or derail dispute settlement processes such as repeated requests for delay, refusals to produce evidence based on claims of confidentiality that are not substantiated, broad requests for evidence going far beyond the confines of a particular dispute, and inflated damage estimates. Disregard for professional courtesy is also evident, in failures to answer correspondence or requests for cooperation in organizing case files or the presentation of evidence, personal attacks on the character of witnesses and attorneys, and demands for security bonds aimed at crippling opposing parties financially. In many instances, this behavior, while perhaps a natural outgrowth of zealous advocacy, becomes what lawyers with experience in Europe and North America would consider an abuse of process. The absence of effective controlling rules has also been seen as contributing to questionable conduct by disputing parties, such as obtaining delays through repeated but unsubstantiated requests to change attorneys, intimidation of witnesses, and what appear to be fraudulent conveyances of assets to avoid paying damage awards.

In the absence of formal rules or informal norms controlling the conduct of attorneys and their clients, lawyer tactics and client behavior are regulated at the discretion of judges and arbitrators. This in turn allows *guanxi* relations between counsel and/or their clients with presiding judges or arbitral officers to determine how a court or tribunal will respond to complaints about abusive conduct. Thus, abusive behavior by clients and counsel becomes the product of formalistic reliance on rules that either permit the behavior or fail effectively to manage it, together with the use of *guanxi* relations to ensure compliant oversight by judicial officers.

This process is justified in theory at least by presumptions about the virtue of judicial decision-makers. In a manner reminiscent of the Confucian system, judges are appointed largely on the basis of Communist Party loyalty and military service rather than legal education. The premise that upstanding and loyal Party members will be immune from blandishments of corruption arrives from Party ideals as well as Confucian tradition.[204] While there is increased recognition of the need to provide clearer rules governing the conduct of judicial officials and laws and regulations have been issued to govern the conduct of judges and lawyers,[205] still

---

204 For an example of rhetoric linking ideological purity with impartial and effective judicial institutions, see "Li Peng Addresses NPC Legal System Seminar," Beijing *Xinhua* Hong Kong Service 30 Aug. 1998 in FBIS-CHI-98-251, 8 Sept. 1998.

205 See e.g., "Supreme Court Promulgates Two Documents," Beijing *Xinhua* Domestic Service 17 Sept. 1998, in FBIS-CHI-98-262, 19 Sept. 1998; "PRC Lawyers Law" (1996), in *China Law & Practice* July/August 1996, pp. 31–41. Also see Patrick Sherrington and Virginia Chan, "New

the barriers between formal compliance with legal rules and process and informal dependence on *guanxi* networks remain important. One senior attorney I spoke with indicated a reluctance to bring cases to the local level courts in China because of corruption problems. Yet this same individual participates actively in the social cum professional intercourse with judicial and arbitral officials that characterizes *guanxi*-building.

The examples of attitudes of survey respondents, the results of case reporting on foreign trade and investment disputes in China, and information gleaned from anecdotal interviews and discussions with lawyers, arbitrators and judges suggest that the conventional approach that juxtaposes the informalism of *guanxi* networks with the role of formal law and legal institutions is misplaced. Rather, the performance of the Chinese legal system and the resiliency of *guanxi* dynamics suggest that the paradigm of complementarity will remain significant. Complementarity between *guanxi* dynamics and formal rules and institutions is made possible by limits in the formal structure of rules and procedures. Where the scope of governance by the formal is limited, an opportunity arises for informal relations to emerge. On the one hand, the operation of formal law and legal institutions in China requires adaptation to local conditions. As well, the formalism that underpins official legal norms requires a mediating mechanism to prevent rigid application of rules to the detriment of substantive fairness. Yet, mechanisms for adaptation and mediation are not themselves incorporated effectively into the formal system, hence the continued role of *guanxi* relations. On the other hand, the *guanxi* dynamic has traditionally been used as a mechanism for protecting individuals and groups against the depredations of powerful but unresponsive officialdom. On the basis of this tradition, *guanxi* will continue to be necessary as a strategy by which individuals and groups seek the adjustments in the application of formalistic law and process.

IMPLICATIONS OF COMPLEMENTARITY OF *GUANXI* AND LAW: APPLICATION AND THE CASE OF CONTRACT LAW

As China continues to be ever-more influenced by the common law traditions of North America, with their attendant lack of formalized rules mediating formal law, the role of *guanxi* is likely to increase. A useful example of this possibility is the Uniform Contract Law, enacted in 1999. This law, for the first time, incorporates many common law principles such as offer and acceptance and good faith in the process of forming contracts, replacing the conventional bureaucratic approval process for determining when contracts are formed and when they are valid. However, China still lacks a body of legal decisions on which can be based interpretations of what is meant by offer, acceptance, and good faith. In the absence

lawyers' law needs further legislative clarification," in *China Law & Practice* July/August 1996, pp. 28–30; Kevin Ying Yue Song, "China's New Law on Lawyers Will Move System Closer to International Standards," in *East Asian Executive Reports* Aug. 15, 1996, pp. 9–14. Also see PRC Judges Law (1995).

of such a body of law, *guanxi* relations are likely to continue to be important in the interpretation of the legal character of contract relations.

Bearing in mind the instrumentalist nature of law making in China, legislation on contracts has generally been an exercise in policy-driven rule making. However, the enactment of the Unified Contract Law in 1999 represented a significant departure from prior approaches to drafting contract laws aimed at preserving the supervisory authority of state bureaucracies. Since 1978, China's economic reform policies have given considerable attention to developing contract law. The Economic Contract Law ("ECL" 1981) was the first such effort, and while it recognized contract rights of the parties, it nonetheless provided significant approval and supervisory authority to state organs.[206] The Foreign Economic Contract Law ("FECL" 1985) offered contracting parties greater authority to select the content of contracts, the governing law, and the forum and process for dispute resolution.[207] However, state control remained strong, through formal approval provisions and proscriptions against conflicts with state interests. The General Principles of Civil Law[208] and China's accession to the Vienna Convention on Contracts for the International Sales of Goods[209] signaled yet further efforts to expand the contract rights available to economic actors, but in essence retained a bureaucratic approval model for contract formation and performance.

The drafting process for the Unified Contract Law reflected a departure from the bureaucratic approval model of contracts to one based on agreement of the parties.[210] After two years of debate, an experts group convened by the NPC Standing Committee issued a "Legislative Proposal" to guide the drafting process.[211] Based on an approach that allowed contracts to be formed based on the agreement of the parties rather than the approval of regulators, the Proposal gave significant autonomy to the parties to determine the content of their agreements. In addressing

206   See Pitman B. Potter, The Economic Contract Law of China: Legitimation and Contract Autonomy in the PRC. Seattle and London: University of Washington Press, 1992.

207   See generally, Jerome Alan Cohen, "The New Foreign Contract Law," in *China Business Review*, July-August 1985 (including translation of "Law of the PRC on Economic Contracts Involving Foreign Interests"); James V. Feinerman, "Legal Institution, Administrative Device, or Foreign Import: The Roles of Contract in the People's Republic of China, in P. Potter. ed., *Domestic Law Reforms in post-Mao China* (Armonk, N.Y.: M.E. Sharpe, 1994).

208   See generally, Henry R. Zheng, *China's Civil and Commercial Law* (Singapore: Butterworths Asia, 1988).

209   Apr. 11, 1980, U.N. Doc. A/Conf.97/18, Annex I (1980), 19 I.L.M. (entered into force Jan. 1, 1988). For discussion of the CCISG's role in unifying private international law, see John Spanogle, "The Arrival of Private International Law," in 25 *Geo. Wash. J. Int'l & Econ.* no. 2 (1991), pp. 477–522.

210   Liang Huixing, "Zhongguo hetong fa qicao guocheng zhong de zhenglun dian" (Points of contention in the process of drafting China's contract law), *Faxue yuekan* (Law Science Monthly) 1996 no. 2, pp. 13–15.

211   "Zhonghua renmin gongheguo hetong fa lifa fangan" (Legislative proposal for PRC contract law), *Zhengda faxue pinglun* (Chengchi University jurisprudence and discussion) 1995 no. 53, pp. 433–443. Also see Pan Weida, "Zhonggong hetong fa zhi jiajiang ji qi weilai fazhan" (The framework and future of PRC contract law), in *Zhengda faxue pinglun* 1995 no. 53, pp. 411–432.

conditions where contracts might be held to be invalid, the Proposal also focused on reasons such as fraud, serious misunderstanding, unfairness, and undue influence that would affect the intent or capacity of the parties to consent to contract terms. While couched in the language of tentative suggestion, the Proposal served notice that future changes in China's contract law would give significant attention to party autonomy and to reducing bureaucratic intrusion.[212] Throughout the drafting process that followed, extending to not less than five separate drafts, a central issue of debate was the extent to which contracts were to be based on bureaucratic approval or party agreement.[213] The fourth and "final" draft released in August, 1998 attempted to reconcile principles of autonomy of contract with public policy concerns of fairness, good faith, and the protection of state interests and social and economic well-being,[214] but further revisions were still required before final enactment at the Second Session of the Ninth NPC, March 15, 1999.

The Unified Contract Law enshrines a basic principle of party autonomy, such that party agreement rather than state approval determines the formation and content of contract. The statute provides that lawfully concluded contracts are effective on conclusion. In a modification of past practice, conclusion of contracts is not delayed until completion of formalities of approval and registration where required by law and administrative regulations. Instead, the new law simply provides that such formalities should be followed. Thus, the absence of contract approval will not necessarily relieve the parties of their contractual obligations unless and until the contract is declared invalid. Also the law does not impose content requirements, but instead allows the parties to determine content.

These general principles on contract autonomy are counterbalanced, however, by requirements that contracts must comply with law and administrative regulation, respect public morality, and avoid disruption of economic order and harm to

---

212 See Chen Xiaojun and Gao Fei, "Zhiding tongyi hetong fa de ruogan fali wenti sikao" (Considerations of several jurisprudential issues in enacting a unified contract law), *Faxue yanjiu* (Studies in Law) 1998 no. 1, pp. 53–59.

213 See generally Jiang Ping, "Drafting the Uniform Contract Law in China," *Columbia Journal of Asian Law* 1996 vol 10, no. 1, pp. 245–258; Liang Huixing, "Zhongguo hetong fa qicao guocheng zhong de zhenglun dian" (Points of contention in the process of drafting China's contract law), *Faxue yuekan* (Law Science Monthly), 1996 no. 2 pp. 13–15; Liang Huixing, "Guanyu Zhongguo tongyi hetong fa caoan di san gao" (Concerning the third draft of China's unified contract law), *Faxue yuekan* (Law science monthly) 1998 no. 2, pp. 47–52; Wang Liming, "Tongyi hetong fa zhiding zhong de ruogan yinan wenti tantao" (Inquiry into various difficult questions in enacting a unified contract law), *Zhengfa luntan* (Political Science and Law Tribune), 1996 no. 4, pp. 49–56 and no. 5, pp. 52–60; Sun Weizhi, "Hetong ziyou de lifa quxiang" (Legislation of Freedom of Contract), *Faxue zazhi* (Law science magazine), 1998 no. 1, pp. 19–20.

214 See "Zhonghua renmin gongheguo hetong fa (caoan)" (Contract Law of the PRC–Draft) (Legal Affairs Committee of NPC Standing Committee, Aug. 20, 1998) (copy on file with the author). The text was published in People's Daily Sept. 7, 1998; "Quanguo renda changweihui fabu tongzhi zhengqiu "Hetong fa (caoan)" yijian" (The NPC Standing Committee issues a circular seeking opinions on the "Contract Law (Draft)"), *Renmin ribao–haiwai ban* (People's Daily–Overseas Edition), September 5, 1998, p. 4. Also see Hu Kangsheng, "Guanyu <<Zhonghua renmin gongheguo hetong fa (caoan) de shouming>> (copy on file with the author).

the public interest of society. As well, the State Administration for Industry and Commerce retains general authority to supervise the formation and performance of contracts, and to act in concert with other government departments to deal with (*chuli*) contracts deemed contrary to state or social interests. The parties' intentions can also be disallowed by state directives – in effect permitting administrative edicts to take on the appearance of voluntary contracts. The statute also imposes liability for parties who conclude bogus (*jiajie*) contracts or negotiate in bad faith, for intentionally concealing key facts or providing false information, or for other conduct that violates principles of honesty and trust. The principles of freedom of contract are limited by provisions that contracts may be held invalid for fraud or coercion that damages state interests; malicious collusion that damages state, collective, or third-party interests; use of legal means for an illegal purpose; violation of the public welfare of society; and violation of mandatory provisions of law or administrative regulations.

What is significant about these limiting provisions is not their basic content, but rather the absence of rules and processes for interpretation. Under the prior system, bureaucratic approvals of contracts served to ensure that within broad limits, the norms governing contract content and performance were relatively stable. Under the new system, such approvals are not formally required such that the normative consistency provided through bureaucratic approval processes is no longer available. With the enactment of the UCL, China's contract system now faces the challenge of providing interpretation of the law's many general principles. Achieving consistent rational interpretation of the law will not be easy, however, not least because the statute reflects differing policy priorities of the diverse communities that contributed to the drafting process. More importantly because state approvals are no longer required for contract formation, there is no unified source of authoritative interpretation of the law's requirement. At the same time, there is no body of law that might give cohesion to decentralized interpretation. The combination of general principles on contract autonomy that depart from established practices of bureaucratic control, together with a lack of binding law that can give meaning to these general principles, will result in increased potential for increasingly unfettered local interpretation.

In such a climate, informal ties between contracting parties will be essential to give effect to their agreements. Moreover, the absence of a body of governing law to impose limits on interpretation will likely expand the opportunities for parties to apply *guanxi* networks to secure favorable interpretations. Thus, in the case of contract relations, the complementarity already evident between *guanxi* and formal law and procedure will likely expand to fill the need for certainty created by the UCL's incomplete sanctioning of contract autonomy.

CONCLUSION

The relationship between China's socialist legal system and the traditional Chinese practices of *guanxi* is one of complementarity rather than conflict. In light of the problems of performance and enforcement in the Chinese legal system, *guanxi* relations play an essential role in providing predictability to legal actors. While the role of *guanxi* can be limited by formal law and legal processes, the formal legal system remains incomplete and would have little effect at all were it not for informal mediating mechanisms such as *guanxi* relations. As China's legal system is increasingly influenced by common law rather than codified civil law traditions, the role for *guanxi* is likely to increase, pending the development of a body of law on which interpretations of general principles and norms might be based. Thus the complementary relationship between *guanxi* and law will continue to characterize the Chinese legal system for the foreseeable future.

10

"IDLE TALK": NEIGHBORHOOD GOSSIP AS A MEDIUM OF SOCIAL COMMUNICATION IN REFORM ERA SHANGHAI

James Farrer

INTRODUCTION: GOSSIP AND *GUANXI*

Early one afternoon (Aug. 27, 2000), I walked into our apartment complex through a narrow gate off a busy thoroughfare in largely working class Northeast Shanghai. The gate is only narrow enough for one person to pass, and at night it is locked. Inside the gate, four retired old men, all over seventy, occupied the two old sofas and several chairs permanently arrayed around the doorway. One white-haired fellow, in a barber chair directly by the door, was having his hair cut by the ancient barber who works at the doorway every day, cutting men's hair for three yuan. Every day, a group of older men and women sit in those sofas watching passersby and chatting. Often their small grandchildren sit with them. As I rounded the corner to enter our own building, a group of retired women and one man were watching the young children play in front of our building. A young mother was hanging her laundry, despite the impending rain. And because it was a rainy day, there were also far fewer people than usual taking in the late afternoon cool outside their apartments. As I walked up the stairs to the fifth floor, I nodded to a neighbor on the stairway. Earlier that day at lunchtime, the neighbor had appeared at our door asking my mother-in-law for a bowl of cooked rice. The neighbors had run out of rice during their meal. Such small occasions for mutual aid are common in the apartment building.

Despite the odd appearance of a blonde foreigner entering an ordinary apartment complex in this part of Shanghai, no one pays much attention to me here. Our story is already well known throughout the neighborhood. I initially moved into my in-laws' apartment in 1995, shortly before I married my wife, a Shanghaiese herself, who had lived here with her parents since the apartment complex was built in 1987. Naturally, neighbors have long passed on their knowledge of our marriage, my Chinese ability, my accommodation to local eating habits, our current residence in Japan, and many other details, such as my occupation in Japan, our income in Japan, my wife's occupation, our plans for children, and so on. Gossip is not only an important activity among neighbors, it is a medium that defines local values and serves as an important source of information about a wide variety of matters of practical concern. Moreover, neighborhood gossip networks in heterogeneous and dense neighborhoods like ours are an important medium for the definition of a local urban culture in Shanghai, a "city people's culture" (*shimin wenhua*) that for most of the reform era has embraced an extraordinarily wide range of class and status positions to include virtually all members of Shanghai society. However, changes in the social geography of Shanghai neighborhoods entail changes in the inclusiveness and heterogeneity of these neighborhood networks and perhaps the end of a common "city people's culture."

My interest in gossip comes out of my field work on sexual culture in Shanghai, conducted from 1994 to 1996 with two two-month follow-up visits in 1999 and 2000. For much of this time I lived with my wife's parents in their three-room flat (*liangshi yiting*) in an ordinary Shanghai apartment block (*gongfang*), a type of community also known by its socialist moniker of "new village" (*xincun*), or "new workers' village." In this chapter, I use this field work experience to reflect on a particular kind of social network that is outside the usual sociological focus on Chinese economic and political networks, networks of neighborhood gossip. During my field work, I realized the importance of gossip as a practice for defining or negotiating normative sexual codes. Gossip seems to be the primary means for communicating about sexual matters. To give readers a sense of these neighborhood conversations, I also focus on the contents of gossip, describing stories local women and men in my neighborhood told about one another, stories that I came to understand largely from roughly two years of living with my mother-in-law as a helpful and entertaining source of local news. I supplement this local material with interviews from residents of other types of neighborhoods in Shanghai. I want to use this field work experience to address one of the common themes in this volume, how the transition to a market economy in China is mediated by social networks, and also how the "market transition" seems to be transforming these social networks as part of a larger ecological process of geographic social stratification in Shanghai.

My perspective is partly inspired by Mayfair Yang's early work on *guanxi* (1994) and her more recent work on a woman's "public sphere" (1999). In essence, I expected to find the latter – a space in which women publicly share information and strategies – in the former – the "rhizomatic networks" of reciprocal interpersonal exchange (i.e., *guanxi networks*). The social exchange I discuss is gossip, the exchange of casual talk about other familiar people, a much under-appreciated communicative activity that most people engage in far more than watching television, reading or many other activities commonly associated with the idea of a "public sphere" (Emler 1994). Gossip, when studied seriously, invalidates the distinction between a critical, rational, and implicitly masculine public sphere and a traditional, emotive, and feminine gendered intimate sphere. As de Sousa writes: "Gossip is inherently democratic, concerned with private life rather than public issues, and 'idle' in the sense that it is not instrumental or goal oriented. Yet it can serve to expand our understanding of life in ways that other modes of inquiry cannot" (de Sousa 1994, p. 25).

When I casually asked my mother-in-law over dinner why so many people were willing to tell her their stories, my father-in-law answered in his typically elliptical fashion, "Mom has good *guanxi* in this building." In the context of the conversation, what he meant was that "Mom" is trusted in the neighborhood. People ask her to do things for them, tell her their personal stories, and trust her with certain tasks, such as keeping a key for an empty apartment or taking their mail to the post office. In turn, she asks for the rare favor or bit of information from her neighbors. Her good *guanxi* rests on her responsible participation in the neighborhood discursive community and on the good reputation that this discursive community has given her. Good neighborhood *guanxi* also can be mobilized for instrumental purposes, as with the bowl of rice, keeping a key, or for more important matters. However, *guanxi* has perhaps been discussed too much in terms of its instrumental uses (*guanxixue*) and not enough in terms of its communicative, moral, and emotive uses. Perhaps thinking about gossip will allow us to see everyday social relations in a different light.

In addition to my specific arguments about neighborhood gossip, I would like to suggest that *guanxi* as an instrumental practice relies on gossip in at least three ways: One is the exchange of information itself. Without adequate information about the members of one's network, it is impossible to mobilize the network for specific purposes. Secondly, gossip is important for establishing and signaling the sentimental bonds (*ganqing*) that define the boundaries of a *guanxi* network. Inclusion in gossip is an important sign of group inclusion. Gossip is not merely a byproduct of community networks, but definitive of community membership, through who is allowed to participate in gossiping (Gluckman 1963; Emler 1994). Finally, gossip is a way of establishing status and moral authority within the group. "Mom's" good *guanxi* in the neighborhood is a consequence of a positive reputation.

Gossip is an effective and important means of communication. In contrast to the passive "publics" created by the mass media, such communities of gossip allow far greater participation and diversity of expression (Post 1994). This might be especially true in China, where access to public mass media is limited, and the topics and perspectives, which can be expressed within it, are limited by political controls. Especially for members of oppressed groups, and especially for women, gossip is an important means of factual inquiry (Ayim 1994) and an important means of social communication (Code 1994; Collins 1994; Schein 1994). Governed by the principles of friendship, reciprocity, and pragmatism that Yang ascribes to *renqing* practice, gossip networks logically constitute a part of the feminine *minjian* Yang is searching for (1994). Based on my observations of gossip in our neighborhood, however, I would argue that while gossip is dominated by women and perceived as a traditional practice of women, men also engage in neighborhood gossip. It seems that age (or retirement status), rather than gender, may be the more relevant criterion for who actually participates in local gossip activities.

Gossip is an effective and important means for negotiating local moral standards. Based on my fieldwork, it seems that sexual norms – and perhaps other social norms as well – are most often discussed through narratives of people with whom the interlocutors feel they have some direct relation. Abstract rules and stories of distant strangers seem unconvincing without such local anecdotal support. In terms of content, gossip can be described as "moral talk" (Taylor 1994), giving concrete operational definition to otherwise rather abstract principles of morality (Sabini and Silver 1982). But gossip is also a special kind of moral reasoning: pragmatic, flexible and attentive to concrete differences (Collins 1994, p. 114). Although gossip tends to support conventional moral codes, the humor of gossip dulls its harsh judgments (Morreall 1994), and the wide experience of gossipers makes them "realistic" about human nature (Ze'ev 1994, p. 19). Gossip allows participants to understand their own situations in a comparative context and gain empathy for the predicaments of others, through which they can begin to revise their moral views (Collins 1994, p. 113). Therefore, even though gossip within a small closed community is likely to lead to judgments that are conservative and conventional, gossip can occasionally be subversive of conventional morality when it provides access to information and models that defy conventional norms (de Sousa 1994, p. 32). As Maryann Ayim writes about women's gossip, "the line between talk that sustains and talk that subverts oppressive norms is an easy one to cross for those who are heavily penalized by such norms" (Ayim 1994, p. 95).

Gossip networks may change along with changes in neighborhood ecology. I propose that as sociologists, we should also consider neighborhood gossip as a feature of the changing ecology of urban spaces (cf. Fischer 1984). In taking this approach, I emphasize the continuing importance of face-to-face networks in urban Shanghai, and also how the changing ecology of urban space in Shanghai is potentially altering and weakening these face-to-face networks. While recent Western literature on urban sociality emphasizes a "routine world of strangers" (Bech 1998, p. 215) and digitally linked virtual "cyberbias" (e.g. Featherstone and Lash 1999), for many residents of crowded Chinese neighborhoods, long-term face-to-face relations among neighbors remain an important context of social life. Following the classic Chicago School formulation, I believe that local living environments qualitatively differ in terms of their *density* and *heterogeneity*, making for different types of involvement in local community life (Wirth 1938). While early Chicago urban ecologists associate the density and heterogeneity of the city with a debilitating moral "disorganization" (Wirth 1938), later participants in this tradition see the diversity and conflict of a "disorderly" urban sociality as beneficial for a viable social order (Sennett 1970; Smith 1979, p. vii). In Shanghai, I see neighborhood gossip as a disorderly medium of communication within which neighbors share and compare personal strategies for dealing with the opportunities of the new market economy. As a constitutive feature of neighborhood life, gossip is also subject to the macro-sociological effects of the market reforms on neighborhood organization in China, through the impact of real estate markets on the ecology of urban residential space.

In sum, I argue that the effects of the market transition on social life in Shanghai are doubly "mediated" by local gossip networks, first through gossip as a medium of communication and second in terms of the ecological transformation of that medium. In the first instance, such networks are a means by which (typically older) men and women communicate and discuss the sexual and career strategies of (typically younger) people in the neighborhood. In this sense, such networks are a medium for negotiating a local cultural response to political and economic regime shifts. The stories shared are the materials with which participants construct a pragmatic and shifting moral order explaining the opportunity structures of the market economy. This argument finds support in the idea that gossip is a "chaotic" or unorganized form of communication particularly suited for finding pragmatic solutions to contentious and complex moral issues (Code 1994). The second point rests on my observation that one of the major effects of the market reforms in China is a transformation of residential space (cf. Dutton 1998, pp. 222–231). The marketization of housing is changing the ecology of neighborhood life and transforming neighborhood social networks. I suggest that new types of neighborhoods that seem to be emerging lack both the heterogeneity and density typical of Shanghai neighborhoods up until recently. This transformation of urban space may be reducing the potential for local networks to act as a socially broad band of communication.

A final methodological point is that the mediating institutions of cultural change during regime transitions, like the transition from state-led to market-led production, are not themselves likely to be products of the new regime, but are more likely to be legacies of older regimes (Wank 1999). I argue that in Shanghai, the new local culture of the market, including this "urban people's culture" of neighborhood gossip, is partly structured by one of the peculiar local legacies of Maoist planning, the "new village" neighborhood. I suggest that it is in this "traditional" and "socialist" sphere of neighborhood gossip that practical information about the market society is exchanged and changing concepts of personal and sexual morality are shared and contested.

A MAOIST NEIGHBORHOOD IN DENGIST SHANGHAI

In my Shanghai fieldwork, I conducted individual interviews, focus groups, and ethnographic observations aiming to understand changing sexual culture in Shanghai (Farrer forthcoming). The focus on sexuality is clearly reflected in the stories I collected. The focus on sexual and intimate matters, however, might not be unrepresentative of neighborhood gossip in general. Gossip is largely about intimate, backstage matters in most societies (Post 1994), and is a major means through which people, particularly women, can engage in informative but relatively protected discussions of sexual matters. I focus on one node in a local gossip network, which serves as a particularistic point of departure for a discussion of more general principles illustrated by this one case. For my discussion of the changing ecology of neighborhood gossip, I also rely on interviews with residents of other Shanghai neighborhoods. Given the limitations of my study, however, this chapter can only make tentative suggestions about neighborhood gossip in general or changes in neighborhood organization on a larger scale.

My in-laws live in what was officially described as a "new workers' village," in an area that in the 1950's would have been on the eastern fringe of the city, but now is well within the boundaries of the city. Our "new village" (*xincun*) consists of fifteen five-story walk-up apartment buildings in a complex that retains the grid-like structure of Shanghai's old-style alleyways (*linong*). This type of housing – the multi-story walk-up apartment building – is now the most common type of housing in Shanghai, accounting for about half of all housing in Shanghai in the mid-1990's. Despite some recent improvements such as additional greenery, our neighborhood is not an aesthetically pleasing environment, lacking the ornamentation and styling characteristic of both pre-1949 structures and of housing built in the late 1990's. The poorly constructed brick and cement apartment blocks were once painted, but are now barren, rain-stained concrete. They are uninsulated and unheated in the cold wet winter. During the 1990's, the state enterprises that owned the housing sold most of the flats to the resident employees, usually at a discount to market price, which depended on employee seniority. By 2000, several well-off families had sold their flats here and were buying new housing in more desirable locations. More typically, many well-off young people have left their homes in the neighborhood for new housing, while their parents remained in the old apartment.

Because of Maoist economic policies there was very little investment in urban housing during the 1960s and 1970s, and with population growth, per capita densities actually increased during the 1970's. Densities in older housing remain especially high. In nearly two years of living here, I have eventually grown comfortable with the ways of crowded Shanghai living. In our apartment, four adults and on most days a young child comfortably share a three-room 32 square-meter apartment. When we are staying here, my wife and I have the small north-facing front room (hot in the summer, cold in the winter). Her parents stay in the main room, which also doubles as a living room. The small dining room in the middle also served as grandmother's bedroom when she was still alive in the mid-1990's. At 8 square meters of floor space per capita (excluding grandmother and the nephew, who were not full-time residents), we were right at the city average in 1995. In the early 1990s, many neighbors thought my in-laws were lucky to have so much space for a family of four. In the early 1990s, it was still very common for adult children to share a room with their parents, for the dining rooms and balconies to be employed as sleeping spaces, even for two married couples to share the same room.[215] By 2000, however, many Shanghaiese lived in far more spacious accommodations than we.

The neighborhood is also very heterogeneous. It was constructed by several state-owned enterprises as employee housing, including a large bank, the public

---

215   From 1990 to 2000, per capita housing space in Shanghai more than doubled from roughly 5 square meters per person to slightly more than 10 square meters per person.

security agency, the military, and a large maritime trading company. Many residents are present or former employees of these work units, including the one where my in-laws worked. Such employees ranged from senior administrators and technical experts to low-level line workers and cleaners, but common work unit ties created bonds of trust, which formed the initial basis for communicative relationships. During the reform era, social and economic distinctions within this group have widened. Managers often have access to extra income from new company sideline businesses. Many low-level workers were laid off. Others in the building have become private entrepreneurs, some successful, others failing. Others have traveled to conduct business or have children living abroad. The fortunes of children in the neighborhood varied dramatically from those who work abroad in prestigious occupations, to those engaging in lowly occupations such as factory work or service labor. Therefore, during the 1980s and 1990s this "new village" complex housed a mix of people who wouldn't be living together in most American communities: workers and managers, unemployed and wealthy, college-educated and illiterate, people who were finding very different "levels" in the "sea" of the market economy. The density of interactions, social heterogeneity of residents, and long-term nature of social ties, which characterized the social networks in "new villages," such as the one where I lived, resulted from cumulative regime changes. Dengist market reforms were recreating the class distinctions that Maoism had intended to eliminate. Nonetheless, Maoist planning had placed members of work units into the same crowded residential spaces, forming the nucleus of social networks that expanded to include neighbors from other work units. This ironic conjuncture of Maoist planning and Dengist reforms for an important period in the 1980s and 1990s created very dense and heterogenous neighborhoods in which a very wide range of people shared living space, social networks, and casual gossip.

The density of interactions between neighbors and their practical involvement in one another's lives were considered intermediate between older traditional alleyways (*linong*) and new high-rise buildings. Residents of Shanghai's older, even more densely populated alleyways and "shanty districts" described neighborly relations in these "new village" public apartment complexes as cold and distant. On the other hand, most of my informants concurred that relations were far more open and sociable in our type of neighborhood than in newer neighborhoods of high-rise commodity housing. Neighbors are able to hear and observe a great deal of one another's activities in the "new village" neighborhood. The narrow alleyways between buildings are neither clearly public nor private. People sleep outside their doorways on hot summer days, and walk about in their pajamas in the narrow spaces between buildings. For an outsider, entering the alleyway is an intrusion into a semi-private space, and residents pay close attention to the activities of both neighbors and strangers.

Surveillance also has a quasi-state aspect in the members of the street committee who man the main gateway to the compound and collect parking fares. The complex was made even less accessible during the time I was there. A large driveway was closed off, and in the evening, all but one gated entrance was closed.[216] Being such a conspicuous outsider, I was at first appalled by the omnipresent formal and informal surveillance, but I gradually realized gossip could be enabling or legitimating for new forms of behavior (sexual behavior being my focus), even as it restrained such behavior in some ways. By this I mean simply that as neighbors' sexual affairs and other peccadilloes become known, and these same neighbors come and go in their daily lives, enduring unscathed the scrutiny of neighbors and state officials, gossip about these cases gradually builds up as a vast reservoir of second-hand experience from which people can pick and chose references, excuses, or deflections for their own problems. Quite literally, alleyway people quickly become wise in the ways of the world, meaning the world of the people living around them. This is an especially rich source of information in our neighborhood, I suggest, because of the density and heterogeneity of the people living in such neighborhoods.

To emphasize the specificity of my case, we can briefly consider alternative neighborhood structures, and their transformation during the reform era. First, not all neighborhoods in Shanghai had the characteristics of density and heterogeneity evident in the "new village" where I lived. There were, for instance, enclaves for high-ranking cadres, and enclaves of university employees, where local gossip might have different contents and rules.[217] More common than these were poor and older neighborhoods in which socialist planning was not such an important factor in the distribution of the population. I conducted extensive interviews among residents of a so-called "shanty district" (*penghuqu*) in an area of Shanghai near my "new village."[218] Residents of this district reported far greater social homogeneity than among residents in my community. Virtually all were from one county in Northern Jiangsu Province, even speaking the same local dialect in the alleyway community. According to informants, only one local resident had ever attended university. Few outsiders were willing to move into the neighborhood, which had a reputation for crime and disorder. Until the neighborhood was demolished in 2000, it remained a tightly knit community similar to many such immigrant neighborhoods in Shanghai before 1949 (Wakeman and Yeh 1992; Lu 1999), dense but not heterogenous. The residents I knew seemed socially isolated from the educated, emigre, and economically successful cases common in the "new village." Such neighborhoods are being demolished at a high rate in Shanghai, with their residents usually scattered

216 The ostensible purpose was to protect the neighborhood from what most people in the neighborhood perceived as increased crime by "outside" workers (*mingong*), but the arrangement also allowed the financially strapped street committee to extract revenue from the increasing number of company cars parked overnight in the alleyway.

217 An informant who grew up in a compound of high-ranking military officials said that resident women (many born outside Shanghai) distinguish their neighborhood from ordinary Shanghai neighborhoods with the argument that they did not engage in idle gossip about one another's personal affairs as do Shanghai's "petty urbanites" (*xiaoshimin*). Whether this characterization is accurate or not it shows the attitude of social elites to this kind of gossip.

218 This term is used to describe communities of private dwellings built up mostly in the 1940s and 1950s (cf. Lu 1995). The people I interviewed from these communities were usually born in Shanghai. Such communities are not to be confused with the communities of contemporary migrant laborers, which I did not study.

among the different new neighborhoods, often far removed from their old homes and former neighbors.[219]

STORIES FROM OUR NEIGHBORHOOD

During the year and a half living in an apartment with my in-laws, I was privy to the neighborhood gossip often passed on to me by my mother-in-law while she cooked lunch for me and my wife's three-year-old nephew who spent his afternoons with us. "Mom" had recently retired from the large state enterprise that built the complex where we lived and for which about a third of the residents worked or once worked, including my wife's father. I didn't directly interview in the complex, thus I report no more than what my mother-in-law could tell me. A fairly typical retiree, she had lived in the complex for ten years, and spent about half an hour a day chatting with neighbors. In the course of a year, my hand-me-down gossip included a large cast of characters in my building. Obviously, these stories don't represent the building statistically, nor do they really represent actual people; rather they should be thought of as discursive constructs, narrative forms for conveying locally relevant information. I present only thumbnail sketches of what were sometimes rather elaborate narratives. These brief descriptions are meant to give readers a sense of the substance of neighborhood gossip, especially in the area of sexual strategies, which as will become clear from reading through them, are not at all unrelated to economic strategies. (I have changed some details to reduce the chance that particular people could be identified.)

- **the girl downstairs who went to Shenzhen,** the special economic zone abutting Hong Kong. Her family liked to show off the expensive gifts she bought them, such as a leather coat for her father. Mom said, "I don't know how she makes her money, but another neighbor said, 'Well that's easy money, all you have to do is loosen your pants.'" Mom was embarrassed when she repeated that line to me, and covered her mouth while she laughed.
- **the girl who married a Japanese.** She ran her own business in Japan and lived in a different city from her husband. Her elderly parents raised her child in the building, and he grew up speaking no Japanese, although I heard other children call him "Japanese," almost an insult in Shanghai. These grandparents reported to my mother-in-law all the gifts their daughter gave them. After we moved to Japan ourselves, they made sure to compare incomes and housing footage.
- **the girl who worked as a hostess in the karaoke club.** Her mother bragged that she could make several hundred renminbi a night in tips. "How could a mother be so stupid as to brag about that," Mom commented.
- **the girl who disapproved of her father's remarriage.** She had moved out, but she insisted on her right to her old room in the apartment, where she stored her old things and denied her father access. The family was Christian, and someone in the family had posted a sticker on the door saying in Chinese, "Jesus will forgive those who sin." We assumed that sticker was just another of the insults exchanged within the family.

219 During the earlier part of the reform era, it was more common for such communities to move back to new housing on the same location (*fangqian*). In such cases, local networks and social customs are often maintained. In recent years, however, an element of price has been introduced into these resettlements, and residents are scattered among different sites according to their ability to pay for a more attractive location.

-   **the girl who married a handicapped man,** and whose parents wouldn't speak to her for a long time thereafter. Her parents were bitterly opposed, and forgave her only after the handicapped husband started pulling in good money by driving one of the small three-wheeled taxis reserved for handicapped drivers.
-   **the star student who now worked in a major bank.** She married a few months before my wife (also a famous top student in the building). A very proper student, she told my mother-in-law that she never went out to dance halls and bars. "These places are too chaotic," she said. Now that she is a bank executive with an uptown apartment, she gives her mother a thousand yuan a month and expensive traditional medicines. "The daughter comes back and everyone treats her like a VIP," Mom said, "Her mother says 'With a daughter like this one who needs a son.' But, I think her son and daughter-in-law aren't happy to hear her talk like that."

These were largely negative examples in my mother-in-law's framing (though given the circumstances the valences of stories could shift from positive to negative as did this last one about the good student who became too 'uppity'). I also heard more positively framed stories:

-   **the son who went to England and got a Ph.D.** His father visited him and came back bragging what a nice clean city London was.
-   **the daughter who went to the U.S.,** became a medical doctor, and married a Chinese-American lawyer. They had just recently bought a house on Long Island. This was almost an ideal case in the eyes of a Shanghaiese mother.
-   **the airline stewardess who flew to America every other week.** She had a boyfriend who was a driver and parked his car in our neighborhood, driving her anywhere she needed to go. (She had a co-worker who was arrested for prostitution, just one example of third- and fourth-hand gossip, which my mother-in-law passed along.)

Then there were simply funny stories:

-   **the nice old Subei (Northern Jiangsu) lady from down the hall.** She always brings back a live chicken for my mother-in-law when she returns from the countryside. Occasionally she comes over to watch TV. While watching a TV program about love and romance, she told Mom, "What is this love and romance stuff. I don't understand it. If my old man dies, he dies. So what?"
-   **the father of the model student who works in a bank.** "He is a retired soldier but acts like a little old lady," Mom said. "He comes complaining to me to get his wife to cook better food for the family. I told him, 'That is your family's business. How can I tell your wife what to do.'" More recently, rumors were spreading that he was flirting with the old women in the building.
-   **the neighbor daughter, who is thirty-one and divorced with a small child.** She went to Eastern Europe doing private business, and now parks a big Toyota Landcruiser in the narrow alley in front of our building. In 1998, her mother was looking for husband for her, and visited the two neighbors whose daughters were in Japan and asked for their help introducing her daughter to a foreigner. She also asked Mom about this idea. By late 1999, the daughter suddenly had a new apartment, and the mother took Mom and several other neighbors to see the apartment. As they entered, they noticed a man's shoes, cigarettes, and other signs that the woman wasn't living alone. Later the couple married, and it turns out that her husband is a wealthy northern businessman.
-   **there was also the good student who married the foreigner with no money** (myself and my wife). Obviously, we were the object of some gossip, the contents of which we can't be sure. My mother-in-law only reported the neighbors' questions, which included their musings about why an American could decide to live in a Chinese apartment

(something they thought impossible), whether I could stand the food, speak Chinese, or use chopsticks. Some wanted to know whether my parents were wealthy, what they did for a living, or how much we earn in Japan.

THE USES OF NEIGHBORHOOD GOSSIP

Gossip as moral discourse

In the neighborhood, a primary use of gossip stories is constructing local standards of normalcy around issues of work, money, sex, and marriage. My initial interest in gossip stories was their use in representing standards of normalcy around sexual practices, including practices that would have seemed deviant before the reform era: working in hostess clubs, extra-marital affairs, premarital cohabitation, or marrying foreigners. In contemporary Shanghai, all of these types of behavior are discussed in neighborhood gossip, and receive some sympathy or approval. Of course, much use of gossip is critical, at least sarcastic. Gossip may be used to condemn or ostracize neighbors for their moral flaws, but I found such strident criticism is unfitting with the live-and-let-live "city people's culture" of reform-era Shanghai. Gossip stories are seldom told with a purely judgmental tone, but rather as a form of enjoyment including humor, jokes that put oneself in a good light through contrast, comparison, association, or just simply because one is privy to some information. Moreover, even the most scandalous stories allow both positive and negative readings. Gossip constrains people's actions through the threat of censure and laughter, but its multivalence offers the possibility of alternative interpretations. The actual meanings individuals attach to stories depend on their *own* circumstances.

Gossip also has empowering or legitimating uses, which may lend themselves to unconventional conclusions. For instance, for the mother of a daughter who married a foreigner or the success stories of women who have moved abroad, gossip carries a lot of weight in conversations with neighbors. The heavy weighting of such stories in my own sample indicates my mother-in-law's interest in such cases. However, even the mother who bragged about how much money her daughter made as a hostess would have a host of positive references as well, especially given the high value placed in the alleyway culture on "face" gained through the gifts of the generous daughter, displaying the two highest virtues in the Shanghai alleyway society (and in Chinese society generally) – wealth and filial piety – which partly negate the shamefulness of how the money is made.

Money, and material wealth more generally, plays a big role in evaluating people's worth in contemporary Shanghai, and seems to have invaded the content of much of alleyway gossip, including stories about sexual matters. The alleyway gossip narratives sketched out here focus on how much money people were making, their material fortunes in love and marriage, and where their money came from. This is "face" in the sense of status – *mianzi* – being able to show off a new leather jacket or a daughter with a medical degree and a suburban American house. This is also how many other Chinese describe the alleyway culture of Shanghai, obsessively concerned with minor differences in income and consumption, a caricature with some truth. This kind of face – *mianzi* – is what was referenced when a daughter is married, firecrackers explode, and all the neighbors poke their heads out in the alleyway to see what kind of dress she is wearing and what sort of car she is being picked up in. (Our own red Ford at our wedding was a bit of a disappointment.)[220] Sexual scandals are a way of diminishing others' success, but also a way of reconsidering the moral criteria by which materially motivated sexual strategies should be judged. Despite its overall conservative tone, neighborhood gossip also provides a moral universe of characters and narratives within which deviant actions can be normalized.

I thus suggest a "dramatistic" analysis of neighborhood gossip as a rhetoric of moral argumentation (Burke 1989, pp. 135–8; Farrer forthcoming), a mode of analysis that focuses on how actions are made meaningful by reference to a locally constructed set of characters, motives, narratives, and scenes. Neighborhood gossip networks serve as broad bands of communication providing the raw materials for moral argumentation. This is not a deterministic process producing a fixed moral code, but rather a process in which individuals have a wide degree of freedom in establishing their own positions. The stories that I heard were mostly stories of young women and their successes and failures in career and marriage. Each story represents a practical strategy for dealing with increasingly free and competitive choices about careers and money, sex and marriage. Neighborhood gossip is thus a local and active semi-public sphere in which older women in particular are able to share information about issues – particularly the economic and sexual strategies of their children – about which they have little other information. This medium crosses class and status lines, and concerns itself with people whose life circumstances are well understood, without the censorship and interpretations imposed on public media. In all these ways, this local "public sphere" shows itself to be more lively, more subjectively "real" and probably more subversive of public mores than discussions of similar issues in public print and electronic media, which receive the bulk of scholarly attention.

Gossip as information medium

While I initially focused on gossip as a site of moral argumentation, I have come to realize that neighborhood networks are also the source of much practical information. While such information would not normally be considered "gossip," gossip plays a role in making this information available. For instance, in our neighborhood, people have access to a wide amount of information about emigration procedures (including specialized information for visa-overstayers in Japan), a very popular topic of conversation in Shanghai. Knowing which neighbors had

---

220 To be more precise and risk a generalization, *mianzi* also seems important in family judgments, while *lian* is also important in close non-familial relationships. It might be that *mianzi* is relevant in nearly all social relations, while *lian* references the serious judgments of intimate friends and family members.

relatives in which countries, allowed people to gain access to this information. Other useful information exchanged in my neighborhood included details of local real-estate transactions, specific information about teachers at local schools, and small but important matters such as which of the local migrant vegetable vendors are more trustworthy. Again, access to much of this information depended on regular participation in neighborhood discussions, and sufficient knowledge of whom to ask.

We can also consider the place neighborhood gossip occupies in relation to other sources of information and moral discourse. In the case of my mother-in-law, the neighborhood reference group was separate from family networks back in the country town where she grew up, and separate from the stories she read in magazines, the evening newspaper, and saw on television. It seems that these sources – neighbors, family, and media – have different uses, comprising a spatial compartmentalization of information and moral discourses. The particulars of this spatial organization might differ for different families in different local contexts, but my example serves to show how such compartmentalization of discourse pragmatically works in one case.

First, public media have become increasingly important as a source of systematic information. Typically, people in my family used television, newspapers, and magazines to learn about things in which the neighbors and family members had less experience or expertise. In the area of sexuality, health issues were a frequent topic stimulated by newspaper stories, such as news of the adverse effects of coffee consumption on male fertility or the dangers of radiation from computers, which my mother-in-law brought to my attention several times. On the other hand, television dramas also featured narratives similar to neighborhood gossip, and local communication networks could be important in the critical reception of these stories. The media occasionally serve as a window onto issues about which personal disclosures would be too painful, such as the topic of families separated by the Cultural Revolution, which was the subject of *Niezhai* ("Retribution") the most popular television drama in Shanghai in 1995. While it was being shown, my mother-in-law occasionally discussed the fictional characters and stories of *Niezhai* with her neighbors. For instance, the fictional characters in *Niezhai* are a group of children abandoned by their Shanghaiese parents in Yunnan Province after the Cultural Revolution. The children, now teenagers, make their way to Shanghai to work. The neighbors in my building, like many Shanghaiese, contested the ending of the story, which had all the children return to Yunnan, an ending in line with central government controls on internal migration. Local residents hoped some of the children would stay in Shanghai (which they see as the land of opportunity), and argued about which ones would actually stay. Neighborhood discussions thus may be important contexts for contesting and interpreting representations from more public sources.

Family and neighborhood social networks may also serve as different moral reference frames. The compartmentalization of neighborhood gossip and family gossip in our family seem to map roughly onto two different conceptions of "face" in the Chinese language (Hu 1944). Family relationships were important for issues of face in the sense of *lian*, deep face, or family honor. For instance, some matters of sexual conduct were of greater importance when facing the family, but of less importance when facing the neighbors. The family would be concerned that in-laws were raising their children to be moral and dignified, since discipline in parenting reflects on the "quality" (*suzhi*) of the family, a concept closely connected with family honor. While honor also should be maintained in front of neighbors, family members were the more important reference group for this concept.

The media, neighborhood, and family thus resemble separate dramatic spaces in which different casts of characters perform and moral judgments are made according to different rules. The different rules include (but are not exhausted by) the rule of gaining face as status (*mianzi*), which governs most neighborhood judgments of social success: the rule of not "losing face" (*diulian*, to lose honor), which governs judgments of sexual scandals within the family; and the more morally neutral concept of verisimilitude (similarity to commonsense "reality"), which governs judgments of stories and reports in the media. Although I will not argue that this one case can represent all Chinese families, I suggest that neighborhood gossip may have distinct uses as a semi-public sphere for adjudicating personal life strategies, which are discussed from a pragmatic moral perspective.

Instrumental uses of gossip networks

In neighborhoods such as ours, in which people have been living together for more than a decade, information and gossip networks also can be mobilized for more instrumental purposes. For instance, several neighbors had relatives in Japan. These neighbors shared information about a great many practical matters, including many for which there are no official or public sources (particularly for immigrants with no legal residence status in Japan). Sharing information might lead to mutual help. For instance, one neighbor approached neighbors with daughters married to Japanese about the possibility of introducing a Japanese husband to her divorced daughter (another service, international marriage, for which there is no legal public alternative). In this case, it seems the inquiry led to no practical result, and the daughter married a Chinese. In another case, however, a neighbor was able to gain the help of a neighbor to arrange a job for a relative who recently left for Japan. Our own experiences with gaining aid through such networks are limited. My mother-in-law is proud that she does not frequently ask aid from neighbors even in trivial matters such as foodstuff. However, she was also able to use the aid of a neighbor to help a nephew purchase a nearby flat, achieving a discount of a few percentage points from the market price. The transaction was legal, but involved insider knowledge of the particular housing development. She also used neighborhood networks to arrange a research-related interview for my wife.

Such instrumental uses of neighborhood social networks seem to depend on several factors related to neighborhood gossip. One is group inclusion. In a neighborhood setting, only those with whom one regularly speaks are going to be seen as members of one's own group and accessible for requests for aid. A closely related issue is mutual affection. Especially, for the older women residents in the building, not participating in "idle talk" (*xianhua*) would be taken as a sign of social distance. Sharing "idle talk" is a way of building and also displaying social closeness. Then there is the issue of information. People must have some detailed knowledge of other residents in order to know whom they can approach for help on a particular matter. I would thus argue that the practical use of social relationships (*guanxixue*) in the neighborhood depends on the tight social relationships maintained in part through everyday gossip and other forms of conversation.

The pragmatics of gossip

Although I seldom observed the activities of people in my own neighborhood exchanging gossip, I learned from interviews of some of the norms governing its practice in this and other neighborhoods. One norm involves the "openness" of homes to casual visits by neighbors (*chuanmen*). In older Shanghai neighborhoods, it would be considered odd to close the doorways during a warm day. Neighbors casually walk into one another's homes, chatting, even carrying their own bowls of rice and eating out of the dishes neighbors prepared. In the new village, doors might be closed, but casual neighborly visits are common, especially among the retired older women in the building. It would be extremely rude not to warmly welcome a visiting neighbor into the apartment for a chat. Minimally, such chats involve exchanging information about one's own activities and those of one's children, and often extend to sharing stories about other neighbors' activities. It should be noted, however, that for residents of Shanghai's older and more open traditional alleyways, "new villages" such as ours seem far less neighborly than their own neighborhoods in which neighbors have usually lived for a far longer period of time and often share public toilets, kitchens, and other facilities.

Another norm of neighborhood gossip is an informal requirement to disclose certain relevant facts about oneself and one's family. This norm came to my attention when I returned to the neighborhood for our visit in 1999. My wife and mother-in-law were returning to the building when they met a neighbor whose children were working in Japan. Knowing that we were living in Tokyo, the neighbor asked about our situation, including my income at the university. Although my wife considered this to be personal information, and tried to evade the question, it was clear that some sort of answer must be provided or risk injuring good neighborly relations. The neighbor needed this information to judge the relative status of her children, and expected a straight answer. Such exchanges may go beyond merely talking. Given the current interest in real estate, several neighbors have taken my mother-in-law to see new apartments they or their children have bought. Such visits are informative, but it would also be rude for her to refuse. Retired older people can't use business as an excuse to avoid friendly invitations from neighbors. Participation in such little outings further illustrates the role of information sharing in signaling community membership. Being included is a sign of inclusion in the community. Not to participate at all would be a statement of dissociation.

Gender and gossip

Gossip is traditionally regarded as women's activity, both in its negative popular reputation and in more positive discussions by feminist theorists (Ayim 1994; Code 1994; Collins 1994; Schein 1994). To some extent, this is born out in my observations. Women seem to dominate gossip networks in my neighborhood, and men who participate too avidly are more prone to ridicule. It is perhaps no accident that two of the funniest stories I remember about neighbors were the two stories about men told by women (earlier). Moreover, while Chinese men traditionally saw themselves as protectors of front-stage propriety, the back-stage conversations of neighborhood gossip have long been considered the affair of women (Wolf 1972).

Women also seem more often to be the topic of women's gossip. Although they didn't usually participate in this talk, young women were the most popular topics of older women's talk, almost in the same cathartic way these women talked about the television serials they watched. Young women were seen as having chances denied to all previous generations of women.[221] Older women in the alleyway weren't trying to keep their daughters and their neighbors' daughters tied to the alleyway home, but also hoped that they would be married, educated, and modern women living in comfortable surroundings with a husband and a child. This vision of the orderly and materially affluent married life is a morally positive statement of a generally materialistic sexual ethos in Shanghai. The frequent deviations from this ideal, small and large, become hot topics of local gossip.

However, based on observations and interviews in the neighborhood and with residents of other neighborhoods (summer 2000), I have become convinced that age rather than gender is the more important factor in participation in gossip networks. Young working adults have far less time to spend in neighborhood gossip than older retired people, and both men and women usually work. Retirement is a great equalizer in Shanghai; old men and old women are equally reduced to the status of part-time babysitters for their grandchildren. Joint babysitting activities in the alleyway and discussions of grandchildren's and adult children's progress go hand in hand, and men and women both participate in these activities. On the other hand, several factors still make it more likely that women will spend more time in the community chatting with others. First, women retire earlier than men, and they are laid off with greater frequency from state enterprises. They live longer, and they had generally spent more time getting to know neighbors before they retired. It would be misleading, however, to see "idle talk" among older people as conducted exclusively by women.

---

221 It might be the case that the mothers of sons would focus more exclusively on stories of young men, and that the stories I heard were influenced by the fact that my mother-in-law had only daughters.

THE CHANGING ECOLOGY OF SHANGHAI'S
NEIGHBORHOOD NETWORKS

While the previous sections discussed the functions of gossips in a typical Shanghai community, I now want to consider what is happening to the functioning of these neighborhood networks along with the rapid changes in Shanghai's social geography. Throughout the 1990s, over a million Shanghaiese were dislocated through infrastructure projects and other construction. Now, thousands more are moving for the sake of buying new housing. All new housing is now considered commodity housing, even if its initial purchase is subsidized by the purchaser's work unit. Individuals rather than their work units are generally responsible for finding their own homes. New neighbors in most neighborhoods consequently lack the work unit ties that formed the initial basis of neighborhood social networks in the "new villages." This commodification of housing allows greater residential mobility for those who can afford to sell their apartments and move to better housing. Increased job mobility also gives people greater incentive to move. The end result is the demolition of old neighborhoods, the construction of new ones (often further removed from the city center), and the social homogenization of older less-attractive neighborhoods, as those who can afford new housing, move out. As everyone in Shanghai now clearly sees, this movement is leading to the geographic redistribution of the urban population along economic class lines.

One result of these population movements is an apparent weakening of social ties among neighbors in new neighborhoods. Along with the commodification of housing, more and more people are moving into housing where they know none of the neighbors. In Shanghai, it is easy to find people who have made the transition from alleyway life (or "new village" life) to life in a new commercial apartment block. The following excerpt is from a recorded group interview with two men in their mid-thirties about their neighborhood experiences before and after moving. Both are mid-level managers in foreign-owned enterprises. They began the conversation when one of them mentioned the issue of neighborhood gossip:

Zheng: The problem with life in the old alleyway was that people all know each other. You couldn't keep anything secret there. And the buildings themselves were quite poorly constructed. Your neighbors could hear everything you were doing.

Gu: Right, for instance, I ran across this in my old alleyway. My next door neighbor was a businessmen. One day he brought a woman home. He lived on the second floor and I was on the ground floor making dinner [in the communal kitchen]. After a while he came out again with her. Later I walked to the alleyway entrance. Now, I lived in No.5 and a neighbor from No. 1 comes and tells me, 'Hey, your upstairs neighbor just brought a woman in.' I just thought, I hope this guy doesn't tell my neighbor's wife, and they end up in a family fight. That's the way things were in the past. . . .

Zheng: Now in the new apartment complexes there are many cases where neighbors don't even know each other. Even after many years, they don't know them. . . . Older people may get to know each other, but we don't. Young people are busy going to work, coming home. I only know one person there [in the new apartment complex]. We were both doing home decoration, and we spoke to each other that day. Actually I don't even know his name. We just say hello when we run into each other.... On the other hand there are these older people who are already retired, they are out exercising, or taking care of the children. Now when I come home I see them talking together. They seem to know everyone's names. I don't know any of them.

Both Zheng and Gu have made the transition from the alleyway to the commodity high-rise. Like many middle-aged Shanghaise I interviewed, they are both nostalgic for the close ties of the alleyway yet happy to be relieved from the informal surveillance and gossip. The spaces they move into aren't devoid of community life, but it is of a far lower density than in the alleyways they left. Whereas many adults in the alleyway were childhood friends, most working adults in these new communities have little knowledge of one another. Unlike the traditional alleyways and older "new villages," the new commodity housing communities have no custom of casual unannounced neighborly visits (*chuanmen*). With air-conditioning, there are fewer opportunities for casual conversation on long summer nights while catching the breeze (*chengliang*) out in the alleyway. High-rise structures seem particularly prone to isolation, with outdoor spaces that resemble public parks rather than compartmentalized alleyways. In comparison with older alleyways, there are fewer small-scale spaces for residents to gather and gossip in high-rise structures. Older people sometimes move in with their children in these new apartments in order to take care of the grandchildren, but they too lack the extensive overlapping social ties from older neighborhoods.

More ominous is the increasing class segregation of housing in Shanghai along geographic lines. Until recently, changes in residential housing patterns lagged behind the rapid growth in income inequality in Shanghai. During the reform era, the economic and social heterogeneity (e.g., income differences) among neighbors increased, partly building on pre-existing differences in education, status, and political influence. Such heterogeneity within communities was preserved because of the great difficulties of changing housing during the reform era up through the late 1990s. Almost all housing was assigned by work units (which themselves were difficult to switch out of), and social or economic advancement didn't quickly or easily lead to a change of residence. In the mid-1990s, few people were able to buy the expensive new commercial apartments. Therefore, throughout the 1980s and the 1990s, when income levels were rapidly diverging and class distinctions reemerging in our "new village," as in Shanghai generally, most people remained in the same residences assigned by their original work units.

Beginning in the late 1990s, however, geographical class stratification became a reality in Shanghai.[222] What was most astounding to me returning to Shanghai

222   According to a local contractor, housing costs in Shanghai depend largely on the location, since the largest variable element of the price is the "use-rights" of the land. The popularity of the location depends on the usual factors such as proximity to the city center, transportation, quality

in summer (2000) was that real estate prices for various districts and developments are now common knowledge among all classes of Shanghaiese. Housing purchase is the hot topic of the day, especially among those young enough to want a new place and well-off enough to afford it. Moreover, with mortgages as long as thirty years, and down payments as low as 10 percent, more and more people can afford new housing. The range of prices means, however, that people with wide differences in social class are far less likely to be neighbors than under the older government-assigned housing system. New apartment housing in our traditionally working-class and somewhat distant neighborhood costs around 3,600 yuan a square meter. New housing on the edge of the city but still within commuting distance is about 2,000 yuan a square meter. New housing in the more fashionable and convenient areas of the city center costs about 10,000 yuan a square meter. Given that the typical floor area for a newly constructed apartment is around 100 square meters,[223] the total price of a typical new apartment is easy to calculate, with prices in the city center roughly five times higher than prices in the suburbs.[224]

The real-estate market enforces clear and unmistakable distinctions among desirable and undesirable areas of Shanghai. We see the rapid return of pre-1949 social distinctions, with the older foreign concession areas of Shanghai (known as "upper-corner *shangzhijiao*") regaining their status as fashionable and exclusive residential districts. New tracts of gated luxury condominium developments are centered in these areas and their westward extensions. At the other extreme, there are vast stretches of apartment blocks in less desirable suburbs, similar in look and quality to the "new village" where we stay, built to house former residents of old alleyways demolished to make way for new construction projects. Such largely working-class communities are located on the expanding fringes of the city, often far from convenient transportation. A process of class segregation is also occurring in older "new village" neighborhoods. For instance, it is very doubtful that neighbors with high incomes or wealthy children will remain in our "new village" indefinitely, eventually leaving behind those with low and moderate incomes. With an aging population, many older and less attractive housing projects in Shanghai may have increasing concentrations of retirees and other low-income people. Such class and age segregation will reduce the heterogeneity of neighborhood social life.

Shanghai is rapidly changing its shape. What these changes consistently mean, I believe, is a reduction in the density and heterogeneity of neighborhood society. For wealthier Shanghaiese in gated enclaves, local neighborhood networks may

---

of schooling, park land, and more amorphous but important factors such as the reputations of various districts. For instance, our district lies in what is called "low corner" or northeast working-class Shanghai, meaning that in the eyes of many Shanghaiese it will never develop into a desirable place to live.

223 This refers to the "construction area" of the apartment (*jianju mianji*), which is greater than the floor space area discussed earlier.

224 There is also a relatively small market for free-standing villas in enclaves on the edge of the city, and an even smaller and very pricey market for free-standing new or renovated villas in the older central city, but this type of "suburban" housing is rare enough to exclude it from this discussion of neighborhood cultures in Shanghai.

become insignificant as sources of support and information. Based on my own interviews with young upwardly mobile professionals, it seems neighborhood ties may be replaced with workplace ties, sub-cultural ties with like-minded friends, and continued ties with family. These are the patterns found by Fischer among central metropolis dwellers in the United States (Fischer 1982, p. 102). The consequences of these changes are not clear. Discussions among classmates, workmates, and other types of social relations may replace many of the functions of local neighborhood gossip, but the voluntary nature of such networks means that people may more easily avoid the difficult people and unpleasant social exchanges that were part of the everyday fare of dense and heterogeneous neighborhoods. This may be a gain in terms of individual comfort, but a loss in terms of cross-class social communication. Wealthier and younger Shanghaiese may thus organize their lives around increasingly voluntary interest-based subcultures (nightlife, travel, education, etc.), while the urban poor and elderly may be increasingly socially isolated in working-class suburbs with weaker and less heterogeneous social ties than those in the dense communities where they previously lived. Only a minority of the most socially active residents, particularly the young and wealthy, are able to participate in the new urban subcultures built around consumption. The change is gradual. Families remain close together physically and emotionally. Old neighbors sometimes move to new accommodations in the same neighborhoods, but the difficult and troubling relations of alleyway life will no doubt be more easily avoided. Further empirical study is necessary to describe and understand these trends, however.

CONCLUSION: PRODUCTIVE DISORDER

This chapter explores the social functions of neighborhood gossip and how these functions may be influenced by the transformation of Shanghai's residential geography. My personal starting point for this essay is a perception that local gossip – stereotyped in popular discussions as conventional and purposeless – is an underestimated site for the communication of new values and new strategies for coping with the market economy. In the second part of this chapter, I have considered evidence that with urban restructuring, the density and heterogeneity of neighborhood networks are decreasing, and that their productivity as a cultural medium may consequently suffer. I conclude by situating neighborhood gossip within a tradition of sociological debates on the nature of urban sociality.

The first sociological image we have of city life is also that of disorder. Wirth (1938) was typical among early urban sociologists in emphasizing the depersonalization and disorganization arising from the size and density of cities. This critique of social disorganization has been repeatedly questioned by later studies (such as Whyte 1993[1943]; Suttles 1968; Anderson 1978), which reveal the density and diversity of urban life as conditions that give rise to new forms of social order. Arguing for a more positive conception of "disorder," Richard Sennett (1970) points out that dense and heterogeneous neighborhoods like pre-war Halstead Street in Chicago forced residents to deal collectively and personally with a wide range of people and a wide range of discomfiting social problems, producing a direct understanding of and participation in the lives of diverse others. Sennett's dense and heterogeneous neighborhood is a place of productive "disorder."

I would like to relate my own ethnographic vignette of neighborhood gossip to Sennett's sociological polemic in support of "disorderly" urbanism. In a very similar sense to Sennett's argument about "disorderly" neighborhood, Code writes, "An adequate civil society depends on disorderly and disorganized activities such as gossip and play" (Code 1994, p. 100). Code describes gossip as a particularly disorderly form of communication, allowing multiple voices and free participation with no established hierarchies of control. Gossip marks the boundaries of communities, creates bonds among community members, and allows the community to negotiate pragmatic new community norms when faced with challenges like the market reform in China. This is similar also, I believe, to the rhizomatic networks of the feminine *minjian* described by Yang (1994).

Ironically, given its origins in utopian Maoist planning, the socially heterogenous world of the planned "new village" apartment complex became for a time during the reform era the most productively "chaotic" of urban spaces, producing a density and heterogeneity of interactions in which the horizons of material and sexual possibilities were enlarged through the spectacle of neighbors' lives.[225] This proliferation of characters and stories in neighborhood gossip becomes a resource from which people assemble a moral order of pragmatic values. The same alleyway gossip networks that were mobilized in the heavy-handed surveillance of private life under the Maoist regime thus became instrumental in spreading "liberal," market-oriented strategies as the state retreated from total social management.

Sennett also argues that this urban disorder is uncomfortable for residents, who at the first opportunity flee to the order and relative isolation of the U.S suburbs. Neighborhood gossip is one of the very things that people wish to avoid. Similarly, in Shanghai, well-off residents are eager to flee diverse and dense neighborhoods to the relative order and isolation of the high-rise condominium, or, if they are really rich, the suburban Shanghai bungalow, or even the actual American (or Japanese) suburb itself. If the analogy to suburbanization in the United States is appropriate, we can imagine an increasing importance of non-local social networks and virtual experiences of social life – particularly television – as urban Shanghaiese move away from their old alleyway communities.

Sennett's point is that such dense and heterogenous neighborhoods are good for people and good for society, forcing people to deal with one another's problems. I won't venture to make such a judgment given the discomforts of crowdedness, surveillance, and mean-spirited gossip in these neighborhoods. Most young Shanghaiese who can afford it will opt for the comforts and privacy of the commodity apartments. I do agree with Sennett, however, that there is a qualitative difference in social life when people are forced to confront such complexities on a daily basis without the choice of easy avoidance. I also agree that these experiences can be

---

225 Such neighborhoods are not "chaotic" in other ways, however, and include a high degree of local social control and local institutions, such as child care and family planning.

productive of new and pragmatic forms of local moral discourse. The "new village" in Shanghai during the market transition is one of these temporarily "disorderly" sites of cultural communication in which a wide variety of sexual strategies can be shared and compared.

While the non-overlapping social networks of the high-rise-dwelling "suburbanites" may be liberating in a negative sense, they may limit the confusing and creative communications between people of different social classes, different age groups, and different moral conceptions. There might be a greater tendency in more socially homogenous networks for gossip to reinforce conventional sub-cultural standards of morality, whether "liberal" or "conservative." Gossip networks may also become less dense, and gossip less informative. Isolated high-rise urbanites may know of adultery and promiscuity, but more often filtered through the lens of television rather than experienced through the messy but better understood lives of neighbors. In terms of the moral content, this may mean less of the pragmatic irony of the alleyway and more of the therapeutic moralizing of the radio talk shows and television melodramas (Post 1994). Again, such tentative conclusions must be tested and refined through further study.

CONCLUSIONS

11

NETWORKING *GUANXI*[226]

Barry Wellman, Wenhong Chen, and Dong Weizhen

THE SOCIAL NETWORK APPROACH

From metaphor to toolkit

The end of every journey is the beginning of the next adventure. As my tired eyes rest from reading the chapters in this book and my exhilarated soul reflects, I [Contributor Wellman] think back on the wonders I have encountered and think ahead about what to do next. As I basked in the pleasure of learning about *guanxi*, I started thinking about how some of the tools of my trade – social network analysis – might help me and others to delve deeper into its mysteries.

Yet there is a danger sign along the road, a bit old fashioned but still worth pondering: The *Economist* (2000, p. 7) warns that outsiders may find *guanxi* an unfathomable "mystical concept." With the ironic tone of a jaded old China hand, the magazine asserts: "If you don't have the patience to learn about *guanxi* old boy, you might as well pack your bags and go home." Thrilled by what I've learned about *guanxi*, the last thing I want to do is to go home, warned off by a claim that newbies can neither understand *guanxi* nor provide useful advice about studying it. Reading this book has been a wonderful journey, and I do not want to pack my intellectual bags just yet.

My intention is to show how some of the toolkit of my specialty, social network analysis, could lead to new understandings of *guanxi*, both as a phenomenon in itself and in relation to other aspects of Chinese societies. This is not just a case of using an available hammer to fit all nails: The fit between network analysis

226 We thank Eric Fong, Tom Gold, Douglas Guthrie, Hsung Ray-May, Michael Patrick Johnson, Emi Ooka, Ruan Danching, Janet Salaff, Scott Tremaine, and Beverly Wellman for their advice, and Kristine Klement for her assistance. Dong Weizhen provided especially useful insights into Chinese society and detailed advice about earlier drafts. This work has benefited from the long-term research support of the Social Science and Humanities Research Council for our NetLab's studies of social networks. The authors can be reached at wellman@chass.utoronto.ca, wenchen@chass.utoronto.ca, and wdong@chass.utoronto.ca.

and *guanxi* is tight (see also Lin 2001b). Although scholars of *guanxi* often talk about "the social network" as a useful, organizing metaphor, social network analysis – like *guanxi* analysis – has developed beyond the metaphor. I deliberately enter what Kipnis calls "the trap of making *guanxi* either an orientalist gloss for networking" or an *a*cultural, universal necessity."[227] Where area specialists argue for the particularity of their field, paradigm mongers such as me argue for the generality of their approach. I join with many of this book's authors in believing that social network analysis can provide useful ways to study both dyadic, two-person *guanxi* ties, and multi-person *guanxi* networks.[228] Social network analysis can help identify more precisely different aspects of *guanxi* and provide techniques for studying it. Its approach can help develop the analysis of *guanxi* and place it in the perspective of interpersonal relations and exchanges elsewhere in the world (see the articles in Wellman 1999b). Although China is different from Western countries, we should be able to use the same tools to address similar intellectual challenges

ANALYZING *GUANXI*

This book does both an eloquent job of describing *guanxi* and raising further questions about it. The chapters provide much evidence that *guanxi* is more than the bribery and corruption on which Yang's (1994) pathbreaking book and others have focused.[229] *Guanxi* relationships can reduce uncertainty, lower search and other transaction costs, provide usable resources, and increase interpersonal pleasure and a sense of connectedness. They provide informal ways to reduce environmental uncertainty and opportunistic behavior (Standifird and Marshall 2000). *Guanxi* networks are flexible, efficient, available, and custom-tailored sources of social capital that are low in financial cost.

Guanxi is a fundamental web of interpersonal relations permeating Chinese societies that should not be facilely dichotomized into "bad" bribery relations and "good" friendship ties. *Guanxi* forms multidimensional continua of interpersonal

227   Kipnis reports that the query about "an orientalist gloss for networking" "comes from a series of questions posed by Thomas Gold at the conference in which this volume was conceived." All citations in this text that do not include a (year) reference are to chapters of this book. My citations of this book's chapters are indicative, and not exhaustive. As I worked with a pre-publication manuscript, I could not include page numbers.

228   For an introduction to network analytic concepts, techniques and findings, see Wellman 1988; Burt 1992; Scott 1991; Wasserman and Faust 1994; Wellman and Berkowitz 1988; Lin 2001a; Lin (2001b).

229   Moreover, networks of bribery and corruption are not unique to Chinese societies, although their precise manifestations vary between societies. (For example, Israelis call a similar practice "protektzia.") Such practices extend through all societies, as well as between societies. See the "Corruption Perceptions Index" website at http://www.transparency.de/documents/cpi/. For some studies of capitalist, bureaucratic socialist, and post-socialist societies see Danet (1989, 1990), Rose (1998a, 1999b), Rose and Haerpfer (1993, 1998), Sik (1994, 2000), and Sik and Wellman (1999).

behavior rather than a bad/good dichotomy. Instead of sniffing at *guanxi* as a corrupter of rational bureaucratic procedures, or celebrating it as a liberation of human initiative, analysts can concentrate on its characteristics and contexts. Back doors are not the only entry points for *guanxi*.

This book presents a broad view of *guanxi* by:

1. **Demonstrating that *guanxi* is prevalent.** Until recently, this has been somewhat a yes/no debate. As almost always, once you look for something, you usually find it. The question remains, as Guthrie notes, as to how prevalent *guanxi* is and how much it has changed since the coming of Communism and through the various stages of the Communist regime. For example, Sik and Wellman (1999) show the persistence of *guanxi*-like relationships in Hungary throughout the Communist period – to deal with bureaucratic rigidities, material scarcities and personal political insecurities – but also in the post-Communist period – to deal with rapidly changing markets, transmuting institutions, and personal economic insecurities. (See also Kipnis.)
2. **Documenting the characteristics of *guanxi* relationships.** It provides evidence about the extent to which *guanxi* relationships are:
   1. *Composed* of strong or weak ties; kin or friends; gender, life-style and age bound, symmetrically reciprocal, local or dispersed relationships, between status equals or patron-clients. Matters especially addressed by Bian, Farrer, Hanser, Wilson.
   2. *Broadly-supportive* ties providing a variety of assistance or specialized relationships in which different network members provide different types of assistance (see Bian and Lin).
   3. Better understood as discrete two-person *dyads* or as relationships that can only be understood as contingent parts of multi-person *networks* and groups.
   4. Bound up in densely knit *groups* or spread out in more sparsely knit *networks*.
   5. Functioning in similar ways throughout Chinese societies? (see Bian and Ang 1997).
   6. Essentially different from social networks in Western developed societies or analyzable with some (or many) of the same concepts and tools.[230]
3. **Proposing the interplay between the behavioral practice of *guanxi* and internalized norms and values** that may be associated with it. Many authors in this book argue that it is important to distinguish between *guanxi* normative feelings (*renqing/ganqing*) – the sentiment of acting with respect for human feelings – and *guanxi* practices – the supportive behaviors in which people actually engage.[231] There is always a marked disjunction between how people feel and what they actually do (Deutscher 1973; Cancian 1975). Situational ethics, opportunities, and constraints make norm/behavior differences inevitable and often unacknowledged – whether among cadres in China or evangelicals in America. Thus, Hwang (1987) argues that *renqing* depends on the perceived position of relationships in power structures. Potter notes that complex social networks make personal trust more problematic, as individuals must negotiate contingent, sometimes transitory relationships rather than rely on the coherent norm enforcement of an all-encompassing densely-knit group. Although I note these important issues here, I do not address them in this chapter.
4. **Showing how privately interpersonal *guanxi* operates in conjunction** with behavior in public spaces (Farrer), formal bureaucracies (Bian, Guthrie, Hanser, Keister, Li, and Wank), and the legal system (Potter). The authors amply show that *guanxi* is best

---

230 The possibly unique nature of *guanxi* is debated throughout this book, either implicitly or explicitly. See also Tu (1994).
231 Hanser analyzes terminological distinctions between *guanxi* and *guanxixue*, the latter having more connotations of combing behavior and sentiment.

seen as a component of overall Chinese societies – for example, providing leverage on
bureaucracies – rather than as an isolated system of interpersonal relationships (see
also Lin 2001b). Potter does this for the legal system. Guthrie strongly argues that
people's positions in Chinese societies affect how they engage in *guanxi*. Ties spill
over national borders as overseas Chinese use *guanxi* to engage in mainland enterprises
(Segal 1999). *Guanxi* is probably eternal, but I wonder how it operated differently in the
previous system of bureaucratic rigidity from in the current system of fluidly, changing
norms and relationships.[232]

5. **Demonstrating that *guanxi* has remained important** in multiple aspects of recent
   and current Chinese societies (an issue on which all authors except Guthrie agree; see
   also Guthrie 1998). As Hanser argues, *guanxi* can best be seen as part of a person's
   toolkit. Is *guanxi* an asset, to be "banked or deployed as needed to serve the interests
   of the holder in the context of a larger institutional system"? (Hanser). Taken jointly,
   the chapters in this book show what *guanxi* does for individuals, interpersonal ties,
   social networks, organizations, institutions, and regional, sectoral, and overall aspects
   of Chinese societies. But is it central or peripheral to different arenas of Chinese
   societies?

THE SOCIAL NETWORK ANALYTIC APPROACH

From method and metaphor to paradigm and substance

Social network analysis has moved from a suggestive metaphor to an analytic
paradigm. It conceives of social structure as the patterned organization of network
members and their relationships. Analysis starts with a set of *network members*
(sometimes called nodes) and a set of *ties* that connect some or all of these nodes.
Ties consist of one or more specific *relationships*, such as kinship, frequent contact,
information flows, conflict, or emotional support. The interconnections of these ties
channel resources to specific structural locations in social systems. The pattern of
these relationships – the social network structure – organizes systems of exchange,
control, dependency, cooperation, and conflict.

Thinking in network terms leads away from individual-level research perspectives whose inherently social psychological explanatory bases see internalized
norms driving interpersonal relations. Network analysts reason from the whole
to the part, from structure to tie to individual, from behavior to attitude. They
study how social networks work for individuals, for relationships, and for social
systems. Social network analysts study both inter-personal ties between people
(Wellman 1999a) and inter-organizational ties between firms, government departments, etc. (e.g., Mizruchi and Galaskiewicz 1994) and international ties in the
world-system (e.g., Breiger 1981). Such larger-scale analyses either collect data
at the unit of the organization or nation, or else use a "network of networks approach" to treat ties between members of different organizations as ties between
the organizations themselves (Craven and Wellman 1973; Wellman 1988).

---

232   See also Sik and Wellman's (1999) analysis of networks in Communist and post-Communist
      Hungary.

A network is not always – perhaps not often – a group

As Guthrie notes, scholars tend to find what they are looking for because their approach affects how they frame their questions and research design. The network approach provides ways to think about social relationships that are neither groups nor isolated duets. There is no assumption that groups are the normal building blocks of social systems, nor that the absence of groups is a deviant aberration. Groups are not privileged by definition; they are discovered. A group is only a special type of social network, one that is *densely knit* (most people are directly connected) and *tightly-bounded* (most relations stay within the same set of people).

Instead of treating officially defined group or neighborhood boundaries as truly social boundaries, network analyses trace the social relationships of persons or institutions, whomever these relationships are with and wherever they go. In this way, formal boundaries can be tested to see if they are relevant rather than treated as *a priori* analytic constraints. For example, people who spend much time together – at work, in the household, in villages, at markets, in neighborhoods – can be studied as either a group or a social network. Those who study them as groups assume that they know the membership and boundaries of the groups. They might ask how important each group is to its members, how the groups are governed and make decisions, how the groups control members, and the circumstances under which members enter and leave. By contrast, those who treat such entities as social networks can address membership and boundaries as open questions. Frequent participation in a friendship circle might be treated as the basis for membership, but so might be the indirect connections (and resource flows) that friends provide to others outside the circle. The pattern of relationships becomes a research question rather than a given.

This empirical approach to dealing with groups should be useful for studying *guanxi*. China, like much of the world, is experiencing a paradigm shift, not only in the way people perceive society, but even more in the way in which people and institutions are connected. It is the shift from living in "little boxes"[233] to living in networked societies. Members of group-oriented *little-box societies* deal only with fellow members of the few groups to which they belong: at home, in the neighborhood, at work, or in voluntary organizations. They belong to a discrete work group in a single organization; they live in a household in a neighborhood; they belong to a kinship group (one each for themselves and their spouse) and to discrete organizations: professional associations, neighborhood groups, and the like. All of these appear to be bodies with precise boundaries for inclusion (and therefore exclusion). Each has an internal organization that is often hierarchically structured: supervisors and employees, parents and children, party leader, cadre and local resident; union leader and proletariat. In such a society, each interaction is in its place: one group at a time. To oversimplify on purpose, this was the standard description of China before the Dengist turn to a market society.

---

233   In the words of Malvina Reynolds' great song metaphor of 1963.

A key meta-story of this book is the shift in China from a group-based to a network-based society (see also Gold 1998; Lin 2001b). This Chinese experience is far from unique. Throughout the Western developed world and in much of the less developed world, a network society has come into being. In such societies, boundaries are more permeable, interactions are with diverse others, linkages switch between multiple networks, and hierarchies (when they exist) are flatter and more recursive. The change from groups to networks can be seen at many levels. Trading and political blocs have lost their monolithic character in the world system. Organizations form complex networks of alliance and exchange rather than cartels, and workers (especially professionals, technical workers, and managers) report to multiple peers and superiors. Management by network is replacing management by (two-way) matrix as well as management by hierarchal trees (Berkowitz 1982; Wellman 1988, Castells 1996). The Western developed world – and perhaps Chinese societies – have seen the rise of *"networked individualism"*: Individuals – and not groups, kinship units, or households – are the key interpersonal units. Yet individuals are rarely isolated in "lonely crowds" (as Reisman (1950) mistakenly thought). They are more likely to have partial, changing ties to multiple social networks (Wellman 2001).

To be sure, Chinese societies – as others – have densely knit, tightly bounded, publicly functioning work groups and community groups. Yet the chapters by Bian, Farrer, and Wilson show sparsely knit, loosely bounded work and community networks, with only a minority of members directly connected with one another. Even when Farrer shows the persistence of public neighborhood networks in Shanghai, he makes it clear that this is one among multiple, partial networks. Wank notes how Fujianese entrepreneurs deliberately created long-distance business ties. Other research has described how the technocratic graduates of Qinghua University help each other move upward in their business and political careers (Cheng 1994). Such relationships often radiate out in many directions like an expanding spider's web rather than curling back on themselves into a densely knit tangle. It is a *"glocalized"* situation, showing the interplay of local involvements and long-distance connectivity (Wellman and Hampton 1999).

The social network approach can be applied to a wide range of social structures. For example, the approach is able to discover densely knit communities in which almost all community members have a wide range of relationships with each other (e.g., Hinton 1966) as well as the rational bureaucratic organizations that Guthrie describes. But the social network approach especially affords the discovery of other forms of *guanxi* networks – perhaps sparsely knit and spatially dispersed – and other forms of organization – perhaps loosely coupled or virtual (Koku, Nazer, and Wellman 2001). Hence it can help to describe and analyze the operation of *guanxi* as it complements and supplements bureaucratic and formally legal interactions. Instead of an either/or distinction between group membership and social isolation, analysts can study such diversified phenomena as:

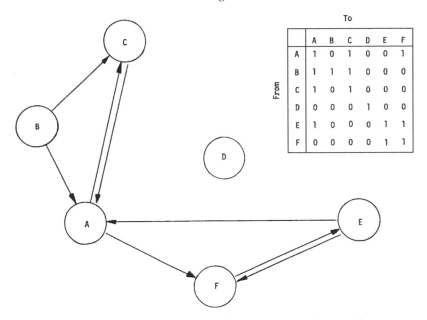

Figure 11.1   Graphical and matrix representation of a network.

- The density and clustering of a *guanxi* network
- How tightly bounded a network is
- Which kinds of people occupy similar roles
- Whether a *guanxi* network is variegated or constricted in its size and heterogeneity
- How narrowly specialized or broadly multiplex are its relationships
- How indirect connections and structural positions affect behavior
- How patterns of connectivity and cleavage channel supportive resources
- The ways in which people and organizations are indirectly connected

The self-conscious, relatively coherent development of social network analysis began in the 1960s (Wellman 1988, 2000). In the past decade, doing social network research has become easier. Information for analysis may be gathered through ethnographic field work, survey research, or archival analysis (finding for example, investment patterns between enterprises – e.g., Mintz and Schwartz 1985). Although network analysts often think about networks as graphs (in which the points represent persons and the lines ties between them), they usually manipulate matrices to analyze the networks (Figure 11.1). They use a variety of statistical and mathematical techniques to tease out selected underlying structural properties of the social system. Network analysts currently have three journals, a professional society, and an annual meeting. They are active in all social science disciplines, mathematics and statistics.[234]

234   The most commonly used software packages for analyzing whole networks are UCINet and its graphical associate. Krackplot, Pajic, Gradap, Multinet, and Structure have also been frequently used. Wellman (1992) and Müller, Wellman and Marin (1999) show how to use standard SPSS and

WHOLE NETWORKS

Patterns of connectivity and cleavage

Whole network analyses describe the comprehensive structure of role relationships in an entire social system, be it a village, a region, an enterprise, a set of enterprises (e.g., the steel industry), or linkages between institutions (e.g., enterprises and bureaucracies). Such analyses provide simultaneous views of the social system as a whole and of the parts that make up the system. They often map social systems, asking, for example, if the systems are socially integrated or if there is an empirically identifiable ruling bloc.

One straightforward approach to studying whole networks is to find who in a population is directly connected with whom. Researchers are able to trace lateral and vertical flows of information, identify senders and receivers of resources, and detect structural constraints (such as decouplings and the shapes of networks) operating on flows of resources. Analysts often want to discover *densely connected* clusters of network members in which most network members are directly connected, and the extreme case of *cliques*, in which all network members are directly connected. Finding clusters and cliques can empirically discover groups whose members cooperate extensively with each other and develop collective identities. Because of the dense interconnectivity within a cluster, resources are often conserved and social control tends to be active. Yet extensive within-cluster involvement can also mean few ties to outside the cluster. As a result, those in densely knit clusters may have difficulties acquiring new information, goods, and other resources from outsiders. They may also lack the external ties necessary for forming coalitions with others to deal with difficulties or opportunities.

Consider, for example, the situation of Overseas Chinese in Toronto. As in other ethnic enclaves, strong ties among members of the Chinese community are often important for successful business start-ups (Portes 1993). These ties tend to develop into densely knit clusters. However, those business people who also have networks outside of the Chinese community tend to have higher income levels (Ooka 2001; see also Ooka and Wellman 2003).

Structurally equivalent role relationships

The hiring practices of many Chinese family businesses show "structural equivalence" (Wasserman and Faust 1994). Key positions at higher levels are often

SAS software to analyze personal networks (i.e., The World According to Garp [or Lee]). The professional society is the *International Network for Social Network Analysis*, which I founded in 1976; the journals are *Connections* (since 1977), the *Journal of Social Structure* (since 2000), and *Social Networks* (since 1978). The International Sunbelt Social Network Conference has met annually since 1980. (See Wellman 1993, 2000 for details.) Precursors of social network analysis go back to Georg Simmel's work in the early twentieth century (see especially 1922, 1950), and a number of scholars in the years between the World Wars (Freeman 2000). For more details, go to the INSNA website, currently http://www.heinz.cmu.edu/project/INSNA.

occupied by close relatives or friends (Kao 1991; Tsui and Farh 1993). Different kin are seen as equivalent in their relationship to the owners.

But structurally equivalent people do not actually have to be related to each other if they occupy similar positions. In the 1980s, Toronto-Chinese sociologist Li Fan asked the residents of an Inner Mongolian town to report who provided resources to each other: gifts, information, and the like. He was then able to use the network analytic technique of *blockmodeling* (White, Boorman and Breiger 1976; Arabie, Boorman and Levitt 1978) to identify the town's elite. Instead of looking for clusters of densely connected people – the usual approach to elite studies in China and elsewhere – Li looked for patterns of role relationships. He manipulated data matrices to identify which townspeople had similar patterns of exchanging resources. The UCINet computer program placed people with such similar patterns in the same "block." It demonstrated substantial differences in structural position according to both ethnicity and organizational position. For example, one elite block consisted of people who received gifts from members of other (analytically constructed blocks) but only exchanged gifts among each other. To be sure, this substantial effort in data collection and analysis revealed party cadres and different ethnic groups to be in distinct positions – not startling findings for the time. But this finding was made inductively – by studying exchanges of resources – and not by deductively assuming that cadres were the elites. Moreover, the analysis sorted the other residents into several blocks, reflecting their position in the town's social structure.[235]

Although Li's actual block model is not available now, Nazer's (2000) block model of a scholarly network provides a good illustration of the approach. Although the core elite members of Block I are not necessarily in direct contact with each other, they seek advice from other Block I members, and to a lesser extent from the members of the other elite group in Block II.[236] Symmetrically, Block II members principally seek advice only from each other, and to a lesser extent from the members of Block I and one member of Block III. The block model shows that Blocks I and II are two distinct social circles that have some advice-seeking connections with each other. By contrast, Blocks III and IV are more isolated because their disciplines are peripheral to the interests of the core. Only one of the members of Block III (Smith) seeks advice from anyone, and the two members of Block IV mainly seek advice from each other.

Indirect ties between persons and organizations

Not only do ties link people and ties link organizations, ties also link people to organizations. People's membership in organizations can be treated as *affiliation*

---

235   The study was done for a graduate course in the Department of Sociology, University of Toronto, but unfortunately has never been published. The town is the same "cowtown" described by Pasternak and Salaff (1993).
236   In this symmetrical matrix, the rows show who seeks advice and the columns show from whom advice was sought.

Table 11.1
Block model of seeking advice

			I					II					III				IV	
			1	2	15	10	9	12	3	8	13	16	7	14	11	4	5	6
			M	A	B	C	H	S	G	S	D	G	S	O	H	M	J	W
I	1	Mann		1		1	1											
	2	Applebaum					1											
	15	Brown	1		1	1	1											
	10	Cook	1		1		1							1				
	9	Hart	1		1	1				1			1					
II	12	Scott			1				1	1	1							
	3	Green			1			1		1		1						
	8	Stone						1	1		1	1	1					
	13	Demore							1	1			1					
	16	Grey							1	1			1					
III	7	Smith		1						1				1	1			
	14	Oldfield		1											1	1		
	11	Hopkins															1	1
	4	Martins													1			
IV	5	Jones											1	1				
	6	Wood												1			1	

$R^2 = 0.32$ Overall networks density $= 0.24$ Standard deviation within blocks $= 0.43$

Source: Nazer (2000) Table 4.4. All names are pseudonyms.

networks and analyzed just like interpersonal networks (Wasserman and Faust 1994). For example, identifying which persons belong to the same or similar organizations can help to discover the gathering places for elites (or dissidents). Indeed, the U.S. Federal Bureau of Investigation (FBI) uses a similar technique for conspiracy cases (Davis 1981).

There is a duality of persons and organizations (Breiger 1974). Just as people belong to organizations, organizations belong to people. If two persons belong to the same organization, they are indirectly linked to each other through their joint membership. Similarly, if a person belongs to two organizations, the two organizations are indirectly linked to each other (Figure 11.2). Matrix multiplication (using

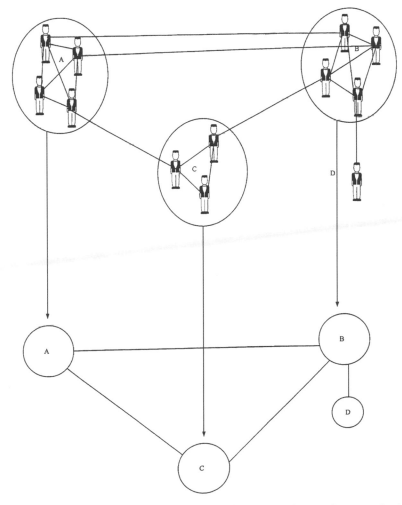

Figure 11.2   A network of networks: From an interpersonal to an interorganizational network. Copyright © Barry Wellman 1988.

UCINet or other software) makes it easy to discover this – and other – indirect ties. For example, North American studies have shown how elites are connected through organizations in a "network of networks," and how organizations are connected when board members are involved in multiple organizations (e.g., Mintz and Schwartz 1985; Carrington 1981; Richardson 1987).

Such analyses are obviously possible for Chinese societies when membership lists are available. They give additional ways to study the business and political relationships investigated by Keister and by Wank (see also Guthrie 1998; Wank 1999). Both within-network centrality and inter-network connectivity affect the market positions of Chinese businesses (Keister 2000). Yet analyses of indirect connectivity do not have to be limited to elites. For example, Mark Chapman (forthcoming) is currently studying how various evangelical Canadian church groups are connected, and David Tindall (1993) has analyzed links among ecologically friendly ("tree-hugger") social movements in British Columbia, Canada. Factory workers (e.g., Walder 1986) and small businesspeople (e.g., Wank) are apt subjects for such analyses.

Indirect ties are also vital for the study of the spread of information and other phenomena (Rogers 1983; Valente 1995): How fast does a rumor about political events in Beijing or a Tibetan town spread? How quickly and to whom does a computer or biological virus disseminate? Are there biases in the spread of such information so that people in certain social network positions are more apt to acquire the information (or virus) more quickly? Does the information eventually spread throughout the entire society, as when Milgram (1967) suggested that the entire world is connected by six or fewer ties? Or does socially structured "decoupling" limits universal connectivity and the concomitant spread of information. For example, not everyone in a school population is chosen as a "friend" or hears all rumors (Rapoport 1979).

Personal networks

Suppose we are interested in which kinds of people get information about jobs, get emotional support, get help with building a home, or get useful business information from friends. In such cases, we are interested in the ties of each person in a population (or a sample of that population). Hence, social network analysts often study *personal networks* rather than whole networks – that is the network *of* Wang, Hsung, or Li – rather than their village or workgroup (e.g., Hwang 1987). Although the personal network approach does not provide information about the structure of the overall social system, it does show how different types of relationships – kin or friend, strong or weak, local or distant – affect the flow of *guanxi* resources to the *focal person* at the center of each network.[237] Figure 11.3, for example, shows the significant interpersonal ties of a typical North American (drawn from Wellman

237   It is possible to move between the whole network and the personal network approaches. Each
       member of a whole network can be analyzed as the center of a personal network (Haythornthwaite
       and Wellman 1996); information about a sample of personal networks can be used to describe

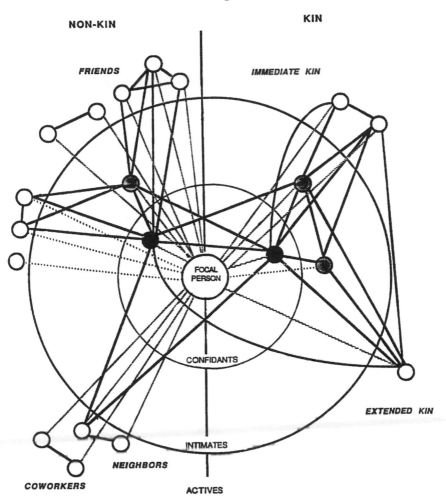

Figure 11.3   Typical North American network. Copyright © Barry Wellman 1988.

and Wortley 1990). She is directly linked with each network member (by definition), and many network members are also significantly tied with each other. She
has a densely knit cluster of kin – three of whom are her socially-close *intimates* –
and more sparsely knit relations among a half-dozen friends and neighbors. One
workmate stands apart, his isolation reflecting a separation of work and social life
in this focal person's life.

There are analytic and epistemological reasons for studying personal networks
(see also Hsung 1998). The personal network approach avoids the problem of a

structural aspects of a large social system. For example, Laumann (1973) does this in describing
interpersonal contact and cleavages between religious and ethnic groups in Detroit, and Ferrand,
Mounier and Degenne (1999) similarly describe class relations in France.

predetermined population boundary. For example, how do you deal with *guanxi* as a long-distance phenomenon (Wilson's concerns in this book) if you limit your analysis only to neighborhood or within-city relationships? Moreover, whole network analyses are not always methodologically feasible or analytically appropriate because such analyses must define the boundaries of a population, compile a list of all the members of this population, and collect a list of all the direct ties (of the sort the analyst is interested in) between the members of this population (Laumann, Marsden, and Prensky 1983). Indeed, as Lin's account of the local and long-distance relationships of entrepreneurs and villagers shows, attempts to impose improper boundaries may lead to analytic confusion. Yet it was common for earlier generations of community sociologists in many countries to ignore non-neighborhood friendships and so declare – wrongly – that urbanites are lonely and isolated (e.g., Stein 1960; see the reviews in Wellman and Leighton 1979; Wellman 1999a).

Personal network studies have documented the pervasiveness and importance of connectivity in Western developed and less developed societies, thereby rebutting mass society contentions (Kornhauser 1959) that development-driven social transformations have produced isolation and alienation. Community, network analysts argue, has rarely disappeared from societies. It has been transformed into new forms, with *guanxi*-like relationships continuing in abundance and vitality even as they have been affected by capitalism, socialism, urbanization, industrialization, bureaucratization, and new transportation and communication technology. Numerous scholars have described how networks link individuals through strong and weak ties, situate them in large social systems, and affect flows of resources to and from them (reviewed in Wellman 1999a). Similarly, the chapters in this book show an abundance of long-distance ties as workers seek jobs (Bian, Hanser, Keister, Wilson), farmers seek markets, and husbands seek wives (Kipnis). Rather than finding self-contained "little boxes," the authors in this book reveal complex webs of relationships, often stretching over substantial differences and radiating out to connect multiple social circles.

STUDYING PERSONAL NETWORKS

Conceptualizing a person's network as the central node linking together complex interpersonal relationships leads to quite different analytic concerns from those focusing on membership in a single, discrete solidarity. It liberates analysts from searching only for vestigial traditional solidarities hanging on in changing societies. Rather than looking to see if what they find measures up to the traditional ideal of densely knit, tightly bounded, broadly based solidarities, analysts can evaluate the ways in which different kinds of social structural patterns affect flows of *guanxi* resources to network members.

Personal network studies mesh well with survey techniques. Researchers interview a sample of respondents, asking them to enumerate the personal and relational characteristics of each member of their network. As the average size of a network in the Western developed world contains more than 1,000 people, generally only the 5–30 strongest ties are studied (see Kochen 1989; Wellman 1999a). To measure network density, researchers typically ask the focal persons in their samples to report about relationships among the members of their networks.

Analysts tend to study these features of personal networks:

- *Composition*: the attributes of network members (e.g., is the network homogeneous or heterogeneous; primarily composed of women or men?)
- *Ties*: the attributes of ties connecting network members to the "focal person" (or ego) of each personal network (e.g., which ties are strong, in frequent contact, between kin?)
- *Contents*: (e.g., who provides job information or emotional support?)
- *Structure*: (e.g., is the personal network densely or sparsely knit; is it better suited for conserving and controlling resources, or for exchanging resources with other social circles?)

Yet, looking at *guanxi* only in personal networks does have its costs:

- It concentrates on strong ties – and sometimes only on strong, *supportive* ties – neglecting the weaker ties that can transmit new information between groups and integrate social systems (Granovetter 1973, 1982, 1995).
- It ignores the ecological juxtapositions with which all people must deal in their residential and social spaces. Even if they are not in a person's network, rapacious politicians may affect the society in which one is embedded, and vigilant residents may make one's neighborhood safe.
- Analyzing the network structure of each personal network is procedurally difficult. This is because software for social network analysis such as UCINet is designed to analyze only one network at a time. Although each personal network can be treated as a whole network, the lack of provision for batch processing means that the data-crunching of hundreds of personal networks must be undertaken one network at a time.
- In a sample survey of any size, interviewing the members of a person's network is impractical because such an approach would increase the sample size enormously. (For example, a sample of 300 persons – each linked with an average of 20 network members – would require 6,000 interviews.) Hence, personal network studies usually rely on surveyed respondents' reports about their network members. This hinders reliability (Bernard, et al., 1984) although no more so than the respondents' reports about other aspects of their behavior. The least reliable and valid survey data are the respondents' reports about the nature of the relationships among the members of their personal networks. Many people just do not know how Cousin Wong feels about Great Aunt Lee.

Differentiated ties

Three basic issues arise in unbundling *guanxi* and analyzing specific types of supportive relationships.

1. Which kinds of guanxi are often conveyed in the same ties? Some of the authors show that social networks provide the basis for interpersonal social capital, what my group has called "*network capital*" (Sik and Wellman 1999; Wellman and Frank 2001; see also Bian's and Lin's chapters). The term is an apt one for this book, with its concentration on relations of work and entrepreneurship. Yet the authors also make it clear that *guanxi* comprehends a variety of supportive relationships:

providing emotional support, helping neighbors, relatives and friends, gossiping about neighbors, and providing a sense of belonging. Farrer and Wilson make such relationships their focus. As Lin notes, analysts cannot assume that all ties provide all types of *guanxi*. In the Western developed world, different types of ties provide different kinds of resources (Wellman 1999a), and *guanxi* analysts should leave open this possibility in Chinese societies (Lin 2001b).

Are the people who help someone find a job the same people who provide emotional support or help with care for the elderly, children, and the infirm? Is *guanxi* support broadly available in a tie, or do different types of ties provide different kinds of support? This is a matter for both ethnographic observation and quantitative analysis using factor and cluster analyses (Hall and Wellman 1985; Wellman and Hiscott 1985; Wellman and Wortley 1989). Both Hsung and Ruan and their associates show important commonalities and differences between Chinese and Western societies in this regard (Hsung and Lin 1995; Hsung 1998; Ruan et al., 1997; Ruan and Zhang 2000; Ruan 2001). In Toronto, our group has found that active network members usually supply only one or two out of the five types of social support – for example, small services and emotional aid, but not large services, companionship, or financial aid. By contrast, Toronto spouses supply each other with all types of social support (Wellman and Wellman 1992). Those network members who provide small services or emotional aid rarely provide large services, companionship, or financial aid (Wellman, Carrington and Hall 1988; Wellman and Wortley 1989; Wellman and Wortley 1990).

2. Which types of dyadic (interpersonal) relationships tend to provide what kinds of guanxi? If *guanxi* support is specialized, it is likely that such specialization is associated with different types of ties. Because personal networks rarely operate as solidarities, people cannot count on all the people in their network to leap in and provide needed help. Hence the provision of network capital partially depends on the social characteristics of network members and the kinds of relationships they have with the person whose network they "belong" to.

The dyadic tie between two persons is at least as important as the network and milieu in which it is embedded (Wellman 2001; Wellman and Frank 2001). This is a major change from pre-industrial society where a wide range of support tended to be available from all sorts of kinfolk and neighbors (Poggioli 1975). In contemporary France, kin and neighbors engage in mutual aid, but friends and neighbors are the confidants (Ferrand, Mounier, and Degenne 1999). By contrast, in Toronto, parents and adult children provide the widest range of support although they rarely supply sociable companionship. Accessible ties – people living or working nearby, or otherwise in frequent in-person or telecommunications contact – provide important goods and services (Wellman and Wortley 1990; Wellman and Frank 2001). The strength of ties is important, with socially close voluntary and multiple-role ties providing high levels of support. Yet Granovetter (1973, 1982) has cogently argued the importance of weak ties for linking sparsely knit communities and providing people with a wider range of information.

Many of the chapters in this book look at how specific kinds of relationships provide specific kinds of support, but there could be more analysis of which types of relationships occur under what kinds of situations. Do similar types of relationships provide similar kinds of support in Chinese and Western developed societies (Ruan and Zhang 2000)? Another comparison would be with other East Asian societies. For example, interpersonal relations in Japan appear to be similar to those in Western societies (Otani 1999; Nozawa 1999).

3. Which sorts of network structures tend to provide what kinds of guanxi? Chinese scholars know even better than Hillary Clinton (1996) that it "takes a village to raise a child." More accurately, it takes a network. As Gold, Hanser, and Lin emphasize, *guanxi* comes from networks as well as from two-person ties. There is more to interpersonal life than just individuals and their one-to-one ties. People are often immersed in milieus filled with companionship, emotional support, or caring for others whose dynamics go beyond the level of the individual alter or tie. There may be group pressures to provide or withhold certain kinds of support. There may be differential access to resources, with some networks better structured than others to hear about problems, mobilize internal resources, or access external resources. Yet as Lin notes, "Despite wide recognition of *guanxi* as [the] nexus of *multilateral* social networks, *dyadic* interaction remains the focus of analytic attention."

There is an interplay between the dyadic relationship and the multiperson network. The specialized provision of support – in the Western developed world and perhaps in Chinese societies – means that people must maintain differentiated portfolios of ties to obtain a variety of resources. They can no longer assume that any or all of their relationships will help them, no matter what the problem is. In market terms, people must shop at specialized stores for needed resources instead of casually dropping in at a general store. This means that people who only have a few network members supplying one kind of *guanxi* have insecure sources of supply. If the relationship ends – if the boutique closes – the supply of that particular type of *guanxi* may disappear.

At the network level of analysis, social network researchers look at the *composition* of the networks (e.g., network size, network heterogeneity, mean frequency of contact, the percentage who are friends) and the *structure* of these networks (e.g., density of links among alters). Such analyses seek to understand how the properties of networks affect what happens in them (and to them). Which attributes of networks tend to occur together? For example, are densely knit networks more supportive, more controlling, or both? The size and heterogeneity of a network (its "range") affect its members' access to resources (Haines and Hurlbert 1992; Burt 1983, 1992). Heterogeneous networks – having a variety of network members with different characteristics – and networks with more socioeconomic resources can better mobilize supportive network capital (Lin 2001).

Nor is it only a question of whether the characteristics of the network, the tie, or the alter independently affect the availability of network capital. Kin may be called on for support when they are enmeshed in densely knit networks, and adult sons are more likely to aid their elderly parents when adult daughters are available (Stone, Rosenthal and Connidis 1998). People navigate nimbly through partial involvements in multiple networks; as members of these networks they are subject to the networks' constraints and opportunities. For example, the helpfulness of ties for job searches is enhanced by membership in resource-rich networks (Bian 1994, 1997; Hsung and Lin 1996; Lai, Lin, and Leung 1998; Lin and Bian 1991).

Instead of total involvement in a single solidary community, the personal mobility and connectivity that are the hallmarks of the industrial and information ages have replaced solidarity with cosmopolitanism. People move through partial specialized involvements with multiple sets of network members. Interactions with network members are between two single people or two couples, or small, informal get-togethers of friends and relatives. These are not simple, homogenous strictures but complex compositions and sparsely knit structures. Most interactions are not in public places, but tucked away in private homes or telecommunications. Relationships are not permanent: Even socially close ties are often replaced within a decade (Wellman et al., 1997). Rather than each network member's providing a broad spectrum of support, people get specialized support from a variety of ties (Wellman 1999a, 2001).

Does this depiction apply in whole or in part to Chinese societies as well as to Western societies? The matter is well worth examining, rather than assuming Chinese exceptionalism. Certainly, Farrer shows the persistence of public, supportive and controlling sociability in a Shanghai neighborhood, and Hanser and Wilson show Chinese networks that extend well beyond neighborhoods provide *guanxi* in sparsely knit, loosely bounded, frequently changing networks. Indeed, migration and trade globalizes *guanxi*, as emigrants move from Hong Kong and China to Canada and Australia (Wong and Salaff 1998; Salaff, Fong and Wong 1999; Dong and Salaff 2000), and Overseas Chinese use the resulting complex networks (Li 2000).

A multi-level approach

Until very recently, the theoretical understanding of the network basis of support/ *guanxi* went far beyond the methodological grasp of social network analysts, constrained by their methodological inability to integrate *analytic* levels into a comprehensive analysis. Technical incompatibilities largely led individual, tie, network, and interactive analyses to develop separately.[238] Quantitative analysts examined separately the effects of either individual characteristics, ties, or the personal networks in which they are embedded. Because many statistical techniques assume independence between units of analysis, they cannot focus simultaneously on different units of analysis. Yet the availability of *guanxi* may well be affected by individual "agency" (self-organized actions on one's own behalf), ties dancing

---

238   See the review in Wellman and Frank's analysis of "network capital" (2001).

interpersonal duets, and the constraints and opportunities provided by networks with different sorts of structure and composition. Not only do people need – and want – to know which kinds of people (an individual-level analysis) and relationships (a tie-level analysis) are apt to provide different kinds of *guanxi*, they also need and want to know the extent to which their social networks as a whole can provide *guanxi* (a network-level analysis).

To analyze such matters, *multi-level analysis* integrates "nested data" into a single statistical model, such as occurs with residents in neighborhoods, children in schools, nation-states in world systems, or, as here, individuals and ties in personal networks (e.g., Sampson in press; Thomése and van Tilburg 1998; van Duijn, van Busschbach, and Snijders 1999; Wellman and Frank 2001). "Multi-level or hierarchical linear models explicitly take into account the nested data and the related dependency structure by incorporating unexplained variables between ties . . . and also between egos" (van Duijn, van Busschbach, and Snijders 1999, p. 188).

As multi-level analysis goes beyond a single focus on the effects of either individual, tie, or network properties on behavior, it engages with the basic social scientific question of *emergent properties*. Is *guanxi* related only to the characteristics of individuals or ties, or is it also related to the characteristics of the personal networks in which these ties are embedded? Does one also have to take into account the characteristics of all network members – will women be more supportive in networks filled with women? – and the social structures in which their ties are embedded – will people be more supportive in densely-knit networks? Are "structural holes" (Burt 1992) – regions of thin connections – as important as densely knit connectivity for successfully acquiring and controlling resources? Bian shows that having trusted informants and controlling access to information is important for getting desired jobs (see also Bian 1999).

Our group's Canadian research suggests that all levels are contingently important for the provision of support. For example, while ties with immediate kin (parents-adult children) are especially supportive, these ties are even more supportive when they are located in networks containing several other immediate kin (Wellman and Frank 2001). The dynamics of the whole are more than the sum of the parts, an accurate way of representing the contemporary network world in which phenomena are inherently multi-level.

A network society

Our group's findings fit the nature of loosely coupled communities and organizations that are not enveloping, binding solidarities. The authors of this book have convinced me that this is as true in China as it is in Canada. Their chapters all portray a significant shift from bureaucratic power to market power (see also Nee 1996; Keister 2000). Both bureaucracies and markets entail social networks to operate. Social network analysis provides analytic tools to move the debate about state power and entrepreneurial markets beyond an either/or discussion. Bureaucracies need interpersonal work-arounds to avoid rigidities (Sik and Wellman 1999) and to make sure that high-status people get "properly" treated. Markets need the social stability and trust-enhancing qualities of interpersonal ties (Cohen 1969; Fong and Dong 1999; White 1981). This suggests that, contra Guthrie, *guanxi* will flourish in China's evolving market society.

Interpersonally, in China as well as the Western world, people are members of multiple networks, and they enact specific ties and networks on an hourly, daily, monthly, and yearly basis. They invest in close ties with immediate kin and good friends, rather than in weaker ties with neighbors and workmates. They can – and do – change ties and networks in response to opportunities, difficulties, and changes in their personal and household situations. Rather than being externally imposed by social control, ties are valued for what they can do instrumentally as well as enjoyed as sociable ends in themselves (Gold 1985; Wellman et al. 1997; Wellman 1999a, 2001).

Under these circumstances, network phenomena can only be facilitating and partially constraining – rarely dominating or controlling. Even though people no longer inhabit solidary groups, they do not function alone. Even though personal networks are fragmentary and loosely coupled, support is given to clusters within a network as well as to an ego. Ties do not operate in isolation. Ties contribute to networks; networks encourage and potentiate ties. The *guanxi* relationship is social in another sense. Support is often given for the general benefit of a household or a network rather than for the specific benefit of the individual. Just as investment is not just zero-sum but builds a fund of capital, *guanxi* can also contribute to the network of which both are members. The network's provision of *guanxi* adds to the fund of network capital circulating in a community as well as benefiting the individual. *Guanxi* is rarely a zero-sum game.

In the West, the network society is changing. In the twentieth century, household-based networks supplanted village solidarities. At present, there is a shift toward *networked individualism*, with the consequent weakening of within-household (and within-single workgroup) ties. This shift is associated with changing marriage patterns, increased geographical mobility, and individually oriented communication technologies such as the mobile phone and personal computer (Wellman 2001). It is probable that Hong Kong, Singapore, and Taiwan are undergoing similar shifts.

The authors of this book have shown that the situation in Mainland China is, as always, more complex – with intertwined social and geographical regions of stability and mobility. Even as the government attempts to control the Internet, millions of Chinese are using it to maintain existing ties, establish new ones, chat in groups, link with the disapora, search for information about jobs, politics, and other matters, and even organize protests and social movements (*Economist* 2001; see also Sheff's [2001] account of Internet growth). It will be interesting to see whether and how the Internet helps to transform the social networks of China that are now often locked in small groups, especially work organizations (*danwei*) and neighborhoods (*juweihui*). Will its potential for less-controlled, less-bounded information and communication promote physical and social mobility? Will it develop voluntary associations that transcend "little boxes" and foster new forms of civic society.

I believe that social network analysis – in combination with multi-level analysis – can contribute to theory, as well as to method and substance in understanding social support in general and *guanxi* in particular. It is an intriguing prospect. As a child of American cultural stereotypes, I grew up believing China to be a land of isolated, broadly supportive, "little-box" village solidarities, as described before World War II by Pearl Buck's *The Good Earth* (1931), updated for the revolutionary Communist era by Hinton's *Fanshen* (1966). The story is continued in this book by Wilson and, in transition, by Kipnis. My young adult life in the 1960s and 1970s was filled with pictures of massed ranks waving little red books – the isolated individual engulfed by the state. This book provides abundant convincing detail that Chinese society is not composed of either little boxes or isolated individuals. It gives us another picture, one that is closer to current Western experience: It shows people spinning, manipulating, using – and by networks of *guanxi*. The authors have ensnared me in their exciting web.

REFERENCES

Ackroyd, S. and J. A. Hughes. 1981. *Data Collection in Context*. New York: Longman.

Alston, Jon P. 1989. *"Wa, Guanxi,* and *Inhwa*: Managerial Principles in Japan, China, and Korea." *Business Horizons*, 32(2), March-April, pp. 26–31.

Ambler, Tim and Morgen Witzel. 2000. *Doing Business in China*. New York: Routledge.

Amsden, Alice H. 1989. *Asia's Next Giant: South Korea and Late Industrialization.* New York: Oxford University Press.

Anagnost, Ann S. 1986. "The Mimesis of Power." Paper presented at the November 22, 1986, conference, "Anthropological Perspectives on Mainland China, Past and Present," Center for Chinese Studies, University of California, Los Angeles.

Anderson, Elijah. 1978. *A Place on the Corner*. Chicago: University of Chicago Press.

Appadurai, Arjun. 1989. "Small-Scale Techniques and Large-Scale Objectives," pp. 250–82, in *Conversations Between Economists and Anthropologists: Methodological Issues in Measuring Economic Change in Rural India,* Pranab Bardhan, ed., Delhi: Oxford University Press.

Appelbaum, Richard. 1998. "The Future of Law in a Global Economy." *Social and Legal Studies* vol. 7, no. 2, June, pp. 171–192.

Arabie, Phipps, Scott Boorman and Paul Levitt. 1978. "Constructing Blockmodels: How and Why." *Journal of Mathematical Psychology* 17: 21–63.

Arias, Jose Tomas Gomez. 1998. "A Relationship Marketing Approach to Guanxi." in *European Journal of Marketing* vol. 32 no. 1/2: 145.

Asad, Talal, ed. 1973. *Anthropology and the Colonial Encounter*. New York: Humanities Press.

Australian Department of Foreign Affairs and Trade. 1995. *Overseas Chinese Business Networks in Asia*. Canberra: Australian Government Publication Service.

Axelrod, Robert. 1984. *The Evolution of Cooperation*. New York: Basic Books.

Ayim, Maryann. 1994. "Knowledge through the Grapevine: Gossip as Inquiry." In *Good Gossip*, edited by Robert F. Goodman and Aaron Ben Ze'ev. Lawrence: University Press of Kansas.

Bailey, F. G. 1991. *The Prevalence of Deceit*. Ithaca: Cornell University Press.

Balazs, Etienne. 1964. *Chinese Civilization and Bureaucracy: Variations on a Theme*. Translated by H.M. Wright. New Haven: Yale University Press.

Barbalet, J. M. 1998. *Emotion, Social Theory, and Social Structure*. Cambridge: Cambridge University Press.

Barnett, A. Doak. 1967. *Cadres, Bureaucracy, and Political Power in Communist China*. New York: Columbia University Press.

Bayraktaroglu, Arin. 1991. "Politeness and Interactional Imbalance." *International Journal of the Sociology of Language* 92: 5–34.

Bech, Henning. 1998. "Citysex: Representing Sex in Public." *Theory, Culture and Society* 15: 3–4, pp. 215–242.

Beijing Xinhua domestic service. 1998. "China: Supreme Court, Procuratorate Report Work." 14 Sept. in FBIS-CHI-98–260, 17 Sept.

Bellah, Robert N., Richard Madsen, William M. Sullivan, Ann Swidler, Steven M. Tipton. 1991. *The Good Society*. New York: Knopf.

Bennett, Gary M. (ed.). 1995. *China Facts and Figures, Annual Handbook*. Gulf Breeze, Florida: Academic International Press.

Berkowitz, S. D. 1982. *An Introduction to Structural Analysis: The Network Approach to Social Research*. Toronto: Butterworth.

Berliner, Joseph S. 1957. *Factory and Manager in the USSR*. Cambridge: Harvard University Press.

Berman, Harold J. 1983. *Law and Revolution: The Formation of the Western Legal Tradition*. Cambridge, Mass. and London: Harvard University Press.

Bernard, H. Russell, Peter Killworth, David Kronenfeld and Lee Sailer. 1984. "The Problem of Informant Accuracy: The Validity of Retrospective Data." *Annual Review of Anthropology* 13: 495–517.

Bi Jifang. 1990. *Zhixie He Daoqian* (Thanking and Apologizing). *Xue Hanyu* (November 1990): 18–19.

Bian, Yanjie. 1994a. *Work and Inequality in Urban China*. Albany, NY: State University of New York Press.

    1994b. "*Guanxi* and the Allocation of Jobs in Urban China." *The China Quarterly* 140: 971–99.

    1997. "Bringing Strong Ties Back In: Indirect Ties, Network Bridges, and Job Searches in China." *American Sociological Review* 62: 366–385.

    1999. "Getting a Job Through a Web of *Guanxi* in China," pp. 225–253 in *Networks in the Global Village*, edited by Barry Wellman. Boulder, CO: Westview.

Bian, Yanjie and Soon Ang. 1997. "*Guanxi* Networks and Job Mobility in China and Singapore." *Social Forces* 75(3): 981–1005.

Bian, Yanjie, and John R. Logan. 1996. "Market Transition and the Persistence of Power: The Changing Stratification System in Urban China." *American Sociological Review* 61: 739–58.

Billeter, Jean-Francois. 1985. "The System of 'Class Status,'" in *The Scope of State Power in China*, Stuart R. Schram, ed., London: School of Oriental and African Studies, 127–169.

Blau, Peter M. 1986. *Exchange and Power in Social Life*. New Brunswick, NJ: Transaction Publishers.

Blau, Peter M., Danching Ruan, and Monika Ardelt. 1991. "Interpersonal Choice and Networks in China." *Social Forces* 69: 1037–1062.

Bloch, Maurice and Jonathan Parry. 1989. "Introduction." In *Money and the Morality of Exchange*, Jonathan Parry and Maurice Bloch, eds. Cambridge: Cambridge University Press.

Bohannon, Paul. 1965. "The Differing Realms of Law." *American Anthropologist* vol. 67, no. 6: 33.

Boisot, Max, and John Child. 1996. "From Fiefs to Clans and Network Capitalism: Explaining China's Emerging Economic Order." *Administrative Science Quarterly* 41: 600–628.

Bonvillain, Nancy. 1997. *Language, Culture, and Communication: the Meaning of Messages*, 2nd edition. New York: Prentice Hall.

Bosco, Joseph. 1994a. "Taiwan Factions: *Guanxi*, Patronage, and the State in Local Politics." In *The Other Taiwan: 1945 to the Present*, ed. Murray A. Rubinstein, 114–43. Armonk: M.E. Sharpe.

——— 1994b. "Taiwan Businessmen Across the Straits: Socio-Cultural Dimensions of the Cross-Straits Relationship." Department of Anthropology, Chinese University of Hong Kong, Working Paper No. 1.

Bourdieu, Pierre. 1977. *Outline of a Theory of Practice*, Richard Nice, trans. Cambridge: Cambridge University Press.

——— 1986. "The Forms of Capital." In *The Handbook of Theory and Research for the Sociology of Education*, ed. John G. Richardson, 241–58. New York: Greenwood.

——— 1990. *The Logic of Practice*. Trans. Richard Nice. Stanford, CA: Stanford U. Press.

——— 1997. *Outline of A Theory of Practice*. Trans. Richard Nice. New York: Columbia U. Press.

Breiger, Ronald. 1974. "The Duality of Persons and Groups." *Social Forces* 53: 181–90.

——— 1981. "Structures of Economic Interdependence Among Nations," pp. 353–80 in *Continuities in Structural Inquiry*, edited by Peter Blau and Robert Merton. Beverly Hills, CA: Sage.

Brightman, Robert. 1995. "Forget Culture: Replacement, Transcendence, Relexification." *Cultural Anthropology* 10(4): 509–546.

Brindley, Thomas A. 1989. "Socio-Psychological Values in the Republic of China (I)." *Asian Thought and Society* vol. XV, no. 42: 98.

——— 1990. "Socio-Psychological Values in the Republic of China (II)." *Asian Thought and Society* vol. XV, no. 43: 2.

Brown, Penelope. 1987. *Politeness: Some Universals in Language Usage*. Cambridge: Cambridge University Press.

Brown, Penelope and Stephen Levinson. 1978. "Universals in Language Usage: Politeness Phenomenon," pp. 56–289 in *Questions and Politeness*, editor Esther N. Goody. Cambridge: Cambridge University Press.

Brugger, Bill and Stephen Reglar. 1994. *Politics, Economy and Society in Contemporary China*. Stanford: Stanford University Press.

Bruun, Ole. 1993. *Business and Bureaucracy in a Chinese City: An Ethnography of Private Business Households in Contemporary China*. Berkeley: Institute of East Asian Studies, University of California.

Buck, Pearl. 1931. *The Good Earth*. New York: J. Day.

Bureau of State Assets Management. January 1, 1995. "Tentative Regulations on Ownership Transfer of State Enterprises," pp. 1 in *Shanghai Economic Daily*. Shanghai, PRC.

Burgess, Robert G. 1982. "Multiple Strategies in Field Research," pp. 163–67 in *Field Research: A Sourcebook and Field Manual*, editor Robert G. Burgess. London: Allen & Unwin.

Burke, Kenneth. 1989. *On Symbols and Society*. Edited and with an Introduction by Joseph R. Gusfield. Chicago: University of Chicago Press.

Burt, Ronald S. 1982. *Toward a Structural Theory of Action: Network Models of Social Structure, Perception, and Action*. New York: Academic Press.

——— 1983. "Range," pp. 176–194 in *Applied Network Analysis*, edited by Ronald Burt and Michael Minor, Beverly Hills, CA: Sage.

——— 1992. *Structural Holes*. Chicago: University of Chicago Press.

Butterfield, Fox. 1982. *China: Alive in the Bitter Sea*. New York: New York Times Books.

Cancian, Francesca. 1975. *What Are Norms? A Study of Beliefs and Action in a Maya Community*. Cambridge: Cambridge University Press.

Carrier, James G. 1997. "Introduction," pp. 1–67 in *Meanings of the Market: The Free Market in Western Culture*, editor James G. Carrier. Oxford: Berg.

Carrington, Peter. 1981. "Horizontal Co-Optation Through Corporate Interlocks." Occasional Paper No. 1, Structural Analysis Programme, Department of Sociology, University of Toronto.

Castel, J. G., A. L. C. de Mestral, W. C. Graham. 1991. *The Canadian Law and Practice of International Trade*. Toronto: Emond Montgomery.

Castells, Manuel. 1996. *The Rise of the Network Society*. Malden, MA: Blackwell.

Cesara, Manda. 1982. *Reflections of a Woman Anthropologist: No Hiding Place*. London: Academic Press.

Chapman, Mark. forthcoming. "No Longer Crying in the Wilderness: Canadian Evangelical Organizations and Their Networks." Centre for Religious Studies, University of Toronto.

Chan, Anita, Madsen, Richard, and Unger, Jonathan. 1992. *Chen Village under Mao and Deng*. Berkeley and London: University of California Press.

Chan, Anita, and Unger, Jonathan. 1982. "Grey and Black: The Hidden Economy of Rural China." *Pacific Affairs*, 55: 3 (Fall), 452–471.

Chan, Kwok-bun. 2000. *Chinese Business Networks: State, Economy and Culture*. Singapore and Copenhagen: Prentice Hall and Nordic Institute of Asian Studies.

Chang, Hui-ching. 1999. "The 'Well-Defined' Is 'Ambiguous' – Indeterminacy in Chinese Conversation." *Journal of Pragmatics* 31: 535–56.

Chee, Kiongtuong, Keeyong Pit. 1998. "*Guanxi* Bases, Xinyong and Chinese Business Networks." *British Journal of Sociology* vol. 49 no. 1: 75–96.

Chen, Lixing. 2000. "Shakaiteki Nettowaaku o Ugokasu Dainamikkusu: Chugoku no Siteki Keizaisha o Siturei to Site" (Dynamics of Social Networks: The Case of Private Business Owners in China). Paper presented at the Conference *The Rise of the Private Business Management and the Social Change in China*. Ehime University, Matsuyama, Japan.

Chen, Weixing. 1998. "The political economy of rural industrialization in China." *Modern China* 24(1): 73–97.

Chen, Wuqing. 1997. "Zhongguoren Guanxi di Youxi Yihan" (The Meaning of Chinese People's *Guanxi* Games). *Shehuixue Yanjiu* (Sociological Research) 2, 103–12.

Chen, Xiaojun, Gao Fei. 1998. "Zhiding tongyi hetong fa de ruogan falu wenti sikao" (Considerations of several jurisprudential issues in enacting a unified contract law). *Faxue yanjiu* (Studies in Law) no. 1: 53–59.

Cheng, Dejun, ed. 1992. *Shewai zhongcai yu falu* (Foreign-related arbitration and law). Beijing: Chinese People's University Press.

Cheng, Lim Keak. 1985. *Social Change and the Chinese in Singapore: A Socio-Economic Geography*. Singapore: Singapore University Press.

Cheng, Lucie, and Arthur Rosett. "Contract with a Chinese Face: Socially Embedded Factors in the Transformation from Hierarchy to Market, 1978–1989." *Journal of Chinese Law* 5(No. 2): 143–244.

Cheng, Tiejun, and Mark Selden. 1994. "The Origins and Social Consequences of China's *Hukou* System." *The China Quarterly* 139: 644–668.

Chiao, Chien. 1982. "*Guanxi*: A Preliminary Conceptualization," pp. 345–60 in *The Sinicization of Social and Behavioral Science Research in China*, edited by Kuo-shu Yang and Chong-yi Wen. Taipei, Taiwan: Academia Sinica.

Chiao, Chien. 1982. "*Guanxi Chuyi*" ["My humble views on guanxi"], in *Shehui ji Xingwei Kexue Yanjiu de Zhongguohua* [Sinicization of social and behavioral science research], Yang Guoshu and Wen Chongyi, eds. Taibei: Institute of Ethnology, Academia Sinica.

Chin, Hui, George Graen. 1997. "*Guanxi* and Professional Leadership in Contemporary Sino-American Joint Ventures in Mainland China." *Leadership Quarterly* vol. 8 no. 4 (winter): 451–65.

Christensen, Garry. 1993. "Sensitive Information: Collecting Data on Livestock and Informal Credit," pp. 124–37 in *Fieldwork in Developing Countries*, editors Stephen Devereux and John Hoddinott. Boulder: Lynne Rienner.

Chu, Godwin C., and Yanan Ju. 1993. *The Great Wall in Ruins: Communication and Cultural Change in China*. Albany: State University of New York Press.

Chu, Lynn. 1990. "The Chimera of the China Market." *Atlantic Monthly* (October): 56.

Clinton, Hilary Rodham. 1996. *It Takes a Village: And Other Lessons Children Teach Us*. New York: Simon and Schuster.

Ci, Jiwei. 1994. *Dialectic of the Chinese Revolution: From Utopianism to Hedonism*. Stanford: Stanford University Press.

Civil Law Office of the NPC Standing Committee on Legal Affairs and CCPIT Secretariat, ed. 1995. *Zhonghua renmin gongheguo zhongcai fa quanshu* (Encyclopedia of arbitration law of the PRC). Beijing: Law Publishers.

Code, Lorraine. 1994. "Gossip or in praise of chaos." In *Good Gossip*, edited by Robert F. Goodman and Aaron Ben Ze'ev. Lawrence: University Press of Kansas.

Cohen, Abner. 1969. *Custom and Politics in Urban Africa*. Routledge and Kegan Paul.

Cohen, Felix. 1970. "The Relativity of Philosophical Systems and the Method of Systematic Relativism," in Lucy Kramer Cohen, ed. *The Legal Conscience: Selected Papers of Felix S. Cohen*. Shoe String Press, New Haven: Yale University Press.

Cohen, Jerome Alan. 1985. "The New Foreign Contract Law." *China Business Review* (Jul./Aug.).

Coleman, James S. 1988. "Social Capital in the Creation of Human Capital." *American Journal of Sociology* 94: S95–121.

Collins, Louise. 1994. "Gossip: A Feminist Defense." In *Good Gossip*, edited by Robert F. Goodman and Aaron Ben Ze'ev. Lawrence: University Press of Kansas.

Cook, Karen S. 1977. "Exchange and Power in Networks of Interorganizational Relationships." *Sociological Quarterly* 18: 62–82.

———. ed. 1987. *Social Exchange Theory*. Newbury Park, CA: SAGE publications.

Cook, Karen S. and Richard M. Emerson. 1984. "Exchange Networks and The Analysis of Complex Organizations." *Research in the Sociology of Organizations* 3: 1–30.

Cool, Karel O. and Dan Schendel. 1987. "Strategic Group Formation and Performance: The Case of the U.S. Pharmaceutical Industry, 1963–1983." *Management Science* 33: 1102–1124.

Cottrell, P. L. 1980. *The Finance and Organization of English Manufacturing Industry*. London: Methuen.

Craven, Paul and Barry Wellman. 1973. "The Network City." *Sociological Inquiry* 43(1): 57–88.

Croll, Elisabeth. 1981. *The Politics of Marriage in Contemporary China*. Cambridge: Cambridge U. Press.

Danet, Brenda. 1989. *Pulling Strings: Biculturalism in Israeli Bureaucracy*. Albany: State University of New York Press.

———. 1990. "*Protektzia*: The Roots of Organizational Biculturalism among Israeli Jews." *Social Forces* (March): 909–932.

Davis, Deborah. 1990. "Urban Job Mobility," pp. 85–108 in *Chinese Society on the Eve of Tiananmen*, edited Deborah Davis and Erza F. Vogel. Cambridge, CA: Harvard University Press.

1999. "Self-employment in Shanghai: A research note." *The China Quarterly* 157 (March): 22–43.

Davis, Roger. 1981. "Social Network Analysis: An Aid in Conspiracy Investigations." *FBI Law Enforcement Bulletin,* December: 11–19.

deBary, Wm. Theodore. 1985. "Neo-Confucian Individualism and Holism." in *Individualism and Holism: Studies in Confucian and Taoist Values,* ed. Donald J. Munro, 331–58. Ann Arbor: Center for Chinese Studies, The University of Michigan.

de Certeau, Michel. 1984. *The Practice of Everyday Life,* Steven F. Rendall, trans. Berkeley: University of California Press.

1986. *Heterologies: Discourse on the Other,* Brian Massumi, trans. Minneapolis: University of Minnesota Press.

DeGlopper, Donald R. 1995. *Lukang: Commerce and Commodity in a Chinese City.* Albany: State University of New York Press.

Deng, Xiaoping. 1984. "On the Reform of Party and State Leadership." In *Selected Works of Deng Xiaoping,* pp. 302–25. Beijing: Foreign Languages Press.

Denzin, Norman K. 1970. *The Research Act: A Theoretical Introduction to Sociological Methods.* Chicago: Aldine Publishing.

de Sousa, Ronald. 1994. "In Praise of Gossip: Indiscretion as a Saintly Virtue." In *Good Gossip,* edited by Robert F. Goodman and Aaron Ben Ze'ev. Lawrence: University Press of Kansas.

Deutscher, Irwin. 1973. *What We Say/What We Do: Sentiments and Acts.* Glenview, IL: Scott, Foresman.

Diamond, A. S., 1971. *Primitive Law, Past and Present.* London: Methuen.

Diamond, Stanley. 1973. "The Rule of Law Versus the Order of Custom." In Donald Black and Maureen Mileski, eds., *The Social Organization of Law.* New York and London: Seminar Press: 318.

Dickson, Bruce J. 1992. "What Explains Chinese Political Behavior? The Debate over Structure and Culture." *Comparative Politics* 25(1): 103–18.

Ding, Xueliang. 1999. "Who Gets What, How? When Chinese State-Owned Enterprises Become Shareholding Companies." *Problems of Post-Communism* 46(3): 32–41.

Dirlik, Arif. 1996. "Critical Reflections on 'Chinese Capitalism' as Paradigm" in *Identities,* vol. 3, no. 3: 303–330.

Dittmer, Lowell. 1995. "Chinese Informal Politics." *The China Journal* 34 (July): 1–34.

Dittmer, Lowell and Lu Xiaobo. 1996. "Personal Politics in the Chinese *Danwei.*" *Asian Survey* 36(3): 246–67.

Dong, Fangzhi. 1998. *Guanxixue Quanshu* (The Complete Book of *Guanxixue*). 2 vols. Beijing: Beijing Tushuguan.

Dong, Jie Lin and Jie Hu. 1995. "Mergers and Acquisitions in China." *Federal Reserve Bank of Atlanta Economic Review* 80: 15–29.

Dong Weizhen and Janet Salaff. 2000. "Just Friends: Social Networks and Middle Class Chinese Immigrants." Presented to the American Sociological Association, Washington, August.

Doreian, Patrick. 1980. "Linear Models with Spatially Distributed Data: Spatial Disturbances or Spatial Effects." *Sociological Methods and Research* 9: 29–60.

Dreyfus, Hubert L., and Rabinow, Paul. 1983. *Michel Foucault: Beyond Structuralism and Hermeneutics,* 2d ed. Chicago: University of Chicago Press.

Duara, Prasenjit. 1988. *Culture, Power and the State: Rural North China: 1900–1942.* Stanford: Stanford University Press.

Dumont, Louis. 1970. *Homo Hierarchicus.* Chicago: University of Chicago Press.

Dutton, Michael. 1998. *Streetlife China.* Cambridge: Cambridge University Press.

Economist, The. 2000. "Tangled Web." "China Survey" section, April 8, p. 7.

Ehrmann, Henry W. 1976. *Comparative Legal Cultures.* Englewood Cliffs, N.J., Prentice-Hall.

Elias, Norbert. 1978. *The Civilizing Process.* Oxford: Basil Blackwell.

Eisenstadt, S. W., L. Roniger. 1984. *Patrons, Clients and Friends: Interpersonal Relations and the Structure of Trust in Society.* Cambridge: Cambridge University Press.

Emerson, Richard M. 1976. "Social Exchange Theory." *Annual Review of Sociology* 2: 335–362.

Emirbayer, Mustafa. 1997. "Manifesto for a Relational Sociology." *American Journal of Sociology* 103(2): 281–317.

Esherick, Joseph and Mary Rankin, eds. 1990. *Chinese Local Elites and Patterns of Dominance.* Berkeley: University of California Press.

Fang Xiaojun, Shan Man, Li Wanpeng, Jiang Wenhua, Ye Tao, and Wang Dianji. 1988. *Shandong Minsu* (Customs of Shandong). Jinan, PRC: Shandong Youyi She.

Farh, Jinglih, M. S. Tsue, Catherine R. Xin and Cheng Bor Shiuan. 1998. "The Influence of Relational Demography and *Guanxi*: The Chinese Case." *Organization Science* vol. 9 no. 4 (July-August): 471–88.

Farina, Anne Judith. 1989. "'Talking Disputes into Harmony:' China Approaches International Commercial Arbitration." *American University Journal of International Law and Policy* 137.

Farrer, James. 1998. *A Sexual Opening in Shanghai.* University of Chicago Dissertation.

Featherstone, Mike and Scott Lash, editors. 1999. *Spaces of Culture: City – Nation – World.* London: Sage.

Fei, Xiaotong. 1949. *Xiangtu Zhongguo* [Folk China]. Beijing University Sociology Department Study Group, 1983, mimeograph. (1949 publication in China by Guan Cha She.)

    1953. *China's Gentry: Essays on Rural–Urban Relations.* Edited by Margaret Park Redfield. Chicago.

    1985. *Rural Life in China,* Beijing: Sanlian Publishing House [in Chinese].

    1992. *From the Soil: The Foundation of Chinese Society* (translated by Gary G. Hamilton and Wang Zheng). Berkeley: University of California Press.

Feinerman, James V. 1994. "Legal Institution, Administrative Device, or Foreign Import: The Roles of Contract in the People's Republic of China," in Pitman Potter, ed., *Domestic Law Reforms.* Armonk, N.Y.: M.E. Sharpe (1994).

Ferrand, Alexis, Lise Mounier and Alain Degenne. 1999. "The Diversity of Personal Networks in France: Social Stratification and Relational Structures," pp. 185–224 in *Networks in the Global Village,* edited by Barry Wellman. Boulder, CO: Westview Press.

Feuerwerker, Albert. 1976. *State and Society in Eighteenth Century China.* Ann Arbor: Center for Chinese Studies.

Fewsmith, Joseph. 1994. *Dilemmas of Reform in China: Political Conflict and Economic Debate.* Armonk, N.Y. and London: M.E. Sharpe.

    1996. "Institutions, Informal Politics, and Political Transition in China." *Asian Survey* 36(3): 246–67.

Fields, Karl J. 1995. *Enterprise and the State in Korea and Taiwan.* Ithaca, NY: Cornell University.

Finder, Susan. 1996. "Litigation in the Chinese courts: a new frontier for foreign business." *China Law & Practice* (Feb): 18–19.

Fischer, Claude S. 1982. *To Dwell Among Friends: Personal Networks in Town and City.* Chicago: The University of Chicago Press.

Foucault, Michel. 1979a. "Governmentality." *Ideology and Consciousness,* no. 6 (Autumn), 5–21.

1979b. *Discipline and Punish: The Birth of the Prison*, Alan Sheridan, trans. New York: Vintage.

1980. *The History of Sexuality*, Robert Hurley, trans. New York: Random House.

1983. "The Subject and Power," in *Michel Foucault: Beyond Structuralism and Hermeneutics*, 2d ed., H. Dreyfus and P. Rabinow, eds., Chicago: University of Chicago Press, 208–226.

Francis, Corinna-Barbara. 1999. "Bargained property rights: The case of China's high-technology sector." In Jean Oi and Walder. Andrew, eds. *Property Rights and Economic Reform in China*, 226–247. Stanford, CA: Stanford University Press.

Frank, Andre Gunder. 1998. *ReOrient: Global Economy in the Asian Age*. Berkeley: University of California Press.

Fraser, Bruce. 1990. "Perspectives on Politeness." *Journal of Pragmatics* 14(2): 219–36.

Fried, Morton H. 1953. *Fabric of Chinese Society: A Study of the Social life of a Chinese County Seat*. New York: Praeger.

Friedman, Edward., P. Pickowicz, M. Selden, eds. *Chinese Village, Socialist State*. New Haven: Yale University Press.

Friedman, Lawrence M. 1975. *The Legal System: a Social Science Perspective*. Englewood Cliffs, N.J.: Prentice-Hall.

Frolic, B. Michael. 1980. *Mao's People*. Cambridge: Harvard University Press.

Fukuyama, Francis. 1995. *Trust: The Social Virtues and the Creation of Prosperity*. New York: The Free Press.

Gadamer, Hans Georg. 1975. *Truth and Method*. New York: Seabury.

1976. *Philosophical Hermeneutics*. Trans. David E. Linge. Berkeley, CA: University of California Press.

Galasi, Peter. 1985. "Peculiarities and Limits of the Second Economy in Socialism (The Hungarian Case)" in *The Economics of the Shadow Economy*, W. Gaertner and A. Wenig, eds. 353–361. Berlin: Springer Verlag.

Gao Cheng-shu. 1999. *Toujianiang [Boss's Wife]: The Economic Activity and Social Implication of "Toujianiang" in Taiwan Small and Medium Enterprises*. Taipei: Lianjing Publishing House [in Chinese].

Garfinkel, Harold. 1967. *Studies in Ethnomethodology*. Englewood Cliffs, New Jersey: Prentice-Hall.

Gates, Hill. 1986. "The Petty Capitalist Mode of Production." Paper presented at the November 22, 1986, conference, "Anthropological Perspectives on Mainland China, Past and Present," Center for Chinese Studies, University of California, Los Angeles.

1996. *China's Motor: A Thousand Years of Petty Capitalism*. Ithaca: Cornell University Press.

Geertz, Clifford. 1964. "Ideology as a Cultural System," in David E. Apter, ed., *Ideology and Discontent*, New York: The Free Press, London: Collier-MacMillan.

1973. "'From the Native's Point of View': On the Nature of Anthropological Understanding." In Clifford Geertz, *Local Knowledge: Further Essays in Interpretive Anthropology*: 55–70. New York: Basic Books.

1983. *Local Knowledge: Further Essays in Interpretive Anthropology*. New York: Basic Books.

1983. "Culture and Social Change: The Indonesian Case," *Man* (n.s.) 19: 511–532.

Gerlach, Michael L. 1992. *Alliance Capitalism: The Social Organization of Japanese Business*. Berkeley: University of California Press.

Giddens, Anthony. 1990. *The Consequences of Modernity*. Stanford: Stanford University Press.

Gilley, Bruce. 1999a. "Loose Connection." *Far Eastern Economic Review*. May 27: 26–7.

1999b. "Marriages on the Rocks." *Far Eastern Economic Review*. October 28: 64–5.

Glendon, Mary Anne. 1985. *Comparative Legal Systems*. St. Paul: West.

Gluckman. Max. 1963. "Gossip and Scandal" *Current Anthropology* 4: 307–16.

1965. *Politics, Law, and Ritual in Tribal Society*. Oxford: Blackwell.

Goffman, Erving. 1955. "On Face-Work: An Analysis of Ritual Elements in Social Inter-action." *Psychiatry* 18(3): 213–31.

Gold, Thomas B. 1985. "After Comradeship: Personal Relations in China Since the Cultural Revolution." *The China Quarterly* 104, December: 657–675.

1989. "Guerilla Interviewing Among the *Getihu*," pp. 175–92 in Unofficial China: *Popular Culture and Thought in the People's Republic*, editors Perry Link, Richard Madsen, and Paul Pickowicz. Boulder, CO: Westview Press.

Golde, Peggy, editor. 1986. *Women in the Field: Anthropological Experiences*. Berkeley: University of California Press.

Goldie-Scott, Duncan. 1995a. *Banking in China*. London: Financial Times Publishing.

1995b. *China's Financial Markets*. London: Financial Times Publishing.

Gomez Arias, Jose Tomas. 1998. "A relationship marketing approach to *guanxi*." *European Journal of Marketing*. 32(1/2): 145–56.

Gong, Huifeng. 1995. *The (Chinese) Stock Market (Gupiao Shichang)*. Shanghai, PRC: Shanghai Yuandong Chubanshe.

Granovetter, Mark. 1973. "The Strength of Weak Ties." *American Journal of Sociology* 78: 1360–80.

1974. *Getting a Job: A Study of Contacts and Careers*. Cambridge, MA: Harvard University Press.

1985. "Economic Action and Social Structure: The Problem of Embeddedness." *American Journal of Sociology* 91 (November): 481–510.

1992. "Economic Action and Social Structure: The Problem of Embeddedness," pp. 53–81 in *The Sociology of Economic Life*, editors M. Granovetter and R. Swedberg. Boulder, CO: Westview Press.

1995. "Coase Revisited: Business Groups in the Modern Economy." *Industrial and Corporate Change* 4: 93–130.

1995 [1974]. *Getting A Job: A Study of Contacts and Careers*. Chicago: University of Chicago Press.

1995. "Afterword." In *Getting A Job* (2nd edition). Chicago: University of Chicago Press.

Gregory, C. A. 1982. *Gifts and Commodities*. London: Academic Press.

Grey, Thomas C. 1983. "Langdell's Orthodoxy." *University of Pittsburgh Law Review* vol. 45, no. 1 (Fall).

Grossman, Gregory, 1977. "The 'Second Economy' of the USSR." *Problems of Commu-nism*. (Sept.- Oct.) 26: 5, 25–40.

1982. "The 'Shadow Economy' in the Socialist Sector of the USSR," in *The CMEA Five-Year Plans (1981–85) in a New Perspective*. NATO, Economics and Information Directorates.

Gu, Yueguo. 1990. "Politeness Phenomena in Modern Chinese." *Journal of Pragmatics* 14: 237–57.

Gumperz, John J. and Stephen C. Levinson. 1996. *Rethinking Linguistic Relativity*. Cambridge: Cambridge University Press.

Guth, DeLloyd, "The Age of Debt, The Reformation and English Law," in D. J. Guth and J. W. McKenna, eds., *Tudor Rule and Revolution: Essays for G. R. Elton From His American Friends*. Cambridge: Cambridge University Press.

Guthrie, Doug. 1997. "Between Markets and Politics: Organizational Responses to Reform in China." *American Journal of Sociology* 102: 1258–1304.

1998a. "The Declining Significance of *Guanxi* in China's Economic Transition." *The China Quarterly* 154 (June): 254–82.

1998b. "Organizational Uncertainty and Labor Contracts in China's Economic Transition." *Sociological Forum* 13(2): 457–494.

1999. *Dragon in a Three-Piece Suit: The Emergence of Capitalism in China*. Princeton, NJ: Princeton University Press.

GYPCBGS (Gongye pucha bangong shi). 1997. *Zhonghua renmin gongheguo 1995 disan ci quanguo gongye pucha ziliao zhaiyao* (Abstracts of the 1989 industrial census of the PRC). Beijing: Zhongguo tongji chubanshe.

Haber, Stephen H. 1991. "Industrial Concentration and the Capital Markets: A Comparative Study of Brazil, Mexico, and the United States, 1830–1930." *Journal of Economic History* 51: 559–580.

Haines, Valerie and Jeanne Hurlbert. 1992. "Network Range and Health." *Journal of Health and Social Behavior* 33: 254–66.

Hall, Alan and Barry Wellman. 1985. "Social Networks and Social Support," pp. 23–41 in *Social Support and Health*, edited by Sheldon Cohen and S Leonard Syme. New York: Academic Press.

Hall, David L. and Roger T. Ames. 1987. *Thinking Through Confucius*. New York: State University of New York Press.

Halpern, Nina. 1998. "Adaptation and decline in Chinese basic-level party organization." Discussion paper. Center for Chinese Research. University of British Columbia.

Hamilton, Gary G. 1989. "Patterns of Asian Capitalism: The Cases of Taiwan and South Korea." Program in East Asian Business Culture and Development, Working Paper Series, 28, Institute of Governmental Affairs, University of California, Davis.

1990. "The Network Structures of East Asian Economies," pp. 105–129 in *Capitalism in Contrasting Cultures*. S.R. Clegg and S.G. Redding, eds. Berlin: Walter de Gruyter.

1991. *Business Networks and Economic Development in East and Southeast Asia*. Hong Kong: Center of Asian Studies, University of Hong Kong.

1996 "The Theoretical Significance of Asian Business Networks." Pp. 283–98 in *Asian Business Networks*. Gary Hamilton, ed. Berlin: Walter de Gruyter.

1996. "Overseas Chinese Capitalism." Pp. 328–42 in Tu Wei-ming ed., *Confucian Traditions in East Asian Modernity*. Cambridge, MA: Harvard University Press.

Hamilton, Gary and Nicole Woolsey Biggart. 1988. "Market, Culture, and Authority: A Comparative Analysis of Management and Organization in the Far East." *American Journal of Sociology* 94 (Supplement): S52–94.

Hamilton, Gary and Kao Cheng-shu. 1990. "The Institutional Foundations of Chinese Business: The Family Firm in Taiwan." *Comparative Social Research* 12: 135–51.

"Han Zhubin Stresses Need to Better Handle Appeals, Tips," Beijing Xinhua domestic service Sept. 25, 1998, in FBIS-CHI-98-271, 28 Sept. 1998.

Hanks, William F. 1996. *Language and Communicative Practices*. Boulder, CO: Westview.

Hardin, Russell. 1982. *Collective Action*. Baltimore: The Johns Hopkins University Press.

Harhoff, D., Stahl, K. and Woywode, M. 1996. "Legal Form, Growth and Exit of West German Firms: Empirical Results for Manufacturing, Construction, Trade and Service Industries." CEPR Discussion Paper No. 1401, London: Centre for Economic Policy Research.

Harvey, David. 1989. *The Condition of Postmodernity*. Oxford: Basil Blackwell.

Haveman, Heather A. 1992. "Between a Rock and a Hard Place: Organizational Change and Performance Under Conditions of Fundamental Environmental Transformation." *Administrative Science Quarterly*. 37: 48–75.

Haythornthwaite, Caroline and Barry Wellman. 1996. "Using SAS to Convert Ego-Centered Networks to Whole Networks." *Bulletin de Methode Sociologique* 50: 71–84.

He Qinglian. 1998. *Xiandaihua de xianjing: dangdai zhongguo de jingji shehui wenti* (Pitfalls of Modernization: Economic and Social Problems in Contemporary China). Beijing: Jinri zhongguo chubanshe.

Henderson, Gail, and Myron, Cohen. 1984. *The Chinese Hospital: A Socialist Work Unit.* New Haven: Yale University Press.

Henry, Stuart. 1983. *Private Justice: Towards An Integrated Theorizing in the Sociology of Law.* London: Routledge and Kegan Paul.

Herschler, Stephen. 1995. "The 1994 tax reforms: the center strikes back." *China Economic Review* 6(2): 239–245.

Hertz, Ellen. 1998. *The Trading Crowd: An Ethnography of the Shanghai Stock Market.* Cambridge: Cambridge University Press.

Hevia, James. 1995. *Cherishing Men From Afar: Qing Guest Ritual and the Macartney Embassy of 1793.* Durham, NC: Duke University Press.

Hinton, William. 1966. *Fanshen.* New York: Vintage.

Ho, David. 1976. "On the concept of face." *American Journal of Sociology* 81, no. 4: 867–884.

Ho, Ping-ti. 1954. "The Salt Merchants of Yangzhou." *Harvard Journal of Asiatic Studies* 17: 130–168.

    1995. Zhongguo lidai tudi shuzhi kaoshi (Investigation on land statistics in Chinese history). Taipei: Lianjing Publishers.

Honig, Emily and Gail Hershatter. 1988. *Personal Voices: Chinese Women in the 1980's.* Stanford, CA: Stanford University Press.

Hsing, You-tien. 1996. "Blood thicker than water: interpersonal relations and Taiwanese investment in southern China." *Environment and Planning A.* 28: 2241–2261.

    1998. *Making Capitalism in China: The Taiwan Connection.* New York: Oxford University Press.

    Forthcoming. "Ethnic identity and business solidarity: Chinese capitalism revisited." In Larry Ma ed. *Geography of Chinese Diaspora.*

Hsu, Jinn-Yu and AnnaLee Saxenian 2000. "The Limits of Guanxi Capitalism: Transnational Collaboration Between Taiwan and the USA." *Environment and Planning* 32: 1991–2005.

Hsung, Ray-May. 1998. "The Concepts of Social Networks and *Guanxi*: The Application to Taiwan Studies." Presented at the Social Networks and Social Capital Conference, Duke University, Durham, NC, October.

Hsung, Ray-May and Lin Ling-Lu. 1995. "Institutional Status, Gender, and Social Resources in Taiwan." Presented to the International Social Network Conference, London, July.

Hu, Hsien-chin. 1944. "The Chinese Concept of 'Face.'" *American Anthropologist* 46: 1 (Jan.-Mar.) 45–64.

Hu, Kangsheng, "Guanyu <<Zhonghua renmin gongheguo hetong fa (caoan) de shouming>> (copy on file with the author).

Huang, Philip. 1985. *The Peasant Economy and Social Change in North China.* Stanford, CA: Stanford University Press.

    1990. *The Peasant Family and Rural Development in the Yangzi Delta. 1350–1988.* Stanford, CA: Stanford University Press.

    1996. *Civil Justice in China: Representation and Practice in the Qing.* Stanford, CA: Stanford University Press.

Huang, Qihai. 2000. "Guanxi di Liliang? Zhongguo Siying Qiye Kuaisu Fazhan Yuanyin Tantao." (The Power of *Guanxi*? An Exploration of the Factors in the Rapid Growth of China's Private Enterprises). Paper presented at the Conference *The Rise of Private Business Management and Social Change in China*, Ehime University, Matsuyama Japan.

Hwang, Kwang-kuo. 1987. "Face and Favor: The Chinese Power Game." *American Journal of Sociology* 92(4): 944–74.

Ikels, Charlotte. 1996. *The Return of the God of Wealth: The Transition to a Market Economy in Urban China*. Stanford, CA.: Stanford University Press.

Jacobs, J. Bruce. 1979. "A Preliminary Model of Particularistic Ties in Chinese Political Alliances: *KanCh'ing* and *Kuanhsi* in a Rural Taiwanese Township." *The China Quarterly* 78: 237–73.

1980. *Local Politics in a Rural Chinese Cultural Setting: A Field Study of Mazu Township, Taiwan*. Canberra: Contemporary China Centre, Research School of Pacific Studies, Australian National University.

1982. "The concept of *guanxi* and local politics in a rural Chinese cultural setting." In *Social Interaction in Chinese Society*. Praeger Publishers.

Janney, Richard W. and Horst Arndt. 1992. "Intracultural Tact Versus Intercultural Tact," pp. 21–41 in *Politeness in Language: Studies in Its History, Theory, and Practice.*, editors Richard J. Watts, Sachiko Ide, and Konrad Ehlich. Berlin: Mouton de Gruyter.

Jefferson, G. H. and Rawski, T. 1994. "Enterprise Reform in Chinese Industry." *Journal of Economic Perspectives* Vol. 8, No. 2: 47–70.

Ji, Li-Jun, Richard E. Nisbett, and Kaiping Peng. 2000. "Culture, Control, and Perception of Relationships in the Environment." *Journal of Personality and Social Psychology* 78(5): 943–55.

Jian, Zhenchang. 1996. "*Dalu nongcun shequ jingying bianhua zhi yanjiu*" (Research on the change of rural community elites in Mainland China). *Gongdang wenti yanjiu* (*Problems of Communist Party*) 22(2): 71–79.

Jiang, Guoxiang. 1991. "Shanghai nongye jingying jizhide youhua he mubiao xuanze" (The improvement and selection of a target model for Shanghai's agricultural management mechanism), *Huadong Shifan Daxue Xuebao* (East China Normal University Journal), no. 1: 16–20.

Jiang, Ping. 1996. "Drafting the Uniform Contract Law in China." *Columbia Journal of Asian Law* vol. 10, no. 1: 245–258.

Jiang, Zilong. 1980. "More About Manager Qiao." *Chinese Literature* 9 (Sept.): 3–39.

1983. "Manager Qiao Assumes Office." In *The New Realism: Writing from China after the Cultural Revolution*, ed. Lee Yee, 56–85. New York: Hippocrene Books.

Joint Publication Research Service. Various years. *China Report.*

Jowitt, Ken. 1983. "Soviet Neotraditionalism: The Political Corruption of a Leninist Regime." *Soviet Studies*. 35(3): 275–97.

Judd, Ellen R. 1994. *Gender and Power in Rural North China*. Stanford, CA: Stanford University Press.

Kan, Ren. April 29, 1996. "Finance Firms Seek Role," pp. 1 in *China Daily*. Beijing, PRC.

Kao, Cheng-shu. 1991. "'Personal Trust' in the Large Businesses in Taiwan: a Traditional Foundation for Contemporary Economic Activities." In *Business Networks and Economic Development in East and Southeast Asia*, ed. Gary Hamilton, 66–76. Hong Kong: Centre of Asian Studies, University of Hong Kong.

Kao, John. 1993. "The Worldwide Web of Chinese Business." *Harvard Business Review* (March-April): 24–26.

Keister, Lisa A. 1998. "Engineering Growth: Business Group Structure and Firm Performance in China's Transition Economy." *American Journal of Sociology* 104: 404–440.

2000. "Exchange Structures in Transition: A Longitudinal Study of Lending and Trade Relations in Chinese Business Groups." Working Paper, Department of Sociology, Ohio State University, September.

Keith, Ronald C. 1994. *China's Struggle for the Rule of Law*. New York: St. Martins Press.

Kelliher, Daniel. 1992. *Peasant Power in China: The Era of Rural Reform, 1979–1989*. New Haven: Yale University Press.

Kenedi, J. 1981. *Do It Yourself: Hungary's Hidden Economy*. New York: Pluto Press.

Kent, Ann. 1993. *Between Freedom and Subsistence: China and Human Rights.* Hong Kong: Oxford University Press.

King, Ambrose Y. C. 1985. "The Individual and Group in Confucianism: A Relational Perspective," pp. 57–70 in *Individualism and Holism: Studies in Confucian and Taoist Values,* edited by Donald J. Munro. Ann Arbor: Center for Chinese Studies, the University of Michigan.

1988. "Analysis of Renqing in Interpersonal Relations (Renji *Guanxi* Zhong Renqing Zhi Fensi)," pp. 319–45 in *Psychology of the Chinese (Zhongguren de Xinli),* edited by Kuo-shu Yang. Taipei, Taiwan: Guiguan Press.

1991. "Kuan-hsi and Network Building: A Sociological Interpretation." *Daedalus* 120: 63–84.

1994. "Kuan-hsi and Network Building: A Sociological Interpretation," in *The Living Tree: The Changing Meaning of Being Chinese Today,* Tu Wei-ming, ed. Stanford, Calif.: Stanford University Press, pp. 109–126.

Kipnis, Andrew B. 1994a. "What's A Guanxi." Paper presented at the 46th annual meeting of the Association for Asian Studies, Boston.

1994b. "(Re) Inventing Li: Koutou and Subjectification in Rural Shandong." In *Body, Subject, and Power in China.* Ed. Tani Barlow and Angela Zito, 201–223. Chicago: University of Chicago Press.

1996. "The Language of Gifts: Managing Guanxi in a North China Village." *Modern China* 22(3): 285–314.

1997. *Producing Guanxi: Sentiment, Self, and Subculture in a North China Village.* Durham, NC: Duke University Press.

Nd. "Zouping Christianity as Gendered Critique: The Place of the Political in Ethnography." Ms. in author's files.

Kochen, Manfred (ed.). 1989. *The Small World.* Norwood, NJ: Ablex.

Koku, Emmanuel, Nancy Nazer and Barry Wellman. 2001. "Netting Scholars: Online and Offline." *American Behavioral Scientist* 44(10): 1752–72.

Kornai, János. 1980. *The Shortage Economy.* Amsterdam: North-Holland.

1986. *Contradictions and Dilemmas: Studies on the Socialist Economy and Society.* Cambridge, MA: MIT Press.

1990. *The Road to a Free Economy.* New York: Norton.

Kornhauser, William. 1959. *The Politics of Mass Society.* New York: Free Press.

Kutsche, P. 1998. "Introduction," pp. 1–12 in *Field Ethnography,* editor P. Kutsche. Upper Saddle River, N.J.: Prentice-Hall.

Lai, Gina, Nan Lin and Shu-Yin Leung. 1998. "Network Resources, Contact Resources, and Status Attainment." *Social Networks* 20: 159–178.

Lamoreaux, Naomi. 1994. *Insider Lending: Banks, Personal Connections, and Economic Development in Industrial New England.* New York: Cambridge University Press.

Land, Kenneth C. and Glenn Deane. 1992. "On the Large-Sample Estimation of Regression Models with Spatial- or Network- Effects Terms: A Two-Stage Least Squares Approach." *Sociological Methodology* 22: 221–48.

Lardy, Nicholas. 1996. "The role of foreign trade and investment in China's economic transformation," pp. 103–20 in Andrew Walder ed., *China's Transitional Economy.* New York: Oxford University Press.

Laumann, Edward O. 1973. *Bonds of Pluralism: The Forms and Substance of Urban Social Networks.* New York: Wiley.

Laumann, Edward O., Peter Marsden and David Prensky. 1983. "The Boundary Specification Problem in Network Analysis," pp. 18–34 in *Applied Network Analysis,* edited by Ronald Burt and Michael Minor. Beverly Hills, CA: Sage.

Lawler, Edward J. and Jeongkoo Yoon. 1998. "Network Structure and Emotion in Exchange Relations." *American Sociological Review* 63(6): 871–94.

Ledeneva, Alena. 1998. *Russia's Economy of Favours: Blat, Networking and Informal Exchanges*. New York: Cambridge University Press.

Lee, Ching Kwan. 1998. *Gender and the South China Miracle: Two Worlds of Factory Women*. Berkeley: University of California Press.

Lee, Hung Yong. 1990. *From Revolutionary Cadres to Party Technocrats in Socialist China*. Berkeley: University of California Press.

Leech, Geoffrey N. 1983. *Principles of Pragmatics*. New York: Longman.

Leff, Nathaniel H. 1976. "Capital Markets in the Less Developed Countries: The Group Principle," pp. 97–122 in *Money and Finance in Economic Growth and Development*, edited by R. McKinnon. New York: Marcel Dekker.

Lever-Tracy, Constance. 1999. "Mismatch at the Interface: Asian Capitalisms and the Crisis." Unpublished paper presented at the Conference, "Chinese Entrepreneurs and Business Networks in Southeast Asia," University of Bonn.

Levi-Strauss, Claude. 1969. *The Elementary Structures of Kinship*, J. H. Bell and J. R. von Sturner, trans. Boston: Beacon Press.

Levy, Marion J. 1949. *The Family Revolution in Modern China*. Cambridge: Harvard University Press.

Li, Lianjiang and Kevin O'Brien. 1996. "Villagers and popular resistance in contemporary China." *Modern China* 22(1): 28–61.

Li, Linda Chelan. 1998. "Guangdong: from Machiavellian flexibility towards the rule of law." *Provincial China* No. 5: 1–17.

"Li Peng Addresses NPC Legal System Seminar," Beijing Xinhua Hong Kong service 30 Aug. 1998 in FBIS-CHI-98-251, 8 Sept. 1998.

Li, Peter S. 2000. "Overseas Chinese Networks: A Reassessment." In *Chinese Business Networks: State, Economy and Culture*, ed. Chan Kwok Bun 261–84. Singapore: Prentice Hall.

Li, Yinhe. 1997. *Nüxing quanli de jueqi* [The sudden rise of women's rights]. Beijing: Zhonggue shehui kexue chubanshe.

Li, Zhi. 1995. *Modern Chinese Business Groups (Zhongguo Xiandai Qiye Jituan)*. Beijing, PRC: Zhongguo Shangye Ban.

Liang, Huixing. 1998. "Guanyu Zhongguo tongyi hetongfa caoan disan gao" (Concerning the third draft of China's unified contract law). *Faxue yuekan* (Law science monthly) no. 2: 47–52.

———. 1996. "Zhongguo hetongfa qicao guochengzhong de zhenglundian" (Points of contention in the process of drafting China's contract law) *Faxue yuekan* (Law science monthly) no. 2: 13–15.

Liang, Shuming. 1949. *The Essential Meanings of Chinese Culture*. Hong Kong: Zheng Zhong Press.

———. 1996. *The Essence of Chinese Culture*. Shanghai: Xueling Publishing House [in Chinese].

Licht, Walter. 1992. *Getting Work: Philadelphia, 1840–1950*. Cambridge, Mass.: Harvard University Press.

Lim, Linda and L. A. Peter Gosling eds., 1983. *The Chinese in Southeast Asia*. 2 vols. Singapore: Maruzen Asia.

Lin, Nan. 1995. "Local Market Socialism: Local Corporatism in Action in Rural China." *Theory and Society* 24: 301–54.

———. 1999. "Building a Network Theory of Social Capital." *Connections* 22(1): 28–51.

———. 2001. *Social Capital: A Theory of Social Structure and Action*. Cambridge: Cambridge University Press.

———. 2001b. "*Guanxi:* A Conceptual Analysis." In *The Chinese Triangle of Mainland-Taiwan-Hong Kong*, edited by Alvin So, Nan Lin and Dudley Poston. Westport, CT: Greenwood Press.

Lin, Nan and Yanjie Bian. 1991. "Getting Ahead in Urban China." *American Journal of Sociology* 97: 657–88.

Lin, Nan and Chi-jou Jay Chen. 1999. "Local elites as officials and owners: shareholding and property rights in Daqiuzhuang," pp. 145–170 in Jean Oi & Andrew Walder (eds.). *Property rights and economic reform in China.* Stanford: Stanford University Press.

Lin, Yi-min. 2000. *Between Politics and Markets: Firms, Competition, and Institutional Change in Post-Mao China.* Cambridge: Cambridge University Press.

and Zhang Zhanxin. "Backyard Profit Centers: The Private Assets of Public Agencies," pp. 203–225. 1999. Chapter 10 in *Property Rights and the Chinese Reform*, edited by Jean Oi and Andrew Walder. Stanford: Stanford University Press.

Lincoln, James R. 1984. "Analyzing Relations in Dyads: Problems, Models, and An Application to Interorganizational Research." *Sociological Methods and Research* 13: 45–76.

Lincoln, James R., Michael L. Gerlach, and Christina A. Ahmadjian. 1996. "*Keiretsu* Networks and Corporate Performance in Japan." *American Sociological Review* 61: 67–88.

Lincoln, James R., Michael L. Gerlach, and Peggy Takahashi. 1992. "*Keiretsu* Networks in the Japanese Economy: A Dyad Analysis of Intercorporate Ties." *American Sociological Review* 57: 561–585.

Link, Perry, Richard Madsen, and Paul G. Pickowicz eds. 1989. *Unofficial China: Popular Culture and Thought in the People's Republic.* Boulder, CO: Westview Press.

Little, Daniel. 1989. *Understanding Peasant China: Case Studies in the Philosophy of Social Science.* New Haven: Yale University Press.

Liu, Binyan. 1983. "People or Monsters?" In *People or Monsters? And Other Stories and Reportage from China after Mao*, ed. Perry Link 11–68. Bloomington: Indiana University Press.

Liu, Jiaqi, Jiang Chunlong and Hu Yi, eds. 1994. *Dangdai daxuesheng zeye zhinan* (Contemporary College Student Guide to Choosing a Job/Career). Harbin: Harbin Gongye Daxue Chubanshe.

Liu, Xin 1998. Reviews of *Producing Guanxi* and *The Flow of Gifts. Journal of Asian Studies* 57(4): 1129–32.

Liu, Zheng, and Song, Dian, et al., 1981. *China's Population: Problems and Prospects.* Beijing: New World Press.

Lo, Ming-cheng and Eileen Otis. 1999. "Toward an Ideal Type of 'Guanxi' Civil Society." *mss.*

Lo, Xiaolin. 1995. "Fenshuizhi: Guangdong difang suiyuandi yingxiang ji jiegou youhua" (Tax sharing scheme: its impact on local tax revenue in Guangdong and upgrading of economic structure). *Nanfang Jingji (Southern Economies)* 5: 38–39.

Local Township Statistical Office. Various years. *Local Township Economic Documents.* Shanghai County: unpublished.

Lovett, Steve, Lee C. Simmons, and Raja Kali. 1997. "*Guanxi* Versus The Market: Ethics and Efficiency." Working paper.

Lu Hanchao. 1995. "Creating Urban Outcasts: Shantytowns in Shanghai, 1920–1950." *Journal of Urban History* 21(5): 563–96.

1999. *Beyond the Neon Lights: Everyday Shanghai in the Early Twentieth Century.* Berkeley: University of California Press.

Lu Jianhua and Dan Guangnai, eds., 1994. "Qingnian laodong jiuye fazhan baogao (A report on the development of youth employment)," in *Zhongguo qingnian fazhan baogao* (Reports on the development of youth). Shenyang: Liaoning renmin chubanshe.

Lü, Xiaobo and Elizabeth J. Perry, eds., 1997. *Danwei: The Changing Chinese Workplace in Historical and Comparative Perspective.* Armonk, NY: M.E. Sharpe.

Lubman, Stanley. 1991. "Studying Contemporary Chinese Law: Limits, Possibilities and Strategy," in 3 *Am. J. Comp. Law* 293.
   ed. 1996. *China's Legal Reforms*. Oxford: Oxford University Press.
   1998. "The Legal and Policy Environment for Foreign Direct Investment in China: Past Accomplishments, Future Uncertainties." *Private Investments Abroad*. New York: Matthew Bender.
Luo, Jar-Der. 1997. "The Significance of Networks in the Initiation of Small Businesses in Taiwan." *Sociological Forum* 12: 297–317.
Luo, Yadong, "Guanxi": Principles, philosophies, and implications." *Human Systems Management* vol. 16(1997), pp. 43–51.
Luo, Yadong, and Min Chen. 1997. "Does *Guanxi* Influence Firm Performance?" *Asia Pacific Journal of Management* 14: 1–16.
Lutz, Catherine. 1987. "Goals, Events, and Understanding in Ifaluk Emotion Theory." *Cultural Models in Language and Thought*. Eds. Dorothy Holland and Naomi Quinn. 290–312. Cambridge: Cambridge U. Press.
Ma Rong, John Wong, Wang Hansheng, and Yang Mu. (eds.) 1994. *Jiushi niandai zhongguo xiangzhen qiye diaocha* (Case Studies in Chinese Township Enterprises in the 1990s). Hong Kong: Oxford University Press.
Ma, Yinchu. 1979. *Xin renkoulun* [New essay on the principle of population]. Beijing: Renmin chubanshe.
Ma, Zhongdong. 1999. "Returned Migrant Labor in China." Working paper. Division of Social Science, Hong Kong Unviersity of Science and Technology.
Madsen, Richard. 1984. *Morality and Power in a Chinese Village*. Berkeley: University of California Press.
Maine, Henry S. *Ancient Law*. London: Oxford University Press (reprinted 1959, copyright 1861).
Malinowski, Bronislaw. 1961. *Argonauts of the Western Pacific*. New York: E. P. Dutton.
Mann, Susan. 1987. *Local Merchants and the Chinese Bureaucracy*. 1750–1950. Stanford, CA: Stanford University Press.
Marx, Karl. 1906. *Capital: A Critique of Political Economy*, S. Moore and E. Aveling, trans. New York: The Modern Library.
Mauss, Marcel. 1967. *The Gift*, Ian Cunnison, trans. New York: Norton.
   1985. "A Category of the Human Mind: The Notion of Person; the Notion of Self," in *The Category of the Person*, M. Carrithers, S. Collins, and S. Lukes, eds. Cambridge: Cambridge University Press, 1–25.
   1990. *The Gift*. Trans. W. D. Halls. New York: W. W. Norton.
Mao, LuMing R. 1994. "Beyond Politeness Theory: 'Face' Revisited and Renewed." *Journal of Pragmatics* 21: 451–86.
McAuley, Mary. 1984. "Political Culture and Communist Politics: One Step Forward Two Steps Back," p. 31 in Archie Brown, ed., *Political Culture and Communist Studies*. Hampshire and London: The MacMillan Press.
Mei, Y. P. 1967. "The Status of the Individual in Chinese Thought and Practice." In *The Chinese Mind: Essentials of Chinese Philosophy and Culture,* ed. Charles A. Moore 323–39. Honolulu: East-West Center University of Hawaii Press.
Menning, Garrett. 1997. "Trust, Entrepreneurship and Development in Surat City, India." *Ethnos* 62(1–2): 59–90.
Merton, Robert K., *Social Theory and Social Structure* (revised and enlarged edition), New York: Free Press (1965), reprinted in Robert M. Cover and Owen M. Fiss, *The Structure of Procedure*, Mineola, N.Y.: Foundation Press (1979), p. 377.
Milgram, Stanley. 1967. "The Small-World Problem." *Psychology Today* 1: 62–67.
Mintz, Beth and Michael Schwartz. 1985. *The Power Structure of American Business*. Chicago: University of Chicago Press.

Mizruchi, Mark S. 1989. "Similarity of Political Behavior Among Large American Corporations." *American Journal of Sociology* 95: 401–424.

1992. *The Structure of Corporate Political Action: Interfirm Relations and Their Consequences.* Cambridge, MA: Harvard University Press.

Mizruchi, Mark and Joseph Galaskiewicz. 1994. "Networks of Interorganizational Relations," pp. 230–254 in *Advances in Social Network Analysis*, edited by Stanley Wasserman and Joseph Galaskiewicz. Thousand Oaks, CA: Sage.

Moore, Barrington, 1978. *Injustice: The Social Bases of Obedience and Revolt.* White Plains, N.Y.: M.E. Sharpe.

Morreall, John. 1994. "Gossip and humor." In *Good Gossip*, edited by Robert F. Goodman and Aaron Ben Ze'ev. Lawrence: University Press of Kansas.

Müller, Christoph, Barry Wellman and Alexandra Marin. "How to Use SPSS to Study Ego-Centered Networks." *Bulletin de Methode Sociologique* 69 (Oct., 1999): 83–100.

Munn, C. W. 1981. "Scottish Provincial Banking Companies: An Assessment." *Business History* 23: 19–41.

Nader, Laura. 1969. *Law in Culture and Society* Chicago: Aldine Press.

Nathan, Andrew J. 1973. "A Factionalism Model for CCP Politics." *China Quarterly* 53 (Jan.): 34–66.

1976a. "Reply." *China Quarterly*. 65 (Jan.): 114–7.

1976b. *Peking Politics 1918–1923:Factionalism and the Failure of Constitutionalism.* Berkeley: University of California Press.

1993. "Is Chinese Culture Distinctive? – A Review Article." *Journal of Asian Studies* 52(4): 923–36.

Nathan, Andrew and Kellee S. Tsai. 1995. "Factionalism: A New Institutionalist Restatement." *China Journal* 34 (July): 157–92.

Naughton, Barry. 1992. "Implications of the State Monopoly Over Industry and Its Relaxation." *Modern China* 18: 14–41.

1995. *Growing Out of The Plan: Chinese Economic Reform, 1978–1993.* New York: Cambridge University Press.

Nazer, Nancy. 2000. "The Emergence of a Virtual Organization: How an *In*visible College Becomes Visible." Doctoral dissertation, Department of Sociology, University of Toronto.

Nee, Victor. 1989a. "A Theory of Market Transition: From Redistribution to Markets in State Socialism." *American Sociological Review* 54: 663–81.

1989b. "Peasant Entrepreneurship and the Politics of Regulation." In *Remaking the Economic Institutions of Socialism: China and Eastern Europe*, ed. Victor Nee and David Stark, 169–207. Stanford: Stanford University Press.

1991. "Social Inequalities in Reforming State Socialism: Between Redistribution and Markets in China." *American Sociological Review* 56: 267–82.

1992. "Organizational Dynamics of Market Transition: Hybrid Forms, Property Rights, and Mixed Economy in China." *Administrative Science Quarterly* 37: 1–27.

1996. "The Emergence of a Market Society: Changing Mechanisms of Stratification in China." *American Journal of Sociology* 101: 908–49.

Nee, Victor and Rebecca Matthews. 1996. "Market Transition and Societal Transformation in Reforming State Socialism." *Annual Review of Sociology* 22: 401–435.

Nickum, James E. 1978. Labour accumulation in rural China and its role since the Cultural Revolution. *Cambridge Journal of Economics* 2, no. 3: 273–286.

North, Douglass C. 1990. *Institutions, Institutional Change and Economic Performance.* Cambridge: Cambridge University Press.

1993. "Economic Performance through Time." Paper prepared for presentation as the Prize Lecture in Economic Science in memory of Alfred Nobel, December 9, 1999.

Nozawa, Shinji. 1999. "Marital Relations and Personal Networks in Japan: Cultural Context and Structural Effect." Working Paper. Department of Sociology, Shizuoka University,

Numazaki, Ichiro. 1992. *Networks and Partnerships: The Social Organization of the Chinese Business Elite in Taiwan*. Unpublished PhD dissertation, Michigan State University.

Oberschall, Anthony. 1996. "The Great Transition: China, Hungary, and Sociology Exit Socialism into the Market." *American Journal of Sociology* 101: 1028–1041.

O'Hearn, Dennis. 1980. "The Consumer Second Economy: Size and Effects." *Soviet Studies*, 32: 2 (April), 218–234.

Oi, Jean. 1988. "The Chinese Village, Inc." In *Chinese Economic Policy: Economic Reform at Midstream*, ed. Bruce Reynolds, 67–87. New York: Paragon House.

    1989. *State and Peasant in Contemporary China: The Political Economy of Village Government*. Berkeley: University of California Press.

    1990. "The Fate of the Collective After the Commune," pp. 15–36 in *Chinese Society on the Eve of Tiananmen: The Impact of Reform*, edited by Deborah Davis and Ezra Vogel. Cambridge, MA: Harvard University Press.

    1992. "Fiscal Reform and the Economic Foundations of Local State Corporatism in China." *World Politics* Vol. 45, No. 1: 99–126.

    1996. "The role of the local state," pp. 170–87 in Andrew Walder ed. *China's Transitional Economy*. New York: Oxford University Press.

    1999. *Rural China Takes Off: Institutional Foundations of Economic Reform*. Berkeley and London: University of California Press.

Oksenberg, Michel. 1970. "Getting ahead and along in Communist China: The ladder of success on the eve of the Cultural Revolution." In *Party Leadership and Revolutionary Power in China*, ed. John Wilson Lewis, 304–47. Cambridge: Cambridge University Press.

    1976. "The Exit Pattern from Chinese Politics and Its Implications." *China Quarterly* 67 (Sept.): 501–18.

Olson, Mancur. 1965. *The Logic of Collective Action*. Cambridge, MA: Harvard University Press.

    1982. *The Rise and Decline of Nations*. New Haven: Yale University Press.

Ong, Aihwa. 1997. "Chinese Modernities: Narratives of Nation and of Capitalism." In *Ungrounded Empires: The Cultural Politics of Modern Chinese Transnationalism,* ed. Aihwa Ong and Donald Nonini 171–202. New York: Routledge.

Ong, Aihwa. 1999. *Flexible Citizenship: The Cultural Logics of Transnationality*. Durham: Duke University Press.

Ooka, Emi. 2001, "Testing Ethnic Resources on Income Attainment among Chinese Self-Employed in Toronto." *Asia and Pacific Migration Review*: forthcoming.

Ooka, Emi and Barry Wellman. 2003. "Does Social Capital Pay Off More Within or Between Ethnic Groups? Analyzing Job Searchers in Five Toronto Ethnic Groups" Forthcoming in *Inside the Mosaic,* edited by Eric Fong. Toronto: Toronto University Press. Preliminary version at http://ceris.metropolis.net/Virtual%20Library/economic/ookawellman1.html.

Ortner, Sherry B. 1984. "Theory in Anthropology Since the Sixties." *Comparative Studies in Society and History* 26:126–166.

Otani, Shinsuke. 1999. "Personal Community Networks in Contemporary Japan," pp. 279–97 in *Networks in the Global Village*, edited by Barry Wellman. Boulder, CO: Westview Press.

Peet, Richard and M. Watts eds. 1996. "Introductory chapter." *Liberation Ecologies: Environment, development, and social movements*. New York: Routledge.

Pei, Xiaolin. 1998. "Township-village enterprises, local governments, and rural communities," pp. 110–35 in Eduard Vermeer, F. Pieke and W-L Chong eds. *Cooperative and Collective in China's Rural Development: Between State and Private Interests*. New York: M. E. Sharpe.

Pelto, Pertti J. and Gretel H. Pelto. 1978. *Anthropological Research: The Structure of Inquiry*. Cambridge: Cambridge University Press.

Peng Qingen. 1996. "Guanxi Ziben he Diwei Huode" (*Guanxi* Capital and Status Attainment). *Shehuixue Yanjiu* (Sociological Research) 4: 53–63.

Perdue, Peter. 1987. *Exhausting the Earth: State and Peasant in Hunan, 1500–1850.* Cambridge, MA: Harvard University.

Pfeffer, Jeffrey. 1981. *Power in Organizations*. Cambridge, MA: Ballinger.

Pfeffer, Jeffrey and Gerald R. Salancik. 1978. *The External Control of Organizations: A Resource Dependence Perspective*. New York: Harper and Row.

Pieke, Frank N. 1995. "Bureaucracy, Friends, and Money: The Growth of Capital Socialism in China." *Comparative Studies in Society and History* 37 (3): 494–518.

Post, Robert. 1994. "The Legal Regulation of Gossip: Backyard Chatter and the Mass Media." In *Good Gossip*, edited by Robert F. Goodman and Aaron Ben Ze'ev. Lawrence: University Press of Kansas.

Pan, Weida, 1995. "Zhonggong hetongfa zhi jiajiang ji qi weilai fazhan" (The framework and future of PRC contract law), in *Zhengda faxue pinglun* no. 53, pp. 411–432.

Parish, William L., and Ethean Michaelson. 1996. "Politics and Markets: Dual Transformations." *American Journal of Sociology* 101: 1042–59.

Parry, Jonathan. 1986. "The Gift, The Indian Gift and the 'Indian Gift.'" *Man*, 21: 3 (Sept.), 453–73.

Pasternak, Burton and Janet Salaff. 1993. *Cowboys and Cultivators: The Chinese of Inner Mongolia*. Boulder, CO: Westview.

Podolny, Joel M., James N. Baron. 1997. "Resources and Relationship: Social Networks and Mobility in the Workplace." *American Sociological Review* 62: 673–693.

Poggioli, Renato. 1975. "The Oaten Flute," pp. 1–41 in *The Oaten Flute: Essays on Poetry and the Pastoral Ideal*, Cambridge, MA: Harvard University Press.

Polanyi, Karl. 1944. *The Great Transformation*. New York: Rinehart and Company.

1957. "The Economy as Instituted Process," in *Trade and Market in Early Empires*, Karl Polanyi and Conrad Arensberg, eds. Glencoe, Ill.: The Free Press, 243–270.

Portes, Alejandro. 1998. "Social Capital: Its Origins and Applications in Modern Sociology." *Annual Review of Sociology* 24: 1–24.

Portes, Alejandro and Julia Sensenbrenner. 1993. "Embeddedness and Immigration: Notes on the Social Determinants of Economic Action." *American Journal of Sociology* 98 (6): 1320–50.

Potter, Pitman B. 1992. *The Economic Contract Law of China: Legitimation and Contract Autonomy in the PRC*. Seattle and London: University of Washington Press.

1994. "Civil Obligations and Legal Culture in Shanghai: A Survey of the *Getihu*." *Canadian Journal of Law and Society* (Fall).

1994. "Riding the Tiger: Legitimacy and Legal Culture in Post-Mao China." *The China Quarterly* (June).

1999. "The Chinese Legal System: Continuing Commitment to the Primacy of State Power." *The China Quarterly*, no. 159: 673–83.

Potter, Pitman B. and Michael Donnelly. 1996. "Cultural Aspects of Trade Dispute Resolution in Japan and China." *Asia Pacific Foundation*.

Potter, Sulamith. 1983. "The Position of Peasants in Modern China's Social Order." *Modern China*, 9: 4, 465–499.

Potter, Sulamith Heins and Jack Potter. 1990. *China's Peasants: The Anthropology of A Revolution*. New York: Cambridge University Press.

Powell, Walter W. and Laurel Smith-Doerr. 1994. "Networks and Economic Life," in *The Handbook of Economic Sociology*, Neil Smelser and Richard Swedberg, eds. Princeton: Princeton University Press, pp. 368–402.

Pye, Lucian W. 1968. *The Spirit of Chinese Politics: A Psychocultural Study of the Authority Crisis in Political Development*. Cambridge: MIT Press.

1985. *Asian Power and Politics: The Cultural Dimensions of Authority*. Cambridge: Belknap Press of Harvard University Press.

1992a. *Chinese Negotiating Style: Commercial Approaches and Cultural Principles*. Westport, CT: Quorum Books.

1992b. *The Spirit of Chinese Politics* (new edition). Cambridge: Harvard University Press.

1995. "Factions and the Politics of *Guanxi*: Paradoxes in Chinese Administrative and Political Behaviour." *China Journal* 34 (July): 35–53.

Qi, Tianchang, ed. 1991. *Hetong an li pingxi* (Discussion of contract cases). Beijing: Chinese University of Politics and Law Press.

Qiao, Jian. 1982. "'Guanxi' Chuyi" (My Preliminary Opinions About *Guanxi*). In *Shehui Ji Xingwei Kexue Yanjiu di Zhongguohua* (The Sinicization of Social and Behavioral Science Research), ed. Yang Guoshu and Wen Chongyi, 345–60. Taipei: Institute of Ethnology, Academia Sinica.

"Quanguo renda changweihui fabu tongzhi zhengqiu 'Hetong fa (caoan)' yijian" (The NPC Standing Committee issues a circular seeking opinions on the "Contract Law (Draft)"), *Renmin ribao – haiwai ban* (People's Daily – Overseas Edition) September 5, 1998, p. 4.

Quinn, Naomi and Dorothy Holland. 1987. "Culture and Cognition." In *Cultural Models in Language and Thought*. Ed. Dorothy Holland and Naomi Quinn. Cambridge: Cambridge University Press.

Rankin, Mary Backus. 1986. *Elite Activism and Political Transformation in China, Zhejiang Province, 1865–1911*. Stanford, CA: Stanford University Press.

Rapoport, Anatol. 1979. "Some Problems Relating to Randomly Constructed Biased Networks." Pp. 119–136 in *Perspectives on Social Network Research*, edited by Paul Holland and Samuel Leinhardt. New York: Academic Press.

Rawski, Thomas G. 1999. "Reforming China's Economy: What Have We Learned?" *The China Journal* 41:139–56.

Redding, S. Gordon. 1990. *The Spirit of Chinese Capitalism*. Berlin: Walter de Gruyter.

1993. *The Spirit of Chinese Capitalism*. Berlin: Walter DeGruyter.

1996. "Weak Organizations and Strong Linkages: Managerial Ideology and Chinese Family Business Firms," pp. 27–42 in *Asian Business Networks*. Gary Hamilton, ed. Berlin: Walter de Gruyter.

Redfield, Robert. 1950. "Maine's Ancient Law in the Light of Primitive Societies." *Western Political Quarterly* 3: 586.

Reform. 1993. *Zhongguo Jingji Tizhi Gaige Nianjian (Yearbook of China's Economic System Reform)*. Beijing, PRC: Gaige.

Reisman, David, with Reuel Denney and Nathan Glazer. 1950. *The Lonely Crowd*. New Haven, CT: Yale University Press.

Reynolds, Malvina. 1963. "Little Boxes." In *Malvina Reynolds Songbook*. New York: Schroeder Music.

Richardson, RJ. 1987. "Directorship Interlocks and Corporate Profitability." *Administrative Science Quarterly* 32: 367–86.

Riley, Nancy E. 1994. "Interwoven Lives: Parents, Marriage and Guanxi in China." *Journal of Marriage and the Family* 56(4): 791–803.

Riskin, Carl. 1987. *China's Political Economy*. New York: Oxford University Press

Rogers, Everett. 1983. *Diffusion of Innovations*. New York: Free Press.

Rosaldo, Michelle Z. 1984. "Toward an Anthropology of Self and Feeling." In *Culture Theory: Essays on Mind, Self, and Emotion*. Eds. Richard A. Shweder and Robert A. Levine, 137–157. New York: Cambridge U. Press.

Rose, Richard. 1998a. "Getting Things Done with Social Capital." In *Studies in Public Policy*, No. 303, Glasgow: Centre for the Study of Public Policy, University of Strathclyde.

1998b. "Getting Things Done in an Anti-Modern Society: Social Capital Networks in Russia. In *Studies in Public Policy,* No. 304, Glasgow: Centre for the Study of Public Policy, University of Strathclyde.

Rose, Richard and Christian Haerpfer. 1993. "Adapting to Transformations in Eastern Europe." In *Studies in Public Policy,* No. 212, Glasgow: Centre for the Study of Public Policy, University of Strathclyde.

Rose, Richard and Christian Haerpfer. 1998. "New Democracies Barometer V." In *Studies in Public Policy,* No. 306, Glasgow: Centre for the Study of Public Policy, University of Strathclyde.

Ruan, Danching. 1993. "Interpersonal Networks and Workplace Controls in Urban China." *The Australian Journal of Chinese Affairs* 29 (Jan.): 89–105.

2001. "A Comparative Study of Personal Networks in Two Chinese Societies." In *The Chinese Triangle of Mainland-Taiwan-Hong Kong*, edited by Alvin So, Nan Lin, and Dudley Poston. Westport, CT: Greenwood Press.

Ruan Danching, Dai Xinyuan, Linton C. Freeman, Yunkang Pan and Zhang Wenhong. 1997. "Personal Support Networks in China and the Netherlands." Working Paper. Department of Sociology, University of California, Irvine.

Ruan Danching and Zhang Wenhong. 2000. "What is Universal about Friendship Ties?" Presented to the International Sunbelt Social Networks Conference, Vancouver, Canada, April.

Sabini, J. and M. Silver. 1982. *Moralities of Everyday Life*. New York: Oxford University Press.

Sahlins, Marshall. 1972. *Stone Age Economics*. New York: Aldine.

Saich, Tony. 1991. "Much ado about nothing: party reform in the 1980s," pp. 149–74 in Gordon White ed. *The Chinese State in an Era of Economic Reform: The Road to Crisis*. London: Macmillan.

Salaff, Janet, Eric Fong and Wong Siu-lun. 1999. "Using Social Networks to Exit Hong Kong." pp. 299–329 in *Networks in the Global Village*, edited by Barry Wellman. Boulder, CO: Westview Press.

Sampson, Robert J. In press. "Beyond Social Capital: Structural Sources and Spatial Embeddedness of Collective Efficacy for Children." *American Sociological Review*.

Sampson, Steven. 1983. "Rich Families and Poor Collectives: An Anthropological Approach to Romania's 'Second Economy.'" *Bidrag til Oststatsforskning* [Contributions to East European research] (Uppsala), 11: 1, 44–77.

1985. "The Informal Sector in Eastern Europe." *Telos*, no. 66 (Winter), 44–66.

Sargeson, Sally. 1999. *Reworking China's Proletariat*. New York: St. Martin's Press.

Saywell, Trish. 1999. "Risky Business." *Far Eastern Economic Review*. January 21: 53.

Schell, Orville. 1989. *Discos and Democracy: China in the Throes of Reform*. New York: Anchor Books.

Schoppa, Keith. 1982. *Chinese Elites and Political Change: Zhejiang Province in the Early Twentieth Century*. Cambridge, MA: Harvard University Press.

Schroeder, Peter. 1992. "Territorial actors as competitors for power: The case of Hubei and Wuhan, pp. 283–307" In K. Lieberthal and D. Lampton, eds. *Bureaucracy, Politics, and Decision Making in Post-Mao China*. Berkeley: University of California Press.

Schurmann, H. Franz. 1968. *Ideology and Organization in Communist China*. Berkeley: University of California Press.

Scott, John. 1991. "Networks of Corporate Power: A Comparative Assessment." *Annual Review of Sociology* 17: 181–203.

1991. *Social Network Analysis*. London: Sage.

Seliktar, Ofira. 1986. "Identifying a Society's Belief Systems," pp. 321–22 in Margaret Herman, ed., *Political Psychology*, San Francisco and London: Jossey-Bass (1986).

Sennett, Richard. 1970. *The Uses of Disorder: Personal Identity and City Life*. New York: W.W. Norton.

Sha, Yexin, Li Shoucheng, Yao Mingde. 1983. "If I Were for Real." In *The New Realism: Writings from China after the Cultural Revolution*, ed. Lee Yee, 261–322. New York: Hippocrene Books.

Shao, Chongzhu, ed., 1998. *Zhonggong fantan daan zhongan* (Big cases and serious cases on the Chinese communists fight against corruption). Hong Kong: So far (xiafeier) publishers.

Shaw, Victor N. 1996. *Social Control in China: A Study of Chinese Work Units*. Westport, CT : Praeger, 1996.

Shen, Guanbao. 1993. *Ichang qiaoqiaode geming* (A Quiet Revolution: Industries and Society in Southern Jiangsu Villages). Kunming: Yunnan People's Publisher.

Sherrington, Patrick, Virginia Chan. 1996. "New Lawyers Law needs further legislative clarification" in *China Law & Practice* (Jul./Aug. 1996): 28–30.

Shi, Xian-min. 1997. "Institutional Building and the Labor Market Structure in Shenzhen." Unpublished manuscript. Shenzhen Institute of Social Research.

Shirk, Susan. 1993. *The Political Logic of Economic Reform in China*. Berkeley: University of California Press.

Shue, Vivienne. 1988. *The Reach of the State: Sketches of the Chinese Body Politic*. Stanford, CA: Stanford University Press.

Si, Xiaotan, 1995. "CIETAC Arbitration: Joint Venture Case Studies No. 1," in China Law & Practice, ed., *Dispute Resolution in the PRC: A Practical Guide to Litigation and Arbitration in China*, Hong Kong: China Law & Practice, p.139.

Sik, Endre. 1994. "Network Capital in Capitalist, Communist, and Post-Communist Societies." *International Contributions to Labor Studies* 4: 73–70.

2000. "The Bad, the Worse and the Worst: Guesstimating the Level of Corruption." Presented to the Princeton University-CEU Joint Conference on Corruption." TARKI, Budapest, April.

Sik, Endre and Barry Wellman. 1999. "Network Capital in Capitalist, Communist and Post-Communist Countries." Pp. 225–254 in *Networks in the Global Village*, edited by Barry Wellman. Boulder, CO: Westview Press.

Silin, Robert H. 1972. "Marketing and credit in a Hong Kong wholesale market." In W. E. Willmott, ed. *Economic Organization in Chinese Society*. Stanford: Stanford University Press.

Silver, Allan. 1990. "Friendship in commercial society: Eighteenth-century social theory and modern sociology." *American Journal of Sociology* 95, no. 6: 1474–1504.

Simmel, Georg. 1922 [1955]. "The Web of Group Affiliations," pp. 125–95 in *Conflict and the Web of Group Affiliations*, edited by Kurt Wolff. Glencoe, IL: Free Press.

1950. *The Sociology of Georg Simmel* Glencoe, IL: Free Press.

1990. *The Philosophy of Money* (2nd ed.). London: Routledge.

Simons, Lewis M. and Michael Zielenziger. 1994. "Enter the Dragon." *San Jose Mercury News*, June 26–9.

SJCYJS (Shujichu yanjiushi) 1982. *Dangqian woguo gongren jieji zhuangkuang diaocha ziliao* (A Collection of Survey Findings on the Current Situation of Workers in Our Country). Beijing: Zhonggong zhongyang danxiao chuban she.

Smart, Alan. 1993. "Gifts, Bribes and Guanxi: A Reconsideration of Bourdieu's Social Capital." *Cultural Anthropology* 8(3): 388–408.

1998. "Economic Transformation in China: Property Regimes and Social Relations." In *Theorizing Transition: The Political Economy of Post-Communist Transformations*, editors John Pickles and Adrian Smith. London: Routledge.

1998. "*Guanxi*, Gifts, and Learning from China: A Review Essay." *Anthropos* 93: 559–65.

1997. "Oriental Despotism and Sugar-Coated Bullets: Representations of the Market in China," pp. 159–94 in *Meanings of the Market: The Free Market in Western Culture*, editor James G. Carrier. Oxford: Berg.

1999a. "Predatory Rule and Illegal Economic Activities," pp. 99–128 in *States and Illegal Practices*, editor Josiah M. Heyman. Oxford: Berg.

1999b. "Doing business across the Hong Kong border: Economic culture in theory and practice. Pp. 158–186 in *Qiaoxiang Ties: Interdisciplinary Approaches to 'Cultural Capitalism' in South China*, editors Leo Douw, Cen Huang and Michael Godley. London: Kegan Paul International.

Smart, Josephine. 1989. *The Political Economy of Street Hawking in Hong Kong*. Hong Kong: Centre of Asian Studies.

Smart, Josephine, and Alan Smart. 1991. "Personal Relations and Divergent Economies: A Case Study of Hong Kong Investment in China." *International Journal of Urban and Regional Research* 15(2): 216–33.

1992. "Capitalist Production in a Socialist Society: The Transfer of Production From Hong Kong to China," pp. 47–61 in *Anthropology and the Global Factory: Studies of the New Industrialization in the Late Twentieth Century*, editors Frances A. Rothstein and Michael Blim. New York: Bergin and Garvey.

1998. "Transnational Social Networks and Negotiated Identities in Interactions between Hong Kong and China," pp. 103–29 in *Transnationalism From Below*, editors Michael P. Smith and Luis E. Guarnizo. New Brunswick: Transaction Publishers.

1999. "Failures and Strategies of Hong Kong Firms in the PRC: An Ethnographic Perspective." *The Globalization of Chinese Business*, editors Henry W. Yeung and Kris Olds. New York: Macmillan.

2000. "Failures and Strategies of Hong Kong Firms in China: An Ethnographic Perspective." In *Globalization of Chinese Business Firms*. Henry Wai-chung Yeung and Kris Olds. London: Macmillan.

Smith, Arthur H. 1894 (1970). *Chinese Characteristics*. Port Washington, N.Y.: Kennikat Press.

Smith, J. C., David N. Weisstub. 1983. *The Western Idea of Law*. London and Toronto: Butterworths.

Smith, Michael. 1979. *The City and Social Theory*. New York: St. Martin's Press.

Smelser, Neil. 1959. *Social Change in the Industrial Revolution*. Chicago: University of Chicago Press.

Solinger, Dorothy. 1983. "Marxism and the Market in Socialist China: The Reforms of 1979–1980 in Context," *State and Society in Contemporary China*, Victor Nee and David Mozingo, eds., Ithaca: Cornell University Press, 194–219.

Solomon, Richard H. 1969. "Mao's Effort to Reintegrate the Chinese Polity: Problems of Authority and Conflict in Chinese Social Processes." In *Chinese Communist Politics in Action*, ed. A. Doak Barnett, 271–361, Seattle: University of Washington Press.

1971. *Mao's Revolution and the Chinese Political Culture*. Berkeley: University of California Press.

1999. *Chinese Negotiating Behavior: Pursuing Interests Through 'Old Friends*. Washington, D.C.: United States Institute of Peace Press.

Song Defu. (ed.) 1994. *Dangdai zhongguo de renshi guanli* (Government Personnel Administration in Contemporary China). Beijing: Dangdai zhongguo chuban she.

Song, Kevin Ying Yue. 1996. "China's New Law on Lawyers Will Move System Closer to International Standards." *East Asian Executive Reports* Aug. 15: 9–14.

Sonoda, Shigeto. 1995. "Chugoku Shakai no 'Kankeishugi' teki Kosei" (The Structure of *"Guanxi*-ism" in Chinese Society). *Nihon Gendai Chugoku Shakai Nenpo* (Japan Contemporary Yearbook of Chinese Society): 50–65.

Spanogle, John. 1991. "The Arrival of Private International Law," in 25 *Geo. Wash. J. Int'l & Econ.* 477.

Staber, Udo, Howard E. Aldrich. 1995. "Cross-National Similarities in the Personal Networks of Small Business Owners." *Canadian Journal of Sociology* vol. 20 no. 4 (fall): 441–67.

State Labor Department of China. 1996. *Projections of Labor Growth Patterns.*

State Statistical Bureau of the People's Republic of China. 1993. *China Statistical Yearbook 1993.* Beijing: China Statistical Information and Consultancy Service Center and International Center for the Advancement of Science and Technology Ltd.

Strachan, Harry W. 1979. "Nicaragua's *Grupos Economicos*: Scope and Operations" in *Entrepreneurs in Cultural Context*, edited by S. M. Greenfield, A. Strickon, and R. T. Aubey. Albuquerque, NM: University of New Mexico Press.

Strathern, Marilyn. 1983. "Subject or Object? Women and the Circulation of Valuables in Highland New Guinea," in *Women and Property, Women as Property*, R. Hirschon, ed., London: Croon Helm, 158–175.

Stein, Maurice. 1960. *The Eclipse of Community*. Princeton, NJ: Princeton University Press.

Stone, Leroy O., Carolyn J. Rosenthal and Ingrid Arnet Connidis. 1998. *Parent-Child Exchanges of Support and Intergenerational Equity* Ottawa: Statistics Canada.

Sun, Liping. 1996. "'Guanxi', Shehui Guanxi yu Shehui Jiegou" (*'Guanxi'*, Social Relations and Social Structure) *Shehuixue Yanjiu* (Sociological Research), 5: 20–30.

Sun, Longji. 1983. *Zhongguo Wenhua de "Shenceng Jiegou"* ["Deep structure" of Chinese Culture]. Hong Kong: Taishan Publishing Company.

Sun, Lung-kee. 1987. *Zhongguo Wenhua de Shenceng Jiegou.* (The Deep Structure of Chinese Culture). 2nd edition. Hong Kong: Ji Xian She.

Sun, Weizhi. 1998. "Hetong ziyou de lifa quxiang" (Legislation of Freedom of Contract), *Faxue zazhi* (Law science magazine), no. 1: 19–20.

"Supreme Court Promulgates Two Documents," Beijing Xinhua domestic service 17 Sept. 1998, in FBIS-CHI-98–262, 19 Sept. 1998.

Suttles, Gerald D. 1968. *The social order of the slum; ethnicity and territory in the inner city.* Chicago: University of Chicago Press.

Swidler, Ann. 1986. "Culture in Action: Symbols and Strategies." *American Sociological Review* 51: 273–86.

Szelenyi, Ivan. 1982. "The Intelligentsia in the Class Structure of State-Socialist Societies," pp. S287–326 in *Marxist Inquiries*, M. Burawoy and T. Skocpol, eds. (supplement to American Journal of Sociology, 88). Chicago: University of Chicago Press.

1983. *Urban Inequalities under State Socialism*. London: Oxford University Press.

Tanzer, Andrew. 1994. "The bamboo network." *Forbes*. July 18: 138–44.

Taylor, Gabriele. 1994. "Gossip as Moral Talk." In *Good Gossip*, edited by Robert F. Goodman and Aaron Ben Ze'ev. Lawrence: University Press of Kansas.

Taylor, Michael. 1982. *Community, Anarchy, and Liberty*. Cambridge: Cambridge University Press.

Thomése, Fleur and Theo van Tilburg. 1998. "Neighbouring Networks and Environmental Dependency: Differential Effects of Neighbourhood Characteristics on the Relative Size and Composition of Neighbouring Networks of Older Adults in the Netherlands." Working Paper. Department of Sociology, Vrije Universiteit Amsterdam.

Thompson, James D. 1967. *Organizations in Action: Social Science Bases of Administrative Theory.* New York: McGraw-Hill.

Tien, H. Yuan. 1973. *China's Population Struggle*. Columbus: Ohio State University Press.

Tindall, David. 1993. "Collective Action in the Rainforest: Networks, Social Identity and Participation in the Vancouver Island Wilderness Preservation Movement." Tampa: International Sunbelt Social Network Conference.

Tolnay, Stewart E., Glenn Deane, and E. M. Beck. 1996. "Vicarious Violence: Spatial Effects on Southern Lynchings." *American Journal of Sociology* 102: 788–815.

Tong, Chee Kiong and Yong, P. K. 1998. "Guanxi Bases, Xinyong and Chinese Business Networks." *British Journal of Sociology* vol. 49, no. 1: 75–96.

Tong, Chee Kiong and Chan, Kwok Bun. 1999. "Networks and Brokers: Singaporean Chinese Doing Business in China." Unpublished paper presented at the Conference "Chinese Entrepreneurs and Business Networks in Southeast Asia." University of Bonn.

Trappe, Johannes. 1989. "Conciliation in the Far East." *International Arbitration* 5(2): 173.

Tsou, Tang. 1976. "Prolegomenon to the Study of Informal Groups in CCP Politics." *China Quarterly* 65: 98–114.

Tsui, Anne S., and Larry J. L. Farh. 1997. "Where *Guanxi* Matters: Relational Demography and *Guanxi* in the Chinese Context." *Work and Occupations* 24: 56–79.

Tu, Wei-ming. 1981. "Neo Confucian Religiosity and Human Relatedness." *Religion and the Family in East Asia*, eds. George deVos and Takao Soufue, 111–24. Osaka: National Museum of Ethnology.

1994. *The Living Tree: The Changing Meaning of Being Chinese Today.* Stanford, CA: Stanford University Press.

Tung, Rosalie L. and Verner Worm. 1997. "The Importance of Networks (Guanxi) for European Companies in China." Working Paper Number 3, Asia Research Center, Copenhagen Business School.

Turner, Stephen. 1994. *The Social Theory of Practices: Tradition, Tacit Knowledge and Presuppositions.* New York: Polity Press.

Unger, Jonathan. 1996. "'Bridges': Private Business, The Chinese Government and the Rise of New Associations." *The China Quarterly* 147 (Sept): 795–819.

Uzzi, Brian. 1996. "The Sources and Consequences of Embeddedness for the Economic Performance of Organizations: The Network Effect." *American Sociological Review* 61: 674–98.

Valente, Thomas. 1995. *Network Models of the Diffusion of Innovations.* Cresskill, NJ: Hampton Press.

van Duijn, Martijtje A.J., Jooske T. van Busschbach, and Tom A.B. Snijders. 1999. "Multilevel Analysis of Personal Networks as Dependent Variables." *Social Networks* 21(2): 187–209.

Varga, Csaba, ed., 1992. *Comparative Legal Cultures.* NY: New York University Press.

Vickery, Greg, 1994. "International Commercial Arbitration in China," 5 *Australian Dispute Resolution Journal* 75.

Vogel, Ezra. 1965. From Friendship to Comradeship: The Change in Personal Relations in Communist China. *The China Quarterly* 21: 46–60.

1967. "From Revolutionary to Semi-Bureaucrat: The 'Regularization' of Cadres," *China Quarterly* 29 (Jan. March): 36–60.

1989. *One Step Ahead in China: Guangdong under Reform.* Cambridge, MA: Harvard University Press.

Wakeman, Frederic. 1975. "Introduction: The evolution of local control in late imperial China." In F. Wakeman and C. Grant, eds., *Conflict and Control in Late Imperial China.* Berkeley: University of California Press.

Wakeman, Frederic, and Wen-hsin Yeh. 1992. "Introduction," pp. 1–14 in Frederic Wakeman, Jr. and Wen-hsin Yeh, ed., *Shanghai Sojourners.* Berkeley: Institute for East Asian Studies/ University of California Press.

Walder, Andrew G. 1986. *Communist Neo-Traditionalism: Work and Authority in Chinese Industry.* Berkeley: University of California Press.

1992. "Property Rights and Stratification in Socialist Redistributive Economies." *American Sociological Review* 57: 524–39.

1992. "Local bargaining relationship and urban industrial finance," pp. 308–32 in Kenneth G. Lieberthal and David M. eds. *Bureaucracy. Politics. and Decision Making in Post-Mao China*. Berkeley: University of California Press.

1995. "Local Governments as Industrial Firms: An Organizational Analysis of China's Transitional Economy." *American Journal of Sociology* vol. 101 no. 2: 263–301.

1995. "The quiet revolution from within: Economic reform as a source of political decline," pp. 1–24 in Andrew Walder, ed., *The Waning of the Communist State: Economic Origins of Political Decline in China and Hungary*. Berkeley: University of California Press.

1996. "Markets and Inequality in Transitional Economies: Toward Testable Theories." *American Journal of Sociology* 101: 1060–73.

1996. "China's transitional economy: interpreting its significance," pp. 1–17 in Andrew Walder ed. *China's Transitional Economy*. Oxford University Press.

Wang, Cunxue. 1993. *Zhongguo jingji zhongcai he susong shiyong shouce* (Practical handbook of Chinese economic arbitration and litigation). Beijing: Development Press.

Wang, Fei-ling. 1998. *From Family to Market: Labor Allocation in Contemporary China*. Lanham, MD: Rowman & Littlefield.

Wang, Gungwu. 1979. *Power, Rights and Duties in Chinese History*. Canberra: Research Schools of Social Sciences and Pacific Studies, Australian National University.

Wang Hongcai, editor. 1987. *Hunyin Fa Jiaocheng* (A Course in the Marriage Law). Beijing: *Falu Chubanshe*.

Wang, Liming, 1996. "Tongyi hetongfa zhidingzhong de ruogan yinan wenti tantao" (Inquiry into various difficult questions in enacting a unified contract law), *Zhengfa luntan* (Political Science and Law Tribune), no. 4 (1996), pp. 49–56 and no. 5 (1996) pp. 52–60.

Wang, Minglu. 1986. "Unhealthy Tendency." In *Policy Conflicts in Post-Mao China: A Documentary Survey, with Analysis*, eds. John P. Burns and Stanley Rosen, 148–59. Armonk: M. E. Sharpe.

Wang, Rong. 1991. "Earnings and Education in Urban China in 1991," PhD dissertation, University of California, Berkeley.

Wang, Shaoguang. 1995. "The Rise of the Regions: Fiscal Reform and the Decline of Central State Capacity in China," pp. 87–113 in Andrew Walder, ed., *The Waning of the Communist State: Economic Origins of Political Decline in China and Hungary*. Berkeley, CA: University of California Press.

Wang, Xin. 1989. "'Guanxiwang' di Jingji Fenxi" (Economic Analysis of *Guanxiwang*) *Xinhua Wenzhai* (Xinhua Digest). March 2: 49–52.

Wank, David L. 1994. "The Institutional Culture of Capitalism: Social Relations and Private Enterprise in a Chinese City." Paper presented at the annual meeting of the Association for Asian Studies, Boston, March 23–27.

1995. "Bureaucratic Patronage and Private Business: Changing Networks of Power in Urban China," pp. 153–183 in Andrew Walder (ed.) *The Waning of the Communist State: The Economic Origins of Political Decline in China and Hungary*. Berkeley: University of California Press.

1996. "The Institutional Process of Market Clientelism: *Guanxi* and Private Business in a South China City." *The China Quarterly* 144: 820–838.

1999a. *Commodifying Communism: Business, Trust, and Politics in a Chinese City*. New York: Cambridge University Press.

1999b. "Producing Property Rights: Strategies, Networks, and Efficiency in Urban China's Nonstate Firms, pp. 248–72 in *Property Rights and Economic Reform in China*, ed. Jean C. Oi and Andrew G. Walder. Stanford: Stanford University Press.

Ward, Barbara. 1972. "A small factory in Hong Kong: Some aspects of its internal organization." In W. E. Willmott, ed., *Economic Organization in Chinese Society*. Stanford: Stanford University Press.

Wasserman, Stanley and Katherine Faust. 1994. *Social Network Analysis: Methods and Applications*. Cambridge: Cambridge University Press.

Watson, James L. 1980. "Transactions in People: The Chinese Market in Slaves, Servants and Heirs." In *Asian and African Systems of Slavery*. Ed. James L. Watson, 223–250. Oxford: Basil Blackwood.

Weber, Max. 1946. *From Max Weber*. New York: Oxford University Press.

1958. "Class, Status, Party," pp. 180–195 in *From Max Weber: Essays in Sociology*. Edited by H.H. Gerth and C. Wright Mills. New York.

1951. *The Religion of China: Confucianism and Taoism*. Translated by H.H. Wright. New Haven.

Weidenbaum, Murray. 1996. "The Chinese Family Business Enterprise." *California Management Review*, 38(4): 141–56.

Wellman, Barry. 1988. "Structural Analysis: From Method and Metaphor to Theory and Substance." Pp. 19–61 in *Social Structures: A Network Approach*, edited by Barry Wellman and S. D. Berkowitz. Cambridge: Cambridge University Press.

1992. "How to Use SAS to Study Egocentric Networks." *Cultural Analysis Methods* 4(2): 6–12.

1993. "An Egocentric Network Tale." *Social Networks* 17(2): 423–436.

1999a. "The Network Community," pp. 1–48 in *Networks in the Global Village*, edited by Barry Wellman. Boulder, CO: Westview.

1999b. ed., *Networks in the Global Village*. Boulder, CO: Westview Press.

2000. "Networking Networkers: How INSNA (the International Network for Social Network Analysis) Came to Be." *Connections* 23, 1: 20–31.

2001. "Physical Place and Cyber Place: The Rise of Networked Individualism." *International Journal for Urban and Regional Research* 25: forthcoming.

Wellman, Barry and S. D. Berkowitz (eds.). 1988. *Social Structures: A Network Approach*. Cambridge: Cambridge University Press.

Wellman, Barry and S. D. Berkowitz (eds.) 1997. *Social Structures: A Network Approach*. Greenwich, CT: JAI Press.

Wellman, Barry, Peter Carrington and Alan Hall. 1988. "Networks as Personal Communities," pp. 130–84 in *Social Structures: A Network Approach*, edited by Barry Wellman and S. D. Berkowitz. Cambridge: Cambridge University Press.

Wellman, Barry and Robert Hiscott. 1985. "From Social Support to Social Network," pp. 205–222 in *Social Support*, edited by Irwin Sarason and Barbara Sarason. The Hague: Martinus Nijhoff.

Wellman, Barry and Kenneth Frank. 2001. "Network Capital in a Multi-Level World: Getting Support from Personal Communities." Forthcoming in *Social Capital*, edited by Nan Lin, Ron Burt, and Karen Cook. Chicago: Aldine De Gruyter.

Wellman, Barry and Keith Hampton. 1999. "Living Networked On and Offline." *Contemporary Sociology* 28(6): 648–54.

Wellman, Barry and Barry Leighton. 1979. "Networks, Neighborhoods and Communities." *Urban Affairs Quarterly* 14: 363–90.

Wellman, Barry, Renita Wong, David Tindall and Nancy Nazer. 1997. "A Decade of Network Change: Turnover, Mobility and Stability." *Social Networks* 19(1): 27–51.

Wellman, Barry and Scot Wortley. 1989. "Brothers' Keepers: Situating Kinship Relations in Broader Networks of Social Support." *Sociological Perspectives* 32: 273–306.

1990. "Different Strokes From Different Folks: Community Ties and Social Support." *American Journal of Sociology* 96: 558–88.

Wellman, Beverly and Barry Wellman. 1992. "Domestic Affairs and Network Relations." *Journal of Social and Personal Relationships* 9: 385–409.

White, Harrison C. 1981. "Where Do Markets Come From?" *American Journal of Sociology* 87(3): 517–547.

White, Harrison, Scott Boorman and Ronald Breiger. 1976. "Social Structure from Multiple Networks: I Blockmodels of Roles and Positions." *American Journal of Sociology* 81: 730–80.

Whiting, Susan H. 1998. "The Mobilization of Private Investment as a Problem of Trust in Local Governance Structures." In *Trust and Governance*, eds. Valerie Braithwaite and Margaret Levi, 167–93. New York: Russell Sage Foundation.

Whyte, Martin K., and William Parish. 1984. *Urban Life in Contemporary China*. Chicago: University of Chicago Press.

Whyte, William Foote. 1993 [1943]. *Street Corner Society: The Social Structure of an Italian Slum*. Chicago: University of Chicago Press.

Wilkinson, John. 1997. "A New Paradigm for Economic Analysis?" *Economy and Society* 26: 305–39.

Williamson, Oliver E. 1975. *Markets and Hierarchies: Analysis and Antitrust Implications*. New York: Free Press.

Williamson, Oliver E. 1985. *The Economic Institutions of Capitalism*. New York: Free Press.

Wilson, Scott. 1997. "The cash nexus and social networks: mutual aid and gifts in contemporary Shanghai villages." *The China Journal* no. 37: 91–112.

Wirth, Louis. 1938. "Urbanism as a Way of Life." *American Journal of Sociology* Vol. 44, July.

Wolf, Margery. 1968. *The House of Lim*. New York: Appleton-Century-Crofts.

1972. *Women and the Family in Rural Taiwan*. Stanford, CA: Stanford University Press.

1992. *A Thrice-Told Tale: Feminism, Postmodernism and Ethnographic Responsibility*. Stanford: Stanford University Press.

Wolfinger, Russ. 1993. "Generalized Linear Mixed Models: A Pseudo-Likelihood Approach." *Journal of Statistical Computation and Simulation* 48: 233–43.

Wong, Christine, P. W. 1985. "Material allocation and decentralization: impact of the local sector on industrial reform." in Elizabeth Perry and Christine Wong, eds. *The Political Economy of Reform in Post-Mao China*. Cambridge: Harvard University Press.

1987. "Between plan and market: the role of the local sector in post-Mao China," in *Journal of Comparative Economics* 11: 385–398.

Wong, Siu-lun. 1988. *Emigrant Entrepreneurs: Shanghai Industrialists in Hong Kong*. Hong Kong: Oxford University Press.

1991. "Chinese Entrepreneurs and Business Trust." Pp. 13–29 in Gary G. Hamilton (ed.) *Business Networks and Economic Development in East and Southeast Asia*. Hong Kong: Centre of Asian Studies, The University of Hong Kong.

1997. "Trust and Prosperity: The Role of Chinese Family Enterprises in Economic Development." T. T. Tsui Lecture, at the University of Hong Kong on February 3, 1997 and at the Australian National University on February, 1997.

1999. "Gender and Trust: Re-inquiring into the internal dynamism of Chinese family enterprises", paper presented at 6th Conference on Modernization and Chinese Culture–Chinese Sociology and Anthropology toward the 21st Century, Wujiang City, China, November 2–7, 1999, [in Chinese].

Wong, Siu-lun and Janet Salaff. 1998. "Network Capital: Emigration from Hong Kong." *British Journal of Sociology* 49(3): 258–73.

Xie, Yu and Emily Hannum. 1996. "Regional Variation in Earnings Inequality in Reform-Era Urban China." *American Journal of Sociology* 101: 950–92.

Xin, Catherine R. and Jone L. Pearce. 1996. "*Guanxi*: Connections as Substitutes for Formal Institutional Support." *Academy of Management Journal* vol. 39 no. 6 (Dec.): 1641–58.

Xin, Chun. 1983. "'Guanxixue' he Guanxixu" (*Guanxixue* and the Study of *Guanxi*). *Shehui* (Sociology), 3: 48–9.

Xing, Yixun. 1980. *Quan yu Fa*. (Power and Law). Beijing: Zhongguo Xiju Chubanshe.

Xu, Jiangmin. 1992. "Lun chi he zai xiangzhen qiye fazhanzhong de zuoyong" (On the use of eating and drinking in the development of rural enterprises), *Shehui* (Society) no. 7: 23–35.

Xue, Muqiao. 1981. *China's Socialist Economy*. Beijing: Foreign Language Press.

Yan, Yunxiang. 1992. "The impact of rural reform on economic and social stratification in a Chinese village." *The Australian Journal of Chinese Affairs* 27: 1–23.

   1996a. *The Flow of Gifts: Reciprocity and Social Networks in a Chinese Village*. Stanford, CA: Stanford University Press.

   1996b. "The culture of guanxi in a North China village." *The China Journal* no. 35: 1–23.

   1997. "The Triumph of Conjugality: Structural Transformations of Family Relations in a Chinese Village." *Ethnology* 36(3): 191–212.

Yang, Lien-sheng. 1957. "The Concept of 'Pao' as a Basis for Social Relations in China." In *Chinese Thought and Institutions*, ed. John K. Fairbank 291–309. Chicago: University of Chicago Press.

Yang, Martin. 1945. *A Chinese Village: Taitou, Shantung Province*. New York: Columbia U. Press.

Yang, Mayfair Mei-hui. 1986. "The Art of Social Relationships and Exchange in China." Ph.D. diss., University of California, Berkeley.

   1988. "The Modernity of Power in the Chinese Socialist Order." *Cultural Anthropology*, 3: 4 (November), 408–427.

   1989. "Between State and Society: The Construction of Corporateness in a Chinese Socialist Factory." *Australian Journal of Chinese Affairs* no. 22 (July): 31–60.

   1989. "The Gift Economy and State Power in China." *Comparative Studies in Society and History* 31(1): 25–54.

   1994. *Gifts, Favors, and Banquets: The Art of Social Relationships in China*. Ithaca: Cornell University Press.

   ed. 1999. *Spaces of Their Own: Women's Public Sphere in Transnational China*. Minneapolis: University of Minnesota Press.

   2000. "Putting Global Capitalism in its Place: Economic Hybridity, Bataille, and Ritual Expenditure." *Current Anthropology*.

Yang, Yiyin. 1995. "Shixi Renji Guanxi ji qi Fenlei: Jian yu Huang Guangguo Xiansheng Shangque" (Examining Interpersonal Relationships and their Classification: and a Discussion with Mr. Hwang Kwang-kuo). *Shehuixue Yanjiu* (*Sociological Research*) 5: 18–23.

Yang, Yiyong. 1997a. "Zhongguo jiuye wenti jiqi zhengce xuanze (China's employment problems and policy choices)," in *Zhongguo xin shiqi shehui fazhan baogao (1991–1995)* (*Reports on Societal Development in China in the New Era, 1991–1995*), Lu Xueyi and Li Peilin, eds. Shenyang: Liaoning renmin chubanshe, pp. 320–350.

   1997b. *Shiye chongjibo – Zhongguo jiuye fazhan baogao* (Unemployment Wave – A report on the development of employment in China). XX: Jinri chubanshe.

   1998. "1997–1998 Nian: Zhongguo jiuye xingshi fenxi yu zhanwang (1997–1998: An Analysis and Forecast of China's Employment Situation)," in *Zhongguo shehui xingshi fenxi yu yuce* (Analyses and Forecasts for China's Social Situation), Ru Xin, Lu Xueyi and Shan Tianlun, eds. Beijing: Shehuikexue wenxian chubanshe.

Ye, Wenfu. 1983. "General, You Must Not Do This!" In *The New Realism: Writings from China after the Cultural Revolution,* ed. Lee Yee, 86–91. New York: Hippocrene Books.

Yeung, Henry W. C. 1997. *Transnational Corporations and Business Networks: Hong Kong Firms in the ASEAN Region*. London: Routledge.

Yi, Gang. 1994. *Money, Banking, and Financial Market Emergence in China*. Boulder, CO: Westview.

Young, Susan. 1995. *Private Business and Economic Reform in China*. Armonk: M.E. Sharpe.
Yu Shao-xiang. 2000. *I was Mou Qi-zhong's Lawyer*, Xi'an: Shanxi Normal University Press [in Chinese].
Ze'ev, Ben. 1994. "The Vindication of Gossip." In *Good Gossip*, edited by Robert F. Goodman and Aaron Ben Ze'ev. Lawrence: University Press of Kansas.
Zelizer, Viviana A. 1994. *The Social Meaning of Money*. New York: Basic Books.
Zhai, Xuewei. 1996. "Zhongguo Renji Guanxi Wangluozhongde Pinghengxing Wenti: Yixiang Gean Yanjiu." (The Question of Balance in Chinese People's *Guanxiwang*: A Case Study Research) *Shehuixue Yanjiu (Sociological Research)*, 3: 78–87.
Zhang, Everett Y. 1998. "*Goudui*/Thickening the Relationship With the State: Constructing Entrepreneurial Masculinity."
Zhang, Haipang and Wong Dingyuen, eds. 1995. *Hueshang yanjiu* (Research on Hue Merchants). Anhui: People's Publication.
Zhang, Haipang and Zhang Haiying, eds. 1993. *Zhongguo shida shangbang* (Ten Merchant Gangs in China). Anhui: Huangshan Press.
Zhang, L-Y. 1999. Chinese central-provincial fiscal relationships. budgetary dcline and the impact of the 1994 fiscal reform: an evaluation. *The China Quarterly* 157 (1): 115–140.
Zhang Hou-yi and Ming Li-zhi, eds. 1999. *Reports on the Development of the Chinese Private Enterprises*. Beijing: Social Sciences Documentation Publishing House, [in Chinese].
Zhang, Huilong. 1990. *She wai jingji fa anli jiexi* (Analysis of Sino-foreign economic law cases). Beijing: Youth Publishers.
    1992. *New Selections of the Foreign-Related Economic Cases in China*. Shanghai: Economic Information Agency.
Zhang, Yongchang. 1991. "Nongcun 'jianfang re' de shehuixue toushi" (A sociological perspective on the 'building craze' in the countryside), *Shehui* (Society) no. 4: 22–23.
Zhao, Shukai, and Associates. 1997. "Modes of Organization for Peasant Migrant Labor." *Sociological Research* (no. 3).
Zheng, Henry R. 1988. *China's Civil and Commercial Law*. Singapore: Butterworths Asia.
Zheng, Yefu. 1986. "Connections." In *The Chinese: Adapting the Past, Building the Future*, ed. Robert F. Dernberger, et. al., 351–61. Ann Arbor: Center for Chinese Studies, University of Michigan.
"Zhonghua renmin gongheguo hetongfa (caoan)" (Contract Law of the PRC – Draft) (Legal Affairs Committee of NPC Standing Committee, Aug. 20, 1998), in *People's Daily* Sept. 7, 1998.
"Zhonghua renmin gongheguo hetongfa lifa fangan" (Legislative proposal for PRC contract law), *Zhengda faxue pinglun* (Chengchi University jurisprudence and discussion) 1995 no. 53, pp. 433–443.
Zhou, Kate Xiao. 1996. *How the Farmers Changed China: Power of the People*. Boulder, CO: Westview Press.
Zhou, Xuegang, Nancy Brandon Tuma and Phyllis Moen. 1997. "Institutional Change and Job-shift Patterns in Urban China, 1949 to 1994," *American Sociological Review* 62 (June): 339–365.
Zito, Angela. 1984. "Re-presenting Sacrifice: Cosmology and the Editing of Texts." *Ch'ing shih wen-t'i* 5(2): 47–78.
    1997. *Of Body and Brush: Grand Sacrifice as Text/Performance in Eighteenth-Century China*. Chicago: University of Chicago Press.
Zweig, David. 1989. *Agrarian Radicalism in China, 1968–1981*. Cambridge, MA: Harvard University Press.
    1992. "Urbanizing rural China," in K. Lieberthal and D. Lampton eds. *Bureaucracy. Politics. and Decision Making in Post-Mao China*, 334–363 Berkeley: University of California Press.

INDEX

age: as analytical category, 22; as determinant of who engages in gossip, 199, 201, 212; as factor in *guanxi practice*, 143–4
agriculture: mutual aid in, 163; shift to hired labor in, 173–4; in village economy, 167
Ang, Soon, 127

backyard profit centers, 69. *See also* corruption.
bao. See reciprocity.
Beijing: study of job changes in, 119–26
Bian, Yanjie, 13, 19, 38, 127, 137, 140–1, 152, 154, 156, 158, 160, 165, 226; critique of research, 40–5, 47–9
Bosco, Joseph, 16
Bourdieu, Pierre, 7, 23
bureaucracies, 223, 223, 239–40
business scale: and differential networks, 111–13

Canada, 232
cash economy, 164n132, 174–7; shift from barter to, 167–8; and instrumentality, 174–6
Chapman, Mark, 232
Chinese Communist Party (CCP): rejection of *guanxi* by, 4; impact of on research, 22
Chinese International Economic and Trade Arbitration Commission (CIETAC), 187
Ching Kwan Lee, 151
Chu, Godwin, 166
class and status: and assessment of value of *guanxi practice*, 102–3; as source of reputation, 106; segregation as result of housing marketization, 213–6
clientelism, 164, 180; patterns of competition and, 108–115
Code, Lorraine, 217
Coleman, James, 135
collective enterprises, 109n91, 110, 123, 124

command economy: decline of, 65
communicative practice theories, 23–5
Confucianism, 10, 62–3, 64, 127
contract enforcement: strong ties as factor in, 132–3
contract law: as example of complementarity of *guanxi* and law, 191–4
corruption, collusion, and whistle-blowing, 71–4, 105, 108, 114, 222. *See also* backyard profit centers.
Croll, Elisabeth, 31–2
Cultural Revolution, 87, 209
culture: as context for understanding *guanxi*, 4, 64

Deng Xiaoping, 8, 62
dependent economic relations: defined, 82–3; cultivated by managers, 85–6, 88, 89, 93
Diamond, A.S., 181
dyads: and *guanxi*, 223, 236–7

economic reform: impact of on *guanxi*, 37–8, 47–55. *See also* reform era.
Economic Contract Law (1981), 192
education: as factor in job searches, 144–5, 146, 151–6, 161
Ehrmann, Henry, W., 181
emotions: Chinese and Western styles contrasted, 27, 33. *See also ganqing; renqing*.
employment. *See* labor market.
enclave enterprises, 68
entrepreneurs. *See* private enterprise.

face (*mianzi*), 4, 9, 175, 177, 207, 210; defined, 166; extra village *guanxi* as source of, 176
Fairwell (*Yuanhua*) Group, 114
Farrer, James, 19, 20, 226
Fei Xiaotong, 10, 118, 164, 165

Fengjia village (Shandong Province), 24, 30, 32
Fischer, Claude, 216
foreign firms: and dispute resolution, 185–8; and
  job procurement methods, 123
Foreign Economic Contract Law (1985), 192
France, 236
Fried, Morton, 8
Friedman, Lawrence M., 181

ganqing (sentiment), 4, 17, 165; and material
  obligation, 24–5, 27, 30–1; practices of
  avoidance of, 28–33, 34. *See also* emotions;
  renqing.
Geertz, Clifford, 23
gender: as analytical category, 22, 23; and
  female *guanxi* networks, 24, 33. *See also*
  gossip: gender and; women.
Gerlach, Michael, 93
getihu, 183–4. *See also* private enterprise and
  entrepreneurs.
Giddens, Anthony, 165
gifts economy, 13, 14, 137, 139; and ledgers,
  170, 175
Gluckman, Max, 181
Gold, Thomas, 16–17 166n134
gossip, 20; gender and, 198, 199, 212; as
  information medium, 208–10; instrumental
  use of networks, 210–11; as moral discourse,
  207–8, 217; pragmatics of, 211–12
Granovetter, Mark, 40–1, 119, 120, 140, 142,
  158, 236
groups: in social network analysis, 225–6
guanxi: defined, 6, 21–2, 25–33, 180, 222–4;
  inequality as characteristic of, 9; as
  information or influence, 152, 156, 159; as
  uniquely Chinese, 9–13, 24–5, 33, 37, 127,
  140, 142. *See also* strong ties; weak ties;
  instrumentalism and instrumental ties; *guanxi*
  practice; ganqing; renqing.
guanxi capitalism: as solution for weaknesses in
  transitional economy, 133–5
guanxi networks: scope of, 61–4
guanxi practice (*guanxixue*), 59–60, 74, 223;
  cultural and structural factors, 60–2; defined,
  6, 21, 139; and dependent economic relations,
  82–3; distinguished from *guanxi*, 79–80, 92,
  139; and economic exchange, 80–2; and
  variations in individual effectiveness, 66–74;
  changing expectations of, 137–8; and job
  searches, 143; importance of for new
  businesses, 101–2, 109–111; as public,
  communicative practice, 24; in reform era,
  64–6; rejection of by managers, 83–5; social
  exchange in Maoist era, 62–4; impact of
  social position on, 46–7; as unprofessional,
  157–8; and weaknesses in emergent labor
  markets, 128–33. *See also* instrumentalism
  and instrumental ties.

Guthrie, Douglas, 14–15, 17–18, 137, 139–40,
  142, 147, 157, 160, 223, 224, 225, 226;
  critique of, 97–104, 115

Haikou: study of job changes in, 119–26, 130,
  131
Hainan Car Incident (1984), 108
Hamilton, Gary, 12
Hanks, William, 23, 33
Hanser, Amy, 19, 224
Ho, David, 166
Hong Kong, 165
housing: marketization of and social networks,
  201, 213–6; in new workers' village, 198,
  202–4; and shanty districts, 203, 204
housing construction and remodeling: and
  shifting forms of aid, 163, 170–2
Hsing You-tien, 16, 52–3, 176
human capital: versus *guanxi* in hiring practices,
  41–2
human feelings. *See renqing.*
Hwang, Ang, Soon

Individual Business Policy, 109n91
Inner Mongolia, 229
instrumentalism and instrumental ties, 59, 163,
  174, 175, 177, 199; in analysis of *guanxi*,
  13–17, 139; increase in reform era, 65–6, 71.
  See also guanxi networks; *guanxi practice.*
international joint ventures: and information
  flow, 128; job procurement methods in, 123
Internet, 240
intersubjectivity, 33

job allocation system: in pre-reform era, 40, 119,
  134, 141, 145, 161; in reform era, 41. *See also*
  labor market.
job fairs, 147, 150, 156
job procurement methods, 120–6; formal
  searches, 146–8
job qualifications. *See* human capital.
job specificity, 138, 144, 151, 153–4
Ju Yanan, 166
judicial behavior: and *guanxi*, 188–91

Kao, John, 127
Keister, Lisa, 18–19, 232
kinship networks: in rural areas in reform era,
  71
Kipnis, Andrew, 8, 16, 17, 166n134

labor market 168; in 1990s, 144–5; and
  employer demands, 138, 145–8; *guanxi* in, 18,
  39, 45–55; and network theory, 140–1; in
  pre-reform era, 64; transition to, 126–7;
  uncertainty in during transition, 81. *See also*
  human capital; job procurement methods; job
  allocation system.

laws and regulations, 52; as opposite of *guanxi*, 97, 98, 99–103, 180; use of *guanxi* to avoid complying with, 93, 108; *guanxi* as part of legal culture, 180–3, 194–5, 223; *guanxi* and legal attitudes and behavior, 183–91; contract law and *guanxi*, 191–4; formality and informality in, 184–5; performance and enforcement, 184

lending and banking, 77–9, 81, 93
Li Fan, 229, 236
Liang Shumin, 10, 118
Lin Yimin, 16 17–18, 118, 234
Lincoln, James, 93
local networks: as alternative to *guanxi* networks, 107–9, 113–15

Mao Zedong: social exchange milieu under, 62–4
market economy: strategic value of gossip in negotiating, 200–1, 216
marketization, 97–8; impact of on behavioral controls, 64–5; impact of on lending and trade relations, 88, 95
Mauss, Marcel, 26
merit-based hiring, 138
methodology. *See* theory and methodology.
mianzi. See face.
migrant labor: and information flow, 128; job procurement methods of, 125–6; and trust between employer and employee, 131
Milgram, Stanley, 232
mobility, 141, 161; workplace and regional, 138, 148–51
money exchange: as substitute for mutual aid in village life, 163
morality: gossip as means of defining and enforcing, 200, 207–8, 217
mutual aid in village life, 163; shift from to hired labor and cash gifts, 170–4, 177

naofang ("stiring up the bridal chamber" ritual). *See* weddings: and *ganqing* avoidance.
Naughton, Barry, 126
Nazar, Nancy, 229
Nee, Victor, 104, 135
network theory, 140–43
networking skill thesis, 58, 59, 74
networks. *See* economic networks; *guanxi* networks; local networks; personal networks studies; social networks; social network analysis; whole network analysis.
new workers' village: density and diversity in, 202–3
non-state-owned enterprises, 69

Oi, Jean, 14
Oksenberg, Michel, 15
overseas Chinese, 12, 16, 165, 127, 228

particularistic tie. *See guanxi.*
Pearson, Margaret, 52
personal network studies, 234–5; differentiated ties, 235–8; multi-level approach to, 238–9
place (*difang*): as defining factor in new business networks, 98. *See also* local networks.
Polanyi, Karl, 26
political culture, 4
Potter, Jack M., 27, 28
Potter, Pitman, 19–20, 223, 224
Potter, Sulamith Heins, 27, 28
private enterprise and entrepreneurs: use of *guanxi practice* by, 103–4, 105, 109–111; job procurement methods in, 124; perceptions of, 104–8. *See also getihu.*
professional workers: mobility, 150–1, 153
property rights, 82
psychology of *guanxi* production, 24–5
Pye, Lucian, 9, 11, 15

reciprocity (*bao*) and reciprocal obligations , 4, 43–4, 57, 59. *See also ganqing*: and material obligation; *renqing.*
Redding, S. Gordon, 10
reform era: change in cultural context of *guanxi* in, 64
renqing (human feelings), 59, 165–6; cash gifts as, 170; as components of *guanxi*, 4; and instrumentality, 174–6, 177
reputation (*mingyu*), 185, 199; as defining factor in new business networks, 97; face as, 166; as substitute for *guanxi practice*, 105, 106–7, 113
residence permits (*hukou*): as limit on job mobility, 149, 160
resource dependence theory, 80, 81, 82, 83, 89, 92
Riley, Nancy, 16–17

school ties: as factor in lending and trade relations, 79, 82, 87–8, 89, 96
Sennett, Richard, 216
sentiment. *See ganqing.*
Shanghai, 163, 167, 176, 183–4, 197–218; study of job changes in, 119–26; and urban culture, 198
Shenzhen: study of job changes in, 119–26, 129, 131
Sik, Endre, 223
Silver, Alan, 175
Simmel, Georg, 164, 165
skills marketability, 138, 144, 151, 152–3
slavery: and *ganqing* avoidance, 28–9
Smart, Alan, 8, 166n134
social capital: compared to quanxi, 7; face as, 166
social exchange; creation of indebtedness, 79–80, 92; values and rules of, 60–2

social exchange theory, 81
social network analysis, 20, 221–2, 224–7
social network capital, 133–5
social position: impact of on use and perception of *guanxi*, 46–7
social relationships: Western contrasted with Eastern, 26, 27
Solomon, Richard, 10
special economic zones, 112
State Administration for Industry and Commerce: and contract law, 194
state-owned enterprises (SOEs): factors shaping use of *guanxi* in, 66–74
strong ties, 59, 64, 66, 138, 140–141, 155, 159, 235, 223; defined, 58n42; *guanxi* as, 118, 142–3; and job procurement, 118–19, 121–2, 122, 123, 124,125, 125, 127; as trust enhancing, 131
subsidiary establishments (of public-sector organizations): and information flow, 128; job procurement methods in, 122–3
Sun Lung-kee, 24–5
Swindler, Ann, 143, 157

Taiwan, 53
taxation, 68
theory and methodology, 78–9, 144; block models, 229–332; in current scholarship, 17–18; in study of hiring practices, 39–45; in critique of Guthrie, 98–104; of particularistic ties and shift to cash economy, 164–7; quantitative data on lending and trade in business groups, 86–96
Tianjin: study of job changes in, 119–26
ties: and tie strength thesis, 58, 59, 74; differentiated and *guanxi*, 235–8; in multilevel analysis, 239. *See also* strong ties; weak ties; instrumentality and instrumental ties.
Tindall, David, 232
township-based enterprises: and collusion, 72–3
trade relations, 77–9, 93
transaction cost economics, 80–1
trust: as factor in labor market, 130–2; law as response to lack or, 180
Tu, Wei-ming, 10

United Contract Law (1999), 192, 193
urbanization: and networks as rural/urban bridge, 70

village life: changes in agricultural mutual aid, 173–4; changes in forms of aid for housing construction, 170–3; changes in *guanxi* networks, 168–9; changes in local economy, 167–8; changes in social exchange, 169–70

Walder, Andrew, 14
Wang Fei-ling, 145, 147
Wank, David, 15–16, 19, 52, 53, 78, 165, 226, 232
Ward, Barbara, 165
Watson, James, 29
weak ties, 140, 141, 142, 223; and job procurement, 118–19, 121–2, 123, 124, 126, 142
Weber, Max, 164, 165
weddings: and *ganqing* avoidance, 26, 30, 31–2
Wellman, Barry, 20, 223
whole network analysis: indirect ties between persons and organizations, 229–32; patterns of connectivity and cleavage, 228; personal networks, 232–4; structurally equivalent role relationships, 228–9. *See also* personal network studies.
Wilson, James, 28–30
Wilson, Scott, 19, 20, 226
Wirth, Louis, 216
women: and job mobility, 149, 151; and marriage customs, 26, 31–2; in Chinese slavery system, 29. *See also* weddings: and *ganqing* avoidance; gender; gossip: gender and.
Wong Shiu-lun, 165, 166n134
Wuxi: study of job changes in, 119–26

Xiamen, 98, 104, 107–8, 109–15

Yan, Yunxiang, 9, 16, 165, 166, 168, 174, 176
Yang, Martin, 31
Yang, Mayfair, 12–13, 43, 52, 58, 79, 97, 138–9, 156–7, 158, 159–60, 165–6, 174, 176, 198, 199, 217, 222
youth: in changing labor environment, 144–145; and labor market reform and employer demands, 145–8; use of social connections, 143–4; and workplace and regional mobility, 148–51; and job specificity and skill marketability, 151–6

Other books in the series (*continued from page iii*)

14. David Wank, *Commodifying Communism: Business, Trust, and Politics in a Chinese City*
15. Rebecca Adams and Graham Allan, *Placing Friendship in Context*
16. Robert L. Nelson and William P. Bridges, *Legalizing Gender Inequality: Courts, Markets and Unequal Pay for Women in America*
17. Robert Freeland, *The Struggle for Control of the Modern Corporation: Organizational Change at General Motors, 1924–1970*
18. Yi-min Lin, *Between Politics and Markets: Firms, Competition, and Institutional Change in Post-Mao China*
19. Nan Lin, *Social Capital: A Theory of Social Structure and Action*
20. Christopher Ansell, *Schism and Solidarity in Social Movements: The Politics of Labor in the French Third Republic*